Flags of our Fathers

Flags of our Fathers

JAMES BRADLEY
with Ron Powers

BANTAM BOOKS
New York   Toronto   London   Sydney   Auckland

FLAGS OF OUR FATHERS

A Bantam Book / May 2000

Book design by Casey Hampton.
Maps created by Mary Craddock Hoffman.

Library of Congress Cataloging-in-Publication Data
is on file with the publisher.

ISBN 0-553-11133-7

Published simultaneously in the United States and Canada

Bantam Books are published by Bantam Books, a division of Random House, Inc. Its trademark,
consisting of the words "Bantam Books" and the portrayal of a rooster, is Registered in U.S.
Patent and Trademark Office and in other countries. Marca Registrada. Bantam Books, 1540
Broadway, New York, New York 10036.

PRINTED IN THE UNITED STATES OF AMERICA

BVG   10   9   8   7   6   5

Mothers should negotiate between nations.
The mothers of the fighting countries would agree:
Stop this killing now. Stop it now.
—YOSHIKANI TAKI

CONTENTS

1. Sacred Ground 1
2. All-American Boys 15
3. America's War 55
4. Call of Duty 73
5. Forging the Spearhead 99
6. Armada 121
7. D-Day 149
8. D-Day Plus One 169
9. D-Day Plus Two 179
10. D-Day Plus Three 193
11. "So Every Son of a Bitch on This 199
    Whole Cruddy Island Can See It!"
12. Myths 213
13. "Like Hell with the Fire Out" 227
14. Antigo 249
15. Coming Home 263
16. The Mighty 7th 279
17. A Conflict of Honor 297
18. Movies and Monuments 315
19. Casualties of War 329
20. Common Virtue 339
    Acknowledgments 355
    Interior Photo List and Credits 357
    Notes 361
    Bibliography 365
    Index 367

One

SACRED GROUND

The only thing new in the world is the history you don't know.

—HARRY TRUMAN

IN THE SPRING OF 1998, six boys called to me from half a century ago on a distant mountain and I went there. For a few days I set aside my comfortable life—my business concerns, my life in Rye, New York—and made a pilgrimage to the other side of the world, to a primitive flyspeck island in the Pacific. There, waiting for me, was the mountain the boys had climbed in the midst of a terrible battle half a century earlier. One of them was my father. The mountain was called Suribachi; the island, Iwo Jima.

The fate of the late-twentieth and twenty-first centuries was being forged in blood on that island and others like it. The combatants, on either side, were kids—kids who had mostly come of age in cultures that resembled those of the nineteenth century. My young father and his five comrades were typical of these kids. Tired, scared, thirsty, brave; tiny integers in the vast confusion of war-making, trying to do their duty, trying to survive.

But something unusual happened to these six: History turned all its focus, for 1/400th of a second, on them. It froze them in an elegant instant of battle: froze them in a camera lens as they hoisted an American flag on a makeshift pole. Their collective image, blurred and indistinct yet unforgettable, became the most recognized, the most reproduced, in the history of photography. It gave them a kind of immortality—a faceless immortality. The flagraising on Iwo Jima became a symbol of the island, the mountain, the battle; of World War II; of the highest ideals of the nation, of valor incarnate. It became everything except the salvation of the boys who formed it.

Chapter opener: James Bradley on the beach of Iwo Jima, April 1998.

For these six, history had a different set of agendas.

Three were killed in action in the continuing battle. Of the three survivors, two were overtaken and eventually destroyed—dead of drink and heartbreak. Only one of them managed to live in peace into an advanced age. He achieved this peace by willing the past into a cave of silence.

My father, John Henry Bradley, returned home to small-town Wisconsin after the war. He shoved the mementos of his immortality into a few cardboard boxes and hid these in a closet. He married his third-grade sweetheart. He opened a funeral home; fathered eight children; joined the PTA, the Lions, the Elks; and shut out any conversation on the topic of raising the flag on Iwo Jima.

When he died in January 1994, in the town of his birth, he might have believed he was taking the unwanted story of his part in the flagraising with him to the grave, where he apparently felt it belonged. He had trained us, as children, to deflect the phone-call requests for media interviews that never diminished over the years. We were to tell the caller that our father was on a fishing trip. But John Bradley never fished. No copy of the famous photograph hung in our house. When we did manage to extract from him a remark about the incident, his responses were short and simple and he quickly changed the subject.

And this is how we Bradley children grew up: happily enough, deeply connected to our peaceful, tree-shaded town, but always with a sense of an unsolved mystery somewhere at the edges of the picture. We sensed that the outside world knew something important about him that we would never know. For him, it was a dead issue; a boring topic. But not for the rest of us. Me, especially.

For me, a middle child among the eight, the mystery was tantalizing. I knew from an early age that my father had been some sort of hero. My third-grade schoolteacher said so; everybody said so. I hungered to know the heroic part of my dad. But try as I might I could never get him to tell me about it.

"The real heroes of Iwo Jima," he said once, coming as close as he ever would, "are the guys who didn't come back."

John Bradley might have succeeded in taking his story to his grave had we not stumbled upon the cardboard boxes a few days after his death.

My mother and brothers Mark and Patrick were searching for my father's will in the apartment he had maintained as his private office. In a dark closet they discovered three heavy cardboard boxes, old but in good shape, stacked on top of each other.

In those boxes my father had saved the many photos and documents that came his way as a flagraiser. All of us were surprised that he had saved anything at all.

Later I rummaged through the boxes. One letter caught my eye. The cancellation indicated it was mailed from Iwo Jima on February 26, 1945. A letter written by my father to his folks just three days after the flagraising.

The carefree, reassuring style of his sentences offers no hint of the hell he had just been through. He managed to sound as though he were on a rugged but enjoyable Boy Scout hike: "I'd give my left arm for a good shower and a clean shave, I have a 6 day beard. Haven't had any soap or water since I hit the beach. I never knew I could go without food, water or sleep for three days but I know now, it can be done."

And then, almost as an aside, he wrote: "You know all about our battle out here. I was with the victorious [Easy Company] who reached the top of Mt. Suribachi first. I had a little to do with raising the American flag and it was the happiest moment of my life."

The "happiest moment" of his life! What a shock to read that. I wept as I realized the flagraising had been a happy moment for him as a twenty-one-year-old. What happened in the intervening years to cause his silence?

Reading my father's letter made the flagraising photo somehow come alive in my imagination. Over the next few weeks I found myself staring at the photo on my office wall, daydreaming. Who were those boys with their hands on that pole? I wondered. Were they like my father? Had they known one another before that moment or were they strangers, united by a common duty? Did they joke with one another? Did they have nicknames? Was the flagraising "the happiest moment" of each of their lives?

The quest to answer those questions consumed four years. At its outset I could not have told you if there were five or six flagraisers in that photograph. Certainly I did not know the names of the three who died during the battle.

By its conclusion, I knew each of them like I know my brothers, like I know my high-school chums. And I had grown to love them.

What I discovered on that quest forms the content of this book.

The quest ended, symbolically, with my own pilgrimage to Iwo Jima. Accompanied by my seventy-four-year-old mother, three of my brothers, and many military men and women, I ascended the 550-foot volcanic crater that was Mount Suribachi. My twenty-one-year-old father had made the climb on foot carrying bandages and medical supplies; our party was whisked up in Marine Corps vans. I stood at its summit in a whipping wind that helped dry my tears. This was exactly where that American flag was raised on a February afternoon fifty-three years before. The wind had whipped on that day as well. It had straightened the rippling fabric of that flag by its force.

Not many Americans make it to Iwo Jima these days. It is a shrine of World War II, but it is not an American shrine. A closed Japanese naval base, it is inaccessible to civilians of all nationalities except for rare government-sanctioned visits.

It was the Commandant of the Marine Corps, General Charles Krulak, who made our trip possible. He offered to fly us from Okinawa to Iwo Jima on his own plane. My mother, Betty, and three of my brothers—Steve, then forty-eight, Mark, forty-seven, and Joe, thirty-seven—made the trip with me. (I was forty-four.) Not everyone in the clan could. Brothers Patrick and Tom stayed at home, as did sisters Kathy and Barbara.

Departing Okinawa for the island on a rainswept Tuesday aboard General Krulak's plane, we were warned that we could expect similar weather at our destination. But two hours later, as we began our descent to Iwo Jima, the clouds suddenly parted and Suribachi loomed ahead of us bathed in bright sun, a ghost-mountain from the past thrust suddenly into our vision.

As the plane banked its wings, circling the island twice to allow us close-up photographs of Suribachi and the outlying terrain, the commandant began speaking of Iwo Jima, in a low voice, as being "holy land" and "sacred ground." "It's holy ground to both us and the Japanese," he added thoughtfully at one point.

A red carpet was rolled out and waiting for my mother as she stepped off the plane, the first of us to exit. A cadre of Japanese soldiers stood at strict attention along one side; U.S. Marines flanked the other.

General Krulak presented my mother to the Japanese commandant on the island, Commander Kochi. We were, indeed, the guests of the commander and his small garrison. American forces might have captured Iwo Jima in the early weeks of 1945, but today the island is a part of Japan's sovereign state.

Unlike in 1945, we had landed this time with their permission.

A visitor is inevitably struck by the impression that Iwo Jima is a very small place to have hosted such a big battle. The island is a trivial scab barely cresting the infinite Pacific, its eight square miles only about a third the mass of Manhattan Island. One hundred thousand men battled one another here for over a month, making this one of the most intense and closely fought battles of any war.

Eighty thousand American boys fought aboveground, twenty thousand Japanese boys fought from below. They were hidden in a sophisticated tunnel system that crisscrossed the island; reinforced tunnels that had rendered the furiously firing Japanese all but invisible to the exposed attackers. Sixteen miles of tunnels connecting fifteen hundred man-made caverns. Many surviving Marines never saw a live Japanese soldier on Iwo Jima. They were fighting an enemy they could not see.

We boarded Marine vans and drove to the "Hospital Cave," an enormous underground hospital where Japanese surgeons had quietly operated on their wounded forty feet below advancing Marines. Hospital beds had been carved into the volcanic-rock walls.

We then entered a large cavern that had housed Japanese mortar men. On the cavern wall were markers that corresponded to the elevations of the sloping beaches. This allowed the Japanese to angle their mortar tubes so they could hit the invading Marines accurately. The beaches of Iwo Jima had been preregistered for Japanese fire. The hell the Marines walked through had been rehearsed for months.

We drove across the island to the old combat site where my father had been wounded two weeks after the flagraising. I noticed that the ground was hard, and rust-colored. I stooped down and picked up one of the shards of rock that littered the surface. Examining it up close, I realized that it was not a rock at all. It was a piece of shrapnel. This is what we had mistaken for natural terrain: fragments of exploded artillery shells. Half a century old, they still formed a kind of carpet here. My father carried some of that shrapnel in his leg and foot to his grave.

Then it was on to the invasion beaches, the sands of Iwo Jima. We walked across the beach closest to Mount Suribachi. The invading Marines had dubbed it "Green Beach" and it was across this killing field that young John Bradley, a Navy corpsman, raced under decimating fire.

Now I watched as my mother made her way across that same beach, sinking to her ankles in the soft volcanic sand with each step. "I don't know how anyone survived!" she exclaimed. I watched her move carefully in the wind and sunlight: a small white-haired widow now, but a world ago a pretty little girl named Betty Van Gorp of Appleton, Wisconsin, who found herself in third-grade class with a new boy, a serious boy named John.

My father walked Betty home from school every day for the stretch of the early 1930's when he lived in Appleton, because her house was on his street. When he came home from World War II a decade and a half later, he married her.

Two hundred yards inland from where she now stood, on the third day of the assault, John Bradley saw an American boy fall in the distance. He raced through the mortar and machine-gun fire to the wounded Marine, administered plasma from a bottle strapped to a rifle he'd planted in the sand, and then dragged the boy to safety as bullets pinged off the rocks. For his heroism he was awarded the Navy Cross, second only to the Medal of Honor.

John Bradley never confided the details of his valor to Betty. Our family did not learn of his Navy Cross until after he had died.

Now Steve took my mother's arm and steadied her as she walked up the thick sand terraces. Mark stood at the water's edge lost in thought, facing out to sea. Joe and I saw a blockhouse overlooking the beach and made our way to it.

The Japanese had installed more than 750 blockhouses and pillboxes around the island: little igloos of rounded concrete, reinforced with steel rods to make them virtually impervious even to artillery rounds. Many of their smashed white carcasses still stood, like skeletons of animals half a century dead, at intervals along the strand. The blockhouses were hideous remnants of the island defenders' fanaticism in a cause they knew was lost. The soldiers assigned to them had the mission of killing as many invaders as possible before their own inevitable deaths.

Joe and I entered the squat cement structure. We could see that the machine-gun muzzle still protruding through its firing slit was bent—probably from overheating as it killed American boys. We squeezed our way inside. There were two small rooms, dark except for the brilliant light shining through the hole: one room for shooting, the other for supplies and concealment against the onslaught.

Hunched with my brother in the confining darkness, I tried to imagine the invasion from the viewpoint of a defending blockhouse occupant: He created terror with his unimpeded field of fire, but he must have been terrified himself; a trapped killer, he knew that he would die there—probably from the searing heat of a flamethrower thrust through the firing hole by a desperate young Marine who had managed to survive the machine-gun spray.

What must it have been like to crouch in that blockhouse and watch the American armada materialize offshore? How many days, how many hours did he have to live? Would he attain his assigned kill-ratio of ten enemies before he was slaughtered?

What must it have been like for an American boy to advance toward him? I thought of my own interactions with the Japanese when I was in my early twenties. I attended college in Tokyo and my choices were study or sushi. But for too many on bloody Iwo there were no choices; it had been kill or be killed.

But now it was time to ascend the mountain.

Standing where they raised the flag at the edge of the extinct volcanic crater, the wind whipping our hair, we could view the entire two-mile beach where the armada had discharged its boatloads of attacking Marines. In February 1945 the Japanese could see it with equal clarity from the tunnels just beneath us. They waited patiently until the beach was chockablock with American boys. They had spent many months prepositioning their gun sights. When the time came, they simply opened fire, beginning one of the great military slaughters of all history.

An oddly out-of-place feeling now seized me: I was so glad to be up here! The vista below us, despite the gory freight of its history, was invigorating. The sun and the wind seemed to bring all of us alive.

And then I realized that my high spirits were not so out of place at all. I was reliving something. I recalled the line from the letter my father wrote three days after the flagraising: "It was the happiest moment of my life."

Yes, it had to be exhilarating to raise that flag. From Suribachi, you feel on top of the world, surrounded by ocean. But how had my father's attitude shifted from that to "If only there hadn't been a flag attached to that pole"?

As some twenty young Marines and older officers milled around us, we Bradleys began to take pictures of one another. We posed in various spots, including near the "X" that marks the spot of the actual raising. We had brought with us a plaque: shiny red, in the "mitten" shape of Wisconsin and made of Wisconsin ruby-red granite, the state stone. Part of our mission here was to embed this plaque in the rough rocky soil. Now my brother Mark scratched in that soil with a jackknife. He swept the last pebbles from the newly bared area and said, "OK, it should fit now."

Joe gently placed the plaque in the dry soil. It read:

TO JOHN H. BRADLEY
FLAGRAISER FEB. 23, 1945
FROM HIS FAMILY

We stood up, dusted our hands, and gazed at our handiwork. The wind blew through our hair. The hot Pacific sun beat down on us. Our allotted time on the mountain was drawing short.

I trotted over to one of the Marine vans to retrieve a folder that I had carried with me from New York for this occasion. It contained notes and photographs: a few photographs of Bradleys, but mostly of the six young men. "Let's do this now," I called to my family and the Marines who accompanied us up the mountain as I motioned them over to the marble monument which stands atop the mountain.

When the Marines had gathered in front of the memorial, everyone was silent for a moment. The world was silent, except for the whipping wind.

And then I began to speak.

I spoke of the battle. It ground on over thirty-six days. It claimed 25,851 U.S. casualties, including nearly 7,000 dead. Most of the 22,000 defenders fought to their deaths.

It was America's most heroic battle. More medals for valor were awarded for action on Iwo Jima than in any battle in the history of the United States. To put that into perspective: The Marines were awarded eighty-four Medals of Honor in World War II. Over four years, that was twenty-two a year, about two a month. But in just one month of fighting on this island, they were awarded twenty-seven Medals of Honor: one third their accumulated total.

I spoke then of the famous flagraising photograph. I remarked that nearly everyone in the world recognizes it. But no one knows the boys.

I glanced toward the frieze on the monument, a rendering of the photo's image.

I'd like to tell you, I said, a little about them now.

I pointed to the figure in the middle of the image. Solid, anchoring, with both hands clamped firmly on the rising pole.

Here is my father, I said.

He is the most identifiable of the six figures, the only one whose profile is visible. But for half a century he was almost completely silent about Iwo Jima. To his wife of forty-seven years he spoke about it only once, on their first date. It was not until after his death that we learned of the Navy Cross. In his quiet humility he kept that from us. Why was he so silent? I think the answer is summed up in his belief that the true heroes of Iwo Jima were the ones who didn't come back.

(There were other reasons for my father's silence, as I had learned in the course of my quest. But now was not the time to share them with these Marines.)

I pointed next to a figure on the far side of John Bradley, and mostly obscured by him. The handsome mill hand from New Hampshire.

Rene Gagnon stood shoulder to shoulder with my dad in the photo, I said. But in real life they took the opposite approach to fame. When everyone acclaimed Rene as a hero—his mother, the President, *Time* magazine, and audiences across the country—he believed them. He thought he would benefit from his celebrity. Like a moth, Rene was attracted to the flame of fame.

I gestured now to the figure on the far right of the image; toward the leaning, thrusting figure jamming the base of the pole into the hard Suribachi ground. His right knee is nearly level with his shoulder. His buttocks strain against his fatigues. The Texan.

Harlon Block, I said. A star football player who enlisted in the Marines with all the seniors on his high-school football team. Harlon died six days after they raised the flag. And then he was forgotten. Harlon's back is to the camera and for almost two years this figure was misidentified. America believed it was another Marine, who also died on Iwo Jima.

But his mother, Belle, was convinced it was her boy. Nobody believed her, not her husband, her family, or her neighbors. And we would never have known it was Harlon if a certain stranger had not walked into the family cotton field in south Texas and told them that he had seen their son Harlon put that pole in the ground.

Next I pointed to the figure directly in back of my father. The Huck Finn of the group. The freckle-faced Kentuckian.

Here's Franklin Sousley from Hilltop, Kentucky, I said. He was fatherless at the age of nine and sailed for the Pacific on his nineteenth birthday. Six months earlier, he had said good-bye to his friends on the porch of the Hilltop General Store. He said, "When I come back I'll be a hero."

Days after the flagraising, the folks back in Hilltop were celebrating their hero. But a few weeks after that, they were mourning him.

I gazed at the frieze for a moment before I went on.

Look closely at Franklin's hands, I asked the silent crowd in front of me. Do you see his right hand? Can you tell that the man in back of him has grasped Franklin's right hand and is helping Franklin push the heavy pole?

The most boyish of the flagraisers, I said, is getting help from the most mature. Their veteran leader. The sergeant. Mike Strank.

I pointed now to what could be seen of Mike.

Mike is on the far side of Franklin, I said. You can hardly see him. But his helping young Franklin was typical of him. He was respected as a great leader, a "Marine's Marine." To the boys that didn't mean that Sergeant Mike was a rough, tough killer. It meant that Mike understood his boys and would try to protect their lives as they pursued their dangerous mission.

And Sergeant Mike did his best until the end. He was killed as he was drawing a diagram in the sand showing his boys the safest way to attack a position.

Finally I gestured to the figure at the far left of the image. The figure stretching upward, his fingertips not quite reaching the pole. The Pima Indian from Arizona.

Ira Hayes, I said. His hands couldn't quite grasp the pole. Later, back in the United States, Ira was hailed as a hero but he didn't see it that way. "How can I feel like a hero," he asked, "when I hit the beach with two hundred and fifty buddies and only twenty-seven of us walked off alive?" Iwo Jima haunted Ira, and he tried to escape his memories in the bottle. He died ten years, almost to the day, after the photo was taken.

Six boys. They form a representative picture of America in 1945: a mill worker from New England; a Kentucky tobacco farmer; a Pennsylvania coal miner's son; a Texan from the oil fields; a boy from Wisconsin's dairy land, and an Arizona Indian.

Only two of them walked off this island. One was carried off with shrapnel embedded up and down his side. Three were buried here. And so they are also a representative picture of Iwo Jima. If you had taken a photo of any six boys atop Mount Suribachi that day, it would be the same: two-thirds casualties. Two out of every three of the boys who fought on this island of agony were killed or wounded.

When I was finished with my talk, I couldn't look up at the faces in front of me. I sensed the strong emotion in the air. Quietly, I suggested that in honor of my dad, we all sing the only two songs John Bradley ever admitted to knowing: "Home on the Range" and "I've Been Working on the Railroad."

We sang. All of us, in the sun and whipping wind. I knew, without looking up, that everyone standing on this mountaintop with me—Marines young and old, women and men; my family—was weeping. Tears were streaming down my own face. Behind me, I could hear the hoarse sobs coming from my brother Joe. I hazarded one glance upward—at Sergeant Major Lewis Lee, the highest-ranking enlisted man in the Corps. Tanned, his sleeves rolled up over brawny forearms, muscular Sergeant Major Lee looked like a man who could eat a gun, never mind shoot one. Tears glistened on his chiseled face.

Holy land. Sacred ground.

And then it was over. Time to board the vans and head back down Suribachi.

My brothers and I became like young boys in our last moments at liberty on the mountain. We scrambled down the slopes to collect souvenir rocks. Steve took photos of Joe, Mark, and me peeing over the side of Suribachi, a gesture several Marines had made on the day the flag was raised. Finally, we gathered the photographs I had retrieved from the van and tossed them into the wind over the mountainside. Images of our loved ones and of the six boys, distributed across the sacred ground.

Then I turned to face the Marine contingent, the uniformed strangers who had now become our friends—become part of our family.

"Thanks for being here," I said to them. And then the Bradleys turned away, leaving the mountain, and soon the island, to its heroic ghosts.

Two

ALL-AMERICAN BOYS

All wars are boyish, and are fought by boys.
　　　　　　　　　　　—HERMAN MELVILLE

.

BUT, NO. NOT GHOSTS. That was the point, I reminded myself, the point of my quest: to bring these boys back to life, or a kind of life, to let them live again in the country's memory. Starting with my father, and continuing with the other five.

That is how we always keep our beloved dead alive, isn't it? By telling stories about them; true stories. It works that way with our national past as well. Keeping it alive by telling its stories.

I'm not a professional scholar or researcher, but I figured that if I could somehow dig deep enough—find enough other boxes, in a manner of speaking—I might be able to achieve this. I knew that I could not do it alone. I would need other people, relatives and comrades of these six figures, to help me restore flesh and blood and bones to their dim outlines.

I started simply. I bought a book about Iwo Jima and read it. Then another. And another. I have since lost count.

I found names in those books; the names of the boys shoving that flagpole aloft.

Back in my office, I started to trace them. I wanted to talk to people who had known and loved them.

I phoned city halls and sheriff's offices in the towns of the flag-raisers' births and asked for leads that would put me in touch with any of their relatives. I dialed the numbers, often with my heart in my throat. I waited through the rings for that first "Hello?" from a widow, or a

---

Chapter opener: Franklin Sousley with his dog.

sister, or a brother of one of the boys whose hands had gripped that pole on Suribachi.

It would take them a moment to comprehend who I was and why I was calling. But inevitably they opened up—as they had not opened up to phone calls from strangers, or to the press.

These calls, these conversations began to consume my days. Then my weeks, and months. Entire seasons. I widened my phone searches to include living veterans of Iwo Jima. I wanted their memories, too.

I had to take on a business partner to ease the workload at my company so that I could spend more time in this search for the six boys' pasts. Eventually I began to travel to the places where they had lived.

As you read this, I am probably still searching. I will probably never stop.

But I have found most of what I wanted to know.

I wanted to know them as Marines, as fighting men who were also comrades. But more than that, I wanted to know them as boys, ordinary shirttail kids before they became warriors.

I wanted to know their family histories. And I wanted to know how "The Photograph" affected their families' lives down into the present time. As a flagraiser's son who had lived in the uneasy shadow of that photograph—a shadow cast by an image that itself was never visible in our household—I knew something about its lingering power within a family. I hungered to know what the Bradley household might have had in common with those of the other five.

The questions I asked generated many tears. But they opened up some bright, glowing chambers of the past as well.

The whole topic of boyhood, for example. Here was a many-faceted realm I had not quite expected to enter, but one that gave me endless fascination nonetheless: the lost realm of American boyhood in the years just before the Second World War.

Most of them, after all, were scarcely out of boyhood when they enlisted. Their lives up until then had been kids' lives: hunting, fishing, paper routes; the movies, adventure programs on the radio, altar duties at church; first wary contact with girls. And, since money was scarce, helping out in their fathers' businesses and tobacco fields; lending a hand in the coal mine, at the mill.

Hard times aside, the 1930's was a terrific decade to be an American boy, whether in the hills of Kentucky or on the gridirons of south Texas or astride the carnival calliope in small-town Wisconsin. Boyhood then was a deeply textured universe all its own, a universe of possibility and hope. Of fervent patriotism as the distant, hazy war clouds gathered.

An American boy's life in the thirties, whether at work or at play, was about connection and community in ways that are hard to imagine today. It was about dreams, vivid and optimistic dreams of a future as radiant as Buck Rogers's cosmos. As such, these dreams provided powerful incentives for courage and loyalty in battle in the minds of thousands of ex-boys in uniform—boys very much like the figures in the photograph.

They were so different, these six: the whooping young Texas cowboy astride his white horse; the watchful Arizona Indian on his reservation; the happy-go-lucky Kentucky hillbilly skinny-dipping in the Licking River; the serious Wisconsin small-towner walking with his third-grade sweetheart under the shade trees; the handsome New Hampshire smoothie checking his profile in the drugstore window; the sturdy Czech immigrant playing his French horn in the teeming Pennsylvania steel mill town. All forming their dreams of a future that was not to be.

And yet so similar.

They were nearly all poor. The Great Depression ran through their lives. But then so did football, and religious faith, and strong mothers. So did younger siblings, and the responsibility of caring for them.

Nearly all were described again and again as quiet, shy boys, yet boys whom people cared about. Boys who somehow made a difference in their families and their communities.

Nearly all generated memories among brothers and sisters and childhood sweethearts that remained as crystalline at century's end as at the moment they occurred.

And all of them together illuminated a great deal that was wonderful and innocent in an America that was soon to leave behind its own childhood forever.

John Bradley: Appleton, Wisconsin

My father's earliest childhood images were dominated by exposed human hearts: the Sacred Heart of Jesus, the Sacred Heart of Mary. Hearts at once human and divine, looming bloodred and out of scale from the open chests of figures who gazed with odd serenity from the large paintings in the Bradleys' household. Iconic figures, among the most recognizable images in human history. Blood and redemption. Agony and healing. Life in death, and death in life. Sacrifice and salvation through faith.

Blessed Mother help us, the grown-ups in young Jack's household prayed, and *Sacred Heart of Jesus, I place my trust in thee,* to the holy presences represented in the paintings.

These images, with their rich, warm colors and vivid gestures, must have made a strong impression on the boy who became my father. Kind, lovely faces, reassuring and constant. The Jesus painting survived into the Antigo home of my own childhood. Symbols of the Catholic faith, an old and European Catholic faith now transplanted to the sunlit fields of 1920's Wisconsin.

My father was born in 1923 in Antigo, the sturdy little town where he would return to sire his own family, and where he would die. He attended St. John's Catholic School, where all eight of his own children would later enroll. But when he was seven, his father, James J. Bradley, moved the family about ninety miles southeast to Appleton, a graceful little city of 16,000 on the Fox River. Jesus and Mary and their visible sacred hearts made the journey with the family.

My dad's mother, Kathryn, Germanic, anxious and worrying, the sister of a priest, had bought those images—standard-issue reprints, purchased at a religious-goods store—and hung them on the living-room wall. Kathryn was the religious worrier in the family; in fact she was the worrier-at-large. She worried about her children's future in the faith, she worried about money, she worried: *What will the neighbors think?* As is so often the case with worriers, she worried about everything except what eventually went wrong.

James J. Bradley, my dad's father, didn't worry about much at all. A veteran of the trenches in World War I, he was a hardworking railroad man, a laborer in a coal depot, a bartender. An Irish-American good-timer, the kind of guy you'd call from the bar to settle a bet about some baseball statistic or other, and he'd give you the straight goods, off the top of his head.

A good man, all around, caught up in bad economic times. In Antigo, James Bradley, Sr., had proudly worn a railroad man's uniform and plied his skills in a variety of jobs on the freight trains that crisscrossed the state. The Depression cut deeply into rail freight, and layoffs crippled the livelihoods of James and many of his fellow "Rails." It was then that he uprooted his family for the more prosperous environs of Appleton.

There, he found work, and also had the misadventure of his career. During a shift as an engineer, he took a curve one day with a little too much throttle, and a boxcar filled with cabbages yawed and spilled all over the wayside. His buddies at the bar turned it into a hilarious local legend, and crowned him with the nickname "Cabbage."

James Bradley struggled hard to rebuild his family's middle-class comforts. Ever the optimist, he sired five children—my dad, "Jack," was the second eldest—and ever the pragmatist, he expected each one, the boys especially, to help out with the household income. Jack and his older brother, James Jr., had newspaper routes throughout their childhoods. When they came home after making their collections each week, they often placed their money on the mantel. That money, perhaps along with the Blessed Mother, helped keep the family fed.

Like nearly every kid of his era, my father grew up wearing hand-me-downs, neat and clean clothes but hand-me-downs, from various cousins and uncles, and aspiring for more. He was a friendly boy, with a ready smile, but he never said much. Talking drew attention, the last thing he wanted. Later, a virulent case of acne deepened his pain at being observed.

He took refuge, with his pious mother, in the Catholic church. It was there, from his vantage point as altar boy, murmuring the Mass prayers in Latin, that he started to notice certain men who seemed to radiate a success and prosperity that belied the general hard times. One of these was his cousin, Carl Shutter. Carl wore handsome suits and fine neckties, and sold insurance for the prestigious Northwestern Mutual Life. Young Jack began to seek out men like Carl Shutter, ask their advice on matters of life. He noticed that these established businessmen—these lawyers and salesmen and bankers—liked him for that. It gave him a sense of his own developing style.

A particular category of businessmen caught his eye at church: the funeral directors of Appleton. These men, Jack thought, had a special way of walking up the aisle amid the incense-smell at Mass or during a funeral service: confident, in control, but always accessible. They seemed so at ease, so first-name familiar with everybody, and everybody seemed to know and respect them. The reason, he quickly came to understand, involved service: The funeral directors were not merely men selling a commodity; other than clergy, they were the ones most intimately in touch with the townspeople in their times of sorrow and need.

Jack Bradley understood service. That's what an altar boy was, a "server." And now here were these models of service well into adulthood. By his early teens, Jack Bradley was working part-time at an Appleton funeral home. He was going to be one of these respected, dignified men of service.

Meanwhile, life in Appleton, Wisconsin, seemed to lilt along almost in defiance of the Depression, or any other unwelcome intrusion. Everyone felt the pinch, but everyone took strength from the town's resilient economic assets and its harmony of place. The town was caught in the lingering twilight of a prior time, a way of life less typical of the Depression than of the Belle Epoque. This era was fading fast in America; but in Appleton no one seemed to notice.

In those straw-hat years between the two world wars, Appleton seemed to embody just about everything that made America worth fighting and dying for. Its very name bespoke its atmosphere of ripe, unblemished enchantment.

Its terrain came out of some diorama of American plenty: low, rolling hills of soil rich and dark with wheat-growing fertility; bordering forests of thick hardwood trees, especially the cherished white pine, good for furniture-making and for paper stock. All of this sumptuous land cut through by a deep clear rushing river, the Fox, whose fish-filled waters had drawn genera-tions of Indians and, later, the great tides of European immigrants, Dutch and German, flowing west in their caravans of prairie schooners.

Appleton was incorporated in 1853 with a population of 1,200, and its aura of quiet radiance, a place apart, never diminished over the ensuing century and a half. Demand for paper from its mills increased dramatically when an inventor in the metropolis to the south, Milwaukee, began to manufacture the typewriter in 1873.

The hardworking Middle-European settlers brought their burgher values to the town and the countryside around it. They made it a land of beer, cheese, bratwurst, and church spires; a land where education was valued, progress honored, government clean, houses neat, children obedient, homes happy, and churches sturdy and impressive.

Appleton boasted the first telephone in all Wisconsin, and the first house to be illuminated by incandescent light in any city beyond the East Coast. In 1911 President Taft brought it into the limelight again by biting into the four-foot-high "Big Cheese" that was Appleton's entry in the National Dairy Show in Chicago.

A little girl named Betty Van Gorp, who grew up to become Mrs. John Bradley, remembers 1930's Appleton in more intimate and enchanting terms.

It was a town of manicured lawns and clean streets with no litter, my mother has told me. A town where women swept their sidewalks and the slam of a screen door could be heard for blocks. And where people sat in swings or on the steps of their front porches on tree-shadowed sum-mer evenings, listening to the cricket-song swell up from the grass, and watching the first fireflies of twilight, and greeting their neighbors who strolled by.

Mothers made hot breakfasts in cold houses for their children in winter-time; Cream of Wheat or pancakes or eggs and toast and, always, hot chocolate. No meat on Fridays for the Catholic families, which was nearly everybody. Friday dinners were potato soup, creamed tuna on toast, soft-boiled eggs broken over mashed potatoes, creamed peas.

Betty Van Gorp could hear the clip-clop of horses' hooves as they pulled the milk wagon or the ice wagon along Appleton's leafy streets. She could hear the whining screech of the streetcar as it stopped to pick up passengers. A ride into downtown was a nickel. On those crickety summer evenings, she often heard the creak of somebody's rope swing. That creaking rope-swing sound stayed with her through the decades.

When Betty Van Gorp was in third grade she found a new companion to walk her home from St. Mary's Catholic School along the wide, tree-lined streets. A new boy in town, a serious, quiet boy named Jack Bradley. She liked Jack, although she wasn't quite sure whether he *liked* her back or just liked her: Sometimes in class she was obliged to pass along notes that he had written for the inconvenient Janet Jones. Still, by fourth grade she felt bold enough to send him a homemade Valentine with "Guess Who?" written on it. She appreciated the fact that Jack never cussed, even when it was so cold you wanted to scream at the weather. "Dad gum" was the worst that ever came out of his mouth.

Other Appleton kids gravitated to Jack Bradley as well. Bob Connelly joined the Boy Scouts with him and went on camporees. Most of the kids in the troop couldn't afford the full uniforms. Bob recalled that Jack made do with just the neckerchief.

Jack Puffer remembered that in eighth grade, Jack would find a way to make him laugh during those tense minutes when the Dominican nun was on the prowl in the classroom. Many times, Jack Puffer got a stick across his fingers for it, but he didn't really care. Jack Bradley was great to be around.

Baseball in summertime. Then a drink from one of the "bubblers," the water fountains, that were on every corner downtown. Tackle football in winter. No money for football uniforms; the kids wore their knickers. Swimming in Lake Park. Hitching a ride there by jumping on a boxcar in the ravine. The carnival once each summer; the *oop-oop* of the calliope and the smell of buttered popcorn.

It seemed an ideal life in an ideal town. But even ideal towns have their dangers and their sorrows; their abrupt reminders of the fragility of the beating human heart.

When Jack was ten years old a catastrophe struck the household of the sort his worrying mother could not have foreseen. It was a frigid winter morning, and his sister Mary Ellen, five years old and just awake, was playing near a large electric heater that had been plugged into an outlet in the kitchen. When the child leaned over the device's coils, the tassels of her nightdress brushed against them and caught fire. Within seconds her clothing was ablaze; the front of her body seared. Jack, nearby, screamed and filled a bucket with water to douse his sister. Their mother had been in the basement shoveling coal into the furnace. She rushed upstairs—*Blessed Mother, please help us!*—and rolled the howling girl in scatter rugs.

A doctor was summoned. Examining the girl, he concluded that her burns were not severe enough to merit hospitalization. He recommended bed rest. The family placed her on a sofa, where she lay for several days.

The doctor visited her each day. But she grew weaker, and within a week the Bradley family buried Mary Ellen. Young Jack Bradley felt responsible for her death. He regretted it for the rest of his life, this medical corpsman who dashed through machine-gun fire to give plasma to wounded and dying Marines. He regretted that he could not have responded better to his sister's mortal screams.

Only as a grown man and a veteran of military medical training did my father realize that it might not have been the burns themselves that had killed Mary Ellen. Likely, it was pneumonia, made more virulent by her lack of movement on the couch.

The family struggled on. Mary Ellen's sisters, Marge and Jean, tried to fill the vacuum left by the ravaged little girl. Childhood death was not an uncommon event in the America of those times. But this fact did not make acceptance any easier. Those who observed Kathryn afterward noticed that some of the life had gone out of her.

In her grief, she drew sensitive young Jack, who most resembled her, even closer to her bosom. She became his counselor, and Jack, her protégé. Jack Bradley grew up religious, responsible. Eager to be of service.

When Jack was nineteen he knew he was about to be drafted, so he devised a plan to enlist in the Navy and avoid land battle. His plan, he was sure, would allow him to be of service but to stay far from the bullets. Little did he realize it would lead him directly to one of history's bloodiest battles.

Franklin Sousley: Hilltop, Kentucky

The mountains are high and steep in eastern Kentucky, blue-shadowed and cut by nearly vertical hollows and plunging river gorges. It is a majestic but lonesome pocket of America. Those hollows have a way of swallowing up the people who come to live there—like the English settlers of two centuries ago who poured westward through the Cumberland Gap on the Wilderness Road. They looked up at those deep hollows and just melted into them, forming little clusters of community that grew as distinct and isolated from one another as islands on a vast upended ocean.

The hollows swallow up people, and even history: Some of the speech patterns you hear today in those high little outposts are preserved from Daniel Boone's time, and those patterns in turn were transported across the Atlantic from the England of Shakespeare.

The names, too: Go there and open up a family Bible, and look at the names entered on its flyleaf through the generations. Good British names like Cochran, and Peck, and William, and James, and Harrison.

And Sousley. Franklin Runyon Sousley.

I love that name; I love the melody of it. It has that twang of Appalachia about it. But beneath that twang, if you listen closely, you can hear the cadences of an older, refined speech pattern. "Franklin Runyon Sousley" reminds you that the hillfolk of Kentucky still carried in their culture the calcified rhythms and accents of Old English, carried across the Atlantic and into the mountain wilderness.

The Sousley roots go deep in Kentucky. The original Franklin Sousley was born in 1809, the year another Kentuckian by the name of Lincoln entered the world. In October 1829 that Franklin had a son, George, who eventually purchased the Holy Bible that still remains in the family, with all those English names inscribed. They were farmers—corn, wheat, tobacco—all the way down to Duke, who married Goldie Mitchell, a pretty girl with a nice, tight, red-haired perm, in November 1922. They set about the hard but productive life of raising tobacco outside the village of Hilltop. They would work the land, have a family, and maybe prosper.

Their first son, Malcolm, came ten months later, then Franklin with his red hair on September 19, 1925. The family home was just a cabin, four small rooms heated by a potbellied stove. They had no electricity and the outhouse was out back.

It was a hardworking farming life for the Sousleys, mostly tobacco, but the hay needed to be cut, cows meant milk for the children, and the vegetables were whatever Goldie could coax from the garden.

When Franklin was just three, death struck the family for the first time. Five-year-old Malcolm died in Goldie's arms, of appendicitis.

Now Franklin was the only son and his mother drew him closer in her grief. As the boy grew she took him along with her as she indulged in her favorite pastime—fishing in the Licking River. With his buoyant personality and perpetual grin, he was a balm for his mother's sadness.

And there were plenty of chores to do. Duke and Goldie were constantly working, always struggling to pay the few bills an unheated cabin and small family could generate.

When he was old enough, Franklin attended the two-room schoolhouse in nearby Elizaville. In May of 1933, when Franklin was almost eight years old, his brother Julian arrived. But just a year later his father Duke could no longer make it to the fields. "Daddy's sick" soon yielded to "Daddy's gone," as Duke succumbed to diabetes at the age of thirty-five. Now Franklin, just nine, found himself the man of the family, with a mother to comfort, a tiny brother to help care for.

The special mother-son bond between Goldie and Franklin deepened, but it wasn't lost in gloom. Goldie, only in her early thirties, had already lost a son and a husband. But she didn't mope. She displayed the implacable optimism, the will to go on that was transferred to Franklin, even through these dark days of hurt. She explained her misfortune as "the Lord's way" and said that "someday He will tell me why they were taken from me."

Goldie didn't smother her son in sadness, but encouraged him to revel in life's joys. And Franklin took the lesson to heart.

This is what people remember most about Franklin. His laughter, his good humor, his ability to put smiles on the faces of all around him. With a busy life, up early for school and to bed late at night after the chores, it seemed he had little time for play, but Franklin Sousley made the most of it.

His grades at school were perfect—an unbroken perfect string of C's. "He was an average student," Winifred Burden remembered years later. "And he was a typical country child. He didn't stay after school to play athletics, because he had to go home and work on the farm. Frankly, us city kids looked at the country kids as different and didn't socialize with them. But Franklin was different. He was nice to everybody with that big smile of his. And everyone liked Franklin."

But as soon as school was done, it was back to work on the farm. Emogene Bailey lived down the road from Franklin, and remembers him clearly over half a century later. "When I picture him," she recalled, "I see him doing farm chores, hay and corn and tobacco, vegetable gardens, mowing lawns, always busy."

Franklin was a dutiful son, finishing all his chores for his mother, or maybe for a slice of his favorite treat, Goldie's Black Jam Cake. He was five feet ten inches tall and weighed 150 pounds in high school, and he could do all the heavy chores she needed done. He was a hard worker, baling hay, bundling that tobacco with those big hands of his—"the biggest hands I ever saw on a human," a Marine in his outfit would later say of him, "like two big hams hanging there."

With his busy life and all the chores that had to be done, the strongest impression he left with his friends in Fleming County is that of a fun-loving, playful boy.

That squared with Aaron Flora's view. "Franklin was in it for a good time," he said. "Fishing, swimming, skinny-dipping, snipe-hunting, where you take some poor fool out in the night and leave him holding a bag in the holler, waiting for you to drive the snipes at him. He was in if it was a good time."

Another time, he and Franklin were shooting off fireworks, and by the time they got to the Roman candles, Franklin was having so much fun he aimed one right square up a buddy's ass.

He was as daring as he was silly. He'd fight a running sawmill and he'd jump buck-naked into a half-frozen creek on a dare.

His close friend J. B. Shannon remembers Franklin as "a big freckle-faced boy with bright red hair. A rambunctious young man, not afraid of anyone."

There was that dewy Halloween night when he and J.B. rounded up a couple of cows and prodded them onto the Hilltop General Store porch and strung up some wire so they couldn't get back off, and then treated them to some Epsom salts. "Those cows shit on the porch all night," J.B. fondly remembered nearly a lifetime later.

The boys liked Franklin and so did the girls. Marion Hamm remembers that "Franklin was just fun, a tremendous guy. I never knew of him being a bad boy. We laughed so much with him always telling jokes."

So many of his friends and sweethearts remember his constant laughter. And he liked to dance, and that broke some ice with the girls.

Marion tried to find words to describe what it was like being around Franklin Sousley, and then shook her head. "You can't imagine how much fun that boy was," she said. And then she brightened up with a memory: "The most fun was when it snowed at Christmas. Franklin would get his family's horse and wagon and we'd get on the sled and go out to the farm and cut Christmas trees and sing carols, and we'd ride around and distribute those trees, so everyone would get one at the same time."

As Franklin ripened to young manhood, his ventures with the girls stayed innocent. "Franklin liked the girls and we'd chase them," J. B. Shannon remembers. "But did we make progress? Well, we were young innocent boys and we thought we did. At least we'd brag about it, lie about it to each other."

The Second World War hovered in the far distant background of Franklin's boyhood. News of its great battles and gossip about the fates of local service- men filled the air at Hilltop as he cavorted and studied and helped Goldie in her struggles with the farm. There is no indication that Franklin paid it much attention. He was only six when Japan invaded Manchuria; Hitler's sweep through Europe had begun when he was only thirteen. By the time he'd graduated from high school, in June of 1943, there was reason to be hopeful in both theaters. The staticky radio broadcasts that he and Goldie listened to—when they weren't tuned in to Waite Hoyt calling the Cincin- nati Reds on summer afternoons and evenings; Goldie was a big baseball fan—were telling tales of victory both in Europe and in the Pacific.

In the first American land battle of the war the Marines had captured Guadalcanal that past February, and the Germans had surrendered at Sta- lingrad. In March, the British Eighth Army under Montgomery broke through the Mareth Line in Tunisia; a couple of months later, German and Italian troops surrendered there. The Allies were driving toward Sicily at about the time Franklin's small graduating class was receiving its diplomas. And from the Pacific, the radio commentators had been sending stirring re- ports of U.S. Navy and Marine victories with names such as Midway and Tarawa.

All of that sounded just fine to the people in the hills and hollows of eastern Kentucky. Franklin began dating in his last year of high school, es- corting Frances Jolly or Marion Hamm to church, to the movies, or just for a walk in the woods.

But upon graduation, Franklin Sousley was more concerned with finding a way to shore up his struggling mother's finances than dating or fighting for his country. Goldie came first, so he went straight to work at a Frigidaire plant in Dayton, across the Ohio border to the north. He lived in a small apartment at 107 Park Drive.

He was sending money back home to Goldie from his paycheck as an eighteen-year-old staker and propeller assembler in Plant No. 2 when, in January 1944, Uncle Sam sent him a telegram. On that day, rather than ac- cept his fate as an Army infantryman, Franklin Sousley—the hijinking hill boy who'd fight a running sawmill—made up his mind to become a U.S. Marine.

It had been a jolt for Goldie when Franklin had gone off to Dayton, far- ther away from Hilltop than she had ever traveled. When she learned that the man in her life was off to the Marines, all she could do was hope for the best and pray to her Lord.

Now eighteen-year-old Franklin, who had smiled his way throughout his difficult boyhood, was off to another world. He spoke of his "duty as a man," but his friend J. B. Shannon remembers that Franklin was "just a big country boy, unafraid of anything."

Franklin was a "good ol' boy" off to fight in the "good war." What could possibly go wrong?

Harlon Block: Rio Grande Valley, Texas

Harlon Block is the figure with his back turned to the world. He's there struggling with the base of the pole, his face invisible. He was the Seventh-Day Adventist who had been taught "Thou Shalt Not Kill," who was out in the Pacific doing his duty. For almost two years the country didn't know it was Harlon in the photo. But his mother, Belle, knew. Belle, who had begged him not to go to war. She knew. He had rejected her pleadings not to fight, but as he experienced the killing in the Pacific her teachings came back to him.

But by that time it was too late. He was committed.

He was from a place they call simply "the Valley." It's the Rio Grande Valley at the bottom of Texas, the far eastern end. Harlon Block was born on a farm there, outside of McAllen, down near the knife-blade tip of Texas where the Rio Grande empties into the Gulf of Mexico.

It's hot in the Valley, but not the dry heat of much of Texas. It's hot and humid there, semitropical, with palm trees growing.

The farm had been something of a compromise between his parents, Ed Block and the former Ada Belle Brantley. Especially for Belle. Ed and Belle had been married in San Antonio in 1917. Ed promptly went off to fight in France in World War I. Just as promptly, he was laid low with both the measles and the mumps. Recuperating in England, he was tapped as an ambulance driver, and spent the rest of his service days ferrying hideously wounded men from the docks to the hospitals in London.

While he was away at war Belle lived frugally and saved the money he sent her. She took courses and became a practical nurse. When Ed returned, Belle spent another portion of the money on tuition for a business course for him. Belle liked the city and saw herself as the wife of a successful businessman there.

Ed passed the course and gave city life a try. He sold real estate and was moderately successful. But Ed dreamed of farming, his first love. One day he saw a get-rich flyer touting the Rio Grande Valley. Thanks to the technology of irrigation, a land boom was about to detonate there: Citrus orchards and cotton fields would overtake the sagebrush. Ed bought forty acres sight unseen and tore off his necktie once and for all. Belle was disappointed; she had no desire to work on a farm. But Ed was enthusiastic and painted a picture of a ground-floor opportunity. He was a practical man and made a down-to-earth case for a new life, living off the land. Belle was a young woman with strong convictions of her own, but she was also idealistic, a bit of a dreamer, and she was swayed by her forceful husband. She overcame her doubts and agreed to go along. It would be the first of many compromises for Belle.

The Valley is a seventy-mile stretch of land carved by the Rio Grande River between Mission, Texas, in the west and Brownsville, Texas, in the east. A separate part of Texas with its own weather system, its own way of life.

A drive along two-lane Route 83 in the 1930's of Harlon's youth would reveal a flat, lush land dominated by small farms, large cultivated fields, and the occasional town of 1,000 to 2,000 people. Where the land was not tilled, mesquite and palm trees held sway.

There was no industry in the Valley; everyone was involved in agriculture, working the soil. What was growing depended upon the seasons, of which there were two: summer and winter.

It was mostly summer in the Valley, from March to October. The hot and humid weather came from the southeast, borne on winds from the Gulf of Mexico. Cotton was king during the Valley's summer, a crop that flourished despite the lack of rain. Fathers and sons would pick cotton by hand on days that regularly saw temperatures of over one hundred degrees with ninety percent humidity.

From Thanksgiving to March, the "northers" brought cooler weather. Temperatures would fall and the humidity would ease. The people of the Valley called this season "winter" and complained of the "cold" if the temperature dipped below fifty degrees.

Citrus and "row vegetables" were planted and then harvested. In the winter the Valley was a grand garden of grapefruit, navel oranges, lemons, limes, carrots, beets, broccoli, and cabbage.

Ranching and oil were small contributors to the Valley's economy, unlike the rest of Texas. There were no wide-open grazing spaces; cattle were raised on feedlots. Some oil was found in the western part of the Valley, but the gushers were far away.

The small Valley farmers were hardly affected by the Depression. The country had an appetite for all they could produce, and the numerous harvests meant work for all.

On the other side of the Rio Grande is Mexico, and the Mexican influence was evident throughout the Valley. Spanish-style white stucco buildings with red tile roofs were part of the landscape. Tacos, tamales, and enchiladas were eaten alongside hamburgers and hot dogs. Twenty percent of the population was Mexican; they lived together in their Catholic enclaves and mixed easily with the majority Protestant Anglos.

Everyday social life revolved around farm, school, and church. Annual celebrations at the county fairgrounds were for displaying prize beets or carrots or pigs. Floats with agricultural themes would follow the high-school band as it marched down the paved main streets. The "Style Show" consisted of ladies modeling fashions made from local produce—carrot and beet "diamonds" shimmering against an eggplant-skin-and-date-palm dress. One lucky girl would have her life transformed as she proudly accepted the title "Citrus Queen."

The Valley was a small part of Texas with small farms and small towns. A youngster's grade-school class would consist of eight students. A large high-school graduating class might number forty-five. It was a place where everyone knew their neighbors' dogs.

The Blocks struggled at first. The newly built farmhouse caught fire and burned to the ground. Ed had to take a job as a farm laborer and rent a small house while they got back on their feet. Belle had an idea to make some money. She suggested they buy a cow every two months with Ed's earnings. Soon, the Blocks were in the dairy business.

And soon they had a family. Ed Jr. arrived in 1920, followed by Maurine two years later, and Harlon in 1924. Later came three more boys: Larry, Corky, and Melford.

As a middle child in a large family, with a brother four years older and a sister two years older, Harlon didn't have to be a trailblazer. He could follow along in his older siblings' footsteps.

The chores started small and gradually for young Harlon. At first he would open the gates as his older brother, Ed Jr., brought the cows in to be milked. Then, as he grew, Harlon, his parents, his brother Ed Jr., and his sister, Maurine, milked fifteen cows apiece every morning starting at three A.M. Maurine would cool the raw, unpasteurized milk. She and Belle would wash the milk bottles and fill them. Then Ed Sr. would be off on his route selling his milk for five cents a quart. "That is how we survived the Depression," was the way Maurine remembered it toward the end of the century.

Harlon was a good helper. He always completed his chores without complaint. He took orders well, fit in as part of the family.

Belle was determined to do right by her family, and she tried to be happy on the farm. But it was difficult for her. She missed the city, but loved her husband and children. So she made the best of it. Fine-featured and dark-haired, she was bred for the city. The Valley's hot, damp climate had her red-eyed and runny-nosed from asthma and hay fever all the time, and the work at the milking stool hurt her back. Maurine recalled how her mother began to suffer bouts of depression: Toward evening she'd walk outside the farmhouse, stare off into space for half an hour, have a conversation with herself, and then come back.

Perhaps it was Belle's longing for another life that made her open to the preachings of the Seventh-Day Adventist Church. Early in their move to the Valley, Belle became a fully accepting practitioner of the vivid Protestant strain that assumed a seven-day creation of the Earth, a Great Controversy between Jesus Christ and Satan, and a millennial return of Christ into history, at which moment the dead will awaken, evil will vanish, and time will end. Belle accepted, too, her denomination's strictures against alcohol, narcotics, and unclean foods; against swearing and unchastity; and against violation of the Ten Commandments—including the Commandment that stipulated, "Thou Shalt Not Kill."

All Christians shared a belief in that Commandment, but the Seventh-Day Adventists took it to heart. Their founder, William Miller, had been an Army officer in the War of 1812, but the killing he witnessed caused him to become a skeptic. Adventist boys were taught they must never carry guns or knives because the Lord would offer them all the protection they needed. And Seventh-Day Adventists had a long record of refusing to fight in time of war. They never faltered in their support of their country, but they served in the medical corps as conscientious objectors.

But being an Adventist didn't just mean heeding prohibitions. It meant being an active force to help your fellowman. The Adventists were well represented in the healing and helping professions as nurses, doctors, and teachers.

Belle was a nurse and put in long hours nursing terminal patients in their homes during their last days. She used her hard-earned money to pay the tuition of her children at the local Adventist school. Knowing her children were being brought up in the protective fold of her church, she felt her sacrifices were worth it.

Ed converted too, donning a respectable suit for church services on the "Seventh Day," Saturday. He followed his wife's lead in the family's religious life, as many men do. But Belle was the true literal believer who lived the word of her Bible. She was always ready to help, and others sensed it. A series of kids who needed a break came to stay with the Blocks over the years. Like young Herbert Savage, who was not welcome in his own home, they showed up at Belle's door asking for room, board, and a new start in life. A local girl who had been raped walked four miles in the dark to seek out Belle's loving help.

Harlon was the child most influenced by Belle and her beliefs. He grew up feeling sure of what was right and wrong. He accepted that the Bible was the literal word of God; the Ten Commandments an absolute guide. Harlon was confident with this ordered view of the world. He was smart—he skipped second grade—and entered his teenage years a chesty, likable boy, somehow at the center of everything. And a free spirit. Often when his chores were finished he was off horse-racing bareback with his Mexican pal Ben Sepeda in McAllen. "Harlon rode a white horse, a solid white horse," Ben remembers. "Harlon was daring and determined. We'd ride bareback over to my house. My mom would make us corn tortillas and jellied tomatoes. Harlon used to bring a jar along to take some jellied tomatoes back with him."

Harlon was sure of himself and his beliefs. He didn't feel he had anything to prove. And Harlon couldn't be cowed. His friend Russell Youngberg remembers the time that somebody vandalized a stepladder at the Seventh-Day Adventist school. Harlon and his buddy Russell were among the three suspects. The principal called them into his office and told them they couldn't play on the playground until they'd fixed the stepladder. Russell Youngberg kept quiet, but Harlon spoke right up. He was terse and to the point: "We didn't do it, and we won't fix it, and you can't make us, and it ain't fair."

The straitlaced principal reddened, but held his tongue. And Harlon Block's Seventh-Day Adventist education had approached the beginning of its end.

In Harlon's sophomore year the mysterious vandal struck again, writing obscenities on the wall of an outhouse next to the school. The principal launched his inevitable inquisition. When he got to Harlon, the boy nonchalantly allowed that he knew who'd done it, but he wasn't going to tell. For this, the principal kicked him out of school.

Harlon, and apparently the whole family, were ready for a change. They moved to the neighboring town of Weslaco, a flat, square speculator's grid slapped down on the Valley floor. Its name was a crunching of its founding firm, the W. E. Stewart Land Company.

At Belle's insistence the other Block children continued at the Adventist school. But Harlon didn't want to return. He felt he had absorbed all they had to teach him. More important, Harlon was athletically inclined and the Adventist school did not have a sports program. He wanted to make his mark in the sport that attracted the local crowds and created excitement in Weslaco, indeed, in all of Texas: football. Harlon wanted to be in on the action, part of a team.

Belle didn't like such talk. She felt Harlon should make an effort to get back into the Adventist school. And football! Well, football was a game of violence and the games were on Friday night, the beginning of the Sabbath, so football was out of the question.

Belle presented her views forcefully to Harlon, who shrugged noncommittally like all teenage boys who are being told what to do. Belle appealed to Ed to discipline the boy, to focus him back on the church and get his mind off football. Ed, who thought Adventism was all well and good but didn't take it as literally as Belle, didn't see the harm in attending a public school. And he was excited by the idea of his son playing football.

Belle was aghast. They argued, but Ed pointed out that they didn't have to decide this right away: Because of the difference in the schools' schedules, Harlon had a seven-month delay before he could enter Weslaco High School. So Ed bought some time and told Belle he'd talk with Harlon as they worked together hauling oil.

A few years earlier, as the Depression deepened, milk prices had sagged. Oil had been discovered forty miles west of McAllen, and Ed had a money-making idea. He bought one, then two, finally four new oil trucks. The Rado refinery in McAllen gave anyone with a truck free gasoline if they'd haul the crude from the oil fields. It made for long, grueling days but Ed was a hard worker with a family to feed.

As his sons matured, he got every one of them involved in hauling crude oil from the hill-country wells to the refinery in McAllen. So when Harlon had time on his hands and was old enough—before he was old enough, Belle thought—Ed enlisted him as one of his drivers. It was brutal work: long trips several times a week, even weekends.

Harlon took the remainder of the school year off to haul oil with his father. Belle was alarmed, but Harlon relished the independence and the opportunity to do man's work. He and his father shared the labor and grew close—"best friends," as Ed would later say. Harlon was the perfect number-two man, ready to take over when the need arose.

Ed loved nothing more than Harlon's company, and he was torn when their months of working together drew to a close. But he couldn't wait to cheer his most athletic son as he starred on the gridiron.

Belle felt she was losing Harlon—he was the only Block child to leave the Adventist school—so she worked hard to involve him in the daylong Sunday socials—"convenings"—the church held. But Harlon was good-looking and gregarious and attracted the attention of the girls.

Belle was troubled by what she saw as the waywardness of her son. And she was horrified when Harlon brought home a .22-caliber rifle. A gun in Belle's home! Harlon's friends all had guns to shoot rabbits in the fields, and Harlon wanted to have some fun. Belle came home one day to find Harlon innocently instructing his younger brothers in its use. Belle told Ed he must discipline Harlon, and Ed spoke to him, but his heart wasn't in it. What was so wrong about a Texas boy having a little gun? Belle's ideals were compromised a little more.

And there were many times when Belle wasn't told of Harlon's hijinks. Harlon's brother Mel remembers when Harlon and some friends, in an attempt to make their own liquor, mixed yeast and grapefruit juice in mason jars and hid them behind a pillar in the barn. "For two weeks those jars were exploding," Mel told me. "We found this concoction dripping all over the barn. Dad thought it was funny. Mom never found out."

Harlon's developing brawn made him a natural for the Weslaco High football squad when he transferred there. He quickly became a star despite a certain naïveté regarding the game's finer points. Leo Ryan recalled a practice early in Harlon's first season when the two of them had drawn their equipment from the team manager and were ambling out to the hard-dirt field. Leo noticed that his friend was limping along on bowed legs. "Hey, big guy," he said, "what's the problem?"

Harlon spoke right up: "My *thaghs* hurt." He glanced down to a point below Leo's waist. "I sure wish I had me some of those *boards* you have in your thaghs."

Leo had to think about that for several moments before he realized that Harlon was referring to the protective pads in Leo's uniform pants.

Harlon was tough; he could take it. In one game the archrival Donna High School players somehow learned of the painful boils covering

Harlon's back and shoulders. The Donna boys pounded on Harlon but he
didn't flinch. Harlon caught a breathtaking pass that scored the winning
touchdown against Weslaco's biggest rival.

In fact, Harlon spearheaded Weslaco to an undefeated season. With him
as punter, pass-catcher, and blocking back, the Panthers ground their way
through every other team in the Valley with an offense as dry and drab as
the red dirt under their cleats. They quick-kicked a lot out of the short punt
formation, and as far as Leo Ryan could remember, they had only one running play. It was called "Harlon's play," which was strange in that it called
for Harlon to block out for the fullback Glen Cleckler. But when the Panthers needed an artillery strike—a pass to gain some first-down yardage—
Harlon's big milk-hauling hands were usually wide open and ready for
the ball.

Harlon, the middle child, loved being part of a team, going along with
the guys. He was a real contributor, but not a leader or initiator. He wasn't a
quarterback calling the plays or a team captain. His main job was to block
for others, to be a real teammate.

He played hard enough to catch the attention of the editors of the
student newspaper, the *Weslaco Hi-Life*: "Hard-hitting, pass-catching, 165
pounds, 5 feet 11 inches describes Harlon Block, right end of the Panther
line. Although this is his first year in Weslaco High School and his first
year of athletics, he is probably one of the more natural athletes in the
Valley."

Harlon made "All South Texas" along with Leo Ryan and B. R. Guess in
that undefeated 1942 gridiron season. Leo always felt that the team might
have triumphed in the Texas playoffs if their bus hadn't been confined to
the Valley by the gasoline shortage. Still, it was a team to remember. Their
photograph appeared in the local papers, all open collars and parted hair
and confident grins.

But Belle hadn't seen Harlon star on the gridiron. Belle insisted the
family observe the Adventist Sabbath from Friday sunset to Saturday sunset. During Harlon's Friday-night football games she sat quietly at home,
concerned for his soul. This proud Christian woman never could quite
enjoy the way Harlon was throwing himself into life as a budding young
man. She was fearful for his spirituality; she seemed to worry that she was
losing him. He was playing around too much; he was always gone, Belle
complained to Ed.

Harlon was a hell-raiser in Belle's eyes, but he was pretty tame by most
people's standards. He was bashful in groups and blushed at off-color jokes.
Leo Ryan said Harlon worried about his looks and never thought the girls

liked him—"Y'all go on ahead without me, now; I'm not gonna get a date," he would tell Leo and the guys.

But the girls sensed something special in him. His brother Ed Jr. told me that the girls flocked to Harlon. And in many of the curling black-and-white photographs of Harlon that I've managed to collect, there is a happy-looking young woman standing close to him.

But the dalliances were innocent, kid stuff. His favorite girl, the one many think he might have married after the war, was Catherine Pierce. "We'd go to the movies together," Catherine remembered. "And we'd go to church functions. We liked each other, we dated, but we never so much as held hands."

Harlon would soon be off to war, soon be a symbol to the world of male bravado. But it's doubtful that in his short life Harlon Block ever kissed a girl.

Ira Hayes: Gila River Indian Reservation, Arizona

I came to realize that much of what there is to know about Ira Hayes can be gleaned by studying him on the flagraising photo.

First of all, his silence, his utter quietness. Sit and look at the photo for an hour, an afternoon, a day. Sit quietly with Ira's not addressing you. Then you know the utter silence that was Ira Hayes, a boy whose favorite game was solitaire.

For another clue look at Ira's position on the photo. He's the last figure to the left, the boy whose hands can't quite reach the pole. That's Ira, different, apart from the rest, unable to grasp the pole just as he was unable later to get his hands around his life.

If you feel you don't know enough about Ira, you know how I felt in the summer of 1998. I had interviewed many people—school chums, ex-Marines, his three living relatives—but I still didn't have a handle on him. I didn't know who he was, what made him tick. So I flew to Arizona in search of the "real" Ira Hayes. And I learned that he cannot be found.

I drove south out of Phoenix until I was on the Pearl Harbor Highway, as Interstate 10 is called as it nears Ira's reservation. I drove through the dry, silent heat along flat pink desert land, a plain of mesquite bushes and deep green saguaro cactus that recedes until it hits the Santan Mountains.

I drove until the four-lane highway crossed a meandering ravine about fifteen yards wide. A sign marked the ravine. It read: GILA RIVER. I pulled my car over and looked down from the highway into what used to be the Gila riverbed. I saw only a wide, dry, empty nothingness. The Gila River hadn't flowed under that highway for decades.

I gazed out at Ira's land, the Gila River Indian Reservation. It's not big, with maybe 15,000 inhabitants. Framed by the mountains in the distance, a glance gives you the feeling you can see it all. Behind me, as I stood over-looking the dry riverbed, cars, RV's, and campers of my society whooshed by. Sometimes a horn sounded to warn me not to back up onto the busy highway. The noises contrasted with the stillness, the utter silence of the reservation before me. After looking down once more at the river that wasn't a river, I got back into my car, off to find Ira Hayes.

Ira was a Pima Indian, a member of a small, proud tribe that had inhab-ited this quiet land for centuries. He was born Ira Hamilton Hayes on January 12, 1923, to Nancy and Jobe Hayes. He was the oldest of the six Hayes children. Two children, Harold and Arlene, died as babies. Two other children died before they were thirty, Leonard in a car crash and Ver-non of spinal meningitis. Ira made it to thirty-two years of age. Nancy and Jobe lived longer than all their children except Kenny, who was born in 1931 and was sixty-seven when I met him.

At birth Ira was already "apart," separated from other Americans by law and custom. Arizona, a state for only eleven years at the time of Ira's birth, did not recognize Pima Indians as citizens. Pimas could not vote; they could not sue anyone in the courts. ·

The home Ira was born into was a one-room adobe hut built of mesquite posts and arrowhead rock. Sturdy and economical, it faced east in the tradi-tional way, so that each morning its occupants, opening the door, were greeted by the rising sun. A well-swept canvas rug covered the dirt floor; upon it stood a woodstove, a table and chairs, iron bedsteads with corn-shuck mattresses. An American flag graced one wall; religious paintings and a Bible were always in evidence.

The front of the house had a traditional *vato*, a shady arbor under which to relax and entertain visitors. Outside, to the west stood a carrel, shed, and storehouse. Built to last for centuries, the Hayes home would still be stand-ing today if it hadn't been destroyed by vandals in the early 1990's.

Subsistence farming, cotton-growing, basket-weaving, the chopping and selling of mesquite branches to white town-dwellers for firewood—these were the hard features of survival for most Pima Indians during Ira's boy-hood. Jobe Hayes was a farmer, a cotton harvester, and a chopper of weeds.

From Jobe, Ira inherited his complete and utter silence. "He was a quiet man," Ira's niece Sara Bernal remembered of Jobe. "He would go days without saying anything unless you spoke to him first." And Kenny Hayes, Ira's only living brother, who himself rarely speaks, said only: "My dad hardly ever talked."

As a little boy, as a young man, and later as an adult, Ira was a quiet person. He didn't feel any compulsion to make conversation, to break any ice. He could be in another's presence for hours not talking, silent as the mountains overlooking his reservation. As his boyhood friend Dana Norris told me, "Even though I'm from the same culture, I couldn't get under his skin. Ira had the characteristic of not wanting to talk."

And in Ira's Pima culture being quiet and self-effacing was encouraged. "In our culture, it's not proper for a Pima to seek recognition," tribal leader Urban Giff explained to me. Or as Dana Norris put it, "We Pimas are not prone to tooting our own horns." But Ira wasn't just quiet; he was a silent island unto himself, already separate from his other Pima friends.

Yet when Ira did speak he displayed a keen mind and an impressive grasp of the English language.

It was his mother, Nancy, a devout Presbyterian, who read to him from the Bible when he was a youngster. Nancy ran an ordered home, volunteered in the community, and was a pillar of the church, which was just a stone's throw from the Hayeses' front door.

Nancy saw to it that Ira and his siblings got the best education available. All his life Ira devoured all kinds of books. He was the most prolific letter writer of the six flagraisers. And when it was time for high school she sent them as boarders to the Phoenix Indian School.

But Ira's literacy wasn't a rarity. His tribe had a long history of being an advanced culture, compared to other Indian tribes and even white settlers.

"Pima" means "River People," and for over two thousand years the Pima had lived by the Gila River as successful and peaceful farmers. Before the time of Christ, they had organized an extensive network of irrigation canals to bring water to their crops. Excavations have identified over five hundred miles of canals built by the year 300 B.C. One book on the Pima states that they had "ruins that crumbled when Rome was still young."

In 1864 a group of white settlers made the first contact with the Pima. They were escorted by the Commander of the Army of the West, Colonel Stephen Kearny. Colonel Kearny posted guards among the settlers as they mingled with the Pima. But as he later wrote, instead of encountering "wild Indians," he was surprised to admit that the Pima "surpassed the Christian nations in agriculture" and were "immeasurably before them in honesty and virtue."

The praise is impressive, coming as it does from an unsentimental warrior more accustomed to slaughtering Indians than tipping his hat to them.
But Kearney had it right: He found himself beholding a settled culture, in
the southern half of what is now Arizona, that had brilliantly harmonized
land, water, crops, and domesticated animals to create a peaceable kingdom
of plenty and of virtue.

Central to all this was the art of bringing water to a dry, rainless place:
Over the centuries, the Pima canals drained water from the Gila and distributed it skillfully through fertile fields of wheat, corn, squash, beans, mel-
ons, and cottonwood trees. The tribe seemed to take its character from the
Gila's deep, generous flow: Unwarlike and rarely invaded, Pima Indians
were a sharing people who offered their bounties to other nations and, in
time, to the forty-niners and other white nomads making their way across
the desert in prairie schooners, headed for California.

This latter gesture may have been a mistake. It drew attention to the
paradise the tribe had painstakingly created for itself. In return for the
Pimas' generosity and even protection under attacks by Apaches, the mi-
grating Easterners who settled in Arizona began to help themselves to the
same water sources that sustained the peaceful culture.

By the 1870's, and despite lip-service assurances from the U.S. government, the Pimas' agricultural system was disrupted. In the 1890's, agents of
the U.S. Geological Survey arrived with plans to rectify the situation. But
they wouldn't listen to the suggestions of the Pimas who had successfully
farmed there for centuries. Instead, the United States tore up the canals and
replaced them with an unworkable and destructive system.

In 1930, former President Calvin Coolidge dedicated the Coolidge Dam
on the Gila River. He smoked a peace pipe—a custom unknown to the
Pima, but gratifying to the newsreel cameramen—and declared that the
dam would save the Pima nation from poverty. The Gila's table continued
to fall; not a drop went to the Pima. And so things went, until finally the
only way that one could determine that a stream had once flowed through
these dry precincts was by looking at that sign beside a bridge on the Pearl
Harbor Highway that promised a "Gila River."

The remarkable thing, given the decades of thievery and ruination of the
Pimas, is the legacy of dignity and forbearance that prevails amid their ex-
ploited culture. For three quarters of a century, the Pimas had fed starving
whites, protected whites against attack by other tribes, never killed a white
man, and never robbed one. Moreover, they obligingly took up the names,
the clothing, the religion, and the rules and regulations of their exploiters.

In 1917, even though they were not U.S. citizens and thus exempt from military service, a majority of young Pima men waived this right and enlisted to fight in France. Matthew Juan, a Pima, was the first Arizona soldier killed in action in World War I, a fact all Pima young men were proud of.

Ira Hayes's people are watchers and listeners, not talkers. The voices are spare as they describe Ira, usually referring to what he wasn't, as if he never revealed who he really was at heart.

"Ira wasn't playful, he wasn't competitive," recalled Dana Norris.

"Ira didn't go in for games," his cousin Buddy Lewis remembered.

"The other Hayes boys would tease me," his niece Sara Bernal recalled, "but not Ira. He was quiet, somewhat distant."

And when they do describe a distinctive trait of his, it's always the same: Ira's total silence, his self-effacement:

"Ira was very shy," Buddy Lewis told me. "He preferred to stay in the background."

"Ira didn't speak unless spoken to," said Sara Bernal. "He was like his father."

"Ira was a quiet guy," Dana Norris confirmed. "Such a quiet guy."

After grade school on the reservation, Ira went to board at the Phoenix Indian School. There he mixed with Indians of other tribes but retained the sense of himself as distinct, a proud Pima. "He'd come and hang out with his Pima friends," Dana Norris remembers. "He felt most comfortable around his own kind."

In three days on Ira's reservation I spoke with many people who knew Ira. They told me the outlines of Ira's life; they remember the boy, but he was so totally self-contained they just shook their heads when I asked them about Ira's attitudes, his beliefs, any distinguishing traits.

Esther Monahan remembered him clearly. A fellow Pima, she attended the Phoenix Indian School with Ira. She saw him daily in their Pima homeroom. But she couldn't recall Ira's ever saying anything. Anything at all. She told me:

"Ira wasn't like the other guys. He was shy and wouldn't talk to us girls. He was much more shy than the other Pima boys. The girls would chase him and try to hug him, like we did with all the boys. We'd catch the other boys, who enjoyed it. But not Ira. Ira would just run away."

In time, Ira's school day would begin with news of faraway battles. "Every morning in school," Eleanor Pasquale remembers, "we would get a report on

World War Two. We would sing the anthems of the Army, the Marines, and the Navy."

Ira enlisted in the Marines nine months after Pearl Harbor, when he was nineteen. His community sent him off to war with a traditional Pima ceremony.

Fifty-six years later, I was embraced by a similar Pima ceremony on my visit to Arizona. It was a dinner at the Ira Hayes American Legion Post, about a mile from where Ira's house once stood. I listened to young and old Pima speakers relate proud stories of their culture and felt the warm embrace of community we rarely experience in our Anglo gatherings.

Near the end of the ceremony I was asked to come onstage, and Eleanor Pasquale presented me with a Pima painting. In the center is the legendary Pima figure Su-he (pronounced *Soo-heee*), and in the background is the famous flagraising photo.

Eleanor, a dignified lady who knew Ira, explained the significance of the painting to me. Su-he is a stick figure in the center of a maze. The maze represents all the challenges of life and the center is where peace and security reside. "Like Su-he, if you keep going you can find the center, your peace."

And what about Ira in the background, I asked.

"We hope in death he has now found his peace," she answered. "The peace that he couldn't find on this earth."

Rene Gagnon: Manchester, New Hampshire

He is the figure hidden by my father in the photo. He stands shoulder to shoulder with John Bradley, only the tip of his helmet and his two hands visible. And in his life he often remained in the background, obscured by others. He was shy, unaggressive, not a standout type of guy. He had little to say when asked a question.

He never imagined life as something to grab hold of and shake. Molded by huge unseen corporate and military forces, he saw his life as that which "they" decided it should be. Life was a question of "luck" or "contacts."

He wasn't a man's man, he never chummed with the guys. The only steps he took in his life were at the suggestion of the women in his life, his mother and later his wife. He always lived with one of them, and other than his time in the Marines, he spent no time out on his own. He followed his wife's advice in search of the lucky break that never materialized. He listened to her until it was too late. And by then he was trapped for good.

Rene Gagnon arrived on March 7, 1925, the only child of French-Canadian mill workers Henry and Irene Gagnon. French Canadians formed a dense ethnic enclave on the west side of Manchester, New Hampshire, in those years; a "Little Canada" in which French was the language and Catholicism the religion. In at least some cases, the menfolk's notions of propriety were markedly more European than the surrounding Yankee Puritan norm.

Rene might eventually have had some siblings, and a chance at a more self-assured childhood, had not Irene Gagnon decided to take him for some fresh air in his stroller one day during his infancy. Their jaunt might have been unremarkable had not Irene spotted Henry Gagnon strolling along the same street. Henry was in the company of another woman. The other woman, like Irene, was pushing a stroller. In the stroller was another infant—Henry's, but not Irene's.

Irene not only divorced Henry; she never allowed him back into her house or her life. She never discussed him with Rene. Rene's own son, Rene Jr., told me that he believed his father never met the old man until after he had returned home from the war.

Strikingly handsome with his lean Gallic face and dark hair and brows, Rene grew up under the coddling influence of Irene. Her life consisted of her job in the mills and her son. She often brought him to work with her to show him off, to be cooed over by the other women. People remember him as a quiet boy, always in the background. He paid attention to the Holy Cross nuns at St. George's grade school, but he did little that people could later remember.

His friend Jules Trudel knew him for years; they attended St. George's together. They played together, walked to school together, sat near each other in the classroom. But when asked to describe Rene or to recall any remarkable incidents, Jules could only say what people would say about nondescript Rene all his life: "He was a nice guy."

The mill. Of all the six flagraisers, it was Rene Gagnon whose life was the one most defined, if not overwhelmed, by forces far larger than himself. Among these were the forces of massed corporate labor: regimented and mechanized, and given architectural form by Rene's hometown. He was born in Manchester, a heavy and sprawling industrial metropolis on the decline in the 1930's, but still the home city to the largest textile-mill complex in the world.

In this regard Rene and his future sergeant, Mike Strank, two young ethnic Americans, shared a powerful formative experience—at least on the surface. Each came of age in a kind of living Thomas Hart Benton mural: a teeming workers' hive that typified the sprawl and belch of American industry in the 1930's. But in fact the two mill towns were vastly different. Franklin Borough, Pennsylvania, where Strank grew up, was a tough coal miner's and steelworker's town, masculine and riotous with fire and smoke and noise. The Manchester mills covered even more territory—triple lines of dark redbrick buildings, each six stories high, stretching for miles below the Amoskeag Falls. But no smoke billowed, no sparks flew from these mills. For nearly a century they had hummed sedately, turning raw thread into gingham cloth—five million yards of it a week at prime production, enough to put a band around the earth every two months.

Rene probably didn't reflect on it, but he was in on the final years of Manchester's century-long epoch as a cradle of industry. That epoch indirectly shaped much of the boy's sense of himself in relation to the world.

The Amoskeag Mills had thrived since 1819, when the advent of the power loom made the complex the largest of its sort on the globe. Manchester itself was a creature of the Amoskeag Manufacturing Company; plotted out by its entrepreneurs in 1837, just as Weslaco was plotted out for the citrus boom in 1919. Throughout the nineteenth century, the Amoskeag drew swarms of textile workers to its site on the Merrimack River about fifty miles north of Boston. Many of these were French Canadians. They poured down in trainloads, tens of thousands over the years, lured by a market for skilled labor that tapped their cultural roots.

In the process they improvised a kind of technocorporate community flavored, and protected, by the dictates of mass commercial production. Accepting the benevolent control of their gigantic employer, content with its definition of them as the "corporation's children," these rural men and women (and their children) adapted themselves to the terrain—both physical and psychological—of their new urban life. They molded to the almost medieval landscape: the harsh mill yards, the endless solid walls of factory buildings, the heavy wrought-iron gates, the dwarfing scale of architecture. They took for granted the social regimentation of their lives; they accepted the notion that a kind of unseen but always attentive power ruled over them.

It was the perfect spawning-ground for life in a mass society—civil or military.

By Rene Gagnon's time, Amoskeag had lost its grip as an industrial monolith. The main product of its mills was cotton gingham, and by the late 1920's consumer demand for gingham had shifted to the emerging synthetic materials, such as rayon. Amoskeag never saw it coming and was too unwieldy to adapt. The mills shut down. In 1937 much of the infrastructure was bought up by a group of Manchester citizens and sold off to more than twenty small, independent industries.

The largest of these was the Chicopee Manufacturing Company, makers of gauze and cheesecloth for such products as medical bandages. Irene secured a job at Chicopee and later brought Rene with her. The fortunes of the city declined, but the lucky workers at Chicopee clung tightly to their jobs, grateful for the security of employment in one more large, paternal, benevolent corporate system. None was more grateful than Irene Gagnon, who told her son how "lucky" she was that "they" had given her a job.

Life inside the corporate fortress had its pleasures. A boy growing up there could bask in the glitter of company-town commerce, the long shopping streets with their glowing lights and snazzy entertainments, their metropolitan bustle and flair.

Thursday nights were shopping nights in Manchester, as in other workers' towns in mid-century America. Paychecks were issued on Thursdays, and the stores and banks stayed open late those nights. People got dressed up and went promenading along Elm Street, where the shops beckoned under the streetlights.

I can imagine Rene Gagnon combed and spiffed up and checking his reflection in the plate-glass windows, hurrying along to meet his friends at the Palace Theater on Hanover Street. He would have walked from his mother's house on Hollis Street, where the rows upon rows of "corporation" houses were always in view. "Layered living," somebody called it. Very much like a vast military camp.

At the Palace, ten cents apiece would buy the boys three hours of cowboy double features, a Gene Autry and a Roy Rogers if they were lucky, plus cartoons and maybe a Buck Rogers serial. On a Saturday morning his gang might have joined seventeen hundred shrieking, jostling kids at the State Theater, an art deco palace with terrazzo floors, to see a special showing of Shirley Temple's new movie.

He might have taken a trolley car, but he wouldn't have been driven: Manchester in the 1930's was not a car town. As a boyhood pal of Rene's recalled to me, "On a hot summer day, if you had ten cars come through town, that was a lot of cars." Horses and wagons still filled the streets back then, the rubberless steel-rimmed wheels grinding on the cobblestones and giving the city its distinctive noise.

In the summer, after school let out in June, short pants and brush haircuts would replace knickers and pompadours. Then it would be a season of baseball, track meets, local talent shows. Peanut-butter sandwiches for lunch and homemade fudge at night.

Winters were even more fun. It snowed a lot in New England in the 1930's, just as it did in Wisconsin and Kentucky; and Rene Gagnon made as much out of the snow as John Bradley or Franklin Sousley did. The town fathers used to block off hilly Sagamore Street with wooden horses after a snowstorm, and hang out kerosene lanterns for illumination, and people would come there with their sleds. Mostly children, but some grown-ups, too. On a good night or weekend afternoon maybe two hundred boys and girls would be flashing down the hill in stocking caps on their Flexible Flyers.

When Rene was old enough, Irene brought him to the mills in his free time so they could be together more. He worked alongside his mother and many other women in the same vast room, performing the same repetitive tasks day after day. He was a "doffer." Doffers took care of the bobbins. Bobbins were cylinders, placed on spindles to receive the cotton thread as it spooled during the mechanized weaving process. There were about 700,000 spindles, servicing some 23,000 looms, humming along in the rows of buildings during the Manchester mills' peak years. When a bobbin was fully wound with thread, the doffer would lift it off its spindle and replace it with an empty cylinder. It was unchallenging work Rene could do.

Irene was happy with her secure life in the mill and her tidy home. She sang the praises of this life to her son and encouraged him to come to work with her whenever he could. Rene began to join his mother during her lunch hour, abandoning his friends in the school cafeteria. After two years of high school, he dropped out so that he could concentrate on being a doffer full-time.

Rene worked alongside his mother and her friends now. Having her boy by her side night and day must have pleased Irene. But there were other women there, younger girls who were attracted to her dark, handsome boy.

Irene was particularly concerned by a young, aggressive girl who had her eye on Rene. Her name was Pauline Harnois and she seemed to cast a spell over Irene's boy, ready to take control, which she was used to having. As her sister Anita later remembered, "Our dad got sick at a young age and my mother had to work in the mills. Pauline was the oldest in a family of four and she had to take a lot of responsibility at a young age. She liked to be in control. Her position in the family, her responsibility formed her. She was always in control."

Like a leaf in the tide, Rene was swept along with whatever current took him and he spent more time with Pauline than Irene would have liked.

One December Sunday when he was sixteen, the world beyond the mill town broke through the routine clip-clop and spindle-hum. A bunch of the guys were all in somebody's den, listening to a football game on a big Halson radio, when the voice of President Roosevelt interrupted and started talking about a date that would live in infamy. The next day the Manchester *Union-Leader* paperboys were brandishing editions whose headline was just one word: "WAR!"

Rationing began not long after.

Rene Gagnon listened to this news, read about it, shrugged, and went back to the mill and his mother and Pauline Harnois. It was all beyond his control. He kept on working. Life went on: the mill, his mother, Pauline, the bright lights along Elm Street.

Rene Gagnon kept on working right up until his Army draft notice arrived in May of 1943. Then he enlisted in the Marines and submitted to the third large, outside influence that would mold his life.

Irene didn't want to lose her boy, but she thought it would do him good to get away from that Harnois girl. What Rene didn't tell his mother was that he had already made a fateful decision. At the age of seventeen he comforted the sad Pauline with the promise that he would marry her when he returned from the war.

Mike Strank: Franklin Borough, Pennsylvania

He was the enigma: the immigrant who became the ultimate fighting Yank; the cerebral little boy from the tough mill town who grew up to be the protosergeant; the physical intimidator who turned out to be the tough shepherd of his flock. The "old man" of his company, who would not live to see twenty-five. Of all the six, I find him the most complex, the most elusive study in contrasts. That is, until I study the small part of him that is visible in the photograph: his right hand. Mike Strank's right hand tells me everything I need to know.

He is behind and to the left of Franklin. His right shoulder is pressed against Franklin's left. Their torsos are conjoined; their arms are reaching upward. Each boy has his left hand on the flagpole, and Franklin has his right hand on it as well. But the key to the image, at least for me, is Mike's right hand closing on Franklin's wrist. It is an image of almost unbearable delicacy and gentleness. That is Mike: the protector. The veteran Marine in the group, helping the tyro. When that shutter clicked on Suribachi, it caught Sergeant Mike in an absolutely characteristic moment. He was reaching out to give support to a younger boy in the critical chain of action.

Among the flagraisers, Mike is the one larger-than-life hero. When old comrades talk to me about Mike they become young men again. "A Marine's Marine" is the phrase they all get to sooner or later. They speak of the strapping man. Yet violence is not the key to Mike Strank; it is not what men valued about him. What they valued—what makes their spines stiffen in admiration fifty years after the battle—was his leadership. That, and his quality of love.

"He was the finest man I ever knew," said one platoon-mate who went on to become a national business leader. "The best of the best," said one who went up Suribachi with him. "The kind of Marine you read about, the kind they make movies about," said another.

A Marine's Marine. But not because of his ferocity in combat—although he was a cool and deadly fighter. Not because he screamed, "Follow me and we'll kill a lot of Nips!" or ranted about "dying for your country." Mike Strank earned respect by emphasizing the well-being of his young charges, at least to the extent possible in the face of torrential gunfire.

"Follow me," Sergeant Mike used to tell the boys in his squad, "and I'll try to bring all of you back safely to your mothers. Listen to me, and follow my orders, and I'll do my best to bring you home."

He was born Mychal Strenk on November 10, 1919, in Jarabenia, Czechoslovakia. A friend of the family, Ann Basophy, who was born in the same small farm village, recalled that Vasil and Martha Strenk subsisted in a one-room house with a dirt floor, along with Vasil's parents and grandparents.

The following year Vasil emigrated to America and changed his last name to Strank. Sponsored by an uncle, Alex Yarina, he passed through Ellis Island and made his way to the Pennsylvania mining and steelworking town of Franklin Borough, on the Conemaugh River sixty-five miles east of Pittsburgh and two miles east of Johnstown.

Franklin Borough, chartered in 1868, was at its peak population in 1920: 2,632 people. A complex built in 1898 by the Cambria Iron Company and soon to be taken over by Bethlehem Steel offered plenty of hard work for gritty, industrious immigrants: twenty-two open-hearth furnaces, two mills for rolling sheared plates, a universal plate mill, and a continuous bar mill. Three years later Bethlehem would add business offices, five blast furnaces, a billet mill, a slab mill, a powerhouse, boilers, a chemical laboratory, a sintering plant (in which iron could be heated into a steely mass without melting), and a steel car department.

At their height, the Bethlehem mills and mines around Franklin Borough employed more than 18,000 workers. They clustered in soot-caked towns and villages throughout Cambria County and along the western slope of the Alleghenies. Franklin Borough became a safe haven for East Central European immigrants and their offspring; by the early 1930's they would form a majority in the little town, a village-within-a-village, really. They would provide three of the town's six civil officers and half the members of the Franklin Fire Department.

Vasil worked the mines for three years before he could afford to send for Martha and the baby. They followed him to America in early 1922. Three-year-old Mychal passed innocently under the portals of Lady Liberty, the most recognizable image of America until he and his comrades supplanted it twenty-three years later.

By the end of that year Mychal had a brother, John. Pete would follow in 1925, with sister Mary still eight years in the future.

The family lived in a two-room rental apartment inside the Slavic enclave. The rooms were a kitchen and a bedroom. To Martha especially, this was luxury: a castle, she said, compared with what they had endured back in Jarabenia. Mike, John, and Pete shared one bed; their parents slept close by in the other. Vasil trudged off to the mine at three P.M. every day in his lamp-hat and fatigues, carrying a pail that had a thermos of water in the bottom and his lunch on top. He wore the same clothes all year round, returning home black with coal dust from head to toe. But proud. This was progress!

Franklin Borough offered the Strank family a symbolic vision of America, but a far different one than quiet Appleton offered the Bradleys. Here was a fiery, noisy landscape of New World mechanization. The whole town could see the vast skeletal structures of the mills. Many families lived virtually next door. The mines, cut into the banks of the hills, completed the enveloping industrial view. Night never came to the mill town; the blast furnaces with their open hearths blazed away twenty-four hours a day.

The day, on the other hand, could seem like a perpetual twilight. The coal-dust haze from the mines formed a thick presence in the sky, blotting out the sun. The first duty for any Franklin family upon waking was to sweep the front and back porches free of the soot that had fallen overnight like black snow. A woman who grew up there remembered walking through "an inch of crunch" on her way to school every day.

Life in the town reflected this pounding, gritty pace of constant sweat and production. When the Stranks arrived, Franklin boasted fourteen beer gardens, but no church, and no doctor. Yet the Eastern Europeans who toiled there did not see any of this as deprivation. For them, it was a new chance in a new and vigorous land; a chance to rise, or at least for their children to rise. They preserved their culture and their religious values in the two-room rented dwellings where they lived under the steel mills' glare, each little apartment building a link in the improvised chain of a new community.

Without realizing it, Vasil Strank might have begun the molding of his eldest son into a Marine's Marine right in the bosom of his tiny household.

Mychal—now renamed Mike—shared a bed with his brothers John and Pete. Returning from his late shift at the mine as he did, at about one in the morning, Vasil seldom saw his three little boys awake—they would leave for school while he was still sleeping, and he would be gone to begin his shift by the time they returned. This routine could not have been easy for Vasil. "His family was really the boys," his son John recalled.

And Vasil abided by a strict Old World value system. Discipline in the family was paramount. When one of the boys had misbehaved, Martha would report it to Vasil upon his return home at night, and he would wake up a few hours later, along with the boys, to administer punishment.

Vasil insisted on a special rule for this punishment: No matter which boy had committed the offense, all three would be disciplined equally. In this way, Vasil thought, he could transfer the burden of discipline from himself to the boys; make them see that they had a shared interest in the good behavior of each.

Vasil probably did not know that he had intuited one of the fundamental principles of military training; in particular, Marine training. Roughly fifty percent of procedure in a Marine basic-training program is about disconnecting the young American boy from his concept of himself as a unique individual, a lone operator. He is remolded into an integer in a team. Shared responsibility—an abiding sense of the unit—is essential to survival in combat. Thus, if a recruit should faint from exhaustion during a forced march, the rest of his unit is trained to run in circles around his body until he comes to. Equal discipline.

As the eldest of the three brothers, and the brightest—his intellectual skills would soon blaze brilliantly to the surface—Mike not only grasped the concept of teamwork and equal responsibility, he became a liaison between his father and his two younger siblings, an explainer of his father's rules and wishes to Pete and John. In short, a sergeant.

Mike Strank resembled his mother, as Jack Bradley resembled his. Like Jack, Mike absorbed his mother's fervent Catholic faith. Before bed each night, he and his two brothers would kneel on the floor, before a vivid painting of The Last Supper, and say their evening prayers in Slovak. They looked out for one another. They took to making sure they wore the same color shirt to school each day. Like uniforms.

Slowly, the Strank family gained a foothold. While Vasil labored, and Martha raised geese on the hill behind the apartment, plucking the feathers to make pillows, the boys attended school, where they picked up the new American language. Schools were good around Franklin Borough and Johnstown; Bethlehem Steel, a benevolent despot, paid for good buildings and teachers and even an indoor swimming pool. But no one could completely shield the immigrant children from nativist bigotry. Ann Bosophy, the Stranks' fellow immigrant from Jarabenia, recalls cringing on the schoolroom floor after being struck by her first-grade teacher. Her sin was unthinkingly slipping into the Slovak tongue.

Mike never made that mistake. He did not know English when he began first grade; by the end of the year he was so proficient in it that he skipped the second. He even learned to joke around in the new tongue. He took up the French horn and learned it. Quickly. It was amazing, his relatives said: The boy never forgot anything. He could open the evening newspaper, read a page of it, and the next morning tell you exactly what all the articles said. A photographic memory.

He was shy around girls, Ann Strank, Pete's wife, recalled. Not outgoing. You would only notice him if you knew him. But then, not many of the boys in that town were at ease with girls, or vice versa. Men, he liked. Men, he understood. And men liked and understood Mike Strank.

His shyness had nothing to do with timidity. He saved his brother John's life in the mines once. It happened in 1933, when Mike was fifteen and John was eleven. Coal miners' children were allowed to go inside the tunnels sometimes, during breaks, and collect random shards of coal to fuel their families' stoves. One day, Mike and John were walking along in the darkness, feeling for lumps of coal. John, trailing his big brother, was idly

banging his coal shovel against the wall. On one bang the shovel made contact with an exposed high-power wire. John screamed, but could not let go;
the electricity fused his hand to the shovel. Mike spun and hurled his body
against the little boy like a football lineman throwing a block, knocking
him free. John fell to the ground screaming in terror, but safe from the
deadly current.

A few years later, during the second Johnstown Flood of 1936, Mike
calmly faced a current of a different kind. With most of the townspeople in
near-panic as the Conemaugh River waters rose dangerously near the peak
of the 1889 disaster, Mike calmly made his way down the steep incline to
have a look for himself. Scrambling back up, looking bored and deadpan, he
told his rapt little brothers, "It's gonna come, and it's gonna go. And that's
just the way it is." The little brothers were awed and calmed by Mike's air of
detachment.

By 1933 the Stranks had saved enough money to buy, for cash, a ten-
room duplex on the side of a hill above the Conemaugh. The family kept
five rooms for itself and rented out the other five. This would prove Vasil's
greatest claim on the good life in America. The Stranks were living in
unimaginable luxury now: When Mary came along a little later that year,
she was delivered by an actual midwife. Her arrival in the family gave the
three boys an expanded cycle of duties at night: One would wash the dishes,
one would dry them, and the third would take the baby out for a stroll.
(Jokester Mike at times would turn this into a Three Stooges routine, slipping his dried dishes back into the sink for John to wash all over again.)

Games of marbles on the kitchen floor. Touch football on the hard town
streets; leather basketballs heaved at quivering hoops tied to telephone
poles. Pennies saved for baseball cards and the collection plate. At night,
the three brothers sprawled near the kitchen stove, studying—Mike tutor-
ing each of them in turn. "Mike would help Pete and me with our home-
work," John Strank remembered. "He'd tutor us on the floor, near the stove
where it was nice and warm." The good life for the Stranks began to feel as
though it would never end.

It seemed that the mills, like the rest of America, would keep on expand-
ing forever, belching ever-brighter flames. Franklin Borough had grown so
confident of its unending prosperity that it built a new municipal building,
so opulent in its gleaming white brick that it was nicknamed the Taj Mahal.
The movie star Gene Kelly had come to town; he did a song-and-dance routine with the local sheriff at its dedication.

But things were not destined to go on like that forever. The year of the
"Taj Mahal" dedication and Gene Kelly's soft-shoe was a year of upheaval.
The year was 1929.

The Depression had sunk into eastern Pennsylvania well before Mike Strank graduated from high school in 1937. Soup kitchens had replaced the bustling activity in the mines and the mills; a steelworkers' strike had failed badly. Thousands of Slavs foraged for new jobs.

The smoke, dust, grime, and blackened skies of Mike's childhood seemed permanent features of the landscape. Even for a bright boy like Mike, college was beyond hope, the costs unimaginable. (His "Ambition," as noted in his 1937 high-school yearbook, was: "To Be President.")

Some workers had come to Franklin Borough while he was in high school; men who said they belonged to something called the WPA. President Roosevelt had created it so that people could work their way out of poverty. These WPA men had built a band shell in the town; sidewalks; some sewers. Mike learned that the men were being paid the impressive sum of fifty-seven dollars a month. He decided that he would see what Mr. Roosevelt had available for him.

He ended up in a similar brainstorm of the President's, one that perfectly suited his energy and developing physique: the Civilian Conservation Corps. The CCC was designed to wean young men off street corners by getting them involved in shoring up the nation's natural environment. Through the 1930's, youthful CCC workers planted millions of trees across America; they released nearly a billion game fish into the country's rivers and lakes; they built wildlife shelters, created camping grounds, and dug thousands of miles of canals for irrigation and transportation.

But the CCC had a greater function—one that did not fully reveal itself until America went to war. It served as a premilitary training experience for some three million boys, many of whom would flood into the armed services after Pearl Harbor. Administered by the Army, the CCC introduced its recruits to camp life, to military discipline, to physical fitness, and to a sense of loyalty to comrades and to a cause.

All this was certainly true of Mike Strank. The former French horn player, scholar, and good Catholic boy disappeared into the CCC in 1937 weighing 140 pounds and reemerged two years later a strapping 180, tanned and handsome. He had headed first for the Petrified Forest in Arizona; then he came back to Pennsylvania, working as a laborer on highway projects for another year.

He would have stayed on happily in the CCC, swinging an ax and hauling concrete under the great American sun, but the government denied his application for an extension: His father had by then found work a couple of days a week, and the family was no longer technically destitute.

Mike Strank was nineteen now. The year was 1939. In Europe, Hitler's legions were overrunning his Czech homeland, making slaves of his people.

Mike decided to join the Marines.

He didn't have to do it. He could have avoided military service altogether, given his Czech citizenship. Brother John always puzzled over the fact that the Marines allowed him in at all: Apparently, no one checked out his nationality.

Mike enlisted on October 6, 1939. He was the only one of the six flag-raisers to sign up before America entered the war. But soon the brainy Czech boy would transform himself into a prototype American fighting man: a tough, driven, and consummate leader, advancing without complaint toward what he came to understand was his certain death.

Three

AMERICA'S WAR

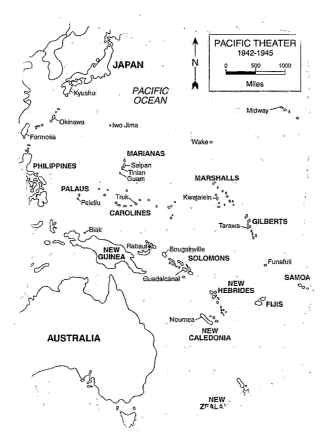

PACIFIC THEATER
1942-1945

0   500   1000

Miles

JAPAN

Kyushu

PACIFIC
OCEAN

Okinawa   • Iwo Jima

Formosa

Midway

Wake

MARIANAS

PHILIPPINES   Saipan
Tinian
Guam

MARSHALLS

PALAUS

Truk   Kwajalein

Peleliu

CAROLINES

Biak   Tarawa   GILBERTS

NEW   Rabaul   Bougainville
GUINEA   SOLOMONS   Funafuti

Guadalcanal   SAMOA

NEW
HEBRIDES

FIJIS

Noumea

AUSTRALIA   NEW
CALEDONIA

NEW
ZEALAND

> *What kind of people do they think we are? Is it possible they do not realize that we shall never cease to persevere against them until they have been taught a lesson which they and the world will never forget?*
>
> —WINSTON CHURCHILL, ON THE JAPANESE, 1942

WHEN IT STRUCK, it must have seemed a plot twist out of some futuristic movie, but this time for real.

A sleepy American Sunday afternoon in early December, Yuletide season in the air, roast chicken dinners finished, and the dishes washed, family radios tuned to Sammy Kaye's *Sunday Serenade* on the NBC Red Network, or a *Great Plays* presentation of *The Inspector General* on the Blue, or perhaps the pro football game between the Washington Redskins and the Philadelphia Eagles . . .

And then suddenly urgent bulletins crackling through static. The future had begun.

The shocking interruptions started at 2:25 P.M.

John Daly of the NBC Red was on the air first: *"The Japanese have attacked Pearl Harbor, Hawaii, by air!"* Five minutes later an anonymous announcer elaborated over both NBC systems:

> From the NBC newsroom in New York! President Roosevelt said in a statement today that the Japanese have attacked the Pearl Harbor . . . Hawaii from the air! I'll repeat that . . . President Roosevelt says that the Japanese have attacked Pearl Harbor in Hawaii from the air. This bulletin came to you from the NBC newsroom in New York.

Chapter opener: Map of the Pacific Theater. It appears in its entirety on page 61.

As the afternoon wore on, the bulletins multiplied and a vast radio audience built: as many as eighty million listeners by one estimate. Some of them heard an anonymous announcer describing the tumultuous damage by telephone from the roof of radio station KGU in Honolulu. After a bomb narrowly missed the broadcast tower the man screamed: *"This is no joke! This is real war!"*

The following day, most of those same listeners, including hundreds of thousands of children, tuned in again to hear President Franklin Roosevelt intone the six-and-a-half-minute speech whose key phrases would resound in American folklore:

> *Yesterday, December 7, 1941—a date which will live in infamy—the United States of America was suddenly and deliberately attacked by naval and air forces of the Empire of Japan . . .*
>
> *With confidence in our armed forces, with the unbounding determination of our people, we will gain the inevitable triumph, so help us God!*

No joke. The real thing.

Before Pearl Harbor America had looked across the Atlantic for an enemy. Adolf Hitler was the enemy we feared and Japan was dismissed as only a threat. But after the "day of infamy," newspaper maps of the Pacific and Asia were scrutinized at the kitchen tables of America.

Now America was in a World War, a "two-ocean war." Across the Atlantic, in Europe, the U.S. would be fighting in support of and with an allied force. But for years, Russian, English, and French troops would do most of the fighting and take the brunt of the beating. And it would be Stalin's troops who would really beat Hitler: seventy-five percent of the German troops who died fighting in World War II were killed by Russian troops.

Against Japan, however, America would stand virtually alone in the Pacific. Japan had violated American soil, and the first and last American battles of World War II would be fought there. The Pacific War would be "America's War."

America went to war in 1941. The Europeans had been fighting since 1939. But for millions of Asians, World War II had begun a decade before, in 1931.

Earlier in the century, Japanese civilians had lost control of the government to the military. Intent on making Japan into a world power, the military became preoccupied with Japan's one glaring weakness: Japan had almost no natural resources, and its industrial base was at the mercy of imports whose supply lines could be cut. Japan, they argued, had to acquire a secure resource base to guarantee its industrial security.

To the military, this goal was important enough to alter the very structure of Japanese society. The entire nation had to be militarized for the goal, and military thinking and training were imposed on each citizen.

The military squeezed the Japanese populace in an iron vise. On one side was a militarized educational system that prohibited free thought. Schools became boot camps complete with military language and physical discipline. Youth magazines carried jingoistic articles such as "The Future War between Japan and America." The final examination at the Maebashi middle school in March of 1941 required the students to discuss the necessity for overseas expansion. "It was commonplace for teachers to behave like sadistic drill sergeants, slapping children across the cheeks, hitting them with their fists, or bludgeoning them with bamboo or wooden swords. Students were forced to hold heavy objects, sit on their knees, stand barefoot in the snow, or run around the playground until they collapsed from exhaustion."

The other side of the vise was a regimen of draconian "thought control" laws that constrained all civilians. Imprisonment and torture were the fates of anyone who questioned authority.

Using the deceptively neutral term "Greater East Asia Co-Prosperity Sphere," Japanese propaganda claimed that Japan's aim was to free its neighbors from white colonial rule. Instead, Japan, like Nazi Germany, used a master-race mentality and a highly mechanized war machine to subjugate those it claimed to be freeing.

Tokyo enslaved "those peoples who lacked the capacity for independence," and stole their national resources. The Japanese attitude of superiority is evident in a document from the Imperial Rule Assistance Association entitled "Basic Concepts of the Greater East Asia Co-Prosperity Sphere": "Although we use the expression 'Asian Cooperation,' this by no means ignores the fact that Japan was created by the Gods or posits an automatic racial equality."

The nation "created by the Gods" initiated "co-prosperity" by raining terror down on Manchuria and China. With official approval and chilly detachment the Japanese army bombed Chinese cities and slaughtered everyone in its way, including unarmed men, women, and children.

Japan's first conquest was Manchuria in 1931. Then, to consolidate control of Manchuria, Japan attacked China in 1937.

The Japanese army employed ruthless tactics in China. Japanese airplanes bombed defenseless civilians. Rats infected with deadly bacteria were systematically released among the populace, making Japan the only combatant to use biological warfare in World War II. The Japanese army raped and pillaged with full encouragement from its superiors. But China is a vast country, and despite millions of casualties, Japan's war became a debilitating war of attrition.

And Japan's relations with China's allies, especially the U.S., became strained. Then, in 1939, war in Europe appeared to offer Japan a fortuitous way out of its dilemma.

Awed by the German blitzkrieg into France in May of 1940, Japan pushed into French Indochina. Japan's military leaders calculated that Hitler's attack on the Soviet Union in the summer of 1941 would be successful. They argued that now was the time to capture other resource-rich Asian countries. Japanese militarists reasoned that the U.S. and the U.K. would be preoccupied by the German thrust and would not dare to allocate large military resources to Asia. Hawks argued that the American public would not support a long war far from its shores. A slowly tightening American economic boycott of critical exports to Japan hastened the decision to act.

Japan's principal war aim was the conquest of European colonial empires in Asia. These empires would give Japan the resources it needed, and fostered a hope that a surrounded China would capitulate.

With a thoroughly militarized citizenry, an experienced army, and an immense navy, Japan was confident it could control the Pacific as its sphere of influence.

After disabling the U.S. fleet at Pearl Harbor, Japanese forces thrust southward toward Australia, overrunning Wake Island, Malaya, Singapore, the Philippines, and what is now Indonesia. Japanese forces soon controlled the Pacific battlefield. Only Australia in the south remained unconquered.

The Japanese army had even humbled the United States Army. On December 7, hours after hearing the news from Hawaii, General Douglas MacArthur sat in the Philippines, stunned, seemingly unable to give a command to mobilize the largest fleet of warplanes in the South Pacific. When nearly two hundred Japanese bombers arrived over Manila, ten hours after the Pearl Harbor attack, they simply obliterated this fleet, which sat in convenient clusters on the tarmac.

MacArthur was soon forced to withdraw 65,000 Filipinos and 15,000 American troops from a defense of Luzon and into the mountains of the

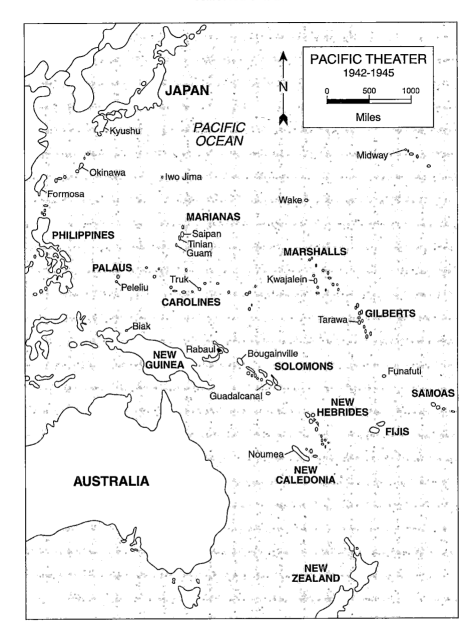

PACIFIC THEATER
1942-1945

Bataan peninsula. They retreated in the face of a converging Japanese naval and infantry force. President Roosevelt, realizing the Bataan defenders were doomed, ordered MacArthur, America's most decorated soldier of World War I, to flee by boat to Australia under cover of darkness.

"The battling bastards of Bataan," as the trapped troops styled themselves, held out, starving, until April 3, 1942—Good Friday. They surrendered, the most crushing defeat in American military history. The emaciated survivors were driven sixty-five miles on foot for three days in lacerating heat to a prison camp: the infamous Bataan Death March. Some 15,000 prisoners perished en route. They succumbed to thirst, starvation, exposure, and the merciless abuse of the Japanese soldiers, who whipped, beat, and shot those who stumbled or paused to lap at water in some roadside stream.

But if the men in charge of America's Pacific forces were temporarily stunned by the onslaught, America's boys were spoiling for vengeance.

Robert Leader, who later served with John Bradley in Easy Company, recalled his youthful indignation on that shocking Sunday afternoon: "We were *so mad* at the Japanese for bombing Pearl Harbor. They bombed on a Sunday, we went to school on Monday and they piped in President Roosevelt's 'Date of Infamy' speech. A bunch of us boys got together and said, 'Let's join up!' " He added, "I was never interested in killing people, but I believed that our country had been violated."

Hundreds of thousands of his contemporaries believed likewise.

Enlistment centers were overwhelmed by the flood of eager enlistees. The entire nation, in fact, seemed overnight to have snapped out of its Depression-era lethargy. Everyone scrambled to be of help. Rubber was needed for the war effort, and gasoline, and metal. A women's basketball game at Northwestern University was stopped so that the referee and all ten players could scour the floor for a lost bobby pin. Americans pitched in to support strict rationing programs and their boys turned out as volunteers in various collection "drives." Soon butter and milk were restricted along with canned goods and meat. Shoes became scarce, and paper, and silk. People grew "victory gardens" and drove at the gas-saving "victory speed" of thirty-five miles an hour. "Use it up, wear it out, make it do, or do without" became a popular slogan. Air-raid sirens and blackouts were scrupulously obeyed. America sacrificed.

For several horrifying months it seemed to be in vain. By the summer of 1942 the Japanese military had conquered a swath of territory that dwarfed Adolf Hitler's most fervent expansionist dreams.

So it was with great alarm that on July 4, 1942, American reconnaissance discovered a Japanese construction brigade building an airstrip on Guadalcanal, a jungle island near the southern tip of the Solomon Islands chain, to the northeast of Australia. An entrenched Japanese force there would spell disaster for Australia and the remaining allies in the South Pacific.

America knew it had to draw the line on this dangerous southern thrust. But who would take a stand? The British, Chinese, and American armies had all been defeated by Japan's Imperial Army. The Japanese appeared to be supermen, impossible to stop.

It was at this critical stage of the war that the United States Marine Corps burst onto the scene as a new kind of fighting force uniquely designed to wage a new kind of warfare.

The Marines had until then been an obscure fringe of the American armed forces. Organized as an internal security and marksmen adjunct of the Navy in 1798, the Marine Corps had never played a significant role in American military history. As recently as the spring of 1940, the Marines had numbered only 25,000 enlisted men.

But by then, forward-thinking military strategists had long since perceived the coming importance of Marines in twentieth-century warfare.

It was in the early 1920's that a veteran Marine officer of World War I by the name of Holland M. Smith (nickname: "Howlin' Mad") assembled a team of officers to reconceive the Marines' mission. Smith, a man at once pugnacious, profane, and professorial, proposed that the business of mounting continental land offensives was the historic province of the Army, and should remain so. But the ominous stirrings in the Far East, Smith insisted, suggested that a great many American boys must soon be trained to master a more exacting array of combat skills. These skills would coalesce around the concept of amphibious warfare: troops disembarking from large ships, speeding toward enemy beaches under heavy fire, and charging ahead to enemy-held islands. Smith and his colleagues foresaw that the islands would be in the Pacific; the enemy, Japan.

Amphibious landings are the most difficult military operations in warfare. In 1915, a British-led Allied force attempted a sea-based landing at Gallipoli in Turkey; the thrust ended in disaster. After that, most military experts agreed amphibious operations were impossible against modern, mechanized weapons.

Howlin' Mad thought otherwise. Over two decades, he and his staff created, refined, and rehearsed the modern science of amphibious warfare. There were four Army divisions in the South Pacific when the urgency arose for an amphibious expedition to seize Guadalcanal. But this battle called for the preeminent amphibious warriors in the world. It was time to send in the Marines.

The Marines waded onto Guadalcanal on August 7, 1942. Caught by surprise, the Japanese did not at first oppose their landing. The Marines streamed in and unloaded their supplies until the Japanese navy finally counterattacked. After losing four ships, the U.S. Navy fled. The Marines ashore were abandoned, standing alone against an enemy that had never been defeated.

For weeks these isolated Marines fought off attacks by Japanese ground troops as unopposed Japanese air and naval power struck at them day after day.

The Marine commander, Alexander Vandegrift, rallied his men. They were Marines, he exhorted them, and "this will be no Bataan." Fighting against seemingly impossible odds, living on two meals a day of captured Japanese rice, the Marines secured the island by December. Some 23,000 Japanese were killed; another 13,000 were evacuated. Japan had suffered its first defeat of the war.

And the Marines had won a place in the heart of America. Guadalcanal was a fight won by teamwork, but also by heroes, whose exploits became instant legends. Heroes such as Sergeant John Basilone, a rugged New Jerseyite who had enlisted in the Marines after telling his mother, "The Army isn't tough enough for me." With "Death Before Dishonor" tattooed on his arm, he had led eight hundred of his comrades in a nonstop seventy-two-hour firefight in October against several thousand Japanese, winning the fight that helped change the course of the battle and thus the war.

After the enemy had destroyed one of Basilone's sections, leaving only two men still in action, the sergeant grabbed a damaged gun, repaired it by feel in pitch darkness, under withering fire, and manned it himself, holding the line until replacements arrived.

Later, with his ammunition running low and his supply lines cut off, the sergeant charged through enemy lines carrying a hundred pounds of urgently needed shells for his gunners. They remained in action and virtually annihilated the Japanese regiment.

For that heroism, Sergeant Basilone became the first enlisted Marine to be awarded the Medal of Honor in World War II. Offered an officer's commission after touring the United States to promote the sale of war bonds, Basilone turned it down and asked to be sent back to the Pacific. "I wasn't scared," he said, in a quote that resounded among the younger troops. "I didn't have time to be. Besides, I had my men to worry about."

The Marines had stunned the Japanese and handed them their first military defeat of the war. But it was perhaps an even greater psychological defeat.

Japanese troops had long been told they were racially and morally superior to the soft and materialistic Western man. Guadalcanal proved otherwise.

For the Marines, Guadalcanal revealed a disquieting truth: America's War would be fought on the most primitive level, a war fought like no other.

In the fall of 1942 America was fighting two very different enemies.

The battles in North Africa were between Westernized armies who fought by the "rules." Ernie Pyle assured his millions of American readers that there the Germans were fighting "a pretty clean war." The German Panzer leader Hans von Luck called it the "always fair war," and when, years later, the German radio-television network ORTF produced a film on the campaign, its title was *The War Without Hate*.

Gentlemen's agreements suspended hostilities for the day at five o'clock each afternoon, and each side held its fire for medics to care for the wounded.

Combat was fierce, casualties were heavy, and passion ran high when fighting the Germans. But rules were followed and a sense of restraint existed in Europe that was absent in the Pacific.

The Marines headed for Guadalcanal had heard of the atrocities committed by the Japanese army over the years. In 1938 *Life* magazine published photographs, smuggled out by a German businessman, of Japanese atrocities in Nanking.

Nanking, capital of China, had fallen to the Japanese on December 13, 1937. As the Japanese entered the capital, only unarmed civilians remained. The victorious troops plastered the city with billboards featuring a smiling Japanese soldier handing a bowl of rice to an appreciative Chinese child. The poster proclaimed the peaceful intentions of "co-prosperity." But instead the Chinese suffered an orgy of torture and death.

In less than a month Japanese troops, with the encouragement of their officers, killed up to 350,000 Chinese civilians. Pregnant women were marched to one killing field where Japanese placed bets on the sex of the fetus about to tumble from its mother's womb, cut by a samurai sword. In another area of town drunken soldiers laughed and tossed babies in the air to be skewered on the ends of their buddies' bayonets. Dogs grew too fat to walk, feasting on the corpses in the streets.

Three hundred fifty thousand: That amounted to more civilians dying in one city in one month than died in entire countries during the entire war. In six years of combat France lost 108,000 civilians; Belgium 101,000; the Netherlands 242,000. The Japanese in Nanking killed even more than the atomic bombs later would. (Hiroshima had 140,000 dead, Nagasaki

70,000.) The Japanese "loot all, kill all, burn all" scorched-earth policy in North China would eventually reduce the population from forty-four million to twenty-five million. Co-prosperity indeed.

The U.S. Army had encountered the Japanese army's ways in the Philippines and Burma. Stories of buddies found trussed like pigs, disemboweled with their severed genitals in their mouths circulated, as did horrifying accounts of boys staked in the hot sun, forced to endure the voracious bugs who savored the honey rubbed into the prisoner's eyes and mouth.

However, the Marines on Guadalcanal had not experienced the atrocities firsthand and found them hard to believe. Until they mistakenly extended a hand of mercy to the Japanese.

On August 11, Frank Goettge led a patrol to rescue a Japanese unit on an isolated spit of ground on Guadalcanal. Marine intelligence had reported sighting a white flag, and a captured Japanese sailor said the unit was unable to maintain itself and inclined to give up.

Goettge called for volunteers to rescue the Japanese unit. Twenty-five, including an interpreter and a Navy surgeon, stepped forward.

Landing on the beach identified by the informant, Goettge announced he was there to help the trapped Japanese. His offer was met by withering gunfire. After hours of fighting only one Marine managed to escape and swim away. As he looked back at the bloody shore, he could see the glint of Japanese swords hacking his buddies' bodies.

A Marine patrol later found the mutilated corpses. They had been violated in the worst possible manner. Chunks of flesh with the Marine Corps symbol tattooed on them had been hacked off arms and stuffed into their mouths. The Marines began to realize they were fighting a war of no rules.

What shocked Marine sensibilities the most was the Japanese treatment of their noncombatant corpsmen. U.S. Navy medics would respond to calls for help from wounded Japanese who would cry "Corpsman! Corpsman!" in English. When the corpsmen came to their aid, they were then either treacherously shot by the wounded Japanese or blown up by hand grenades concealed on their bodies.

America's War in the Pacific would be a war without quarter, fought with no rules. It would be a primitive battle, a fight to extinction.

The Japanese fighting man believed he was fighting in the proud tradition of ancient samurai. But this was not the case.

Bushido, the "Way of the Warrior," had for centuries been the honored code of Japan's proud samurai caste. In the first half of the twentieth century the military romanticized the "Way," calling upon all young men to be will-

ing to die for their Emperor. It was this interpretation of Bushido that motivated the Japanese soldiers to fight to the death in a manner the Marines
judged fanatical.

But this ideal was not the real thing. Rather, it was a corruption of
Bushido.

In the past the Bushido code had been specialized and isolated. The
samurai had always been a small elite within the larger society. For them,
Bushido defined a life of honor and duty. But in the early 1900's the Japanese military set forth an updated version of Bushido. Its aim was to make
warriors of the entire male populace. Death in battle was portrayed as an
honor to the family and a transcendent act on the part of the individual.
Surrender was a disgrace to the soldier and his family.

This vulgarized version of the Warrior's Way would have surprised samurai of an earlier era. Those professional warriors had never advocated a will-
ingness to sacrifice themselves for anyone. A true samurai would slice his
belly open over an issue of honor. But he didn't believe mass suicide in
hopeless situations was sound strategy. As the American General George
Patton phrased it: "No one ever won a war by dying for their country. They
won by making the other son-of-a-bitch die for his."

But the twentieth-century Japanese military wasn't being run by samurai.
The new leaders taught a cult of death, that sacrificing your life is the ultimate beautiful goal. A corruption of Bushido.

The young men the Japanese military drew into its ranks were never
aware of this corruption. They had no outside information on which to
build critical judgments. They were, in effect, brainwashed to believe that
by laying down their lives they were walking in the footsteps of heroic
samurai.

Not surprisingly, the military hierarchy had little respect for the products
of the system they had designed. They referred to army draftees as *"issen
gorin." "Issen gorin"* meant "one yen, five rin," the cost of mailing a draft-
notice postcard—less than a penny.

"They were expendable; there was an unlimited supply for the price of
the postcards. Weapons and horses were treated with solicitous care, but no
second-class private was as valuable as an animal. After all, a horse cost real
money. Privates were only worth *issen gorin.*"

Later in the Pacific campaign, a captured Japanese officer observed American doctors tending to the broken bodies of wounded Japanese soldiers. He
expressed surprise at the resources being expended upon these men, who
were too badly injured to fight again. "What would you do with these men?"
a Marine officer asked. "We'd give each a grenade," was his answer. "And if
they didn't use it, we'd cut their jugular vein."

To the Japanese fighting man, surrender meant humiliation. His family would be dishonored, his name would be stricken from the village rolls, he would cease to exist, and his superiors would kill him if they got their hands on him. All in the name of a version of Bushido cynically devised to make young Japanese men fodder for the military's adventures.

Unable to surrender, forced to fight to the death, the young Japanese soldier had no respect for Americans who didn't do the same. So a tragedy occurred in the Pacific. A tragedy brought about by the Japanese military leaders who forced their brutalized young men to be brutal themselves.

Back in America, the dramatic island victory on Guadalcanal and its heroes galvanized a new wave of American boys. The Marines, a volunteer force, had suddenly become the branch of choice, especially among boys who, like Jesse Boatwright, were looking for the biggest challenges: "We felt they sent the Marines to the toughest places, and if it wasn't tough, the Army went in."

Young kids were faking birth certificates and urine samples—not to get out, but to get in. Pee Wee Griffiths made it into boot camp by stuffing himself with bananas. At one hundred eight pounds, the Ohio boy was rejected on his first enlistment try; he was four pounds under the Marine minimum. "They told me to eat as many bananas as I could," Pee Wee recalled to me. "I ate so many bananas, it felt like thousands. But it only put two more pounds on me. But when I told them how many I'd eaten they must have felt sorry for me; they let me in."

James Buchanan signed with literary visions of war crowding his thoughts. He'd been inspired by the book *Guadalcanal Diary*, published just as he came of age.

And then there was Tex Stanton, a dark-haired boy from the Lone Star State who by rights should not have been a Marine. Tex had a bad right eye. Some young men might have used this as a legitimate excuse to duck service. Tex Stanton found a way around it. Sitting in front of the eye chart during his physical, he managed to hold the "blinder" card in such a way that he could recite the letters twice with his good eye. His impairment was detected during a second physical, but the Texan appealed so strongly that the doctor shrugged and passed him through. He would become an outstanding BAR (Browning Automatic Rifle) man, a close buddy of the flagraisers.

"You went into the Marines because you wanted to be the best," Stanton reminisced to me many years later. "We had the hardest training, hit the hardest spots. We *were* the best."

Their first stop was basic training: boot camp.

It was the mission of boot camp to quickly convert recruits' naive boyish fervor into something American society had never generated before: a mass-produced, numerically immense cadre of warrior-specialists at once technically sophisticated and emotionally impervious to the horrors of battle.

And selfless. These masses of kids from a nation of individualists would have to be processed through a radical redefinition of the Self. No longer would a boy be the center of his sunlit universe—family, friends, neighborhood, town, or city. Now his selfhood would consist of integer in a precision-tooled, many-faceted human war machine.

Battles are won by teams working together, not by heroic individuals fighting on their own. The central function of boot camp was to erase the impulses of individuality and get the recruits thinking as members of a team.

Aware that the American individualistic ethic did not lend itself to easy subordination, the military designed basic training as "intensive shock treatment," rendering the trainee "helplessly insecure in the bewildering newness and complexity of his environment." Individuals had to be broken to powerlessness in order that their collectivity, their units, might become powerful.

As Jesse Boatwright told me, "The first thing you learn is you're training for war and you're not going in alone. War is a team sport. From the general on down, everybody is a team and all of you have to do your part."

William Hoopes remembered that "they break everybody down as an individual. Our drill instructor (DI) would have us fall out at two-thirty or three A.M. He'd say things like, 'Everybody fall out, I don't want to hear any fucking noise except your eyeballs clicking.' "

And Robert Lane recalled, "The discipline was extremely tight. You didn't cough unless you had permission."

"When you first enter the Corps," wrote Art Buchwald, "their only goal is to reduce you to a stuttering, blubbering bowl of bread pudding . . . The purpose . . . is to break you down, and then rebuild you into the person the Marine Corps wants . . ."

"It was a subtle destruction of your civilian mentality," is how Robert Leader remembered it. "And I mean that in a good way. A Marine can't think like a civilian, he has to think differently to be a good fighter."

The erasure of individuality would create malleability to discipline; repetitive actions would instill that automatic response for which the services strove.

And there was more. "Don't get close to anybody," the tilt-brim, chin-strapped drill instructors would warn boys not long removed from earning their World Brotherhood Boy Scout patches. "Because every other one of you sum'bitches is probably gonna get killed!" When a recruit named Eugene Sledge innocently wondered why his sergeant had asked him about scars or birthmarks, the topkick barked back, "So they can identify you on some Pacific beach after the Japs blast off your dog tags!"

They were growing fit; learning drill and marksmanship and weaponry and chain of command, learning to obey. They were learning to repeat simple, vital tasks ad nauseam; learning to live in alternating states of boredom and lethal urgency.

It was a world in which the basic implement of combat, the rifle, was an object of obsession. The rifle was cleaned several times a day. The rifle was a Marine's best friend. The rifle had to be taken apart into its thousand parts and then reassembled, on the double. And then taken apart and reassembled blindfolded. The use of the rifle was mastered—standing, sitting, prone—or else. The rifle, sometimes several of them, was a recruit's bedmate if he screwed up. Above all, the rifle was a *rifle*. Make the dipshit mistake of calling it a "gun" and you got humiliated before the entire company—forced to run up and down in front of your buddies in your skivvies, one hand holding your rifle and the other your gonads, screaming over and over: "This is my rifle and this is my gun! One is for business, the other for fun!"

All militaries harden their recruits, instill the basics, and bend young men to their will. But the Marine Corps provides its members with a secret weapon. It gives them the unique culture of pride that makes the Marines the world's premier warrior force. "The Navy has its ships, the Air Force has its planes, the Army its detailed doctrine, but 'culture'—the values and assumptions that shape its members—is all the Marines have." They call this culture *"esprit de corps."*

"No one can explain esprit de corps," the veteran Jesse Boatwright told me. "They drilled it into you from the word go. You're the greatest, they told us. And they showed us why. They showed us the history of the Marine Corps, the proud history. They made you feel like you were a part of a great chain of events."

For Pee Wee Griffiths, esprit de corps brought him into contact with greatness. "I thought I was special because I had great men among me," he said, "and I thought maybe some day I could be special like them. You looked up to those guys. That's what made us feel proud. Great leaders, great men."

Newsman Jim Lehrer would later write about the special Marine warrior pride ingrained into him in boot camp: "I learned that Marines never leave their dead and wounded behind, officers always eat last, the U.S. Army is chickenshit in combat, the Navy is worse, and the Air Force is barely even on our side."

And becoming a member of this elite force was not automatic.

In boot camp the boys were cautioned: "You are not Marines. You are recruits. We'll see if you will be worthy of the title of United States Marine!"

Earning the title of Marine was an honor recruits strove for. As Robert Lane put it, "You thought the Marines were the best and you had to be the best."

Alone among the U.S. military services, the Marines have bestowed their name on their enlisted ranks. The Army has Army officers and soldiers, the Navy has naval officers and sailors, the Air Force has Air Force officers and airmen—but the Marines have only Marines.

"We felt we were superior to any serviceman," was how William Hoopes summarized the process. "They made you into the best fighting man in the world."

CALL OF DUTY

APPLY, OR WRITE, TO NEAREST RECRUITING STATION

*Those who expect to reap the blessings of liberty
must undergo the fatigues of supporting it.*
                                    —THOMAS PAINE

ON THE DAY JAPANESE BOMBS surprised the sailors at Pearl Harbor there was a six-year spread among the flagraisers-to-be.

Pennsylvanian Mike Strank was the oldest at twenty-one, already a Marine corporal with two years of service. Pima Ira Hayes was an eighteen-year-old sophomore at the Phoenix Indian School with eight months to go before he enlisted in the Marines. Six months younger than Ira, Jack Bradley was a recent high-school graduate and apprenticing his way to a Wisconsin funeral director's license. Harlon Block was seventeen, still a school year away from his senior heroics for the Weslaco Panthers. Franklin Sousley was a sixteen-year-old junior in high school, rushing home to do his chores. Rene Gagnon was only fifteen, in his second and last year of high school, soon to melt into the routine of New Hampshire mill life.

Mike was three years older than Ira, six years older than Rene, large gaps for young boys. The boys would always behold Mike as their grizzled leader, the "old man." The six boys would meet each other for the first time in April of 1944 when they came together at a new camp to form a new Marine division. Each of them arrived there by different paths.

Mike Strank got to the war first.

He had enlisted on October 6, 1939—the only one of the six flagraisers to sign up before America entered the war. He plowed through boot camp

---

Chapter opener: WWII-era U.S. Marine Corps recruiting poster.

at Parris Island, his 180-pound frame taking on hard bulk by the week. Mike was a "born leader," the oldest of the Strank boys, whom Vasil had relied upon to steer John and Pete the right way. Now the Marines quickly recognized his talents.

Mike thrived on the routine and loved this rough-and-tumble man's world. The former French horn player with the photographic memory fit right in with the Marine Corps demands for excellence.

Private First Class Strank sailed first to Guantánamo Bay for additional training in January of 1941. America was at peace, but the Marines had been practicing amphibious assaults against Caribbean islands for over sixteen years by now. Since 1924, Marine leaders had been predicting that their next major challenge would be conquering islands in the Pacific. And they would be ready.

Corporal Strank was back at Parris Island by April of 1941, and he began molding other young Marines at New River, North Carolina (now Camp Lejeune). He became Sergeant Strank two months after Pearl Harbor.

In March 1942 Mike returned home for a short leave. Friends observed that Mike had thrived in the Marine Corps. He had an impressive physique to match his confidence and intelligence. His body rippled with strength, his bright white smile attractive against his dark tan. "Mike changed in the Marine Corps," remembers his brother John Strank. "He had bulked up and was solid muscle."

Three months later he was headed for combat. Not toward Europe as he had hoped, to help avenge his ravaged Czech homeland, but in the opposite direction: He joined the great swarm of young American men hastily assembled, trained, armed, and rushed west to stem the shocking Japanese onslaught in the Pacific.

At about the same time, Ira Hayes was shedding the vestiges of his Pima Indian boyhood at boot camp in San Diego.

He'd enlisted on August 26, 1942. Ira's enlistment surprised many because he certainly wasn't a warrior type. He was quiet, passive, and noncompetitive. "In our culture we don't encourage competition," Dana Norris told me. "We lived in a cooperative society, we leaned on each other, did things together." But somehow Ira got it into his head that he should go off to fight for his country with the Marines.

His mother, Nancy, remembered Ira's determination to be a Marine: "He just made up his mind to go. We didn't want him to go. We wanted him to stay. But he brought home his papers and we signed them. He said he wanted to go and defend us."

The Marine Corps recruiter noticed that Ira already had an arrest record. In the past year he had been jailed twice for being drunk and disorderly. No one remembers how or why Ira began drinking. But the record is there. Perhaps the Corps hoped their discipline would make him change his ways.

His Pima culture had enveloped him on the day before he set forth in America's War. Nancy Hayes invited the tribal elders, church leaders, and choir to dinner in his honor. The guests enjoyed a sumptuous feast— jackrabbit stew, Jobe's favorite dish, cooked in clay pots over flaming mesquite branches; spicy tortillas, fried potatoes, wild spinach, beans whipped into a pudding.

Then each guest spoke to Ira about honor, loyalty, his family, and his people. The Pima abhorred war and all its brutality; but in this instance, the elders agreed that it was necessary.

The choir sang hymns, and each guest embraced young Ira Hayes and said a private good-bye. All prayed for his safety.

His early letters home from San Diego show that his boyish innocence did not vanish overnight. Thoughts of home were on his mind on August 29, 1942, when he wrote his "Dear Folks":

> *I'm really grateful for the big dinner you gave me and the people you invited. Things those old men said are really helpful now when you realize all they said about God taking care of me and I really feel that he is. I'm being a good boy and always will because right now in times like this you have to get on the right way of life.*

And he signed his letter with a sign of his new pride in his position:

> *From a guy who is proud he's a Marine*
> *and in his country's service.*
> *Ira H. Hayes*

And a somewhat later correspondence revealed an earnestness that is especially touching, given the demons that Ira battled later in his life:

> *Today, Sunday, this morning me and another fellow went to church and heard a good sermon. The sermon was "Alcohol versus Christianity." Which was a swell sermon made me cry to think I was once a fool but glad and happy to think that I have redeemed myself before my Lord. Therefore I am not scared in whatever the future brings me.*

The Marine Corps, with its proud tradition, was the perfect organization to introduce this young Pima to the outside world. Ira wrote home that his fellow Marines were "swell guys, the best friends a fellow could have." He would "not take a thousand dollars to separate from them."

And being a Pima and a Marine meant Ira was doubly proud. When he read a newspaper clipping that his mother mailed him about Marine Corporal Richard Lewis, the first Pima killed in action in the war, "Ira wept tears of pride," a fellow Marine recalled.

Marine Corps boot camp is widely recognized as the most demanding recruit training in the world. But Ira wrote home that he enjoyed it and when the other guys complained of sore muscles and aching feet he "felt sorry for them." On the sharpshooter range he scored just six points short of expert. He was so proud of his achievement that he included a small sketch of his sharpshooter's badge in his next letter home.

A sign of how good a Marine Ira was is that when he completed boot camp he applied for and was accepted for parachute training. Jumping out of airplanes in 1942 was a challenging and dangerous business. Marine parachute school accepted only the best candidates. Even though the training was restricted to these elite, there was a forty percent washout rate.

But Ira was determined. His buddy William Faulkner remembered the first time the two of them jumped from an airplane. "He went from brown to white and I went from white to green," Faulkner said. "He hit the ground hard, like a sack of wet cement. We were both scared, but we did it." And Ira wrote to his parents: "Everytime I land and get out of my chute harness, I look up and think did I really do it. Then I thank God for safety and courage."

Ira earned his USMC Paratrooper wings on November 30, 1942. He was proud to be the first Pima to graduate from parachute training. His buddies dubbed him "Chief Falling Cloud." The Marines photographed Ira crouched with his parachute ready to jump from an airplane. The photo caused a sensation back home when it appeared in the Pima *Gazette* and the Phoenix Indian School *Redskin*.

"Everyone in school saw Ira's photo as a paramarine," Eleanor Pasquale remembered. "We were all proud of him. He made us proud to be Pimas." And Ira was proud of his elite status as a paratrooper. He wrote: "I'm glad you are proud of me and I don't blame you. Everybody must think I am a fool. But it means a lot to me. I'll say I'm glad to be here in the Para Battalion. It's been said time and time again around here that the Parachute outfit was the toughest and best equipped outfit in all the branches of the military, that's why we get paid extra."

And he began signing his letters: "Sincerely, a Paratrooper, PFC I. H. Hayes."

He was assigned to Company B, 3rd Parachute Battalion, Divisional Special Troops, 3rd Marine Division. The good boy was now ready for war.

The summer and fall of 1942 had been eventful on fronts far distant from the football fields of south Texas. In August, about the time Harlon was drawing his pads and helmet, massive American air attacks began in Europe, and German planes pulverized Stalingrad.

The North African invasion began in November, around Homecoming time. And in the South Pacific the Marines' stunning victory at Guadalcanal—the first American land battle of World War II—would ignite new waves of patriotism and fighting fervor among ardent, impressionable American boys.

It certainly ignited the Weslaco High Panthers. During their winning season in the fall of 1942, Glen Cleckler had the idea for all of the seniors on the team to enlist in the Marine Corps together after they graduated in May. If Harlon had any qualms about fighting he kept them to himself. It would have been difficult to voice his pacifist background, as he was the only Seventh-Day Adventist on the team. It would have been much more comfortable to go along with his buddies, to be part of the team.

Glen broached the idea with the principal, who not only endorsed it but also arranged for the boys' classes to be accelerated so they could enlist early. Patriotic fever ran high in the Valley.

Harlon told his parents he was going to enlist along with his football buddies. For Belle the news could not have been worse. War. Fighting. Guns. The Marines! Belle pleaded with Harlon to enter the medical service, to avoid the killing. As a Seventh-Day Adventist Harlon had a legitimate out; he didn't have to fight.

If Harlon had stayed in the Adventist school he would have heard other voices of caution. "My brothers went in as conscientious objectors," Harlon's girlfriend, Catherine Pierce, recalls. "They served in the medical corps to help save lives, not to take them. I don't know why Harlon didn't consider that option."

But at Weslaco High School there were no forces to amplify his Adventist background. Just the opposite. There were enthusiastic newspaper articles praising the boys for their patriotism. The high school held a special pep rally, with cheerleaders shaking their pom-poms for the boys as they were introduced to thunderous applause.

"Mr. Block sided with Harlon," Leo Ryan told me. "He said it would make him a man." Belle was beside herself. "She said, 'I won't sign those papers,' " Mel Block remembers. "Dad signed them."

In January 1943 a photo appeared in the Valley newspaper. It was a photo of thirteen Weslaco Panthers, lined up facing Marine Captain D. M. Taft. Captain Taft held a Bible in his left hand; his right hand was up, as were those of Harlon, Leo Ryan, Glen Cleckler, and their other buddies as they took their oath.

For Belle it was a last, painful compromise. The move to the Valley, Harlon leaving the Adventist school, working on the oil trucks, the girlfriends, playing football on the Sabbath, and now joining the Marines, the unit that was known as "the first to fight."

But Harlon had no fear, he wasn't worried. He was part of an enthusiastic team, going along with his buddies. He was eighteen years old, his head full of images about the glory of war. Commandments about killing were only an abstraction.

The recruiter in San Antonio had misspoken. The boys did not stay together. They were split up after boot camp and scattered among various units. It was part of the breakdown of the individual's past life, his remolding as a Marine.

At boot camp near San Diego, Harlon was unfazed. He quickly took to wearing his helmet at a cocky angle and made friends quietly.

Joe Pagac was a bunkmate of Harlon Block's during that training program. The two new buddies had mess duty together, which gave them liberty from night to noon. They visited San Diego just about every night: They went bowling. Sometimes Harlon would tell Joe about what it was like to drive an oil truck to Brownsville. How he loved to play football. He'd talk about how beautiful and green the countryside was in the Valley. (Joe had always thought it was dry.)

Good duty, all in all, mess duty, Joe Pagac remembered. Nothing at all like what they were about to experience.

Like Ira, Harlon was proud of qualifying as a parachutist in the Marines. He invited his brother Ed Block, Jr., then living in San Diego, to come and watch his first jump on May 22, 1943. "I stood outside the fenced-off area to watch Harlon jump," Ed remembered. "That night we celebrated at my house. I asked Harlon how it felt to jump. He said, 'It scared the hell out of me!'

"Harlon also said that he snapped his watchband when he leapt from the plane," Ed continued. "He and some buddies searched the landing area for the watch but couldn't find it. Then a week later in another jump Harlon told me he was floating down and had to spread his legs to avoid landing directly on his watch!"

There was a saying in the Corps that there are only two types of Marines: those who are overseas and those who are about to go overseas. And on November 15, 1943, Harlon shipped out in the distant wakes of Mike and Ira.

The Raiders were the toughest outfit in the Pacific, and Mike Strank quickly became one of the toughest of the Raiders. This was the outfit that introduced "gung ho!" into the American fighting lexicon. The Raiders were legendary risk-taking killers in the South Pacific, the Green Berets of their day. Theirs was the original Mission Impossible: to storm beaches considered inaccessible in advance of larger forces; to launch rapid, surprise raids with light arms against an enemy that always outnumbered them; and to roam behind enemy lines for long periods, cut off from their own command.

Mike was more than six feet tall now, and weighed nearly two hundred pounds, all hard muscle. As the brawny man replaced the wiry miner's boy, the introspective musician gave way to the seasoned, charismatic leader. The intuitive brilliance he'd shown in childhood now focused acutely on the inner subtleties and structures of Marine life. Mike concealed his searching intelligence beneath a rough-and-tumble exterior.

He embraced life in the Raiders on two seemingly contradictory levels. The emerging warrior in him savored their cutting edge of lethal aggression. At the same time, the instinctual big brother in him responded to their strong ethic of cooperation and mutual protection; of working constantly as a seamless unit. That, after all, was what "gung ho" meant: not mindless fanaticism, but constant teamwork and brotherhood.

Mike landed with the Raiders at Uvéa and Pavuvu, where they found little opposition.

Bloody Bougainville was a different story.

Bougainville was a key "hop" in the Pacific command's island-hopping campaign. Guadalcanal had been the first hop, and the capture of Bougainville, the northernmost island in the Solomon chain, would push the Japanese out of the South Pacific once and for all.

Bougainville was a wet hell. As the Marine commander there later wrote, "Never had men in the Marine Corps had to fight and maintain themselves over such difficult terrain as was encountered on Bougainville." There were centipedes three fingers wide whose bite caused excruciating pain for a day, butterflies as big as little birds, thick and nearly impenetrable jungles, bottomless mangrove swamps, man-eating-crocodile-infested rivers, millions of insects, four types of rats larger than house cats, and heavy daily torrents of rain bringing enervating humidity. And sacred skull shrines, reminders of days of cannibalism and head-hunting.

John Monks, Jr., quoting a Marine on Bougainville, described what night was like: "From seven o'clock in the evening till dawn, with only centipedes and lizards and scorpions and mosquitoes begging to get acquainted—wet, cold, exhausted, but unable to sleep—you lay there and shivered and thought and hated and prayed. But you stayed there. You didn't cough, you didn't snore, and you changed your position with the least amount of noise. For it was still great to be alive."

Chuck Ables, who fought on a number of Pacific islands, called Bougainville "the closest thing to a living hell that I ever saw in my life."

There was also the matter of an entrenched Japanese force: a murky army whose numbers and exact distribution were impossible to determine beneath the jungle foliage.

Air attacks on the island began in August of 1943 and continued through the fall. Diversionary landings on nearby islands occurred in October, as distant Marine units hurried to the area, completing the encirclement strategy. Among the arrivals were Ira Hayes, who landed at Vella Lavella in October, and Harlon Block, who hit New Caledonia four days before Christmas. For both these boys, their hard-won parachutists' wings were now matters of ancient history. What they would experience on the island of Bougainville would change their lives forever.

As these great events were thrashing themselves out in the Pacific, a certain mild-mannered young fellow in Appleton, Wisconsin, was preparing, cautiously and under a few critical misimpressions, to do his duty.

Jack Bradley was nineteen in January 1943. Two years out of high school, he had just completed an eighteen-month apprenticeship course in the mortuary arts. But it was clear that he would be drafted at any moment.

Jack's father, Cabbage, the old infantry doughboy who was tending bar in an Appleton hotel, had some advice. Enlist in the Navy, he urged his son. You'll have a clean place to sleep; none of those foul trenches like the ones I endured. (To the fathers of other sons, Cabbage was a little more blunt. Have your son go into the Navy, he told them. He'll die clean and on a full stomach.)

And so on January 13, 1943, my father and Bob Connelly hitchhiked from Appleton down to Oshkosh and signed up with the U.S. Navy. Cabbage had convinced his son and himself that the Navy would take one look at Jack's mortician apprenticeship and escort him to a relatively safe position, such as pharmacist's mate.

Cabbage was half right. The Navy did, in time, take notice of the apprenticeship.

The hometown recruiter had told Jack that he would be stationed at the Great Lakes naval base, not far from Appleton. But the ink was scarcely dry on their signatures when Jack and Bob were assigned to the massive Navy training center in faraway Farragut, Idaho.

The boys' first stop was Milwaukee, where they stood naked together for their physical exams. Then they boarded a troop train with wood-burning stoves for the three-day haul west. Connelly remembered that they sat upright for nearly the whole trip. This wasn't what they'd been expecting, but it was an adventure.

They pulled in, exhausted but in holiday spirits, at four A.M. on February 10, 1943, at Athol, Idaho, to board a Navy bus for Farragut. In their cockiness they assured each other that they were in "Asshole, Idaho."

At Farragut they got their heads shaved, saw their first mountains, came down with a virus called "cat fever," stayed very cold most of the time, drilled in rowboats on a frigid lake, eight guys to a side, and started to imagine the good life on board a ship.

In March, young Jack Bradley received yet another jolt: He had been selected as a Seabee—the Navy engineering cadre that often did its road-building and railroad-repairing work under hostile fire. "Your dad stormed into the office and demanded to know why," Bob Connelly recalled to me. "They told him it was because he was color-blind. Why they wanted color-blind Seabees, your father never could figure out, but he hit the roof. From what he knew, the Seabees worked like hell and fought on land. He told them, 'I'm *not* color-blind! I had a beer last night! Test me again!'

"Your father and I," Connelly concluded, chuckling, "didn't care for guns."

Jack Bradley got his wish. He was not required to join the Seabees. But this bit of luck, which Jack thought would keep him far from the front lines, ensured he would later participate in the worst battle in the history of the Marine Corps.

But Jack had some more good duty in front of him. In the fall of 1943, about the time Harlon sailed off for the South Pacific, Jack Bradley was transferred to Oaknoll Naval Hospital in Oakland, California. This was the type of duty he had imagined.

But he wasn't far from the fighters. It was his job to change the dressings of the burned veterans of Pacific battles, to empty their bedpans, to give them their painkillers, to adjust their IV's. He was new to this work and young-looking to my later eyes, but to his fellow seventeen- and eighteen-year-old corpsmen he exuded a certain maturity. He was called "Doc" now.

Jack thought he had it made, working with the doctors and nurses in clean, ordered rooms. And San Francisco beckoned just across the bay for weekend getaways. Bill Shoemer, who had worked with Jack at his father's funeral home in Appleton, was a fellow sailor who received a letter from his buddy aboard ship: "Jack wrote kidding me about being on duty in the Pacific while he was in Oakland with all kinds of liberty."

But for Jack Bradley, the good life was about to change.

Rene Gagnon enlisted in May of 1943, two months after his seventeenth birthday. Until then, he'd kept on working at the Chicopee textile mills, working right up until his Army draft notice arrived. A friend of his remembered what cinched his decision. It hadn't been the indignation after Pearl Harbor. It hadn't been the inspiration that welled up after Guadalcanal. It had been something a little more. At about the time he got his draft notice, the handsome young boy had spotted the famous Marine recruiting poster and was knocked out by the uniform, by those snazzy dress blues and whites. His attitude, his friend recalled, was essentially: I'm goin' in anyway. So I may as well look good.

After secretly promising Pauline he would come back and marry her, Rene was sent to Parris Island in South Carolina. He made Private First Class in July 1943, and transferred to the Marine Guard Company at the Charleston (South Carolina) Navy Yard. Like his civilian life, his Marine career seemed to be going nowhere in particular. That would eventually change.

There are few direct accounts of what Mike, Ira, and Harlon experienced on Bougainville. We do know that Mike was there longest, fighting on what is always the single toughest day, D-Day.

Mike, the indomitable leader, with the safety of his boys his uppermost goal, now saw too many of his boys fall dead right beside him. He heard their last words, saw the tears that flowed from their eyes just before they closed for the last time.

On November 1, 1943, along with 14,000 other Marines of the 3rd Division, Mike splashed ashore on the island of Bougainville at dawn in high surf. The waves pitched the landing craft this way and that and a number of the boats smashed into each other. For several young Marines, their leap from the craft into the surf was their last living act: They drowned immediately in the deep water.

Mike and the other landing Marines were raked by a devastating cross fire of Japanese machine guns and artillery fire. The Japanese resistance there was far more concentrated than the Marines had been able to detect, and within minutes the churning water was a chaos of blood, bodies, and swamped equipment.

Mike and the landing Marines could see no enemy; none of the invaders could; it would become an all-too-common frustration of sea-to-land assaults in the Pacific campaign. The Japanese were concealed by dense jungle foliage that spilled all the way down to the waterline. And they were protected by another type of shield that would recur from island to island: concrete bunkers. At Bougainville, the preinvasion naval bombardment was supposed to have destroyed these bunker positions, but none of them had been hit. The Navy had played it safe, launching some of the bombardment from a range of over seven miles. As the official Marine history later summarized, "The gunfire plan had accomplished nothing." And because of that, many young Marines were dying all around Mike.

Those who made it ashore had begun a descent into an island hell. A Marine captain later reflected that the day began with "steak and eggs served on white tablecloths by stewards. And three and a half hours and a short boat ride later," he continued, "we were rolling in a ditch trying to kill another human being with a knife."

Sergeant Mike would fight on for two months, until the end of the campaign.

Ira had enlisted wanting to "protect his family," bursting with pride to be a member of a new storied tribe, the Marines. But Ira was a passive boy; no one remembered him ever raising his voice, much less getting in a fight. Now Ira had to kill, not at a distance, as in target practice, but close up.

Ira landed on Bougainville in the early hours of December 3. He and his company walked onto the island unopposed, observed by an unseen enemy. Jack Charles, who fought with Ira, recalled how elusive the enemy was: "Though we spent over a month on Bougainville, engaging the enemy in several firefights, while on patrol and on line with the third Marine Division, I can honestly say, few if any of us ever saw a Japanese. The jungle was that thick. And they always took their wounded and dead with them . . . they were masters at camouflage."

Late on the first day, the leader of the patrolling Company K sent Ira Hayes and a couple of other Marines ahead to scout in the remaining moments of daylight. The boys had groped their way about three quarters of a mile when they came upon a creek. A company of Japanese soldiers was splashing and bathing in the river. The Japanese did not detect the Americans' presence. Vastly outnumbered, Ira and the others crept back and reported their findings to the patrol leader. Company K dug in for the night and tried to keep silent to avoid detection. A monsoon swept in, soaking the tense and terrified boys. They did not dare rise from their soaked foxholes for fear of being picked off by a sniper.

Dawn. And a long, hot day of being pinned down. Company K stayed concealed, rank with its own sweat, watching larger enemy units pass by almost within arm's reach. Night again.

That night Ira's childhood vanished forever. He was sharing a foxhole with Bill Faulkner. Faulkner remembered: "We took turns sleeping and Ira was sitting in one corner with his rifle between his legs and I curled up in another to get a little shut-eye."

Faulkner was jolted awake by bloodcurdling screams. Horrified, he tried to make sense of the violent lashings in the darkness. Ira was struggling with his bayoneted rifle. Impaled on the long knife blade was a Japanese soldier, still screaming. The infiltrator had crept soundlessly to the edge of the foxhole. Then he had sprung with lethal intent toward the two young Americans. In the darkness, he had not glimpsed the point of the blade that was now killing him.

The next morning, what remained of Ira's platoon was ordered to retrieve the bodies of the Marines who had been killed on the hillside the previous day. Machine-gun fire greeted them and dropped several in the now-familiar bloody heaps. They fell back and called for artillery. After forty-five minutes the barrage was lifted and the paratroopers continued on, met by only intermittent snipers.

A Marine named Dobie Fernandez remembered how terrible it was. The rain had been so heavy, he recalled, it had mutilated the corpses to the point of being unrecognizable. And there was that stench, that nearly unendurable stench.

Bill Faulkner remembered it, too. "When we reached the spot where they were, we found the Japs had driven wooden stakes through their arms, chests, and legs, pinning them to the ground. One of the Marines who came with us to get the bodies had a brother who was one of the dead. It's tough seeing your brother like that."

Ira Hayes fought on to the end of the battle, quiet as ever, betraying his emotions to no one. But Ira had the screams of dying men in his head now; his hands had held that bayonet with a struggling, writhing human impaled on it. It's not known if the dreams and memories that haunted him in later life began here. All he would reveal in a letter to his mother from Bougainville was: "I'm okay, thanks to my Lord."

Harlon Block arrived on Bougainville on December 21, just days before the island was declared secure. To boys like Harlon, growing up in quiet 1930's America, there had been little exposure to the horrors of war. There was no TV; movies offered sanitized, heroic images of battle; radio was for entertainment; and even actual pictures of the world were scarce—the first photo magazine, *Life*, didn't hit the newsstands until 1935.

But Harlon Block saw plenty of reality when he fought near "Hellzapoppin' Ridge." Arriving at the battle site, Harlon moved in a macabre world of splintered trees and burned-out brush. The earth was a churned mass of mud and human bodies. The streams were filled with blasted corpses. Dead Japanese snipers hung from trees. Harlon, the Seventh-Day Adventist, was getting his first glimpse of the world's wickedness as he trudged past these remains of friends and enemy dead.

Nor were the Japanese through. As the Marines moved forward, a Japanese machine gun stuttered and the enemy artillery roared, raking the American line. A Japanese counterattack slammed into the Marines' left flank. Harlon Block found himself in close-up combat, hand to hand and tree to tree. With knife, gun, and bare hands, the Texas pass-catcher fought in the confusion of English and Japanese screams. His clear-cut world of right and wrong had dissolved into a brutish fight for survival. The survivors on both sides eventually withdrew to endure another night and fight another day.

Harlon's sweetheart, Catherine Pierce, corresponded with him throughout the war. She remembered that his letters gave her the feeling that the war was traumatic for him. He wrote obsessively of bailing out of planes, of falling into unknown territory. And of Bougainville.

Harlon had enlisted at the age of eighteen, wanting to be one with his Weslaco team. He couldn't imagine the horror that lay behind the concepts of "fighting for your country" and "doing your duty." Now as Harlon learned what his duty really was, the glorious concepts faded away.

Something happened to Mike, Ira, and Harlon on Bougainville. They would never discuss it, never identify exactly what had affected them so. But for the rest of their days death was never far from their thoughts.

The three Pacific veterans sailed home from Bougainville on separate boats that left the second week of January. They would have a month to stare at the ocean and ponder their private thoughts before they arrived in San Diego on February 14, 1944.

At about this time, Franklin Sousley was getting his first taste of life as a Marine. He had entered the Corps on January 5 and reported to the recruit depot in San Diego for boot camp.

One of Franklin's buddies, Tex Stanton, remembers boot camp as "weeks of monotonous training, learning how to march, how to follow orders, how to shoot a rifle, how to be a real Marine."

Tex remembers Franklin as "a big redheaded country boy," serious about proving himself as a Marine. But nobody ever said that war had to be all serious. Not as long as Franklin R. Sousley had anything to do with it.

He quickly noticed something interesting about the lyrics to the stirring anthem that all recruits had to memorize, the "Marine Corps Hymn" ("From the halls of Montezuma/To the shores of Tripoli/We fight our country's battles/In the air, on land and sea"). What Franklin noticed was that those lyrics could be transferred nicely to another tune: specifically, the raucous, rousing tune of the Roy Acuff hillbilly standard, "The Wabash Cannonball" ("Listen to the jingle/The rumble and the roar/As she glides along the woodlands/through the hills and by the shore"). Franklin was glad to belt it out in his high nasal twang for any leatherneck who would listen, slapping an upended rifle as a makeshift bass fiddle. Somehow, he escaped time in the brig for that one.

Franklin left the boys laughing, but in a letter home to his mother, Goldie, he revealed the challenge of being a young man far from home: "I

Mike Strank—First Communion.

Right: Franklin Sousley.
Below: Franklin Sousley's
birthplace, Hilltop,
Kentucky.

Rene Gagnon.

Ira Hayes and his father, Jobe.

Jack Bradley in front of the family home in Appleton, Wisconsin.

Harlon Block and his brothers. *From left to right:* Mel, Ed, Harlon, Larry, and Corky.

Jack Bradley and family. *From left to right:* Kathryn (in the back), Mary Ellen, Marge, Jack, Jim, and Cabbage.

Harlon Block
in his USMC
dress blues.

Ira Hayes in his
USMC service uniform.

Rene Gagnon
in his USMC
dress blues.

Jack Bradley in his
Navy dress blues.

Franklin Sousley
in his USMC
dress blues.

Mike Strank, in
camouflage, on
Bougainville.

believe I am homesick for once in my life. If you had treated me mean before I left, it wouldn't be so hard to forget; but you were so good that when they start raving around here, I think of home."

Franklin was like so many of the millions of country boys who served in World War II for whom a big weekend was playing Ping-Pong at the USO for two days. As his buddy Pee Wee Griffiths remembers, "Franklin was a big overgrown kid with rust-colored hair. He'd lumber along speaking in his Kentucky drawl. He was a big smiling country boy."

In that January of 1944, eighteen-year-old Private First Class Rene Gagnon was serving in a Military Police unit guarding the Navy Yard at Charleston, South Carolina. He had endured a hot and humid boot camp at Parris Island during the summer of 1943. Other "boots" who trained with him would later remember little about him other than he was "a nice guy." But there was one thing. In his dress uniform, the handsome French-American looked "like a movie star."

That January marked the end of Jack Bradley's safe passage through the war. A fellow pharmacist's mate told Jack he was transferred to Field Medical School. This meant he was being transferred to the Marines, to be a combat medic, a corpsman. Not good news. Jack raced downstairs and indeed found his name on the list. He must have been stunned. His strategy had been to join the Navy to avoid fighting with the Army. Now he found himself a member of the most rugged group of warriors in the world.

At Field Medical School (FMS) outside San Diego, Navy corpsmen were trained to care for Marines in battle. FMS had classes in specialized life-saving skills, and Jack was also expected to endure the rigors of battle like any leatherneck. That meant tough Marine Corps conditioning.

"We had been through Navy boot camp," Corpsman John Overmayer remembered. "But with the Marines it was much more rugged. We were learning from hardened combat veterans. We definitely got the message that we would someday have to do under fire what we were being trained to do. The Marines were serious."

"There was culture shock for us Navy guys going into a Marine school," Corpsman Gregory Emery recalled. "The discipline and demands in the Marines are immediate. No boot camp in another service can ever match the Marine Corps. It's immediately obvious, from the very first second."

Jack wore Marine uniforms, Marine dog tags. He watched Marine combat films and learned how to fire his .45-caliber pistol. He rose at dawn to hike with Marines who never slowed down.

He was shown footage of horribly wounded Marines in actual combat. "We learned how to crawl out under fire and rescue injured men," Corpsman Overmayer recalled. "We learned how to make a splint with weeds, paper, twigs, anything."

I asked Mr. Overmayer what he remembered, years later, as the most noticeable difference between his Navy and Marine training. "Pride," he answered immediately. "You felt a different sort of pride being trained in the Marine tradition. The Marines made us feel we were part of a special team."

In February and March of 1944, Jack continued his FMS training while Rene was back east. Franklin was granted a furlough after boot camp, as were Mike, Ira, and Harlon after they docked in San Diego.

To the civilian noncombatant, war was "knowable" and "understandable." Orderly files of men and machines marching off to war, flags waving, patriotic songs playing. War could be clear and logical to those who had not touched its barb.

But battle veterans quickly lost a sense of war's certitude. Images of horror they could scarcely comprehend invaded their thoughts, tortured their minds. Bewildered and numbed, they could not unburden themselves to their civilian counterparts, who could never comprehend through mere words.

These three boys back from their Pacific Heart of Darkness now embraced death. Two were convinced their next battle would be their last. And one lingered on for ten years before he was consumed by his living nightmare.

Ira wrote to his parents when he touched land. His letter, posted from San Diego, was typically upbeat: "Well, I'm back in Dago . . . arrived here Monday with the whole regiment. We get furloughs starting Monday for 30 long days . . . I'll get home the fastest way possible."

He was back on the Gila Reservation a few days after that. Nancy saw the change in him as soon as he stepped off the bus.

At twenty, Ira was stockier, Nancy noticed; he had gained about fifteen pounds of muscle during boot camp and it had stayed on him during the jungle nightmare on Bougainville. The slim, quiet boy had been transformed into a very formidable-looking young man.

But the real change, his mother saw, was in his affect.

He looked old, Nancy thought. Standing there in his green fatigues and his overseas cap. So much older than she remembered. He'd always had a solemn face, his full mouth in repose a natural frown. But now those turned-down corners did not broaden so easily into a smile. Hardly at all, in fact.

Ira had always been a solemn-looking boy, Nancy thought. Now he looked, at times, downright sullen.

Ira never admitted what was bothering him. But in a letter to his mother about Bougainville he first hinted at the memories that would haunt him all his life: "We lost some of our dear buddies . . . which isn't a very good thing to remember."

As Ira's leave drew to a close, his parents once again held a farewell dinner in his honor. The guests were tribal leaders, church elders, and the choir.

After the feasting, the tribal council asked him to speak. Ira slowly stood and addressed the congregation. His words were typically thoughtful and gentle, but they were no longer the words of a boy. A man was talking now, a man who had seen things.

Brotherhood was on his mind. He praised his fellow Marines for their bravery, self-sacrifice, and brotherhood. "They'd never let me down," Ira remarked. Ira concluded by promising never to bring any shame upon his tribe. When he finished speaking, they warmly embraced him. As the choir sang, he cried softly. And then he went back to war.

Mike Strank returned to Franklin Borough worn out by battle and a case of malaria he had contracted on Bougainville.

His friends Mike and Eva Slazich took him out for an evening on the town. They saw a movie, a war movie. Slazich asked his friend what he thought of the movie. Mike Strank remarked quietly: "It isn't really like that."

At the end of the evening Mike turned to his friend and said, "I doubt if I'll ever see you again. I don't think I'll be coming back."

"Don't say that!" replied a shocked Slazich.

Mike was sure that his next battle would be his last. But his parents wanted him alive and in the United States, away from war. One night his father sat Mike down at the kitchen table for a talk. Vasil asked if there was any way Mike could secure a training assignment in the States so they could see him more often.

Mike, tired from malaria, convinced he would never come home again, looked into the eyes of the father he would soon leave for good and said: "Dad, there's a war going on out there. Young boys are fighting that war. And Dad . . . they need my help."

Before departing Franklin Borough for his cross-country trek back to the Pacific, Mike took his little sister aside. He urged her to keep goading their parents, so tentative with the English language, to keep writing letters to him.

"Keep those letters coming," he urged eleven-year-old Mary. "You might not get an answer, but keep 'em coming." Shortly after that he was gone. Little Mary would never see her big brother again.

Harlon Block had gone home to east Texas for what he, too, believed was the last time. On his furlough in the booming citrus country, Harlon did some things that Belle and Ed and his friends would never have conceived. He took long walks in the swampy fields near the Rio Grande, the mosquito-laden fields. He was trying to catch malaria. It wasn't cowardice. Harlon was hoping that the sickness would be a sign from God that he would not have to go back into battle and continue to kill his fellowman.

But the malarial mosquitoes never found his flesh. God was not going to let Harlon Block off the hook that easily. When he realized that, Harlon began to prepare some of those close to him for his eventual death.

Not everyone. He spared Belle and Ed. But he told it to his football buddy Leo Ryan's young wife, Jean. He met Jean in her office at the Sunny Glen Orphanage, associated with the Church of Christ; Jean was executive secretary to the director there. He took her to a café in town. Over coffee, he told her simply: "I don't think I'll be coming back next time. I've had my chances and I think my number will be up next time."

After this, Harlon started telling several other friends and relatives as well.

Catherine Pierce was one. Harlon visited his special girl one afternoon during his furlough; he looked her up at the boarding school in Keene, Texas, where she was completing her senior year. Catherine noticed something different about Harlon right away. He was a little thinner than she remembered, but that wasn't it. He was subdued. But just under that careful surface she could sense strong emotions. She recalled that going back to the Pacific was very much on his mind that sunlit, awkward afternoon. He loved her, but his message was not about her "waiting for him."

He surprised her as he softly said, "I don't think I'll be coming back, Catherine."

"He was a different person," Catherine told me. "Before he went to war he had been happy, with lots of enthusiasm. Now he was quiet, like something was weighing on him.

"I tried to encourage him. I said, 'Oh, Harlon, don't be silly. Nothing is going to happen to you.' But he felt differently. He said with conviction, 'Catherine, I just have this strong sense that I won't be coming back.' "

The idea that young Marines like Mike and Harlon would foresee their deaths in battle, especially after experiencing combat, might seem a normal, even predictable thing. But in fact such thoughts are the exception to the rule. Almost all men in combat are convinced that "the other guy is going to get it, not me." It's not natural to think that death is imminent and to continue to function normally.

A surgeon who later served on Iwo Jima wrote a memoir that included a passage suggesting how rare were Mike's and Harlon's intuitions that they were going to be killed:

As I slowly headed back north in my jeep, one of the frequently used war slogans came to mind. Our Marines were willingly laying down their lives for their country. This statement was sheer nonsense, for the overwhelming majority of the men felt they would be spared, and that it was the next guy that would be killed or wounded. They had no intention of laying down their lives for their country or anything else. Each man believed he would be one of the lucky ones to return home. Those that lost or never did have this feeling of invulnerability would sooner or later crack up.

Hilltop, Kentucky, stirred when their Marine Franklin Sousley arrived home on furlough, proud, with a new focus and direction in his young life.

"When Franklin came home," his friend J. B. Shannon, then a wide-eyed thirteen-year-old, remembers, "it was a big deal for our little community. He stepped off the train in his Marine dress blues looking straight as a string."

"He stopped at my house on his way home," Emogene Bailey remembered clearly years later. "He looked so very handsome in his uniform. I took him out in my backyard and made him pose for a picture. I still have that picture today." Emogene helped Goldie cook Franklin's welcome-home dinner as Franklin entertained his younger brother, Julian, with tall stories in the living room.

On Franklin's last night home he borrowed his aunt's car for a date with Marion Hamm. "He came over to my house and we visited," she remembered. "We took a walk and he told me how proud he was to be a Marine, how excited he was to serve his country in the Corps." At the end of the night he asked Marion to do what so many millions of World War II boys asked of their special girls: "He asked me to wait for him."

Franklin couldn't sleep after he said good night to Marion. He walked over to the Hilltop General Store. "We sat on the porch talking until three A.M.," his chum Aaron Flora remembered. "Franklin told us how great it was to be a Marine."

The next morning Franklin said his sad farewells to his friends and family. They embraced and cried. He presented his mother, Goldie, with a copy of his formal Marine Corps portrait. Then Franklin stepped back. With a big smile he looked Goldie in the eye and proclaimed, "Momma, I'm gonna do something to make you proud of me."

Later that morning he said good-bye to Marion. On the back of the portrait he gave her he wrote:

> Picking a girl
> Is like picking a flower from the garden
> You only pick the best.
> > > Love,
> > > Franklin

His last words to his sweetheart were: "When I come back, I'll be a hero."

At the train station young J. B. Shannon just couldn't bear to say good-bye to his buddy. He considered riding the train to Maysville with Franklin, but it was a quarter each way, big money for a thirteen-year-old in 1944. But as Franklin was boarding his train, J.B. shouted impulsively, "Hey, Franklin, I'll just ride along with you."

"On the train he told me he was just thrilled to be a Marine," J.B. remembered. "He said he was right where he wanted to be in his life, in the uniform of the United States Marines. He said he was fulfilling his dream." In Maysville, J.B. waved good-bye as Franklin's train pulled out of the depot. "He was a hero to me there and then," J.B. told me fifty-four years later.

It was a battle on the tiny atoll of Tarawa in the Central Pacific that would foreshadow the fate of Mike, Harlon, Franklin, Ira, Rene, Doc, and all the Marines fighting America's War.

Tarawa was a tiny one-square-mile spit of sand, only eight hundred yards wide. It was in the Central Pacific, in the Gilbert Island group, north of Bougainville in the Solomons.

Tarawa represented the kickoff of Howlin' Mad Smith's Central Pacific thrust on the "Road to Tokyo," the dramatic opening of a second front in the war against Japan. This was a new theater of sand, coral, and volcanic rock that left the jungles of the South Pacific far behind.

The Central Pacific campaign was unlike the battles in the South Pacific. The Japanese had heavily fortified these island outposts; to capture them, Marines would have to mount offensive thrusts into the teeth of an armed and waiting enemy.

In 1943, there were reasonable military officers in the Pacific who expressed serious doubts whether "any fortified island could ever be assaulted by amphibious forces. These men honestly believed . . . the heavily barricaded enemy atolls of the Central Pacific would prove to be the burial ground of any American force foolish enough to 'leap off the deep end.' "

Howlin' Mad Smith was not among those officers. He knew he was attempting the "toughest of all military operations: a landing, if possible, in the face of enemy machine guns that can mow men down by the hundreds." He knew the battle would be costly in Marine lives. The Japanese had boasted that Tarawa "could not be taken in a thousand years." But Smith was confident his Marines would succeed.

Huge Navy gunships hit Tarawa with the greatest concentration of aerial bombardment and naval gunfire in the history of warfare up to that time. The Navy admiral directing the bombardment even promised he would "obliterate" the island.

But when the first three assault waves of Marines stormed ashore on the morning of November 20, 1943, they realized the Navy bombardment had been ineffective, had only rearranged the sand. Japanese gunfire ripped through their ranks. Confusion reigned.

The Marines pinned down on the shore were in desperate need of reinforcements. Two waves of landing boats full of troops, tanks, and artillery were on their way.

Then disaster struck.

The landing boats hit an exposed reef five hundred yards from shore and were grounded.

It would be forty-four years before physicist Donald Olson would discover that D-Day at Tarawa occurred during one of only two days in 1943 when the moon's apogee coincided with a neap tide, resulting in a tidal range of only a few inches rather than several feet.

The actions of these Marines trapped on the reef would determine the outcome of the battle for Tarawa. If they hesitated or turned back, their buddies ashore would be decimated.

But they didn't hesitate. They were Marines. They jumped from their stranded landing crafts into chest-deep water holding their arms and ammunition above their heads.

In one of the bravest scenes in the history of warfare, these Marines slogged through the deep water into sheets of machine-gun bullets. There was nowhere to hide, as Japanese gunners raked the Marines at will. And the Marines, almost wholly submerged and their hands full of equipment, could not defend themselves. But they kept coming. Bullets ripped through their ranks, sending flesh and blood flying as screams pierced the air.

Japanese steel killed over 300 Marines in those long minutes as they struggled to the shore. As the survivors stumbled breathlessly onto shore their boots splashed in water that had turned bright red with blood.

This type of determination and valor among individual Marines overcame seemingly hopeless odds, and in three days of hellish fighting Tarawa was captured. The Marines suffered a shocking 4,400 casualties in just seventy-two hours of fighting as they wiped out the entire Japanese garrison of 5,000.

When the battle ended, Howlin' Mad Smith toured the island to see the Japanese defenses for himself. Because water lies only four feet below the surface of the Tarawa atoll, the Japanese could not build underground defenses. Instead they built pillboxes aboveground.

Smith, with other officers and Time reporter Robert Sherrod trailing him, examined one of the five hundred pillboxes on Tarawa. Sherrod wrote:

The pillbox is forty feet long, eight feet wide, and ten feet high. It is constructed of heavy coconut logs, six and eight inches in diameter. The walls of the pillbox are two tiers of coconut logs, about three feet apart. The logs are joined together by eight-inch steel spikes, shaped like a block letter C. In between the two tiers of logs are three feet of sand, and covering the whole pillbox several more feet of sand are heaped. No wonder our bombs and shells hadn't destroyed these pillboxes! Two-thousand-pound bombs hitting directly on them might have partially destroyed them, but bombing is not that accurate—not even dive bombing.

The message was clear. The Japanese were building defenses impervious to our bombs. It would take individual Marine riflemen on the ground to charge and neutralize these defenses.

Looking at these Japanese defenses, Smith knew the Marines' road to Tokyo would be a bloody one. The distance between this first major amphibious assault on Tarawa and faraway Tokyo was over eight thousand miles. It presented the greatest challenge in terms of distance in the history of warfare.

In 1812, Napoleon had marched his men fifteen hundred miles to Moscow; in the thirteenth century, Genghis Khan advanced four thousand miles from Mongolia to the shores of the Mediterranean. But those campaigns collapsed because of the distances.

And now the Marines were faced with a campaign twice the distance from New York to San Francisco. Putting it another way, if the Marines had started in Seattle and traveled south, they would have overshot Buenos Aires by a thousand miles.

A grief-stricken General Smith walked to the beach to view for himself young Marines floating facedown in the lagoon and lying along the blood-splattered beaches.

When American civilians later saw newsreels and photos of rows of Marine corpses floating in the surf, most were horrified. "This Must Not Happen Again!" screamed editorials, and one mother wrote a commander, "You killed my son on Tarawa."

Correspondent Sherrod worried that America did not have the stomach for the sacrifices the Marines would have to make to conquer the Pacific. To him it was obvious that the Japanese strategy was to dig in on every island in the Central Pacific to inflict horrendous American losses in the hope that America would give up and negotiate a peace. The Japanese were counting on civilians to blanch at the human cost of advancing on Japan and for the Marines to falter in the face of the fanatical Japanese defenses.

Yet, however much civilian support might have been in doubt, Smith had no doubts about the determination and bravery of his Marines.

And at his last stop on the island, at the high seawall the Marines had to surmount to get onto Tarawa, Howlin' Mad saw an example of Marine valor. Sherrod wrote that the party saw "a Marine who is leaning in death against the seawall, one arm still supported upright by the weight of his body. On top of the seawall, just beyond his upraised hand, lies a blue-and-white flag, a beach marker to tell succeeding waves where to land. Says Holland Smith, 'How can men like that ever be defeated? This Marine's duty was to plant that flag on top of the seawall. He did his duty, though it cost him his life. *Semper fidelis* meant more to him than just a catchphrase.' "

Tarawa was the first major amphibious assault in which U.S. troops faced sustained opposition on the beach. The American victory at Tarawa opened the Central Pacific to a new Marine thrust, with more difficult amphibious island assaults ahead. And it made clear to Marine commanders that many more motivated and well-trained Marines would be needed to win America's War in the Pacific.

So in March of 1944 the Marines issued new orders to six young boys who would someday be world-famous heroes. They were to report to a new camp to become part of a new Marine division. The great events in the Pacific began to draw the six flagraisers toward one another. Soon veterans Ira, Harlon, and Mike, strangers at Bougainville, would be introduced to one another. They would be joined by three other strangers: Franklin Sousley, Rene Gagnon, and a non-Marine, a Navy corpsman attached to their unit, whose name was Jack "Doc" Bradley.

And as these six made their way to their new assignments, a tiny hill far out in the Pacific lay waiting.

FORGING THE SPEARHEAD

> *If the Army and the Navy*
> *Ever look on heaven's scenes*
> *They will find the streets are guarded*
> *By United States Marines.*
> —FROM "THE MARINE'S HYMN"

IT WAS LIKE A CITY, but it was not a city. At least it was like no city the six boys had ever seen or imagined: a low-slung city of men; men and heavy machines and weapons and ammunition. Far greater in size and layout than any of their hometowns, it spread out in an olive-drab glaze over the rolling California land between Los Angeles and San Diego.

Nearly every kid who arrived at the city's gates was awed. "Camp Pendleton was so large I thought there was no end to it," James Buchanan remembered. "I thought it went all the way to New York."

In the prewar years Camp Pendleton had been a small boot camp—a sleepy little base south of Los Angeles, named for Major General "Uncle Joe" Pendleton, the father of Marine training on the West Coast. In March of 1942 the Navy Department radically increased its size by acquiring the adjoining 130,000-acre Rancho Santa Margarita y Las Flores.

Rancho Santa Margarita had consisted of canyons and rolling hills, livestock and grasses and wild Castilian roses and low vegetation, rattlesnakes and fleas. The Pacific Ocean thundered against its westernmost perimeter.

The new Camp Pendleton, with its isolated and rugged terrain, offered the Marines the perfect environment to harden their young men. The future flagraisers would spend the next six months moving about this untamed land, never sleeping in a barracks, never showering indoors, fighting raging wildfires, only occasionally sighting something as civilized as a dirt road. As one of their friends, Grady Dyce, later told me, "We were in the

---

Chapter opener: Franklin Sousley (on the right) and a buddy at Camp Pendleton.

middle of nowhere. All that was out there was rattlesnakes, sheep, and coy-otes. We had to cut the tall grass with machetes."

The new specialized city of specialized military men would mold a high-performing population that in traditional cities required generations to ges-tate. In fact it would have to produce specialists of a level no civic society had ever required: leaders who could make mass life-and-death decisions in split seconds; doctors ready to perform brain surgery at a moment's notice; mailmen delivering to no fixed address; priests whose duties overwhelm-ingly involved last rites; cooks who could serve "customers" by the thou-sands, three times daily; and scores of record-keepers, mechanics, drivers, dog trainers, and others—every one of whom would have to perform his du-ties in sync with the others, in a spirit of total cooperation, and under fire.

Mostly, the city would produce men to return that fire and vanquish the enemy shooters. Its overarching purpose was to quickly transform Doc, Rene, Ira, Mike, Franklin, Harlon, and 21,000 others from standard-issue fighting men into an elite, interdependent martial society that would be moved intact across an ocean to fight an island battle.

Camp Pendleton would see the creation of an entirely new Marine divi-sion. This new division—the 5th—had been activated on November 11, 1943, Armistice Day. In the ensuing months, its pell-mell assembly into a combat-ready force drew on all the energies and know-how of American industrialization.

The urgency surrounding the 5th Division's creation was dictated by harsh military realities. The bloody battle of Tarawa had demonstrated the need for many more Marines trained to rout out well-entrenched Japanese defenders. It would be at Camp Pendleton that the 5th Division learned the skills needed to prevail on the Road to Tokyo.

It was at Camp Pendleton, a crucible of that counteroffensive, that the six flagraisers first came together. They all swept in on the roiling streams of new men who flooded the unreal city every day. The men poured in by the truckful on convoys along Highway 101 and on crowded railroad cars clat-tering along an extension of the Santa Fe line. It was as though the Ameri-can continent was being drained of its young men, and they were flowing here in great rivers.

Mike, Harlon, and Ira reported to the camp at the end of their post-Bougainville furloughs. Forty percent of this new force would be composed of veterans such as they. Doc, Franklin, and Rene represented the remaining sixty percent—young boys just out of basic training. Doc came up in April from his crash course at Field Medical School in San Diego. Franklin arrived from boot camp in San Diego. Rene was shipped over from the camp at Charleston. He joined the Military Police Company at the camp. But within four days, on April 8, Rene was shifted to a new company. A company destined for great hardship and for everlasting renown.

This was Company E, nicknamed "Easy"—a stinging irony, given its fate.

Easy Company consisted of about 250 men. They were divided into a headquarters (or command) section, three rifle platoons, a machine-gun platoon to supplement the rifle platoons, and a 60mm-mortar section to back up the riflemen. Doc was one of two corpsmen assigned to the 3rd Platoon, led by Lieutenant Keith Wells. (Corpsmen remained technically within the Navy, but trained and billeted with the men whom they would watch over in battle.)

Mike, Harlon, Franklin, and Ira were in the 2nd Platoon, led by Lieutenant Ed Pennel. Its forty members were divided into four squads. Sergeant Mike was a squad leader with three corporals reporting to him. One was Corporal Harlon Block, to whom Private First Class Franklin Sousley and Private First Class Ira Hayes in turn reported. Rene was in another of Mike's squads.

Easy Company's boss was Captain Dave Severance, a tall, lean Wisconsin native; a ramrod Marine of exceptional judgment who had shown his mettle in battle, who expressed his authority through calm understatement and unflinching example.

Easy Company was part of the 2nd Battalion commanded by Colonel Chandler Johnson. The 2nd was assigned to the 28th Regiment, commanded by Colonel Harry—"the Horse"—Liversedge.

The new fighting force soon received the honor of its own special moniker: Spearhead. Nearly 600 Marines submitted entries to design a shoulder insignia expressing this name. The winning design, created by a lieutenant named Fergus Young, was a scarlet shield and gold V, pierced by a spearhead of blue.

"Spearhead" was a salute to the division's intended role in the grim island battles that lay ahead. When its training was complete, Spearhead would be thrust to the forefront of the great human tidal wave of hundreds of thousands of Marines fighting their way from island to island as it bore down inexorably on Japan.

Spearhead would fight only one battle. The American high command pinpointed this objective later, in the fall of 1944, although its location and identity would remain top-secret: an ugly little scab of rock and volcano six hundred miles south of the Japanese islands.

And so, its high command, facilities, colors, and shoulder insignia squared away, Camp Pendleton began molding the assault force that would descend upon that ugly, as-yet-nameless scab.

Inspired leadership is a key to the Marines' greatness. Marine officers stress their duty to look after the needs of their men. The mythic Marine "Chesty" Puller once instructed his officers: "Whenever we are at chow-time, the privates will be fed first. Then the noncoms, and the officers last of all."

Robert Leader, in Easy's 3rd Platoon with Doc Bradley, shared his memories of his leader with me: "In the Marines I never saw an officer take a drink before his men drank. Our lieutenant, Lieutenant Wells, would take heavy machine-gun ammo off the back of guys who were struggling. Mortar shells are heavy and Wells would take a couple from a guy to help. There was a loyalty between the men and the officers, between everyone. We knew our officers would go to hell with us."

Joe Rodriguez, who was in the same fire team as Ira and Franklin (they reported to Harlon, who reported to Mike), reminisced about Mike's leadership:

> Everybody idolized Mike. He was a born leader, a natural leader, and a leader by example. Harlon, Ira, Franklin all loved him. Even his lieutenant, Lieutenant Pennel [to whom Mike reported], stood somewhat in awe of Mike.
>
> He led by example; he had been there. He was an experienced fighter, but he never talked about himself. He had real concern for us, he was a big brother to us. We were young boys and he would reassure us. He would say, "I want to bring as many of you back home to your mothers as possible."

Another good example of the leadership talent in the 5th Division was the semimythic warrior who would command the 28th Regiment, to which Easy Company was attached. This was Colonel Harry "the Horse" Liversedge, a towering specimen from Volcano, California, who grew into a six-foot-four Olympic shot-putter and who, in the war, won a Navy Cross for his heroism in the jungle fighting at New Georgia.

By 1942 he was a Raider commander. Now, two years later, he strode among the young boys of Camp Pendleton, an icon who was willing to wade once more into the horrors of battle at their helm.

Harry the Horse's mission at Camp Pendleton was to mold his 3,400 men of the 28th Regiment into a flexible fighting unit. Flexible in that they had to be effective whether they were fighting together as a regiment or as a number of small teams. Whatever he needed—a lone Marine to assault a blockhouse, a three-man fire squad, a forty-man platoon, a two-hundred-fifty-man company, a nine-hundred-man battalion, or a three-thousand-man regiment—all his Marines had to be able to break off or come together as needed.

Colonel Liversedge and the rest of the cadre of officers would assemble and polish its Swiss watch of a fighting force in several tightly calibrated stages. The training began with the simplest and most critical cog in the great fighting machine—the rifleman.

First came the mastery of weapons.

The boys had learned marksmanship in basic training. They had learned (often the hard way) that the Marines venerated the rifle. But now they began to understand that the rifle was *the* essential weapon of combat in this war. The Navy now held sway in the ocean, the Army Air Force was beginning to dominate the skies. But as Tarawa had shown (and as future battles were to show again), no amount of aerial bombing or naval bombardment—regardless of how obliterating it might look from a bombardier's sights or from the deck of a destroyer—was going to dislodge these deeply entrenched Japanese from their obsessively fortified Pacific islands.

It was the rifleman, sloshing ashore in the teeth of murderous fire. It was the rifleman, surrounded by the screams and the floating corpses of his buddies. It was the rifleman, scared and exposed and unprotected by armor of any sort, peering through the smoke and confusion for a glimpse of an individual enemy. It was the rifleman who would determine the outcome of America's War.

The rifleman was the Marine counterpart of the Army infantryman. Every Marine, regardless of his ultimate assignment, would be trained with the rifle. The Marines even had a motto for it: "Everyman a Rifleman." Doc would learn the rifle, even though he was a corpsman. Rene would learn the rifle, even though he was a runner, a messenger. Mike, Harlon, and Franklin would be rifle specialists. As for sturdy Ira, his weapon would be an advanced version; a Browning Automatic Rifle, or BAR. Long and heavy (it weighed about twenty-four pounds), the BAR could be fired either in single shots or in bursts. It held twenty rounds of ammunition, like a machine gun. It produced triple the firepower of a standard rifle. The BAR man was a popular guy to have around in a firefight.

At Pendleton, the young Marines began to learn the complex choreography of rifle combat.

"They'd learn 'fire and movement,' " Dave Severance reminisced to me.

"We played war games. Two rifle companies would fire on a target while another company moved. Then they'd switch off and proceed toward the objective—riflemen like Ira and Franklin doing what Sergeant Strank and Corporal Block told them to do. A key was protection: fire groups protecting one another as they advanced to new positions."

Jesse Boatwright recalled the emphasis on teamwork. "War is a team sport," he said. "From the private on up, you learn how to take orders and do what you're told. To work as a team. To obey the chain of command."

The training was intense. "It was about getting up at reveille and going up in the hills and playing war," Tex Stanton recalled. "We'd crawl and run around in the hills in the hot sun and then walk home." And tedious. "Repetitive and simple," Don Mayer remembered. "It was about doing simple things over and over so that you could do them automatically." And for real. "We fired so much live ammo at Pendleton," recalled Grady Dyce, "that we'd always be starting prairie fires. We were always fighting fires. Even forest fires."

By April, all units were drilling in the field, in the midst of physically draining tactical marches and three-day bivouacs.

Meanwhile, the division's many specialists would gain engineering expertise in state-of-the-art demolitions, mapmaking, land mine use, camouflage, and bridge building. Still others would receive intense training in communications, from enormous vehicle-mounted radio receivers to portable "walkie-talkies." And every boy in uniform was expected to meet the highest standards in conditioning, on both dry land and in the water. Swimming was a heavily emphasized skill. Those who could not swim were taught how. Those who knew how were taught to swim better.

As spring gave way to summer, Spearhead accelerated into the culminating elements of its training agenda. It launched into the first stages of amphibious training: conditioning these thousands of hard-bodied marksmen and technical specialists to move over the sides of massive carrier ships into small landing vehicles—LST's—and then to climb from these into shallow water, and then onto enemy beaches, all under intense hostile fire. Here was where Spearhead's training began to conform most closely to its finely calibrated special mission.

At Camp Pendleton, the troops got their first exposure to the terrifying skill of climbing over the rail of a skyscraper-size carrier ship and into the small LST's far below. They worked with dry-land mock-ups here; steep wooden walls covered with netting. Battle-condition training would come soon enough.

These exercises quickly gave way to full-fledged mock assaults. These games marshaled the division's nine landing teams, each an infantry battalion with guns, armor, and other support elements. In early July, using transports that set sail from San Diego, these units participated in two landing assaults on San Clemente Island off the California coast. At the conclusion of the second landing, the troops immediately reboarded the transports and headed for their final exercise of the Pendleton phase: an assault on what their officers now called "Pendleton Island," and described to them as "a strongly held advance air base of the Japanese in the Western Pacific—a base that menaced U.S. forces."

No one was saying yet just where that "strongly held air base" lay.

It was during these final phases of training, in July of 1944, that a distinguished visitor began to make himself visible at Pendleton. Many of the troops caught sight of him at a distance, observing them through binoculars: a figure wrapped in a dark cape, sitting in a canvas chair beside an enormous black limousine. This was their Commander in Chief, come all the way across the continent from Washington to observe Spearhead; the legendary President whose "Fireside Chats" had kept some of these boys spellbound beside the radio with their families only a few years before. This was Franklin Delano Roosevelt.

Throughout the six months at Pendleton, all of Spearhead's boys, veterans and new Marines alike, sensed a subtle but unmistakable new climate of respect from the brass. Gone was the ritualized domination of boot camp. These Marines were held to strict standards of discipline and physical endurance. But they were no longer mere recruits now; they were certified leathernecks. Crisp professionalism replaced dictatorial fury as the abiding mood of their universe. A year from their first action, the boys of Spearhead were already a brotherhood.

"*Semper Fidelis*—always faithful—it meant you were faithful to the guys around you," is how Easy's Donald Howell put it. "If you didn't have those guys around you in battle, you didn't stand a chance. With another Marine around you, you knew you had a chance."

Robert Leader goes so far as to say this brotherhood involved a deep love: "I believe we were out there fighting for our buddies. It's deceptive because we'd fight over a beer, insult each other's sister, but then we were ready to risk our lives for each other. It's like a domestic fight where the cop goes in and the man and woman, at each other's throats moments before, beat up the cop! No Marine would admit he loved another Marine but it was true. We had a love for each other."

My father typified this brotherhood in many ways. As the senior Navy corpsman of Easy Company, Doc had functional connections with the other five flagraisers. Though technically assigned to the 3rd Platoon, in practice he supervised the seven other corpsmen in the company; he would see to the needs of the entire company in combat. In this way, 2nd Platoon members Mike, Harlon, Ira, Franklin, and Rene came to see Doc not only as a potential lifesaver but as an integral part of their daily lives. He trained as a Marine alongside these boys, and earned their respect as an equal in the service. His platoon commander, Lieutenant Keith Wells, would later give Doc and his fellow medics the ultimate compliment: "My corpsmen were Marines."

Mike Strank, an immensely popular sergeant who had some of the élan, if not the notoriety, of John Basilone, had his own colorful way of expressing brotherhood. Mike was a prototypic "big brother," a tough and fearless warrior who led by example, not by intimidation. Many young Marines idolized Mike. And Mike in turn softened his martinet's aura with frequent outbursts of goofy, profane humor.

A lover of the weekly "liberty" leaves that sent the Marines flocking into nearby towns and bars for fun, Mike was amused at a necessary ritual that accompanied each liberty: the mandatory testing for venereal disease of each man by a medic, as a chaplain stood piously by.

"You'd have to pull out your pecker and let them see if it was going to 'cry,'" was the way Tex Stanton described the testing for telltale fluids. "And one day Mike made up this poem about it."

As Tex recalled the poem, it went:

> Walk right in
> And don't salute
> Down with your skivvies
> And out with your root.
> Skin 'er back and give it a squeeze,
> Do an about-face and stand at ease.

Another hazard of those environs, besides the clap, was the rattlesnakes. The rattlers had not been impressed by all the upheaval and the sudden onslaught of Marines. More than one trooper found himself frantically bashing a coiled diamondback with his rifle. One night a rattler visited a tent occupied by Tex Stanton and Franklin Sousley, among several others. Tex chuckled over it half a century later: "One guy reached up to get a bug off his neck, and it was the snake. He stood up all night after that."

There were other, less lethal annoyances. The men of the 28th Regiment were encamped in a section of Pendleton, ten miles from the ocean, cut by a dramatic canyon. The original Spanish settlers had named it La Cañón de los Rosales, or Rose Canyon, a gesture to the many wild Castilians that carpeted the area. But that name quickly gave way to another one, far more relevant to anyone who had actually camped there: "Cañón Las Pulgas," it came to be called, the Canyon of the Fleas.

The fleas were only part of the fun. Mornings were icy cold (reveille at six A.M.) and the water-showers were colder. It rained a lot that spring, and the boys were often wet.

Through all of this, my father was a calm center, a steadying influence on all the Easy Company boys around him. Just as the famous photograph showed him: there, in the midst of things, lending a hand. At twenty, he was already regarded as "the Old Man" among the corpsmen. He didn't socialize much; scarcely took a drink during liberty. He made himself the company's unofficial barber, cutting guys' hair on request; otherwise he tended to stay in his tent, reading.

When he wasn't crawling on his belly behind his platoon, that is. Most of his time was spent shadowing the riflemen, watching them maneuver, staying a little behind, alert for casualties. Doc, who Cabbage had recommended get a "clean bunk" in the Navy, would spend this year without sleeping in a real bed.

His kindness became his trademark. A Marine named Lloyd Thompson had injured his back severely, but did not report to sick bay. Every morning, Doc Bradley would show up at his tent to help him with his boots so he could meet reveille. James Buchanan always remembered how Doc not only treated him for cat fever, but stopped him weeks later on a company street at Pendleton to ask him how he was coming along. "No one else would do that," Buchanan said. "He was kind."

Father Paul Bradley (no relation) of Brooklyn, the 28th Regiment's Catholic chaplain, recalled that Doc Bradley volunteered to assist in serving his first Mass at the camp—a typical gesture from my service-minded dad. "I asked, 'Does anyone know how to serve Mass?' " the priest remembered. "Doc came forward. He knew all the Latin responses. He continued to be very religious. A lot of the guys went wild, but not Doc. He was very faithful attending the daily Masses."

It was at Camp Pendleton that Doc Bradley met the doomed youth who would become his best buddy in the service and perhaps a key to his lifelong silence on the subject of his World War II experiences. It was here that my father met Iggy.

His full name was Ralph Ignatowski, and the name was nearly bigger than the boy who bore it. Like Doc, Iggy was a Wisconsin product, a baseball-and-bicycle kid, and the youngest of nine children in a close-knit Milwaukee family with strong European Catholic ties. His father, Walter, was born in Poland in 1885; his mother, Frances, in Germany in 1890. Ralph was the favorite in a family that would produce a priest (Father Bruce, the second youngest) and four servicemen. "We loved him so much," his sister Julia said softly to me many years later.

Like Rene Gagnon, Iggy was young, almost unthinkably young, to be in combat training: He was seventeen during the advanced training at Pendleton; eighteen when Iwo was assaulted. Like Franklin Sousley, he seemed to lack the temperament of a warrior; he was a sunny jokester, a warmhearted family boy. His Marine photograph shows an intelligent, open adolescent face, clear-eyed and confident—a handsome face in an affable, jug-eared way. But there was steel beneath that surface gentleness: Ralph had been determined to enlist in the Marines upon graduation from Boy's Tech in Milwaukee in the spring of 1944. But the Marines rejected him because of problems in his urine sample. Ralph could have sat out the war, no questions asked, at that point. Instead he returned to the induction center a few days later bearing a fresh urine sample. This one came from someone else. He made the grade.

And Iggy was proud to be a Marine, as his brother Al Ignatowski related to me years later: "I got a pass from the Army to visit Ralph at Camp Pendleton. I noticed a sergeant chewing out a young recruit. I told Ralph, 'This is so different from the Army. You crucify these guys!' But Ralph's chest just swelled with pride as he replied, 'That's how we Marines do it!' "

At Pendleton, Doc and Iggy gravitated toward each other and quickly teamed up under the Marines' "buddy" system. Although the Marines generally warned their troops against forging too many friendships—knowing that combat would rip huge, heartbreaking holes in these networks—the Corps recommended that each man identify one other who would be his close ally, eyes and ears, his alter ego in combat. And possibly the comforter of the other's parents. On this the two Wisconsin boys formed their bond, a bond that quickly took on a comradely life of its own. They bunked together, ate ice cream together, went on liberty together, and generally came to know each other's deepest hopes, fears, and joys.

Among the other beneficiaries of Doc's kindness at Pendleton was Ira Hayes.

Ira's mother, Nancy, had been right: Something had changed in Ira after

Bougainville. Or if not changed, brought to the surface, grown darkly dominant. The God-fearing "good boy," the earnest, reform-minded son who had wept on hearing the sermon "Alcohol versus Christianity," was slipping back into the grip of the vice that would war with his good instincts and foreshorten his life.

He remained a good Marine (despite a growing paunch that made some wonder, mistakenly, about his endurance) and a respecter of Marines. He still cared about his "good buddies," and would care about them until the end. But his inner circle of "good buddies" was a narrow one—Mike, Franklin, Harlon, and Doc were among its key members—and those outside it trifled with him at their peril. Playful Franklin, who would become a foxhole comrade with Ira under fire, triggered Ira's edgy wit on their first meeting at Camp Pendleton when he asked him innocently: "What nation do you belong to?" "I'm an original American!" Ira fired back. "And that's more than you can say."

Ira respected Mike and Harlon because they, like him, were veterans tested by combat and the knowledge of violent death. His respect for Mike, in fact, bordered on adulation; he would talk to the Czech-born sergeant intimately and intelligently, as he would to no one else. Mike Strank, many recalled, was the only person who could get Ira to truly relax.

His bond with Doc was somewhat different. Like the other Marines, Ira sensed Jack Bradley's gentleness and goodwill. Doc, for his part, sensed the limits of Ira's tolerance, and respected these.

Clifford Langley, Doc's good friend and co-corpsman, recalled being on liberty in Los Angeles one night, in Doc's company, when they came upon Ira, drunk and surly, thrashing about in the grip of two Military Policemen. The two corpsmen talked the MP's into releasing Ira into their care. But that didn't end Ira's wayward night. "We couldn't control him," Langley said. "He was yelling, 'Get away from me, you can't tell me what to do.' Doc finally said, 'If he doesn't want our help, let's let him go,' and we did. He got picked up by the MP's again and thrown into the brig."

Ira often wore a poncho stuffed through his belt—it is visible in the flagraising photograph—in the Pima manner. His bunk was usually sloppy (the whole company would often pay the price, with restrictions on liberty); his shoelaces usually untied.

Ira was mostly silent and his mates could only guess his thoughts. Except for Kenneth Milstead, who heard Ira's pain in the dead of the night:

I would have guard duty with Ira often. We'd be sitting there alone guarding some gate, no one around, just pitch black. Ira was always depressed. Over and over he'd repeat, "I have nothing to go back to. There's nothing

waiting for me at home when I get back." It was just his nature to be de-
pressed. He didn't talk much to most guys, so they couldn't tell, but when he
talked to me it was with this down-in-the-dumps attitude. I would just try to
change the subject and get into something else.

But his letters home frequently revealed a brighter side. In early July,
writing from "Tent City No. 1," he sounded for all the world like a kid at
summer camp: "I'd rather stay in a tent than barracks. In the barracks you
have to keep your place clean all the time . . . What's more we got wooden
decks, 6 men to a tent, lights and we have our own radio."

By the end of the first week in August, his mood had turned fatalistic:
"Well I was offered another chance to go to communication school and be
promoted fast and get away from this rough life. But I said no. My place is
with a rifle. I didn't come in here to lead an easy life. They better get us
overseas quick and the war would be over with. Don't worry about me. I'm a
man now, no young guy."

The "man now" behaved a lot differently from the boy who had been impressed by the sermon on alcohol. George Scott of Easy Company remembered a late night after liberty when he was sitting in the tent talking
quietly with some buddies. Ira lurched into the tent and, without warning,
hurled a bayonet in Scott's direction. It stuck in the ground. "We all looked
up in silence at him," Scott recalled. "He just stood there scowling. I don't
think he intended to hit me. He was just angry. He was generally angry.
There was a chip on his shoulder; he was separated somehow."

Perhaps Ira's unlikeliest pal was Franklin Sousley.

Franklin arrived at Camp Pendleton "bright-eyed and bushy-tailed," as
his Kentucky people would have put it: a good ol' boy of eighteen, rawboned and drawling, his rust-colored hair uncombed. He had grown physically formidable in boot camp; he stood six feet now, all of it muscle and
bone. But the jokey sweetness was still intact: Franklin was as lighthearted
as Ira was dour. He would have his new buddies in stitches within minutes,
singing his homemade songs. His countrified "Marine Corps Hymn" had
become a minor smash around the camp, and now he had written a new
tune: this one a half-comic, half-serious warble called "Oh, Lord, Make
Me Lucky (Take Me Home to Kentucky)." When he wasn't vocalizing,
Franklin was spinning yarns about the country folks back home, folks who
lived in towns with names like Big Bone Lick and Dog Walk.("I never believed those names," mused Joe Rodriguez, "until I went there in 1982 and
saw that it was true.")

His buddies loved to send up his countrified ways. "He was the only one in the whole bunch," Bill Ranous liked to joke, "who thought that K rations tasted good."

Kentucky and his homefolk were never out of his mind. In July he wrote a touching letter to his hardworking mother: "You wrote that you were sick. I want you to stay in out of that field and look real pretty when I come home. You can grow a crop of tobacco every summer, but I sure as hell can't grow another mother like you."

Mike Strank added his own bawdy twists to the good-natured teasing of the Kentucky hillbilly. One Sunday morning, as the sergeant stood talking to some of his fellow veterans in the Easy Company compound, Franklin came loping into view. "Here's a good one," Mike whispered out of the corner of his mouth; then, in a louder, conversational voice, he remarked: "Well, I got my masturbation papers today. Now I can go overseas again."

Franklin, ever on the alert for inside lore, was all ears. "Where," he wanted to know of Mike, "do you get those masturbation papers? I want to go overseas, too." Mike was the picture of helpfulness. He directed the boy to the nearest officer in charge of records. And off Franklin charged, full of high hopes.

Mike Strank functioned on many levels. He was a weekend drinker, a good-time Charlie, and on Monday mornings he was all business again. He was widely regarded as one of the best squad leaders in the regiment: His squad, with Harlon, Ira, and Franklin in it, was also considered among the best in the regiment.

His method was tough discipline leavened with gentleness. During the exhausting hikes up and down Pendleton's canyon trails, just when the boys were groaning at the monotonous sameness of it all, Mike would call a halt, reach into his pack and pull out a chocolate "energy bar," and carve it into small bits. "Here are your pills," he'd tell the boys, who were soon laughing.

Robert Radebaugh loved the memory of the night Mike organized a séance in his tent. There was Strank, surrounded by a bunch of kids with their eyes squeezed shut and their hands suspended just above the surface of a card table. Mike had told the boys that he would make the table talk. He told them he would ask the table questions and it would respond by tapping on the floor. (It was Mike, of course, who was doing the tapping.)

Few seemed to have much fondness for Rene Gagnon. One of the youngest and most sheltered of the Marines in the company, Rene had had little experience in the art of mingling with men, and he never really got a chance to develop it. His comrades-in-arms seemed to recoil from the slight, callow nineteen-year-old almost by reflex. They shook their heads at the pencil-thin mustache he sometimes cultivated; it made him look like nothing so much as a little boy trying to disguise himself as a man. The memories of him, among the guys of Easy Company, are almost unremittingly withering: "He seemed like a guy who didn't want his body hurt." "I didn't like him from the moment I met him." "He had an attitude of indifference. Negative cockiness." "He was looking for the easy way out."

Ira Hayes was toxic in Rene's presence. Ira played solitaire, the card game of choice for this solitary boy. When Rene made the mistake of looking over his shoulder and intoning, "This goes on that," Ira leaped off the bunk and took a swing at him.

And the men in his Company could tick off a whole list of grievances: "He had an irritating attitude. Nothing was ever right. Everything needed fixing. The food wasn't right. The entertainment wasn't right. The command wasn't right. Very negative, very negative."

It fell to Mike Strank to confront Rene's liabilities and turn this weak link into a useful integer in the chain. He rode the boy hard, pointing out every screwup, making him the butt of his jokes and ridicule, until Captain Severance finally noticed the problem and reassigned the boy as a runner, a messenger reporting to headquarters. It wasn't cruelty that motivated Mike; it was the larger goal of saving lives. And with the transfer, Rene remained a functioning member of the company. The other Marines were relieved, and Rene saw no problem in it. "I figured it would be a pretty good deal, getting the jeep and running errands for headquarters," he later said.

Only on liberty was Rene able to enjoy anything even remotely similar to a last laugh. "We used to take Gagnon with us on the town," Rodriguez admitted. "The girls flocked to him. He was real handsome. We'd get his leftovers."

Harlon Block's tour at the advanced training camps was a period of inwardness for the hearty Texas athlete: diligent training and quiet contemplation. He kept close to Mike Strank, whom he admired. The ex-footballer who had once craved some of Leo Ryan's "boards" for his football pants now adapted some of Mike's mannerisms: Like Mike, he wore his helmet cocked to one side. Like Mike, he disdained socks. Like Mike, he cultivated the strange habit of showering with his boots on.

Privately, he continued to wrestle with his Adventist beliefs and their conflict with his military obligations. And with his conviction that from his next mission, he would not return.

On a weekend leave, Harlon hitchhiked up to Dos Palos, California, where Ed Jr. was in flight school to become a weather pilot. That night, as the two brothers sat at Ed's kitchen table under a single lightbulb, Harlon told Ed that after his next assignment he was not coming back.

"He spoke as a patriot," Ed recalled to me. "He wasn't scared about it. But he told me he wasn't coming back. I tried to act like he was fibbing; I pretended that he was joking around. I said, 'You're crazy, Harlon. You're not serious. Don't give me that.' But he was serious. He wasn't joking around."

His sister, Maurine, was the last family member to see Harlon alive. Harlon took a bus trip from Camp Pendleton to Loma Linda to visit her one summer day. It was on this visit that Harlon disclosed what he had been doing in the swamps back in Texas. If he got sick, he told Maurine, maybe it was God's will that he receive a discharge. But after God had not intervened, Harlon made up his mind that it was his fate to do his duty—never mind the torment he felt over the moral implications of battle.

On the morning he left for Camp Pendleton, and then the Pacific, Harlon told his sister what he'd told the others: "Maurine, I'm not comin' back."

"As the bus pulled out," she recalled sadly many years later, "I had the strong intuitive feeling that Harlon was right and I would never see my little brother again."

In their half year at Camp Pendleton, the Marines of the 5th Division had survived fleas, rain, cold, hot sun, bad food, and rattlesnakes; they had learned all that the officers and facilities at the surreal city of men could teach them.

Now it was time to board some ships and sail off into the ocean, toward another training facility, at a destination as yet unnamed, and learn some more.

On September 19—Franklin's birthday, as it happened—the Marines left San Diego harbor in troopships. Their voyage would take two weeks. Many of them would never see their American homeland again. But all of them would get a glimpse of Paradise before the firestorm to come. And yet a second, massive, "specialized city" within that Paradise.

Paradise—Hawaii—looked lush and green and inviting from the rails of the ships dropping anchor in Hilo Bay. Few of these American heartland boys had ever seen anything quite so exotic. One Marine later remembered it as "a huge hunk of green jade shimmering in the dark blue of the Pacific Ocean."

From the cars they boarded on a narrow-gauge railroad bound for their new camp, they could see waterfalls, pineapple trees, fern jungles with their brilliant flora, wild parrots screeching in flight. This was "the Big Island," Hawaii itself.

Their arrival, however, burst the illusion and brought them back to earth—dusty, hardscrabble earth. Spearhead's final destination turned out to be yet another training camp forged from what had been a ranch. This was the former Parker Ranch, the largest cattle empire on American soil. At the outbreak of the war its owner, Richard Smart, agreed to lease its forty thousand acres to the Marine Corps for one dollar a year. Its first major use had been as a respite for the battered and fatigued 2nd Division after the battle of Tarawa in 1943. The leathernecks quickly renamed the grounds Camp Tarawa, and the name held through the remainder of the war.

Camp Tarawa sprawled across terrain that lay between two volcanoes: Mauna Kea and Mauna Loa, whose snowcapped peaks were visible from the hundreds of pyramid-shaped tents soon erected there. The camp was sixty-five miles away from the town of Hilo and sixteen miles from the beach. And on this side of Paradise, at least, the landscape was a far cry from Eden. Shiny slabs of black rock, ossified lava flow, covered much of the ground. Coating the rock were layers of volcanic dust that spiraled up in the whipping wind that never seemed to abate, getting in the boys' eyes, flavoring their food.

"Oh, Camp Tarawa was a miserable place, with those lava rocks and constant dust," recalled Roy Steinfort. "The Red Cross judged it unfit to hold prisoners there. So it was a perfect place for the Marines."

As to the food, the troops-in-training would enjoy none of the beefsteaks that the Parker Ranch had sent out to an appreciative America. "We were on the biggest cattle ranch and on Hawaii," one of them later recalled, "but we never got beef and no pineapple juice." Instead, they would take sustenance with a nightly meal that someone dubbed "SOS," for "shit-on-a-shingle": creamed mutton on toast. Sometimes, for variety, they got mutton meat loaf or mutton stew.

A local woman, a cook named Tsugi Kaiama, came to the rescue of the boys' palates with an inviting delicacy: juicy hamburgers. Each day Tsugi—"Sue"—requisitioned a steer from the slaughterhouse and fed it through her gas grinder. The steak and rib sections added greatly to the flavor, as did her addition of celery and bread crumbs. The Marines queued up for Sue's burgers in lines so long that the townspeople gave up on joining them.

One day Sue spotted a boy who looked like a local; a Hawaiian, perhaps. When he reached the counter she asked him if that was true. No, the boy said, he was an American Indian. He introduced himself as Ira Hayes.

Here, in the final four months before the great armada departed for its still top-secret destination—for the Japanese island known only as "X"—the Marines would fine-tune the ultraspecialized skills they would need for their great challenge. They would learn how to disembark, take the beach, turn left, and cut off the mountain.

"Disembark" hardly suggests the lethal difficulty of the first component in this sequence. It entailed the stomach-wrenching, terrifying process of climbing down the webbing of rope ladders pitched over the sides of the great transport ships—every step of the climb encumbered by heavy packs—and securing a seat in one of the smaller landing crafts that would carry the men into the shallow water and to the edge of the beach. The young men were forced to make their descent as the huge transports bobbed and yawed in the turbulent waves. Some lost their footing and plunged into the water, others found themselves painfully jammed against the ships by a sudden collision of hull against hull.

My father told me about the challenge of this experience once when I was a young man. It was one of the very few times he ever spoke of his wartime life, and that fact made it even more memorable to me.

He told of clinging for dear life to the webbing, trying to choke back nausea and disabling terror, as he followed the back of the next Marine down. "I kept saying to myself, 'If he can do it, I can do it,' " my father told me.

So much of what all these boys would do over the next months, so much of their survival, so much of their sanity in the midst of murderous chaos, would come down to just that: following the back of the next Marine. If he could do it, they could do it.

The maneuvers at Camp Tarawa, with its obsidian terrain and its access to the pitching Pacific surf, were designed, as far as was humanly possible, to make the troops live out the assault on Iwo Jima before they got there; to live it out in their reflexes, their instincts, their dreams. The ideal result of Tarawa was that, once in combat, the boys would not have to think; would not have the mental option of making a wrong move. They would already have done it—psychically speaking—all their lives.

While the boys trained and retrained, their colonels and generals plotted strategy according to specific orders they had received from Washington at a secret conference at Pearl Harbor. The officers dissected and reconfigured this strategy inside a forbidding-looking wood structure next to division headquarters, a building that bore the deceptively innocuous title of "the conference center."

The conference center's windows were blacked out, its shut doors sealed with double locks, its premises cordoned off with barbed wire and the constant presence of armed MP's. No one could enter the conference center without a special pass.

It was inside this dark edifice that a small training staff was told in November of 1944 that "Island X" was Iwo Jima. Fred Haynes, on Harry the Horse's staff, remembers how the training changed at Camp Tarawa after they secretly studied the maps of Iwo Jima:

> We knew we would land on Green Beach, right under Mount Suribachi. And we knew we had to cut Suribachi off.
>
> We found a volcanic hill about the same height as Suribachi, about 550 feet high. We took tennis court tape and marked off a "beach" around this "Suribachi." We then rehearsed the men "landing" on this "Iwo" and getting them across the island to cut off the mountain from the rest of the island.
>
> We had the riflemen—the flagraisers would have done this many times—form into a boat team of twenty-five or so men. Each of these teams lined up a distance away as if they were at sea, headed for the "shore." They walked together until they hit the tape (beach) and then deployed. The 1st Battalion went straight across the island while the 2nd Battalion, with Easy Company, had to swing around immediately to the left and together they would take the hill.
>
> We wore out thousands of pairs of tough rubber shoes going over that rough volcanic rock practicing this. We had a hard time keeping the troops in shoes.

After all the serious practice, Ira Hayes still managed to recapture a vestige of his Pima youth on Camp Tarawa. With his friend Jack Castle he would go looking for horses to ride during rare moments of leisure—an easy task on the vast ranchland, if one was not afraid of riding bareback. "There were no saddles," Castle recalled, "so we'd stand on a rock and jump on the horse's back. You had to hold on to the horse's mane . . . so you wouldn't fall off. Ira was a very good rider and he loved to ride bareback. He'd talk then about being free and roaming the plains, when there were no reservations."

Franklin could not get lucky. He could not get home to Kentucky. So he found a way to bring a little bit of Kentucky to Tarawa.

Bill Ranous smelled something highly peculiar in the company's tent one day, in the general area of Franklin's cot. More than peculiar: something downright rotten. "What's that smell?" he asked Franklin.

Franklin looked around to make sure they were alone. Then he motioned Ranous to come over to the cot. Silently, he raised the blanket to reveal a tub filled with a foul-scented, dark mush.

"What," Ranous asked, "is that?"

"Raisin jack!" Franklin answered proudly. It was, as Ranous soon learned, an alcoholic mash that the young Kentuckian would later strain through a filter to make drinkable: a kind of moonshine.

He'd appropriated the raisins from the kitchen while on KP duty, he explained to Ranous. And he'd added a little yeast, and then waited while nature did the rest: an old folk skill that he'd brought with him all the way from the Appalachians.

"He was real proud of that raisin jack," Ranous remembered.

My father passed his days at Camp Tarawa attending to his duties and thinking of home. From what his friends recalled of him, he clung to his characteristic serenity and the exceptional focus that would guide him through his long and happy life in Wisconsin. A dream burned in his heart, even as a hell on earth brewed on the other side of the ocean: a clear, simple dream of returning home and opening his funeral home. Through all the turmoil that was about to engulf him, he never lost sight of that dream.

Robert Lane remembered Doc's tranquillity in those days. "He was more mature than most guys," Lane said. "He never participated in the drinking bouts. And he used to tell me how he handled people who were suffering the loss of a loved one. He had already done that often in his life, in the funeral business."

In November, the men whose home states authorized absentee voting were allowed to cast their ballots in the general elections. But most of the boys were too young to vote. By that month, infantry regiments were running seventy-two-hour maneuvers, as fighters and dive-bombers roared overhead. The practice landings continued, and continued.

It was in November that Harlon Block made the gesture that would underscore his bond with Belle. The 5th Division announced a plan to make National Service Life Insurance policies available to every man in the ranks. Harlon purchased a ten-thousand-dollar policy. The beneficiary was Belle. Not Ed, and not both his parents, as would have been routine, but Belle. In doing so, he ensured his mother's comfort and freedom in the years beyond his death.

Harlon wrote his mother a letter in November, a few weeks before the ships sailed. In it he imagines what it would be like to be home: "Let's see, the early oranges are already gone, the navel oranges too. About another month and you will be selling the ruby reds." He asks after the football buddies he enlisted with in a group. "Are the rest of the guys that came in when I did OK?"

Thinking of Christmas, he mentions the girl he is convinced he will never see again: "Buy Catherine [Pierce] a present for me and send it out to her. Get anything that would be alright for the occasion. You know more about that than I do."

Harlon instructs Belle to "buy all the kids something, and Dad don't forget him." Then the boy focuses in on his mother, and becomes in his fantasy her Santa: "Above all don't forget yourself. Just go down and buy yourself a new hat, coat, dress and shoes (and purse). Use as much money as you need . . . If I draw any money to amount to anything, I'll send it home."

December 1944. The last Christmas for too many young boys. Then off for the forty-day sail to Iwo Jima. The boys of Spearhead had been expertly trained for ten months. They were proficient in the techniques of war. But more important, they were a team, ready to fight for one another. These boys were bonded by feelings stronger than they would have for any other humans in their life.

The vast, specialized city of men—boys, really, but a functioning society of experts now, trained and coordinated and interdependent and ready for its mission—will move out upon the Pacific. Behind them, in safe America, Bing Crosby sang of a white Christmas, just like the ones he used to know. Ahead lay a hot island of black sand, where many of them would ensure a long future of Christmases in America by laying down their lives.

Six

ARMADA

Don't worry about me, Momma. I'll be OK.
—FROM THE LAST LETTER OF AN
IWO JIMA–BOUND MARINE

THERE WERE NO CHEERING CROWDS to see Mike, Harlon, Ira, Doc, Rene, and Franklin off as they departed Camp Tarawa. To maintain military secrecy they journeyed to the port of Hilo in the dead of night.

Their destination was an "Island X." That's all they knew. For the Marines fighting America's War in the Pacific it was a familiar stereotyped pattern. Months of training, the invasion of an island no one had ever heard of, followed by more training and another invasion.

In Europe troops liberated cities and were cheered as conquering heroes. But the Pacific was a different story. After slogging through fetid jungles and fighting across coral outcroppings, the survivors of battle had only memories of their fallen buddies as they gazed out at the sea from the transports returning them to their base for more training.

But the boys on their way to "Island X" were in for an unusual treat. Along with almost five hundred ships, theirs stopped at Pearl Harbor for a final liberty before battle.

Honolulu!

Mike mingled with old Raider buddies in bars packed wall to wall with leathernecks acting as if they would never see another beer. For many of them, this would be true. Ira and Joe Rodriguez walked down jammed

---

Chapter opener: An onboard briefing held en route to Iwo Jima.

Bishop and King Streets through Honolulu's "Coney Island" where men outnumbered women a hundred to one. Doc and Rene waited in long lines at the USO near the Royal Palace Grounds, where there were writing facilities, game rooms, food and soft-drink bars. Franklin took the opportunity to permanently proclaim his love of the Corps: On Hotel Street he had the Marine emblem tattooed on his right arm.

When a shore barge sidled up to Harlon's ship to take him ashore, he caught sight of a familiar face in the crowd of Marines. He silently climbed down the ladder, jumped into the barge, and surprised his old buddy Glen Cleckler with a slap on the back. Glen Cleckler, the Panther fullback who had churned through the big holes opened up by Harlon's blocking.

The two boys went larking in the city; there they ran into a couple of other Weslaco boys. So many boys from Weslaco! It seemed like the whole Marine Corps was there! "This must be the Big One," the young boys shouted, referring to the invasion of Japan.

But as the group's hilarity wore on into the night, Harlon's mood turned serious. It was while the friends were milling out of a movie theater that he turned quietly to Glen. He slipped his ring off his finger and some photographs out of his pocket and pressed them into Cleckler's hand. "Give this to my mother," he told his buddy. "My luck has run out. I don't think I'm coming back."

Like the others who had heard this, Glen at first laughed it off. He tried to hand the items back, but Harlon looked hurt, so Glen shrugged and kept them. "I didn't know what to make of this," Cleckler told me, "but Harlon was dead serious."

A few days later, just before he left Hawaii, Harlon had one more encounter with a Weslaco Panther teammate, Leo Ryan. Harlon searched for Leo until he found him in a naval hospital tent in "Camp Katland" on Red Top Hill outside Honolulu. Leo was in horrible shape: heavily bandaged and temporarily blinded from the effects of a Japanese shell in the battle of Tarawa.

Leo was lucky to be alive. In fact, he had been left for dead, in a pile of bodies stacked like cordwood that had been his Marine comrades until the 155-millimeter shell had exploded in their midst on Tarawa. The concussion had torn his nose to shreds, changed the wrapping of his face, unhinged one side of his jaw, and blown both eyeballs out of their sockets— they were hanging down his cheeks, held only by their stems, when the corpsman found him.

Unconscious and motionless, he was placed on a pile of corpses. He was in this state when a medic had spotted him and ordered the erroneous telegram notifying Jean Ryan that her husband was dead. Only later, when another medic walked by and noticed movement, was Leo pulled out of the pile, given treatment, and evacuated to Oahu. Against all odds, he not only recovered but also eventually regained his eyesight.

Now, in this hospital tent in a virtual city of hospital tents—they were sectioned off into streets, there were so many—the two boys spoke quietly as a heavy rain fell. The glory of their undefeated football season seemed a long way in the past.

Harlon confessed the same fatalistic thoughts to Leo as he had to the others. He was as calm in delivering them as he had been with his brother Ed and sister Maurine. He had mulled it over: He would do his duty. He would fight. He would die. "I have beat the odds because I haven't been hit yet," he told Leo. "But I won't be so lucky again. My odds have run out."

But there was more. He spoke of his liberty in Weslaco months before as "a gift from God, an act of fate that gave him his last opportunity to tell people that he would not return." Corporal Block then spoke of his reemerging religious beliefs. He realized he had to go out and kill the enemy, but he was not comfortable doing so. Harlon spoke of the validity of the Fifth Commandment, "Thou Shalt Not Kill," and how it was the government that now demanded he kill. "Eleanor Roosevelt had com- plained that the Marines were a bunch of savages after a few had broken up some West Coast bars," Leo remembered. "Harlon was hurt by this, sensi- tive to being taught to kill against his religion and then being branded a killer."

In late January the huge fleet moved slowly out of Pearl Harbor, forming a convoy seventy miles long. Amidst the machinery and manpower on one transport ship, the USS *Missoula*, are six particular boys: six boys with the wind in their hair, unsuspecting of their own impending place in mythic history.

The boys are pushing toward their destiny now. Doc, Ira, Mike, Franklin, Harlon, and Rene are rushing to their appointment with an entrenched, dedicated defender of a sacred homeland. Peaceable American boys, citizen- soldiers about to engage with a myth-obsessed samurai foe. This will not be a mere battle. It will be a colossal cultural collision, a grinding together of the tectonic plates that are East and West. The Western "plate" will be the cream of American democracy and mass-production: in voluntary man- power; in technology, training, and industrial support. The Eastern "plate" will be the elite minions of a thoroughly militarized society whose high priests have taught that there is no higher virtue than death in battle.

The results of this collision will alter the fates of both East and West for the next century to come.

This giant fleet of American warships—a modern armada—churns across the ocean day and night for a journey of four thousand miles. It moves with the inevitability of a railroad schedule. It stops for nothing, it deviates for nothing. The United States, having been surprised at Pearl Harbor and then raked in battle after battle by the onrushing forces of imperial Japan, has finally stabilized and gathered its strength. Now the American giant is fully awake and cold-eyed. It is stalking an ocean, rounding the curve of the earth, to crush its tormentor.

Accommodations on the *Missoula* are less than comfortable. There are only small spaces on the boat to mingle, so most of the men have to remain in their bunks, along with their pack, rifle, and helmet. The boys' sleeping compartment is a cargo hold belowdecks where floor-to-ceiling bunks, twelve to fifteen high, have been installed. Woe to all below when the man on the uppermost bunk gets seasick.

The days are long. Pinochle games dot the fantails and the upper-deck gun platforms. Some of the men squint at paperback books—Perry Mason mysteries, Zane Grey westerns. Others thoughtfully clean and reclean their weapons. Briefings are common; captains and sergeants going over the plan of action on the beach with their huddled squads and platoons, again and again. The troops know their drill. They've practiced it for a year. They go over it again, one more time.

One kid prowls the decks offering to sharpen knives. He'll sharpen anybody's knife. It doesn't matter if he's sharpened it before. It's something to do. Something to pass the hours.

The *Missoula* carries all of Easy Company amidst its 1,500 troops. By the time this fleet converges with a second one, hurrying northward from down near Australia, the total number of ships will exceed eight hundred. They are carrying three reinforced Marine Divisions, the equivalent of the entire ground combat forces of today's Marine Corps. All of these ships, all these men, converging on an eight-mile-square island six hundred miles south of Tokyo.

The movement of over 100,000 men—Marines, Navy support personnel, Coast Guard units—across four thousand miles of ocean for three weeks is a triumph of American industry galvanizing itself in a time of great national peril. At the outset of the war, Japan's naval strength was more than double that of America's. But across the American continent, the idling factories steamed and sparked to life. Most of the vessels came splashing off the industrial assembly lines in the six months before this assault. And they have been augmented by reinforcements from around the globe. The call has gone out to every theater of the World War, and every theater has sent what it could spare. Support has come from MacArthur in the Philippines, from the China and India commands. Eisenhower in Europe looked up from his maps and wondered, "What *are* they doing out there?" and consigned transports that had borne troops from England to the beaches at Normandy.

And it has not been just a matter of hardware. The civilians of America have mobilized behind these fighting boys. Behind each man on board the ships are hundreds of workers: in the factories, in the cities and towns, on the heartland farms. Rosie the Riveter. Boy Scouts collecting paper and metal. The young girl who will become Marilyn Monroe, sweating away in a defense plant.

Here is some of what those mobilized civilians have generated for this tremendous force:

For each of the 70,000 assault-troop Marines, 1,322 pounds of supplies and equipment. Some of it sounds weirdly domestic: dog food, garbage cans, lightbulbs, house paint. Some of its suggests an island business office: duplicating machines, carbon paper, movie projectors. Some sounds like kids' camping gear: toilet paper, socks, shoelaces, paper and pencils, flashlights, blankets. Some begins to suggest a sterner mission: flares, plasma, bandages, crucifixes, holy water, canisters of disinfectant to spray on corpses. And some of it gets exactly to the point: artillery, machine guns, automatic rifles, grenades, and ammunition. The transport ships carry six thousand five-gallon cans of water, a hundred million cigarettes, and enough food to feed the population of Atlanta for a month, or the assaulting Marines for two months.

Two days out of Honolulu the identity of "Island X" is revealed.

Some troops in World War II will have the honor of liberating Paris, others Manila. Easy Company has been assigned an ugly little hunk of slag in the ocean, nearly barren of trees or grasses or flowers. It is a dry wasteland of black volcanic ash that stinks of sulfur ("Iwo Jima" means "sulfur island"). Bulging at its northeast plateau, tapering down to Mount Suribachi at its southwestern tip, it resembles an upside-down pear with Suribachi at its stem. Pilots who had photographed the island from above thought it resembled a charred pork chop.

Mount Suribachi in the south is an extinct volcano, and the lava flow from Suribachi's volcanic eruptions formed the rest of the island, oozing

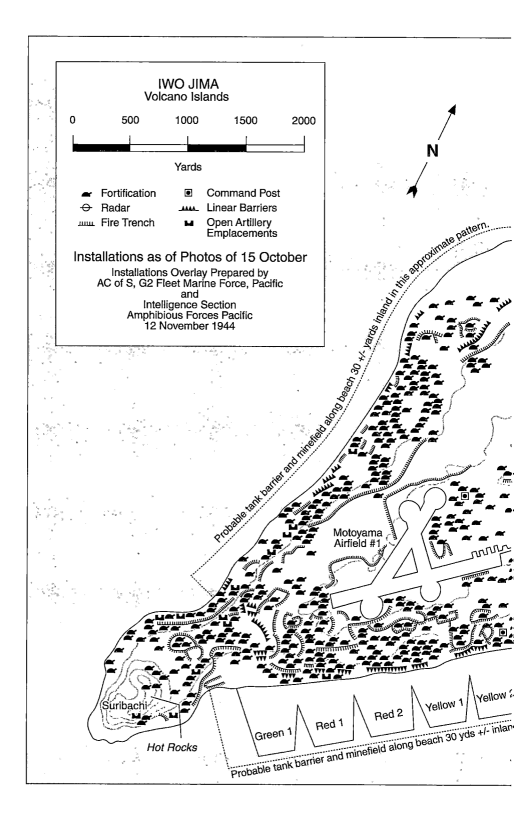

IWO JIMA
Volcano Islands

0   500   1000   1500   2000

Yards

- Fortification   ◙ Command Post
- Radar   ᴧᴧᴧ Linear Barriers
- Fire Trench   ▶◀ Open Artillery
                          Emplacements

Installations as of Photos of 15 October

Installations Overlay Prepared by
AC of S, G2 Fleet Marine Force, Pacific
and
Intelligence Section
Amphibious Forces Pacific
12 November 1944

N

this approximate pattern.

Probable tank barrier and minefield along beach 30 +/- yards inland in

Motoyama
Airfield #1

Suribachi

Hot Rocks

Green 1   Red 1   Red 2   Yellow 1   Yellow 2

Probable tank barrier and minefield along beach 30 yds +/- inland

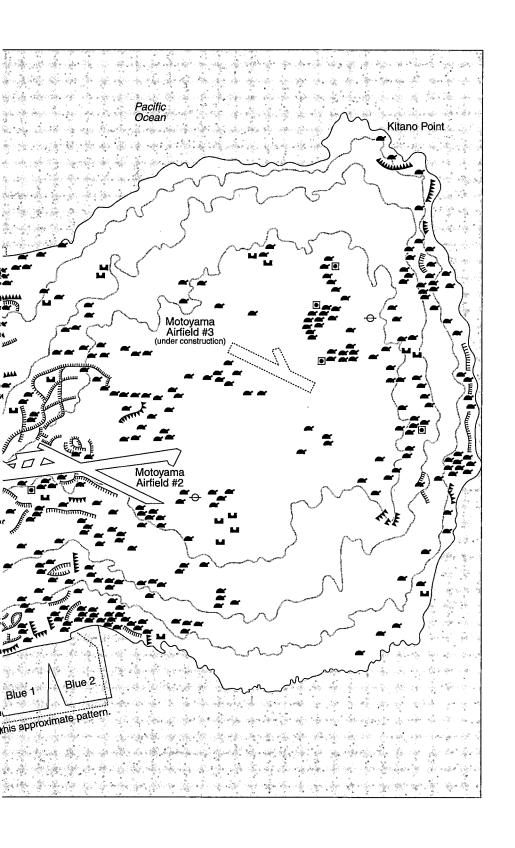

Pacific
Ocean

Kitano Point

Motoyama
Airfield #3
(under construction)

Motoyama
Airfield #2

Blue 1

Blue 2

this approximate pattern.

along the slender neck and pooling out over five and a half miles to a width of two and a half miles at its widest part. The only practical landing beach begins at Suribachi's base and extends two miles along the eastern shore. The land rises, then, as the island's width expands, toward a 350-foot mountain, Motoyama, that commands the northwesterly corner. Plumes of steam-driven, rank sulfur still jet from Motoyama, evidence of volcanic substrata.

Iwo Jima is an ugly, smelly place. Giant boulders, shifting sands, and stinking sulfur beds allow for little vegetation. Hardly a Pacific dream isle, it is covered by some twisted brush and has no fresh water. It is, as one Japanese soldier wrote, "A place where no sparrow sings."

Maps are being unfurled on ships throughout the armada: large, rolled-up, heavily detailed maps, maps designed from aerial photographs of the island, table models made out of rubber, maps designed to be suspended from walls and spread across vast tables.

The maps show the military challenge. They give the combatants their first look at Iwo Jima: a small chunk of land in a triangular shape. Mike, Harlon, Franklin, Ira, Rene, and Doc no doubt pay close attention to the strange little fortified volcanic mountain down near the beach where they'll rush ashore.

The boys, new to combat but seasoned by their year's training, look on alertly, with professional savvy. Some of the veterans and older field officers, who can relate map symbols to direct personal experience, draw back in disbelief. One of them mutters, "It's gonna be rough as a corncob."

I can only imagine what the flagraisers thought as they bent over the Iwo Jima map on the *Missoula*. Stamped "SECRET" and dated November 12, 1944, it was based on "PHOTOGRAPHY FROM NAVY SORTIES 19 AUG. AND 1 SEPT. 1944." They must surely have focused on their landing beach, stamped "GREEN BEACH," adjacent to Mount Suribachi. And they would have seen the designation the mapmakers had given Suribachi: "HOT ROCKS."

Harry the Horse's 28th Regiment, with Easy Company among it, would land closest to Hot Rocks, right under its threatening mass. They were part of the group that would string out in a ribbon of men across the narrow neck of the island, "cutting" Mount Suribachi off from the rest of the island. Then they'd pivot left to take the volcano.

The surface of Iwo was rendered white on the map. But the white was almost totally obscured by little black dots. These black dots represented the armaments that would fire at them as they struggled up Green Beach and raced inland in the shadow of Hot Rocks.

Just about every type of defense available in 1945 was represented by those black dots. All were identified by the key in the lower right-hand corner: Coastal Defense Guns, Dual-Mount Dual-Purpose Guns, Covered Artillery Emplacements, Rifle Pits, Foxholes, Antitank Guns, Machine Guns, Blockhouses, Pillboxes, and Earth-Covered Structures.

Hundreds of black dots, but no buildings. No structures to house the estimated 12,000 Japanese defenders.

Captain Dave Severance had first seen the maps a month before in the conference room at Camp Tarawa. He was astounded by its many overlapping swirls and heavy rectangles and triangles, each figure denoting a weapon emplacement or a fortified blockhouse. Severance's thoughts reeled back through military history. "It scared the hell out of me," he will always recall. "It conjured up images of Civil War battles, row after row of men going up and replacing those who had fallen. I knew we'd get to the top of that mountain, eventually—but how many men was it going to chew up?"

Each boy in the armada reacted differently to knowing the target. Some hoped it would be over quickly, others dreaded a long campaign. Others sharpened their bayonets for the umpteenth time, while a few checked their lucky charms once again.

For good luck Rene tucked a photograph of nineteen-year-old Pauline Harnois, his girlfriend from back in the mills, into the webbing of his helmet. The photo showed Pauline in an evening gown. Pauline, whom he had met working in the Chicopee spinning room. His mother disapproved of Pauline, thinking she was too aggressive, pushing her little boy. But it was Pauline's picture that Rene depended on to protect him in the coming battle.

Mike Strank's protection was his sense of humor. He put on a don't-give-a-damn veneer, coated by his trademark grin and playful sense of humor. He wore his helmet cocked to one side of his head and told jokes in an Old Country dialect that broke up the farmboys and the office clerks.

Joe Rodriguez remembered the day that Mike overheard him sounding off about how poor his parents were during the Depression; how his mother had to make pillowcases out of used flour sacks.

"You guys must have been rich as hell," Strank broke in. "I'll tell you what my mother used to do. When I was a kid my mother made our shorts from flour sacks. You know, it took me almost six weeks after joining the Marines to figure out what that fly was for!"

Early in February the fleet crossed the 180th meridian, the International Dateline, and veterans like Mike initiated the men making their first crossing. They were now in the domain of the meridian's ruler, the Golden Dragon. Mike threw himself into this comic ritual, where Marines were yanked out of their bunks, shaved bald, decked out in ridiculous garb, forced to ingest some unnamed "stinking" matter, and then doused with water hoses as they scampered up and down the decks. The victims were forced to kneel and kiss the bare feet of Neptune, the god of the sea.

Mike was at the center of it, laughing. "He dragged me out of bed while I was seasick," John Fredatovich recalled, "but he let me go when he saw how sick I was. But I still had fun. Everybody was laughing. And Mike was the ringleader."

The younger guys loved this, Rodriguez recalled. Those kids in uniform wanted to be just like him; kids who weren't so sure of themselves couldn't get enough of Sergeant Mike's style.

It is a calculated performance. These admiring boys, many of them still innocent and unsuspecting, are his new younger brothers. They are transparent to him. The grueling training, the close quarters, the liberties, the poker games, the bull sessions about battle—all of that is over now. The cards are on the table. The cores of these kids' beings are visible to Mike. They are ready to give their lives—especially for one another. But most of them don't really know, yet, what that is going to mean. Mike is their shepherd. He has won their confidence. Now he is going to do his damnedest to get them home.

Mike, the immigrant American, is representative of the best of the young leaders in the Pacific. A sergeant, he does not lord his rank over anyone. He embodies the Raider egalitarian ideal of no divisions between the men, no hierarchy.

He eats with his men instead of going to the sergeants' mess. And a few weeks before leaving for Iwo Jima, Captain Dave Severance tries to recommend Mike for the rank of Platoon Sergeant. Mike turns the offer down on the spot, saying, "I promised my boys I'd be there for them."

Despite the hilarity, one frightening aspect of the coming battle stuck in the back of the boys' minds. There was reason to believe the battle for Iwo Jima would be even more ferocious than the others, reason to expect the Japanese defender would fight even more tenaciously.

In Japanese eyes the Sulfur Island was infinitely more precious than Tarawa, Guam, Tinian, Saipan, and the others. To the Japanese, Iwo Jima represented something more elemental: It was Japanese homeland. Sacred ground. In Shinto tradition, the island was part of the creation that burst forth from Mount Fuji at the dawn of history. Modern-day governance honored that tradition: Iwo was part of the Tokyo prefecture. It was only 650 miles from the capital city. The mayor of Tokyo was also the island's mayor. Thus the island was part of a seamless sacred realm that had not been desecrated by an invader's foot for four thousand years.

Easy Company and the other Marines would be attempting nothing less than the invasion of Japan.

Emperor Hirohito was personally alarmed by the prospect of foreign defilement of his realm at Iwo Jima. In May of 1944 he handpicked a trusted commander to defend Japanese honor there, the head of his personal palace guard, Lieutenant General Tadamichi Kuribayashi.

Kuribayashi's ancestors were samurai and had served six emperors over five generations. Hirohito was confident this was the man to save Japan from disgrace.

Kuribayashi was tall for a Japanese, five feet nine inches, husky, and with a small potbelly. He had had a varied career, from Japanese military schools to service in embassies in Canada and Washington to command of combat troops in China and Manchuria.

He was familiar with America and spoke excellent English. As a thirty-seven-year-old captain and deputy military attaché at the embassy in Washington in 1928, he had crisscrossed the United States and studied its people and ways. He knew and respected his enemy.

The night before he flew to Iwo Jima in the second week of June 1944, he had a private meeting with Emperor Hirohito, an almost unheard-of honor for a commoner. It was critical that the barbarians not take Iwo Jima.

The highest personage in his land also handpicked the commander of the Marines. Because of his age, sixty-two, and serious diabetes, it took the personal intervention of President Roosevelt to get the old warrior Howlin' Mad Smith out to battle.

By now, as he sailed to Iwo Jima with the armada, Smith was the "Patton of the Pacific." He was irascible, often profane, and constantly ruffled the smooth feathers of the hidebound Navy, but like Patton, he was a winner. And by early 1945 he had put together an unbroken string of victories over thousands of miles that even Patton would envy.

Unlike all the other combatants in World War II, including the U.S. Army, Smith and his Marines never lost a battle. Wherever a Marine boot stepped ashore in the Pacific, Americans were there to stay.

So Iwo Jima would be the battlefield of the personal representatives of the Emperor and the President. Smith would try to kick in the front door to Japan; Kuribayashi would try to sweep Smith from the sacred doorstep. Kuribayashi respected the Marines' proud record in the Pacific. But he was determined to bury that record in the black sands of Iwo Jima.

By February 11 the 5th Division armada had rendezvoused with the 3rd and 4th Divisions at Saipan. Filling the horizon were over eight hundred ships, pausing one last time before sailing the final seven hundred miles to Iwo Jima. There were more Marines massed here than would be in uniform for the rest of the century.

Just eight months before, the 4th Division had wrested Saipan away from the Japanese. Now long, gleaming white airstrips had replaced the rotting corpses among the cane fields.

The boys of Easy Company watched the gigantic American B-29 Super-fort bombers lumber down the three-mile-long airstrips and lift slowly into the air on their way to bomb the Japanese mainland. They didn't know it, but some of those planes would not return because of a certain Sulfur Island. And it was for this reason that the battle of Iwo Jima had been ordered.

In the fall of 1944 the Joint Chiefs of Staff had rejected General MacArthur's plan to attack Japan via Taiwan and China. Instead, they endorsed Admiral Nimitz's plan of a frontal attack against the Japanese mainland. Preliminary saturation bombing of Japanese military plants and cities was part of the plan.

The biggest obstacle a B-29 pilot faced on his bombing run from Tinian and Saipan to Japan was the lethal triple whammy of danger presented by Iwo Jima. Athwart the direct path to Japan, the island was almost exactly halfway between the Marianas and Japan and boasted two airstrips and a radar station.

As the Superforts approached Iwo on their way to Japan, the radar station would give mainland defenders a two-hour early warning. The gigantic B-29's, lumbering north on their 2,500-mile round trip flight to attack Japan, made easy targets for the small, quick fighter planes based on Iwo.

And lastly, after enduring more antiaircraft fire and dogfights over

Japan, the B-29's, often damaged, would again be forced to face the Iwo-based fighters on their return trip. Too many pilots and crew were being lost to watery graves. General Curtis LeMay, commander of the Twentieth Air Force, warned that his pilots could not sustain these losses much longer.

And it was not only the bombers in the air that were vulnerable. The Army Air Force concluded after the war that Iwo Jima–based planes destroyed more B-29's on the ground, in raids on Tinian and Saipan, than were lost on all the bombing runs over Tokyo.

But the conquest of Iwo Jima was not merely about cutting losses. In Allied hands, the island would take on an offensive value: The B-29's could themselves land there to change crews, discharge wounded, take on fuel. And they could be escorted to their targets by squadrons of Army Air Corps P-51 long-range fighters.

Given these powerful incentives, the island had to be taken at almost any cost.

The Army Air Force was doing its part to soften up Iwo Jima for the Marines. Beginning December 8, B-29 Superforts and B-24 Liberators had been pummeling the island mercilessly. Iwo Jima would be bombed for seventy-two consecutive days, setting the record as the most heavily bombed target and the longest sustained bombardment in the Pacific War. One flyboy on Saipan confidently told Easy Company's Chuck Lindberg, "All you guys will have to do is clean up. No one could survive what we've been dropping."

Some optimistically hoped the unprecedented bombing of the tiny island would make the conquest of Iwo Jima a two- to three-day job. But on the command ship USS *Eldorado*, Howlin' Mad shared none of this optimism. The general was studying reconnaissance photographs that showed that every square inch of the island had been bombed. "The Seventh Air Force dropped 5,800 tons in 2,700 sorties. In one square mile of Iwo Jima, a photograph showed 5,000 bomb craters." Admiral Nimitz thought he was dropping bombs "sufficient to pulverize everything on the island." But incredibly, the enemy defenses were *growing*. There were 450 major defensive installations when the bombing began. Now there were over 750. Howlin' Mad observed: "We thought it would blast any island off the military map, level every defense, no matter how strong, and wipe out the garrison. But nothing of the kind happened. Like the worm, which becomes stronger the more you cut it up, Iwo Jima thrived on our bombardment."

The photographs shocked Smith's Chief of Staff. He would later write: "The prolonged aerial bombardment of Iwo Jima, which was a daily occurrence for over seventy days, had no appreciable effect in the reduction of the enemy's well-prepared and heavily fortified defensive installations."

The air raids were called "softening up" activities. But in fact, Iwo Jima was becoming "harder."

Off Saipan, Doc now learned that whatever terrors the coming battle would hold for him, he would not have to climb down the rope nets he dreaded so much. The first ten waves of the assault force—the tip of Spearhead—were placed on board LST's for the final trip to Iwo. Instead of ropes over the side as they had been trained, Easy Company would walk down to the dark holds of the LST's and board amphibian tractors (LVT's). These tractors would clank down a metal ramp into the sea and then to shore.

A final invasion rehearsal was conducted, with Tinian as the objective. The LST's raced toward shore and swerved away at the last moment. The next time the boys would feel the earth under their feet, it would be on Iwo Jima.

On February 15, the assault troops shoved off from Saipan. It would be a seven-hundred-mile, four-day trip to D-Day, scheduled for February 19.

The weather is balmy during the trip, and most of the men sleep atop the deck of the crowded LST. They are quieter now as battle approaches, more serious. They hone their knives and bayonets, clean and reclean their rifles. Religious services are well attended. At night men hang over the rails staring silently at the phosphorescence of the water as their LST slices through the Pacific.

The armada's momentum is inexorable now, fated, a force of history. Nothing will stop the surge. A man on one of the ships loses his balance, pitches over the side, and finds himself terribly alone in the Pacific Ocean. His craft does not stop. None of the ships stop. He waves his arms in panic. The ships churn past him. His horrified comrades look on as his figure recedes, then vanishes. The armada cannot stop for one man. The armada has an appointment, and means to be on time.

And theirs will be no surprise attack. The day the invaders sail from Saipan, General Kuribayashi orders his men to take their battle stations, and he moves to his command post. "I pray for a heroic fight," he writes.

To the general a "heroic fight" meant one in which all his men would die. There were no medals for survivors in the Japanese army, only for the heroic dead.

More was expected of the Japanese soldier than any soldier in World War II. They were to fight valiantly with no hope for survival. Every man on Iwo Jima knew the island would be his grave.

Kuribayashi had no expectation that he could win the battle. He knew the Americans would throw overwhelming arms and numbers of men at him. And by now he realized the depleted Japanese navy would not sail to his rescue.

His goal was a foreshadowing of the enemy's strategy in Vietnam: to make the battle so costly to the Americans in terms of lives that the civilian leaders in Washington would blanch at the prospect of a later invasion of the Japanese mainland. He had instructed his men that their duty was to "kill ten Americans before you die."

His *issen gorin* had long ago written the final letters that would be delivered to their folks on farms in Kyushu. To his wife, Kuribayashi had written, "Do not expect my return."

The troops had even pooled their money and shipped it to the treasury in Tokyo. Their lives were only worth the cost of a postcard to their military masters—"one yen, five rin"—but perhaps Tokyo had use for their money. They knew they would have no need for it anymore.

All they had to look forward to was the death of as many Marines as possible before they offered their lives for the Emperor.

The Japanese troops on Iwo Jima were hardened veterans. To ensure a solid defense, the army had shipped from Manchuria the veteran 145th Infantry Regiment, crack troops from Kagoshima, for the battle.

All their young lives their heads had been filled by military propaganda, in grade school, high school, and now in the army. Since their youth they had been told how true Japanese heroes always "died with the Emperor's name on their lips." Death on the battlefield was glorified for the home front, but the veterans knew the last word of a boy dying in battle was someone else's name, not the Emperor's. It was the same name all troops throughout history had cried out with their last breath. It was rendered in different tongues, but the meaning was universal. His last word was invariably *"Okasan!"* The German would cry *"Mutter!"* The English and Americans, "Mother!" "Mom!" or "Mommy!"

No matter the similarity in death, in life the Americans and Japanese fought very differently. The Japanese army fought using the most ruthless tactics of any combatant in World War II. Their practice of "no surrender" meant they were unpredictable, as they fought far beyond the limits of a Westerner. On Tarawa only seventeen Japanese soldiers had surrendered. And most of those were captured unconscious, stunned, or weakened by battle. Five thousand Japanese soldiers fought to extinction. Ira, echoing the feelings of many Marines, had recently written his parents, "I would rather fight a Nazi than a Japanese."

The Japanese soldier turned all Western logic on its head. If surrounded, a German would surrender; a Japanese would fight on. If wounded and disabled, an Englishman would allow himself to be taken prisoner; a Japanese would wait and blow himself and his captor up. The Marines could not treat the Japanese soldier as they would hope to be treated. Their only choice was to exterminate him.

Japanese treatment of defenseless prisoners of war alarmed the American fighting man. All armies commit atrocities against their opponents, but these are usually isolated incidents not condoned by higher officials. But Japanese authorities in Tokyo, including the Emperor, condoned a different set of rules to fight their war. Rules that permitted, among other startling actions, slavery, systematic torture, barbaric medical experiments, even cannibalism.

Japanese "hell ships" with their Allied chattel stuffed in dark, stinking holds delivered survivors to China, Korea, and Japan, where they were forced to work as slaves in mines, factories, and farms. Allied slave labor built the "Railroad of Death" over the Kwai River at a brutal cost of three hundred lives per mile.

The Japanese had their counterpart to the Nazi Gestapo: skilled torturers, the Kempei Tai. One of their favorite tricks was to force fistfuls of rice down a POW's throat, insert a water hose down his throat until his belly swelled, and then mercilessly jump on him.

By 1945 the Marines were aware of a number of Japanese atrocities. There was a certain photograph, copies of which were passed among Allied troops in the Pacific. It showed an Australian POW—a pilot, on his knees, blindfolded, with his arms tied behind his back. A Japanese officer towered over him with a raised samurai sword, about to chop the Australian's head off. In the background, smiling Japanese soldiers looked on.

The statistics at the end of the war spoke to the brutal Japanese treatment of anyone within their grasp. Allied POW's captured by the Germans in the European Theater died at a rate of 1.1 percent. But POW's held by the Japanese died at a rate of 37 percent.

Because the Japanese fought by different rules, the Marines changed some of theirs also. I think of Doc, my twenty-one-year-old father-to-be, on that LST sailing to Iwo Jima. He's "Doc" to everyone, a Navy corpsman. But his counterpart in Europe would not recognize him as a fellow medic.

Doc is dressed like any other Marine. But if he had been a medic in the European Theater, he would have worn a red cross on his helmet and expected the Germans to spare him as a noncombatant. Since the Japanese refused to make this distinction, Doc bore no special markings. In Europe the medics were unarmed, according to the Geneva Convention; the Germans usually would not stoop to shooting a corpsman. But Doc and the other medics in the Pacific had been issued .45-caliber pistols to protect themselves. The Japanese targeted corpsmen to prevent them from helping wounded Americans.

Despite his youth, Doc was the senior corpsman for Easy Company. In that capacity he occasionally called the other corpsmen together for a briefing, to relay news, to go over procedures. But briefings got old; there wasn't much news, and by now the other corpsmen knew their procedures.

And so Doc calmed his mind by arranging and rearranging the contents of his "Unit 3," again and again. And again.

A Unit 3 was a corpsman's pouch—a large cloth pouch that the medic would sling across his chest, much like the newspaper bags my father used on his paper route back in Appleton. But this pouch was not meant to bring in dollar bills for young Jack Bradley to put on his parents' mantel. This pouch was meant to save human life. It contained medical supplies. Bandages, adhesives, safety pins, tweezers, and sulfa powder for disinfectant— penicillin, still new and costly, was available only in limited supply then. And like the newspaper boy he had once been, sitting and folding the papers on the curb, Doc would spend hours hunched down someplace on deck, organizing and reorganizing his Unit 3. He memorized the exact place where every item would be; memorized it by touch, so that he could reach for it in the chaos of battle and find it unerringly.

The morphine Syrettes—small tubes with a needle on one end and a dispenser on the other—contained a quarter grain of morphine to be injected into a grievously injured Marine to dull unbearable pain. To calm him so that Doc could work on him. Or just to ease his passage to death.

The thick white swatches of woven cloth for tourniquets. In battle, these would be stained red from blood spurting from severed arteries as the corpsman wrestled one over the stump of a man's missing arm or leg.

The large gauze dressings with their long tie-strings. These were for the hideously but accurately named "sucking chest wounds," wounds that tore open the chest and punctured the lungs. The sucking sound came as the injured man gasped for breath and his chest cavity lost pressure. Doc would have to restrain the victim, applying the dressing over the hole, and hope it was enough until the kid could be evacuated to an aid station.

The hemostats, clamps with flat ends to stick into a gaping wound and tie off a broken artery.

I can imagine my father, Doc Bradley, finally packing up his Unit 3 at the end of the day. Perhaps he hoped it would bring him luck, protect him, that he would be as safe with it slung across his body as he had been with a newspaper sack back in Appleton.

But no matter how he would have tried to imagine that the Marine riflemen would do most of the dying, there was the fact that 414 corpsmen had been casualties of the fighting on Saipan, eight times as many as on Tarawa. At Iwo Jima the figure would double.

Whatever his thoughts as he lay down to sleep on his LST, he didn't know that on Iwo Jima the Japanese soldiers had special rules regarding the treatment of Navy corpsmen like him. They were being trained how to recognize him and make him a priority target. The idea was that if they could kill a corpsman, more Marines would die unattended, bleeding into the sand.

Even better, they were instructed, was to wound a corpsman. Since the Marines valued their corpsmen and felt protective of them, often three or four would rush out to help them, making inviting targets.

And how were the Japanese soldiers trained to recognize Doc Bradley as a medic? By his Unit 3. "Unit three! Unit three!" their instructors would shout, pointing to intelligence photos of young Navy corpsmen running through battle.

Perhaps the biggest fear of the boys, now only days away from their target, was fear of the unknown. How many troops would be on Iwo Jima? Would air and naval bombardment eliminate most? How well dug in were the Japanese?

American intelligence analysts had many aerial photographs of Iwo Jima, but they rarely revealed a Japanese soldier. Because of the island's lack of potable water, they concluded only 13,000 troops could be there. They were off by forty percent. In reality there were 22,000 Japanese.

By the summer of 1944 the Japanese high command concluded that, while they could not win the war outright, they could force America into a negotiated peace. They were confident the American public would not tolerate a long war with growing casualties in the Pacific. So they ordered attrition warfare: fighting that would slow the Americans down and inflict maximum casualties. These tactics would capitalize on two great strengths of the Japanese troops—their ability to dig in and their ability to endure the most god-awful shelling.

In August of 1944 Imperial General Headquarters issued orders calling for "endurance engagement" through the use of "Fukkaku positions," honeycombed underground defensive positions. No longer would the Japanese soldiers mount banzai charges; now they were ordered to fight from heavily fortified underground tunnels and caves.

General Kuribayashi, waiting on the beaches of Iwo Jima for the U.S. armada, not only had absorbed the lessons of the Pacific, but had studied the mistakes Japan's ally Germany had made in the amphibious invasion at Normandy seven months before.

Normandy was a colossal military failure for Hitler, who had spent years building his "Atlantic Wall" as an impenetrable barrier to invasion from the sea. Thousands of troops spread over hundreds of miles were confident their cement bunkers, ocean defenses, barbed wire, and powerful guns would repulse any invader into the sea. Eisenhower's forces leaped over this wall in twenty-four hours.

At Iwo, by contrast, the defenders knew exactly where the invaders would arrive. Only two miles of beach on the entire perimeter was suitable for an assault. All the Marines would have to go through this narrow funnel, all under the deadly gaze of Mount Suribachi.

Kuribayashi had absorbed the central lesson of Normandy: No matter how strong your defense, you cannot stop an American invasion on the beach indefinitely. So over the objections of his subordinates he dismantled the old beach defenses and pulled his guns back. He would not invest in a defense that could be breached in a day. General Kuribayashi was determined to cause as many casualties as possible over the longest possible time.

Kuribayashi concluded attrition was the best he could expect. He would fortify the interior of the island and make it a killing field, hoping the exorbitant casualties would make the Marines falter and perhaps cause the civilians in America to pause in their desire to invade the Japanese mainland. To these ends he ordered that his forces cede the beach to the invaders, and that they move their fortifications underground.

Kuribayashi had sifted the coarse volcanic beach sand through his fingers and figured the men and their machines would bog down there. So he would wait until the beach was crowded with bodies. Then his troops would open fire on the Marines huddled there. Crisscrossing, withering fire would rain down upon a beach so jammed with boys that hardly a bullet could miss.

And anyone who made it off the beach would enter a frightening no-man's-land with the enemy underground, unseen. Bullets would fly from hidden crevices, mortars would arc from holes deep below the surface. Kuribayashi's defenses were designed to make every advancing step hell for the Marines.

He set about building the most ingenious fortress in the history of war-fare. By the time he was finished, Iwo Jima would become the most heavily fortified island of World War II. Kuribayashi transformed Iwo Jima into the equivalent of one huge blockhouse.

Soon the best fortifications specialists in the Japanese army arrived on Iwo: quarry experts, mining engineers, labor battalions, and fortress units. They drew up specifications for the backbone of Iwo Jima's defense—a sub-terranean cave system connected by tunnels.

By the fall of 1944 a veritable city of 22,000 was functioning below the surface of Iwo Jima. Two additional levels of tunnels had been added, above and below the original tier. Tunnels large enough for troops to run through standing up. General Kuribayashi himself would direct the battle from his command center, a bombproof capsule that was seventy-five feet below the surface.

As one officer, Baron Nishi, wrote in a letter to his wife: "When we com-plete our underground rooms we . . . won't even have to worry about the enemy's one-ton bombs."

On Iwo Jima, the defenders constructed fifteen hundred underground rooms. Many were electrified and ventilated. Most had plaster walls. Light-ing ranged from electricity to fuel lamps and candles. They were thirty to fifty feet deep and had stairways and passageways. There was space for stor-ing ammunition, food and water, and other supplies. The caverns had mul-tiple entrances and exits to avoid entrapment.

Underground billets, meeting rooms, communications centers, and even hospitals complete with surgical equipment and operating tables took shape. One hospital could treat 400 men on hospital beds carved into the rock walls.

The blockhouses on the surface were built of thick concrete with steel reinforcing rods. The walls were three feet thick, the ceilings six feet thick.

The Japanese camouflaged the blockhouses with sand. Thus, there were many more than General Smith and his aerial spotters could see from their photographs. The black dots that the boys had observed on their battle maps were only the surface openings of this elaborate system: the tip of the iceberg, the spout of the submerged whale.

The blockhouses were mutually supporting, laid out so that every square inch of the island would be covered by cross fire.

The blockhouses had tiny slits exposing only the muzzles of slender machine guns. Antiaircraft guns pointing at the beaches were hidden in rocky outcroppings. Tanks waited behind six-foot rock walls with only their turrets visible. Coastal defense guns jutted from concrete bunkers.

Snipers were ready in cave entrances and tunnel openings, piles of hand grenades at the ready.

Antipersonnel mines were stockpiled for shallow burial on the landing beaches. Heavier mines would wreak havoc with tanks making their way inland. Rocket launchers and mortar tubes hid under concrete covers with firing apertures. Antiaircraft guns were pointed not at the sky, but forward to meet the oncoming Americans.

The maps on the U.S. ships didn't tell the American boys—mostly teenagers—that they would have to run over ground that hid fifteen hundred underground rooms connected by sixteen miles of tunnels. Running over the heads of 22,000 well-fed troops with plentiful rations that could hold them over for five months. Unable to see an enemy who had a clear view of them.

The Air Force pilot on Saipan was correct when he suggested the boys wouldn't see anyone on the island. But not because of the aerial bombing. It was because the Japanese were not *on* Iwo Jima. They were *in* Iwo Jima.

On February 17, D-Day minus two, ships' doctors reported an outbreak of diarrhea. Young boys were getting anxious.

But no matter what the Japanese had designed as a defense, the Marines figured they had an ace in the hole. Big Navy ships would deliver the real power punch before their arrival. The battleships the boys had seen anchored off Saipan that had preceded them by days to Iwo Jima reassured the Marines: enormous monsters capable of lobbing 2,600-pound shells the size and weight of large automobiles to smash the enemy's blockhouses. Every one of these shells would save many American lives.

The Marines could not know that this ace was about to be trumped—by their own command.

The invasion of Iwo Jima was a Navy operation. General Smith's Marines, were, in effect, the Navy's land troops. Smith and his staff were the world's experts on amphibious assaults. They knew that ten days of Navy shelling by heavy ships was critical before their Marines rushed ashore. Smith requested that amount in an October 24 memo.

The general was stunned at the Navy's reply: Ten days was "impossible." ("Impossible" was a concept that Howlin' Mad was not familiar with.) The Navy would only provide three days' bombardment. Their bureaucratic rationale dumbfounded the Marine general: "due to limitations on the availability of ships, difficulties of ammunition replacement, and the loss of surprise."

Smith knew that the Japanese couldn't be surprised after seventy days of bombing by planes and the sure knowledge of an armada of 880 ships sailing toward them. He was convinced that replaceable ammunition could be found to save irreplaceable lives. But the key was the phrase "the availability of ships."

The Joint Chiefs had made the capture of Iwo Jima the main Allied objective in the Pacific. But the Navy was eager to grab headlines and show that they too, and not only the Army Air Force, could shell mainland Japan. And so ships were diverted to the high-profile but strategically dubious mission of bombing the enemy's homeland.

Smith seethed and fulminated, and made increasingly desperate pleas for more bombardment. Nine days, seven, until he was down to four, just one more day than the Navy had arbitrarily assigned. All his requests were rebuffed. Smith knew three days' shelling would spell death for many of his Marines. But the Navy would have their headlines.

Then at the last moment the Navy added a final insult: There would be even fewer ships available for the shelling of Iwo Jima than agreed upon. Additional ships were "needed" for the shelling of Japan. This further diminished the impact of the bombardment. When his own Navy associates expressed disagreement with this siphoning-off of ships, Vice Admiral Raymond Spruance weakly wrote Smith: "I regret this confusion caused in your carefully laid plans, but I know you and your people will get away with it."

"Get away with it." The flip phrase betrayed the harsh reality. But Smith's Chief of Staff needed no hints. "The cost in Marines killed will be far greater," he wrote, "because naval support has been so weakened as to jeopardize the success of the operation . . ."

And it got worse.

The Navy shelling was scheduled for three days: February 16, 17, and 18. But only February 17 saw a complete day of bombardment.

The problem was the rules the Navy imposed upon the bombardment. Targets were to be shelled only when they were visible and if the results were observable by spotter airplanes.

Ten minutes into day one of the bombardment, clouds rolled in. The shelling was stopped and the Marianas-based bombers returned to their bases without releasing a single payload. Rain squalls on February 18 similarly halted the action.

Marine officers pleaded for just one extra day of shelling. It was about the lives of young Marines, they argued. But Vice Admiral Blandy, in charge of the bombardment, refused and sent this message to his superiors: "Though weather has not permitted complete expenditure of entire ammunition allowance, and more installations can be found and destroyed with one more day of bombardment, I believe landing can be accomplished tomorrow as scheduled."

Smith would always remember that the ammunition lockers in Blandy's battleships still contained hundreds of shells that hadn't been fired because of Navy rules. "If the Marines had received better cooperation from the Navy," he wrote bitterly, after the war, "our casualties would have been lower."

Months before, a Marine officer had summed up the Navy's attitude when he pointed a finger at his Navy counterparts and asserted, "Even though you Navy officers do come in to about one thousand yards, I remind you that you have a little more armor. I want you to know that Marines are crossing the beach with bayonets, and the only armor they'll have is a khaki shirt."

As Easy Company with their khaki shirts neared their destiny, seventy civilian correspondents gathered in the steaming wardroom of the command ship *Eldorado* anchored off Iwo, for a final briefing.

Admiral Kelly Turner told the newsmen that the battle would be rough—"the defenses are thick"—and that Iwo Jima was "as well defended a fixed position . . . as exists in the world today."

Perhaps hopefully, he then added, "We are taking steps, as far as our knowledge and skill and intent are concerned, to reduce these losses as far as we can, to as low a figure as we can."

General Smith nodded as Turner, his superior, took his seat beside him. It was all Howlin' Mad could do to control his disgust. He knew very well the steps the Navy had failed to take.

Now Smith took the podium. He somberly predicted large casualties, a hard fight. As his words sank in among the correspondents he said proudly and quietly: "It's a tough proposition. That's why my Marines are here."

As the Old Warrior sat down his eyes were misty. Iwo Jima would be his last battle, the last time he would command "my Marines."

Then a special guest rose to speak. He was dressed in Marine fatigues with no insignia of rank. He was the big boss, Navy Secretary James Forrestal, out to witness the Navy's largest operation in its history. And he made clear that he knew who would bear the brunt of this campaign:

> In the last and final analysis it is the guy with the rifle and machine gun who wins the war and pays the penalty to preserve our liberty. My hat is off to the Marines. I think my feelings about them are best expressed by Major General Julian Smith. In a letter to his wife after Tarawa he said, "I never again can see a United States Marine without experiencing a feeling of reverence."

The room was still as Forrestal sat down. Howlin' Mad's face beamed with a proud smile.

Admiral Turner broke the silence. "Are there any questions?"

From the back row a correspondent asked, "When's the next boat to Pearl Harbor?"

The Japanese on Iwo certainly did not share Forrestal's opinion of the Marines. These troops had never fought Americans and by their standards the Marines were cowardly, known to refuse the honorable choice of death and choose surrender. The Marines fought for publicity and had materialistic desires, their government pamphlets assured them. And worst of all, they didn't fight with spiritual incentive like the Japanese fighting man, but instead depended upon their material superiority.

Veteran combat correspondent Robert Sherrod, who had landed on Tarawa and who would also land on Iwo, felt differently. He wrote that it was easy to say that American industrial power was winning the war. "But no man who saw Tarawa, Saipan . . . would agree that all the American steel was in the guns and bombs. There was a lot, also, in the hearts of the men who stormed the beaches."

For the boys of Easy Company, their year of special training at Camp Pendleton and Camp Tarawa had prepared them to pay any price for one another, as a team, as a band of brothers. They would fight for their company, their platoon, their squads and fire teams. And it would be the ties at this level that would determine the outcome of the battle. Ira had written home: "There is real friendship between all us boys; and I don't think any of us would take $1000 to separate from the others. We trust and depend on one another and that's how it will be in combat. These boys are all good men."

The Japanese enemy would fight to the death for the Emperor. That motive made them formidable. But these boys would fight to the death for one another. And that motive made them invincible.

As Robert Leader would write as a full professor of fine arts at Notre Dame in 1979:

> *It was like being on a winning athletic team and everyone was playing over his head. Can you possibly imagine the unspoken affection we felt for each other? An affection that allowed men to offer their lives daily for each other without hesitation and, I suppose, without understanding. And yet, to place oneself between danger and one's people is the ultimate act of love.*

Mike, Harlon, Franklin, Ira, Rene, and Doc were about to enter a battle against an underground enemy that had endured the Pacific's most intense bombing of World War II and had not been disturbed. The only way the cave kamikaze could be overcome was by direct frontal assault, young American boys walking straight into Japanese fields of fire.

It would be a battle pitting American flesh against Japanese concrete. The boys would have only their buddies to depend upon, buddies who were willing to die for one another. As soon they would.

The evening of D-Day minus one, February 18, a date that nine years later would become my birthday, my father and the assault troops still could not see their objective. Everything was timed down to the minute. Their churning craft would approach Iwo Jima on schedule, only just before it was time to assault the beaches.

Each boy was quiet now, lost in his private thoughts. Their confidence must have been shaken when, that night, Tokyo Rose named many of their ships and a number of the Marine units. She assured the Americans that while huge ships were needed to transport them to Iwo Jima, the survivors could later fit in a phone booth.

The opposing commanders tried to get some sleep before battle. Howlin' Mad comforted himself with his Bible in his cabin on the *Eldorado*.

Kuribayashi was also in his personal quarters—a system of caves and tunnels seventy-five feet below the surface of Iwo Jima. Lying in his small concrete cubicle. The dim candlelight illuminated the "Courageous Battle Vow" posted on the wall, as he had ordered it posted on the walls of all the bunkers, caves, and blockhouses on the island. It read:

> *We are here to defend this island to the limit of our strength. We must devote ourselves to that task entirely. Each of your shots must kill many Americans.*

We cannot allow ourselves to be captured by the enemy. If our positions are overrun, we will take bombs and grenades and throw ourselves under the tanks to destroy them. We will infiltrate the enemy's lines to exterminate him. No man must die until he has killed at least ten Americans. We will harass the enemy with guerrilla actions until the last of us has perished. Long live the Emperor!

There is no record of what Kuribayashi's last thoughts were before he fell off to sleep that night. But in a broadcast to the mainland on Radio Tokyo he had said, "This island is the front line that defends our mainland, and I am going to die here." And to his son Taro he had written, "The life of your father is just like a lamp before the wind."

But there is one thought he had never shared with the 22,000 men he was about to lead to their deaths. He had written it years before to his wife when he was stationed in the United States, after traveling extensively across America: "The United States is the last country in the world Japan should fight."

Seven

D-DAY

Life was never regular again. We were changed from the day we put our feet in that sand.

—PRIVATE TEX STANTON,
2ND PLATOON, EASY COMPANY

IT BEGAN EERILY, IN THE NIGHT:

A dark Pacific sky cut by hellish red comets, rising and descending in clusters of three, each descent followed by a distant explosion. Sleepless young Marines stood watching atop their LST's, thirteen miles offshore.

To Easy Company's Robert Leader of Cambridge, Massachusetts, it looked like heat lightning on a summer night. Through his daze, he heard a voice in the darkness utter what sounded like a fragment from a dream: "That's Sulfur Island." "What do you mean?" Leader murmured, not turning his eyes from the sky. The speaker beside him, a Navy crewman, replied: "Don't you know? 'Iwo Jima' means Sulfur Island."

The sun rose pink. The sky turned blue and clear. On the horizon, the sulfur island lay wreathed in smoke.

The date was February 19, 1945.

The cooks on the transport ships had provided a gourmet breakfast for the young men about to suffer and die: steak and eggs.

Doc awoke with the others, before dawn. The first words spoken to him were from a veteran: "Me, I'm experienced enough to dodge the bullets. You—well, you'll probably get one right between the eyes."

Mike had spent much of the night watching the shelling. Ed Blankenburger, who'd stood beside him, had been elated: Surely this barrage would all but obliterate the enemy. His optimism was shared by many of the boys. Seventeen-year-old Donald Howell, from Mercer City, Ohio, was so certain

---

Chapter opener: Marines on the beach at Iwo.

there would be no Japanese survivors that he relaxed on board with a book called *House Madam*, about brothels on the West Coast.

And so Blankenburger was surprised when, near dawn, he heard Mike say quietly: "I'm not coming back from this one, Ed."

Over 70,000 Marines—the 3rd, 4th, and 5th Divisions—massed in the ships that had finally arrived at Island X, ready to hit the narrow two-mile beach in successive phases. Awaiting them, dug into the island and out of sight, 22,000 elite Japanese—the Rising Sun—who understood that they were to die.

At seven A.M. the boys of Easy Company walked down the metal steps of LST-481 and into the yawing holds of their assigned amphibious tractors. All the terrifying practice that Doc Bradley had put in scrambling down those treacherous net ladders in Hawaii had gone for naught. But there was plenty of terror left. "I was petrified when we got into those amtracs," Corpsman Vernon Parrish, a close friend of Doc's, recalled. "I was new to battle but I could sense that even the veterans were scared." Parrish's fears were hardly calmed when one veteran, gazing at Iwo, said out of the corner of his mouth: "You don't know what's going to happen. You're going to learn more in the first five minutes there than you did in the whole year of training you've been through."

Now the first waves of tractors were loaded and surging toward the island at full throttle, kicking up white foam behind them, their turbine engines deafening to the helmeted young men packed inside, about twenty to a boat. Behind and above them was an overwhelming American force that controlled the sea and the air: in the sea, the armada at anchor, vessels stretching away from shore for ten miles; in the air, flights of Navy Hellcats swooping low to strafe Mount Suribachi, reshaping its contours with their firepower. In front of them lay the most ingenious and deadly fortress in military history. The Century of the Pacific was about to be forged in blood.

In those final moments before the first landing, many of the troops in the boats could still convince themselves that this was going to be no sweat. They could do this despite the evidence to the contrary around them: the doctors and medics with their surgical instruments and their operating tables ready to be set up on the beaches. The rabbis, priests, and ministers in their midst, prepared to wade ashore and risk their lives to comfort the dying. And the wooden crosses, the Stars of David, the body bags, that later boats would carry.

Maybe all that stuff would not be needed. Wasn't the island being blown to bits even as the amtracs churned toward shore? The enormous battle-wagons out in the ocean were blasting Iwo Jima with sheets of one-ton shells. The concussion of these great guns nearly capsized some of the smaller boats. Howlin' Mad Smith himself would remember it as a barrage that blotted out all light "like a hurricane eclipse of the sun."

In those final moments, a carefree kid aboard Doc's amtrac could still serenade his buddies with Nelson Eddy/Jeanette MacDonald movie tunes. In those final moments, eighteen-year-old Jim Buchanan of Portland, Oregon, could still view the bombing as a beautiful tableau, like in a movie; the island nearly invisible beneath clouds of gray, yellow, and white dust from all the rockets and bombs. He turned to his buddy, a kid named Scotty, and asked hopefully: "Do you think there will be any Japanese left for us?"

Jim Buchanan could not possibly fathom what lay immediately ahead. None of them could.

The bombardment had not touched the subterranean *issen gorin*. They would have to be obliterated individually, up close, at tremendous cost. The Marines were hurtling toward a mutual slaughter that would involve nearly 120,000 Japanese and Americans on- and offshore, consume thirty-six days, kill or maim more than half the land combatants, and assume characteristics unlike anything in twentieth-century warfare.

The battle of Iwo Jima would quickly turn into a primitive contest of gladiators: Japanese gladiators fighting from caves and tunnels like the catacombs of the Colosseum, and American gladiators aboveground, exposed on all sides, using liquid gasoline to burn their opponents out of their lethal hiding places.

All of this on an island five and a half miles long and two miles wide. An area smaller than Doc Bradley's hometown of Antigo, but bearing ten times the humanity. A car driving sixty miles an hour could cover its length in five and a half minutes. For the slogging, fighting, dying Marines, it would take more than a month.

The naval bombardment lifted precisely at 8:57 A.M. At 9:02, just 120 seconds behind a schedule that had kicked in at Hawaii, the first wave— armored tractors, each mounted with a 75mm cannon—lumbered from the waves onto the soft black sands of Iwo Jima.

The first troop-carrying amtracs landed three minutes later, at 9:05 A.M., and behind them came hundreds more, each trailing a white wake. Easy Company rolled in on the twelfth wave at 9:55 A.M. Easy was part of Harry the Horse's 28th Regiment, whose special mission was to land on Green Beach One—the stretch nearest Mount Suribachi, just four hundred yards away, on the left—and then form a ribbon of men across the narrow neck of the island, isolating the fortified mountain and ultimately capturing it. This assignment meant that Easy Company would be part of a 2,000-man force fighting a separate battle from the main assault: Some of the 5th and the entire 4th Division would fan out toward the right and progress northward along the island's length to engage the bulk of its defenders. Before the battle ended, part of the 3rd Division, originally seen as a reserve force, would be rushed into action.

The 28th's was no small mission. As Howlin' Mad Smith would later declare: "The success of our entire assault depended upon the early capture of that grim, smoking rock."

And so the great tragic funneling from wide ocean to narrow beach had begun: hordes of wet, equipment-burdened boys slogging from the water, forming a tightly packed mass on the two-mile strip of beach. Targets in a shooting gallery.

The boys squinted upward at their assigned routes and the ugly, stunted mountain beyond. The beach slanted upward from a point some thirty yards from the edge of the surf; it rose in three terraces, each about eight feet high and sixteen feet apart. In peaceful times it might have resembled a gently curving amphitheater. In this context it was an amphitheater of death. The boys would have to climb not on hard white sand but on soft black volcanic ash that gave way and made each upward step a lingering effort.

The first wave of Marines and armored vehicles hit the shores. The vehicles bogged down immediately in the absorbent maw. The troops moved around them and began their cautious climb, unshielded, up the terraces.

It was all so quiet at first.

Perhaps the optimistic young Marines had been right. Perhaps it was over already. Donald Howell recalled, "When the landing gate dropped I just walked onto the beach. I was confident. Everyone was milling around. I thought this would be a cinch."

The "cinch" lasted about an hour. The false calm was part of General Kuribayashi's radical strategy: to hold off from firing at once, as every other Japanese force had done in the island campaign, and wait until the funneling attackers had filled the beach.

Easy Company had been ashore some twenty minutes and in their assembly area when the slaughter began.

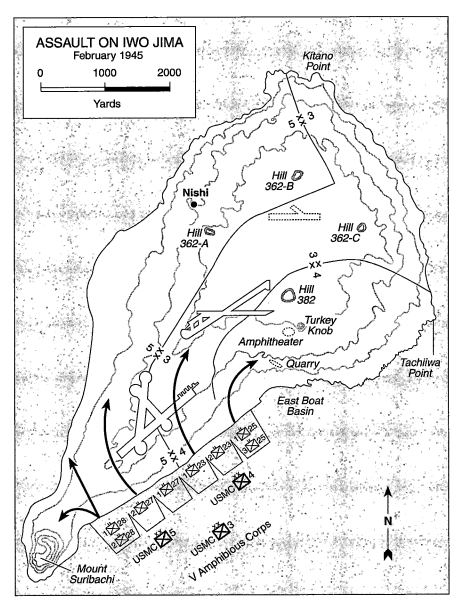

ASSAULT ON IWO JIMA
February 1945

0   1000   2000

Yards

Kitano Point

Nishi

Hill 362-B

Hill 362-A

Hill 362-C

Hill 382

Turkey Knob

Amphitheater

Quarry

Tachiiwa Point

East Boat Basin

USMC

V Amphibious Corps

Mount Suribachi

N

Smoke and earsplitting noise suddenly filled the universe. The almost unnoticed blockhouses on the flat ground facing the ocean began raking the exposed troops with machine-gun bullets. But the real firestorm erupted from the mountain, from Suribachi: mortars, heavy artillery shells, and machine-gun rounds ripped into the stunned Americans. Two thousand hidden Japanese were gunning them down with everything from rifles to coastal defense guns. "It was so loud it was almost like it was quiet," one stunned Marine remembered. To Lieutenant Keith Wells, Doc's 3rd Platoon leader, Suribachi turned into a monstrous Christmas tree with blinking lights. The lights were gun barrels discharging ammunition at him and his men.

There was no protection. Now the mortars and bullets were tearing in from all over the island: General Kuribayashi had designed an elaborate cross fire from other units to the north. Entire platoons were engulfed in fireballs. Boys clawed frantically at the soft ash, trying to dig holes, but the ash filled in each swipe of the hand or shovel. Heavy rounds sent jeeps and armored tractors spinning into the air in fragments. Some Marines hit by these rounds were not just killed; their bodies ceased to exist.

More than Marines. "I was watching an amtrac to the side of us as we went in," Robert Leader remembers. "Then there was this enormous blast and it disappeared. I looked for wreckage and survivors, but nothing. I couldn't believe it. Everything just vaporized."

In the same boat with Leader was Doc Bradley.

The boys on the beach scrambled forward. It was like walking through a pile of shell corn, said one. Like climbing in talcum powder, said another. Like a bin of wheat. Like deep snow.

Advancing tanks crushed those of the wounded who could not get out of the way. Others, unwounded, were shoved to their deaths by those behind them. "More and more boats kept landing with more guys coming onto the beach," said Guy Castorini. "You had to just push the guy in front of you. It was like pushing him to his death."

The shock of actual combat triggered bizarre thoughts and behavior. Some Marines dropped into a deep, terror-induced sleep amid the carnage and had to be kicked awake by their officers. Others clung to fastidious habits of civilian life. "I don't smoke," moaned a badly wounded boy who'd been offered a lit cigarette. Jim Buchanan, who had hoped there would be some Japanese left for him, became indignant when he realized what was happening. "Did you see those Japanese firing at us?" he screamed to the guy next to him. "No," the leatherneck answered, deadpan. "Did you shoot them?" "Gee, no," Buchanan replied. "That didn't occur to me. I've never been shot at before."

Phil Ward, leaping out of the amtrac that also contained my father, had a similar epiphany: "We'd had live ammo training in Hawaii, so I was used to the sound of bullets, but suddenly I realized why this was different. 'Goddamn!' I said. 'These people are shooting at me!' "

The beach rapidly turned into a salvage yard of wrecked trucks and Jeeps stuck in the sand or smashed by artillery. The dead piled up along the shoreline. "Coming in, I could see guys lying on the beach," Corpsman Roy Steinfort recalled. "I thought, great! They'll cover our landing. But when we drew closer I saw they were all dead."

Annihilation seemed possible in the hideous first minutes. Radio transmissions back to command quarters aboard the ships raised that specter: "Catching all hell from the quarry! Heavy mortar and machine-gun fire!" "Taking heavy casualties and can't move for the moment!" "Mortars killing us!" "All units pinned down by artillery and mortars!" "Casualties heavy! Need tank support fast to move anywhere!" "Taking heavy fire and forward movement stopped! Machine-gun and artillery fire heaviest ever seen!"

But it was even worse than what the transmissions indicated. No one was out of danger. A five-foot-three Associated Press photographer named Joe Rosenthal, landing with the 4th Division, ran for his life through the hail of bullets. Later he would declare that "not getting hit was like running through rain and not getting wet." Corpsman Greg Emery, crawling on all fours, glanced back at a landing craft coming in; the ramp dropped down; machine-gun fire ripped the interior. Boys fell dead atop each other as they stumbled off the ramp.

The first wave of Easy Company Marines, caught on the terraces in their heavy packs, scrambled for survival. "Like climbing a waterfall," one remembered. Jerry Smith pressed himself as close to the ground as he could, and felt bullets rip through his backpack. "Even the socks in my pack had bullet holes in them," he recalls. The volcanic ash slowed progress and kept the Marines exposed to fire; but in another sense the ash saved lives: It absorbed many of the mortar rounds and shrapnel, muffling explosions and sucking in the lethal fragments.

Lieutenant Ed Pennel's 2nd Platoon nearly lost its way in these early moments of deafening chaos. The unit, with Mike as a squad leader and Harlon, Franklin, and Ira in the ranks, landed far off course, north of Green Beach. Shortly after the bombardment erupted, Harry the Horse summoned Easy Company Captain Dave Severance and ordered him to stand by: "Are you ready to move out?" Liversedge demanded. "All except the Second Platoon that hasn't arrived yet, sir!" Severance replied. "Well, you've got five minutes to find that platoon or you're up for a general court-martial!" the colonel retorted.

The platoon soon rejoined the company. Its wayward landing down the beach had touched off a comic moment before the carnage. Lieutenant Pennel had thought to reorient his men with a show of John Wayne–like gallantry. As the amtrac's ramp went down he yelled, "Come on, men!" and then fell flat on his face into the water-saturated volcanic ash. "The guys ran up my back, laughing," he remembered.

Not everyone was laughing. "I was a very scared son-of-a-gun," Ira wrote later. "Our boat hit solid ground and the ramp went down. I jumped clear of the ramp. About three yards away lay a dead Marine right on the water's edge, shot in the head. He hadn't begun to fight. My stomach turned flip-flops, and I started to get scared all over again."

A tissue of their former lives connected many of the onrushing warriors: ironies, coincidences of place and memory, overlapping fragments of their boyhoods. Wesley Kuhn of Black Creek, Wisconsin, was nineteen years old when he hit the beach. Wesley did not know Doc Bradley, who could not have been more than a few dozen yards away; but he knew Doc's future wife, Betty Van Gorp. Wesley and Betty had been in a school play together in the ninth grade. Wesley's role had been that of the "Kissing Bandit," who'd snuck up and planted a kiss on Betty, who was playing an innocent housewife.

Bodies, body parts, everywhere he looked, recalled Kuhn. "My worst memory is of the first time I saw a man with his chest blown open and dirt trickling in on his vital organs."

There were moments of grotesque humor. Monroe Ozment of Virginia and his buddies were struggling up and over the third terrace, getting picked off by machine-gun and mortar fire, when someone yelled: "Turner got hit!" "Turner was a heavyset guy," Ozment remembered, "and we always kidded him that if he got hit he'd get it in the butt. 'Where'd he get hit?' I shouted, and someone yelled back, 'In the butt!' "

But there were many more moments of unbearable pathos. Nineteen-year-old Corpsman Danny Thomas hit the beach at 10:15 A.M., several paces behind his best buddy, Chick Harris. In training camp, Thomas and Harris were called "the Buttermilk Boys" because they were too young to buy drinks on liberty. "I was charging ahead and saw Chick on the beach, facing out to sea, his back to the battle," Thomas recalled. His buddy was in a strange posture: His head and torso were erect, as though he'd let himself be buried in the sand from the waist down in some bizarre prank. As Thomas rushed past him, he yelled a greeting and saw Chick's hand and eyes move, acknowledging him.

Then Thomas glimpsed something else that made him fall to his knees in the sand, vomiting. The "something else" was blood and entrails. "I vomited my toenails out," Thomas remembered. "I realized that Chick had been cut in two. The lower half of his body was gone." He added, "He was the first person I ever saw dead."

"Buttermilk Chick" was fifteen. He had lied about his age to get into the Marines.

The big shells had blown a few holes in the ash. Guy Castorini and a

few other rookies were in one behind their leader, a veteran named Lundsford. "We had no idea if this was a bad battle or not. One of the guys yelled,
'Hey, Lundsford, is this a bad battle?' Lundsford shouted back, 'It's a fucking
slaughter.' Maybe two minutes later—*Whoom!*—we got hit with a mortar.
I ducked and something dropped on my back and rolled off. It felt like a
coconut or something. I looked down and saw that it was Lundsford's head.
Those were his last words: 'A fucking slaughter.' "

Somehow, the Marines kept advancing. Somehow, discipline held.
Somehow, valor overcame terror. Somehow, scared young men under sheets
of deadly fire kept on doing the basic, gritty tasks necessary to keep the
invasion going.

The calming presence of veterans in their midst was one factor in their
resolve. Another was their year of advanced Marine training in the California and Hawaii camps. "Our training taught us how to conquer fear," was
the way Corpsman Langley put it. "We knew there was a good possibility
that we would die or get wounded. But we knew we had to keep going to
keep from getting killed. You learn there's an awful lot you can do while
having the hell scared out of you."

Mike Strank, true to form, was one of the steadying veterans. In the
opening moments of Japanese mortar fire, when the boys of Easy Company
were still groping their way toward Captain Severance's main unit, Lloyd
Thompson looked up to his right and could not believe what he saw.
"There was Mike, sitting upright, emptying the sand out of his boots. Just as
if nothing was happening." Bill Ranous remembers the same sight: "I had
my face buried in the sand. I looked up and saw Mike sitting straight up
emptying his shoes. What a guy."

Having made his point, Mike was soon shepherding his boys across
the sands to their rendezvous with Dave Severance's unit. Joe Rodriguez
remembers him dashing back and forth among his squad members, cau-
tioning them to spread out: "Don't bunch up! Don't be like a bunch of
bananas!"

It was gestures such as Mike's—probably hundreds of them, most lost to
history—that enabled the Americans to withstand the maelstrom of hidden
firepower, and even to begin inflicting damage of their own.

Damage against what? That was the constant question at Iwo Jima.
There were no targets. The gunners were invisible, protected, creatures of
the underworld. Sergeant Major Lyndolph Ward summed up the frustration:
"The thing that bothered me was you couldn't get your licks in. There was no
visible enemy to shoot at." Even when they claimed a casualty, the Marines
could rarely see it: The Japanese quickly pulled their dead and wounded
back inside the caves and blockhouses. Thus there was little evidence of the

invasion's impact, a detriment to morale. In the days that followed, observers of the battle in spotter planes high above the action would remark that it looked as though the Marines were fighting the island itself.

And yet the Americans did inflict damage that hellish first morning—by the same excruciating means they would continue to inflict it for thirty-six days, until all the 22,000 defenders were wiped out: by exposing themselves to fire, charging the fortified blockhouses and cave entrances, and shooting or incinerating their tormentors at close range.

One of their strategies was to identify "fire lanes." By observing where enemy machine-gun bullets were landing and kicking up ash, a Marine could roughly judge the peripheral limits of a shooter's range: his capacity to swivel the gun left and right from inside his cave or blockhouse. Units of boys, widely spaced, would dash along the outer boundaries of those fire lanes—a great many of them falling dead or wounded under cross fire—until a survivor reached the cave's mouth or the blockhouse's unprotected rear. Then a tossed grenade, an orange sheet from a flamethrower, and the nest was silent.

For a while. An early mistake in the invasion was to assume that a source of enemy fire, once extinguished, was permanently dead. It wasn't. General Kuribayashi's vast tunneling system assured that many Marines were shot as they moved past a "neutralized" nest that had been quickly repopulated from below the ground.

Throughout the bloody morning, fresh troops landed on the beaches. Tangible progress was achieved in the opening hour and a half of combat. By 10:35 A.M., a small group of men from the first assault waves—Company A of the 28th Regiment—had survived a near-suicidal, seven-hundred-yard dash across the island to the western beach. Already Suribachi was cut off from the rest of the island. The reptile's head was alive and deadly, but it had been severed.

How they got there was a portrait of American victory in microcosm. They got there with courage best exemplified by Tony Stein's headlong charge.

Stein was a twenty-three-year-old corporal from Dayton who became the first Medal of Honor winner on Iwo. For the risky mission he'd armed himself with a stinger gun, a light machine gun he'd taken from an airplane and adapted into a rapid-fire gun. When his comrades were stalled on their dash by concentrated Japanese fire, Stein stood upright, drawing the enemy's fire and allowing his buddies to get into position. But Stein was just getting warmed up. His next move was to charge the nearby Japanese pillboxes, alone. He did this several times, killing twenty of the enemy in close-range combat. Out of ammunition, he threw off his helmet and shoes and hurried barefoot to the beach to resupply himself. He did this eight times, carrying a wounded man to safety on each trip. Later in the day he covered the withdrawal of his platoon to the company position, though his weapon was shot from his hands twice.

Meanwhile, other brave boys were doing grunt-work near the shoreline, work that would get the mechanized part of the assault in motion. Oblivious to the storm of lead and steel, some bent down and shoved wire mats under the treads of mired tanks; others calmly climbed into bulldozers to begin roughing out the semblance of a road system.

These were the instincts of training and courage that took hold as the first shock of battle wore off; courage fueled by a fierce kind of love. "There was an incredible bond among guys on that beach," Danny Thomas remembered. "We knew each other and we could rely upon each other, trust one another. We had trained together and we were bonded."

Death became demystified, an occupational hazard. The Marines quickly saw that even heroes could die. Sergeant John Basilone, the Medal of Honor winner who had helped change the course of the Guadalcanal battle, was leading a rifle unit along the beach toward a Japanese emplacement. "Come on, you guys, we gotta get these guns off the beach," he called to his men, and then was obliterated by a mortar shell.

Moments of valor proliferated. Among the heroes were the men sent to give solace. Corpsman Emery yelled "Keep down!" to a fellow medic sitting upright in the sand. Crawling closer, he saw that the man was struggling to tie a tourniquet around the stump of his leg. "Take care of the others, I'll be OK," the injured medic called out. When Emery crawled back past the corpsman several minutes later, he was dead.

"Dead men were lying around," Ira said later, "and the peculiar smell of gunpowder, smoke, and blood was in the air."

Father Paul Bradley went in on the third wave. "I was young," he recalled later, "and didn't think about the danger to me. And I was too busy crawling from dying man to dying man. It was always, 'Father, over here!' Once I was kneeling in the sand administering to a guy who had been hit. There was a loud *thud!* His eyes closed. He'd been hit again and was dead. 'Father, over here!' someone called. I went on to the next one."

One combatant met his fate with supreme elegance. The moment occurred in the air, as the first wave of amtracs headed for shore. The Marine fighter planes were finishing up their low strafing runs, and as the last pilot began to pull his Corsair aloft, Japanese sprang to their guns and riddled the plane with flak. The pilot, Major Ray Dollins, tried to gain altitude as he headed out over the ocean so as to avoid a deadly crash into the Marines headed for the beach, but his plane was too badly damaged. Lieutenant Keith Wells watched it from his amtrac, with Doc Bradley standing by his side. "We could see him in the cockpit," Wells said, "and he was trying everything. He was heading straight down for a group of approaching 'tracs filled with Marines. At the last second he flipped the plane over on its back and aimed it into the water between two waves of tanks. We watched the water exploding into the air."

Military personnel listening to the flight radio network from the ships could not only see Dollins go down; they could hear his last words into his microphone. They were a defiant parody.

> *Oh, what a beautiful morning,*
> *Oh, what a beautiful day,*
> *I've got a terrible feeling*
> *Everything's comin' my way.*

Eight days earlier, en route to Iwo Jima, Major Dollins had received news of the birth of his first child, a daughter. He was the first 5th Division Marine to die in the battle.

In the midst of all this carnage and confusion was my father. My father, with his corpsman's pouch, his Unit 3, slung over his shoulder. The ex-paperboy, on his rounds.

He was busy almost from the moment he touched land—although his fellow medic Cliff Langley was busy even sooner. "Cliff hit the beach about ten seconds before me," Doc told an interviewer some weeks after the battle, "and when I stepped out, he was already treating a casualty." The "casualty" was a lieutenant shot through the jaw, a disabling wound by its appearance. "Do you want to be evacuated?" Langley asked the man. "No, I'm OK, thanks," the Marine bravely mumbled, and ran back into the battle.

Thurman Fogarty, eighteen then, remembered the "welter of blood" that engulfed the Navy doctors and corpsmen as soon as they landed. Fogarty himself was buffeted by the concussions of the big shells coming in and going out, like gusts of a powerful wind. After just a few minutes he fell to the beach and scraped out as much indentation as he could. Doc Bradley was crouched next to him, attending to a small wound in his own leg.

"I happened to look to my left and saw that the Marine next to me had his arm almost blown off," Fogarty said. "It was just dangling from his shoulder. I pointed this out to Doc. He looked up from his own wounds and rolled across my legs to attend the injured Marine. The guy was conscious. Doc calmly put a tourniquet on the stump of the arm and told the guy to hold it. Then he shot him full of morphine and tied the dangling arm to the stump. And then pointed him toward the Aid Station."

After that, Fogarty and my father were separated. Crawling up a terrace, Fogarty spotted a boy whose head had been cut open by shrapnel. The sight nauseated him and he slid into a shell crater to vomit. There again he found Doc, taking care of a man whose chest had been caved in. This sight reactivated Fogarty's heaving. "Doc asked me where I was hit," he later remembered. "I told him I was just sick. He smiled at me and assured me, 'You'll be all right.' "

John Fredatovich, also eighteen, would become Easy's first casualty and had need of Doc Bradley nearly as soon as he broke from the water. He recalled it vividly: "I heard the mortar, then I felt a cold chill, the shock to my nervous system as the shrapnel penetrated my arm and leg. I was sliced open from my knee to my buttocks and under my arm. My femur was smashed.

"Doc came over. He made everyone stay away. He was very forceful and took charge. He gave me blood transfusions as I went in and out of consciousness. Then four Marines carried me away to a place on the beach for evacuation."

The place where Fredatovich lay offered no protection from the hellstorm. Every inch of the beach was an active target. Fredatovich lay on his cot until four P.M., and watched death and destruction explode around him. He saw a boatload of Marines lifted out of the water in a giant flash, and implode into nothingness. He saw other wounded boys on their stretchers get blown to pieces. He saw kids in the beach detail get hit as they unloaded explosives, their flesh fused to the fireball.

The sight that returned to the future teacher most often in memory, however, was a strikingly unlikely one: a glimpse of Harlon Block as Harlon ran past him toward the action.

"I called up to him; I said, 'Hi,' " Fredatovich remembered, "but he just ran on by. It was the look in his eyes that startled me. He had a glazed, blank look. It was as if memories were coming back to him from past experiences. This surprised me. I later studied psychology and I realized that those dilated pupils meant he was shocked by something and was transfixed on some image from his past. It was as if the noise of the mortars transported him to a past memory."

Fredatovich later decided that Harlon was summoning up visions of death: the deaths he'd seen on Bougainville, perhaps. Or perhaps his own.

By noon, the heavy casualties continued but the threat of annihilation

had vanished. Nine thousand troops were ashore, and counting. The Marines were on Iwo Jima to stay.

Through the long afternoon, the American boys held their positions and
even advanced, despite the continuing nightmare of fighting an invisible
enemy. The Japanese cross fire maintained and even increased its prodigious
volume. It came from everywhere on the island; even the artillery near Kitano Point, nearly five miles to the north, was delivering shells in sheets.
From the right flank of the plateaulike land on the eastern beaches came
automatic-weapons fire that swept back and forth. Advancing vehicles
were blown up by aircraft bombs embedded in the sand as tank mines. "Spi-
der traps" and caves linked to the tunneling system were everywhere. They
gave the defenders countless places from which to pop up, fire, disappear,
and surface again somewhere else. The veteran Marine who'd boasted to my
father that he was experienced enough to dodge bullets had not dreamed of
what he'd face. The difference between living and dying was sheer luck,
many survivors said later. You were a target if you moved. And you were a
target if you stayed in place.

Some of General Kuribayashi's technical stratagems could almost have
been lifted from the science-fiction comic books the Marines had read as
boys. Many recalled watching in horror as an orifice would reveal itself
on the side of Suribachi; a yawning hole in what had appeared to be solid
rock. From the hole, the muzzle of a massive gun would appear and discharge a heavy round. Before American artillery could fix on the hole, it
would close again: a reinforced metal shield, operated like a giant retractable
garage door.

And yet, as William Wayne recalled, "We did what we were ordered to
do. We worked our way across the center of that island with machine guns
firing at us. We'd jump into a tank ditch for protection and then our leader
would yell, 'Mine!' and we'd change direction. We'd blast pillboxes, secure
them just like in training. But unlike in training they'd come alive again
and fire at us from the rear.

"But we made it. We completed that day's mission. We got across the
island."

Eight battalions were onshore by the afternoon, as were the tank battalions of two divisions and elements of two artillery battalions.

Getting ashore proved more difficult as the day progressed—and not just
because of the gunfire. John Gramling recalled that his amtrac circled for
hours in the offshore water, the boys tensed for an incoming shell. "We
couldn't get in because of the congestion," he said. "When we hit the beach
there were stacks of bodies." Wesley Kuhn's 'trac encountered bodies well

before it hit the shoreline. "They floated facedown because of the air trapped in their backpacks," he said.

One of the war correspondents aboard the ships, Robert Sherrod, watched the battle through binoculars. To him, the struggling tanks were like "so many black beetles struggling to move on tar paper."

At around five P.M., Sherrod made ready to board a landing craft to take him ashore. He met Keith Wheeler of the Chicago *Times,* returning from the beach. "I wouldn't go in there if I were you," Wheeler advised him. "There's more hell in there than I've seen in the rest of the war put together."

In the midst of this hell, Harlon was crawling through a trench in the late afternoon, leading a line of boys on all fours. Bill Ranous was directly behind him, and collided with him when Harlon stopped abruptly.

"We all looked to see what had stopped Harlon," Ranous recalled. "He was staring at two legs attached to hips with no upper torso. He was just transfixed, staring silently."

To William Wayne, also in the line, the legs were inanimate—something to put out of his mind and move on from. "I was in a survival mode," he said, "and seeing those legs didn't bother me at the time. But to Harlon they were part of a person. He turned to me after a little while and said, softly, 'Why don't we bury him?'"

Variations on such encounters produced varieties of tortured etiquette. Roland Chiasson tumbled into a crater and nearly rolled over a Marine with his right arm blown off. "I felt silly," he recalled. "I didn't know what to say. What do you say to someone who has just lost his right arm?"

Mike Strank had performed heroically, shepherding his boys throughout the day. But his grim fatalism had not left him. Aloise Biggs recalled taking a breather in a shell hole with him in the afternoon. In a matter-of-fact voice, Mike said: "This is my third campaign, and I'm not going to make it through this one."

"I had been through Bougainville," Biggs said, "and I didn't think much of it at the time."

The corpsmen were catching hell along with everyone else. Cliff Langley, Doc's co-medic, was watching six of them in a circle, conferring with one another. A shell landed in their midst. "That was the last of them," Langley said.

By nightfall the beachhead was secured. As the sun set, the shoreline grew even more grotesquely clogged with human bodies: Each Marine returning for supplies from the front brought a dead or wounded man with him. Their groans could be heard up and down the shore as darkness set in. Uncounted numbers of them died there, blasted by shells as they lay on their stretchers, waiting to be evacuated to the hospital ships.

And still there remained work to be done—for the corpsmen, especially. More injured, hundreds more, lay scattered throughout the field of battle. Doc, as senior corpsman for his unit, received reports and assigned help as best he could.

A Company, which had landed first and made the heroic charge across to the western beach, was among the most devastated. "Doc sent me over there," Cliff Langley recalled. "Their corpsmen were gone and they needed help. They'd started the day with two hundred fifty boys and they were down to thirty-seven. They had paid the price for that seven-hundred-yard dash across the island." On arriving, Langley encountered eight "walking wounded" among the casualties. "They were suffering," he said, "and I gave them tags to identify them as casualties so they could be evacuated. They could have left and received Purple Hearts, and held their heads high." But like the lieutenant shot through the jaw in the morning, none of them would go. "They stood there wounded and bleeding," Langley remembered. "But they refused to leave their buddies."

The first night on Iwo Jima brought its own special horrors.

The hellish red comets that had cut the predawn blackness reappeared in the sky, intermixed with streaks of white: tracers; shells from the offshore destroyers (more than ten thousand rounds); phosphorous "star shells" to provide bursts of white light; searchlights to keep Suribachi illuminated; parachute flares that made a *Poof!* sound when they illuminated and then floated down slowly. These flares cast an especially eerie glow over the island. As they wafted downward in the wind, their back-and-forth motions made the shadows move and seem to come alive.

To Danny Thomas, lying in his foxhole on his back, the night sky was a mesh of hot light, a net of crisscrossing fire. "It seemed like you could stick a cigarette up and light it," he said.

The leaders of Spearhead hardly rested. Colonel Harry Liversedge moved his command post two hundred yards nearer the front, to be ready for the next morning's assault on the mountain.

In the waters offshore, boats churned through the night, bringing in more of the living, taking away more of the dying. At the White House, President Roosevelt shuddered when told of Iwo's first day. "It was the first time in the war, through good news and bad, that anyone had seen the President gasp in horror."

The first day's fighting had claimed more than half as many casualties as the entire Guadalcanal campaign: 566 men killed ashore and afloat, and 1,755 wounded. Ninety-nine boys had suffered combat fatigue.

The remaining troops lay as still as they could, trying to sleep, trying not to sleep. They had been trained to shoot any moving object as the enemy. The falling parachute flares illuminated everything; the shadows darted and slid. Any shadow might be a Japanese soldier, crawling softly for the kill.

One surgeon had established an operating theater in what he'd thought was a safe area. With sandbags and tarp, he'd fashioned a makeshift hospital. But as he tried to sleep that night, he heard what sounded like foreign voices below him. Was he dreaming? He dug his fingers into the soft ash and felt for evidence. His fingertips scraped something solid: the wooden roof of a reinforced cavern. The surgeon had built his hospital directly atop the enemy.

Phil Ward remembered that the passwords for that night were based on American-made cars. Uttering "Nash," "Plymouth," "Chevrolet," or "Dodge" at a crucial moment could make the difference between life and death.

"Late in the night," Ward recalls, "a guy put a gun to my head and I forgot all the passwords." Somehow, he was spared.

The first day of the Battle of Iwo Jima had come to an end. There were thirty-five left to go.

Eight

D-DAY PLUS ONE

It is good that war is so horrible, or we might grow to like it.

—ROBERT E. LEE

RAIN GREETED THE BOYS of Easy Company as they awoke and looked out at Suribachi's great squat bulk on Tuesday, February 20. Rain and cold gusts would lash them for the next three days. The surf, mercifully calm during the invasion, had risen with the night winds; it roiled and slammed its ugly gray foam onto the beach in four-foot waves. Now the unloading of equipment would be hampered by more than enemy artillery, and the mood among the high command was grim. "It became a fight against the sea, the surf, the volcanic ash, and the Japanese, all joined in one colossal alliance against us," General Smith would lament in his memoirs.

It had been a chilly, nerve-shattering night. From their position above the western beaches, Mike, Ira, Harlon, and the others could hear the mortar, rocket, and artillery fire from Japanese guns. It did not abate throughout the night. The shells wiped out two casualty stations on the assault beach, killing many already wounded men.

The young Marines had spent the night braced for a banzai charge. General Smith had warned them to expect it. Such attacks—hordes of *issen gorin* rushing insanely through the darkness toward the bivouacked Americans—had been routine tactics in other Pacific island battles. Although terrifying, these charges at least exposed the Japanese soldiers to the Marines' gun sights; usually, the attackers lost many more men than the defenders. "This is usually when we break their backs," Howlin' Mad Smith observed as he gave orders to prepare. But no attack came. This extension

---

Chapter opener: Two Marines on the beach of Iwo Jima.

of Kuribayashi's coolly radical "fill-the-beach-and-then-get-them" strategy withstood the objections of the traditionalists beneath him. Instead, the mortar and big-artillery shells continuing through the night killed more American boys than any banzai charge ever could.

And the stealthy menace implied by the flares' eerie glow was real; not all the shadows were phantoms. At around two A.M. a Japanese grenade had landed in Easy's midst and injured Ed Kurelik and Phil Christman. A weary Doc Bradley felt his way through the darkness on his hands and knees to treat the wounded, shouting his name so that he would not be shot as an enemy.

Richard Wheeler recalled that Kurelik, a Chicago kid, was steamed that the Japanese had not played fair. "I heard somebody coming up the trench and hollered, 'Studebaker,' " Kurelik fumed as Doc bound his wounds, "and then that Jap t'rew a hand grenade!"

The gray dawn illuminated the night's destruction. To the experienced correspondent Robert Sherrod, who thought he had seen all the worst that the Pacific campaign had to offer, it revealed nothing less than "a nightmare in hell." His dispatch continued: "About the beach in the morning lay the dead . . . They died with the greatest possible violence. Nowhere in the Pacific have I seen such badly mangled bodies. Many were cut squarely in half. Legs and arms lay fifty feet away from any body."

Thus, for some Marines who hours earlier had prayed for night, it was now the dawn that proved a blessing.

The 28th Regiment—Harry "the Horse" Liversedge's outfit—had established itself across the narrow neck of the island, isolating Suribachi just a few hundred yards to the south. Now the 3,000 men of the 28th would begin their dangerous advance southward toward the volcano, while the other 33,000 Marines on the island would fight their way north across the island's main mass, toward the airfields and the high fortified ground on the northern rim.

The cost of taking Suribachi would be high, and the 28th braced itself for the grim assignment. Soon after sunrise on D-Day plus one, Colonel Liversedge positioned his 2nd and 3rd Battalions to continue their assault on Mount Suribachi. Easy Company was not among these units. They were held in Regimental Reserve. Easy would retrace their steps of the day before, going eastward to position themselves in the 2nd Battalion area. There, they would assume a backup position from where they could be rushed into the front lines.

The covering bombardment erupted at first light. An air strike screamed in with the dawn; Navy carrier planes looming out of the wet sky to slam the mountain with rockets, bombs, and napalm blobs.

At eight-thirty, Harry the Horse gave the order to attack, and elements of the 2nd Battalion under Lieutenant Colonel Chandler Johnson, and the 3rd Battalion under Lieutenant Colonel Charles Shepard, moved out. As the Marines zigzagged their way through the rain toward Suribachi, shells from halftracks and nearby U.S. destroyers lambasted the mountain. It had little impact on the subterranean enemy. Captain Severance committed Easy's 1st Platoon to the attack early in the day. The platoon leader, Lieutenant George Stoddard, was wounded and evacuated. The ground assault gained less than seventy-five yards through the morning, and those yards were earned the old-fashioned way: via flamethrowers, hand-held guns, and demolitions.

Around eleven A.M. Johnson sent a message to 5th Division Headquarters: "Enemy defenses much greater than expected. There was a pillbox every ten feet. Support given was fine but did not destroy many pillboxes or caves. Groups had to take them step-by-step, suffering severe casualties."

While the attack surged and then stalled, Easy Company, minus the 1st Platoon, continued to pick its way east, always with the mountain and its gunners looming not far away. Contact with the enemy was negligible, except in the case of one Marine from the 3rd Platoon, a blacksmith's son and bona fide eccentric from Montana named Don Ruhl. Ruhl had become something of the company oddball during training; he hated wearing a helmet, lectured his buddies that brushing one's teeth only wears them down, and made no secret that he'd had enough training; he was ready to fight.

On D-Day, Ruhl had shown everyone that he was not kidding. Spotting a cluster of eight Japanese who were fleeing their blown-up blockhouse, the boy charged them by himself, killing one with a bullet and another with a bayonet thrust.

Now, at around eleven-thirty of D+1, Ruhl came loping up to Easy Company's First Sergeant, John Daskalakis, with an equally reckless notion: A Marine lay wounded about forty yards forward of Easy's position, and Ruhl wanted permission to bring him in. Several other Marines and corpsmen had already tried this, and were driven off, many with wounds, by machine-gun fire. Sergeant Daskalakis pointed this out to Ruhl and then told him to go ahead. "He jumped out of the tank trap we were in," Daskalakis recalled, "ran through a tremendous volume of mortar and machine-gun fire, and made it to the wounded man's side. Then he half-dragged and half-carried him back." Ruhl rounded up an assistant and a stretcher and bore the man off, again through heavy fire, to the Battalion Aid station three hundred yards away. Then he sprinted back to the platoon and took his place again.

The beach was still hot. Unlike Normandy's beaches, which fell quiet after twenty-four hours, the Iwo Jima shoreline continued to absorb casualties for days. Corpsman Hector McNeil could never forget the sight of wounded boys on their stretchers being blown to bits by shells. Roy Paramore of Lufkin, Texas, saw Seabees and bulldozer operators killed as he himself unloaded supplies in the firestorm.

Father Paul Bradley and his assistant, Max Haefele, were likewise exposed, preoccupied through the onslaught as they cared for the wounded. Max remembered in particular one young Marine who had stepped on a land mine. "We raised his blanket and saw his legs and one arm were just chopped meat. He wouldn't survive. But he just lay there calmly smoking a cigarette."

But up on the front lines, American boys were avenging these losses with a fury. Some of the fiercest of these "boys" were just that: kids barely out of childhood. Jacklyn Lucas was an example. He'd fast-talked his way into the Marines at fourteen, fooling the recruiters with his muscled physique and martinet style—he'd attended a military academy before signing up. Assigned to drive a truck in Hawaii, he had grown frustrated; he wanted to fight. He stowed away on a transport out of Honolulu, surviving on food passed along to him by sympathetic leathernecks on board.

He landed on D-Day without a gun. He grabbed one lying on the beach and fought his way inland.

Now, on D+1, Jack and three comrades were crawling through a trench when eight Japanese sprang in front of them. Jack shot one of them through the head. Then his rifle jammed. As he struggled with it a grenade landed at his feet. He yelled a warning to the others and rammed the grenade into the soft ash. Immediately, another rolled in. Jack Lucas, seventeen, fell on both grenades. "Luke, you're gonna die," he remembered thinking.

Jack Lucas later told a reporter: "The force of the explosion blew me up into the air and onto my back. Blood poured out of my mouth and I couldn't move. I knew I was dying." His comrades wiped out the remaining Japanese and returned to Jack, to collect the dog tags from his body. To their amazement, they found him not only alive but conscious. Aboard the hospital ship *Samaritan* the doctors could scarcely believe it. "Maybe he was too damned young and too damned tough to die," one said. He endured twenty-one reconstructive operations and became the nation's youngest Medal of Honor winner—and the only high school freshman to receive it.

When I asked him, fifty-three years after the event, "Mr. Lucas, why did you jump on those grenades?" he did not hesitate with his answer: "To save my buddies."

In the midst of battle the Marines buried their dead. Don Mayer, at nineteen, had never before touched a corpse; on this day he dragged body after body out of the surf: kids who'd drowned jumping from their amtracs or who had been hit just as they landed.

Bob Schmidt of Appleton, Wisconsin, was part of Graves Registration. (Like the "Kissing Bandit," he'd grown up near Doc, but didn't know him; in later years they would play golf together.) His unit was supposed to go in on D-Day, but the beach was so full they didn't make it until two P.M. on D+1. "We spent twenty-eight hours in that little amtrac just circling around," Schmidt said. "It was torture. I would doze off and then be awakened by waves of seasickness. All you could see was the carnage of the landing craft being blown up on the beach."

When Bob Schmidt finally went to work, he realized at once that this was a different sort of battle. "I had buried the dead on Saipan," he said, "but the difference was how mangled the bodies were. The Japanese were hitting us with higher-caliber weapons than we had ever seen. On Saipan each Marine was buried in an individual grave. But on Iwo Jima we'd bulldoze a single grave a hundred feet long, ten feet wide. We didn't bury by grave, we buried by rows. We had surveyors plotting the markers."

Chaplain Gage Hotaling could never forget the bleak enormity of these mass burials: "We buried fifty at a time in bulldozed plots. We didn't know if they were Jewish, Catholic or whatever, so we said a general committal: 'We commit you into the earth and the mercy of Almighty God.' I buried eighteen hundred boys."

At about four P.M. on D+1, Easy Company received its order to head for the front with the 2nd and 3rd Platoons, plus company machine-gun squads supporting each platoon.

Its mission was to relieve a unit that had been on line for most of the afternoon and taken many casualties. The 2nd Battalion had clawed its way some one hundred yards toward Suribachi. The winter sun, which had emerged from the clouds late in the day, had now sunk behind the mountain, and the Marines of Easy moved directly into its giant shadow. Many of the young boys were seized with the feeling that the mountain was looking at them; and in fact, it was, with thousands of eyes: those of the 22,000 Japanese who were barricaded under its surface.

Arriving at the front at a running crouch, Richard Wheeler asked a rifleman, flat on his stomach, "How's it going up here?" "We're getting shot to hell!" snapped the shooter. Almost immediately, Easy was experiencing this truth firsthand. Kenneth Milstead, a 2nd Platoon buddy of Mike, Ira, Franklin, and Harlon, had just dropped into a shallow foxhole he'd dug when a shell landed beside him and blew him out again. Blood streamed from the embedded fragments in his face. "I could have been evacuated," Milstead recalled, "but the Japanese had pissed me off. I went from being scared to being angry. That was the day I became a Marine."

Over the boys' heads, rounds from tanks and offshore destroyers slammed into the mountain. "Nothing but noise," Phil Ward recalled. Navy and Marine fighter planes angled in, plastering the steep flanks with napalm that burst in bright orange plumes.

On the ground, under fire, my father prowled, his Unit 3 pouch slung over his shoulder; exposed; looking for wounded.

"Our sick bay was just a rifle in the ground," recalled Dr. James Wittmeier, the battalion surgeon. "Doc Bradley came in with another casualty, and since he had been out with the troops so much I ordered him to rotate to the back and take a breather. He was tired, but he refused to stop. He said, 'I don't want to leave my men. I want to stay with them.' Then he went back to the fighting."

It was a day of heroics and tragedy for Easy Company. Sometimes the two were almost inseparable. As the Marines pushed ever closer to the mountain's base, Lieutenant Ed Pennel spotted five gravely wounded men in open terrain not far from him. They needed immediate rescue, but they lay under withering cross fire. Pennel looked around for a solution. A few tanks were finally lumbering toward the field. The nearest was about a hundred yards away. Lieutenant Pennel took out for it on a dead run. Somehow reaching it unscathed, he grabbed the telephone hanging on its side and guided its driver back to two of the wounded men. Mike, Harlon, Ira, and Franklin dashed to the pair, partly shielded by the tank's bulk, and pulled them into a trench. Pennel directed the driver to back the tank until it straddled the men, who were then pulled inside through the escape-hatch door. The lieutenant then guided another tank toward the other three wounded men, and repeated the risky operation twice more. He received a Navy Cross for his valor.

And Don Ruhl remained in a fighting mood.

A large Japanese gun was in place about seventy-five yards from the company's right flank. A company next to Easy had taken seven casualties in an attempt to rush and neutralize it. Now the toothbrush-hating Ruhl and a buddy came up to Lieutenant Keith Wells, the 3rd Platoon leader, and offered their services. As dozens of their fellow Marines watched, the two boys sprinted across territory that had cost other American boys their lives. Reaching the big gun, they found its emplacement unoccupied. The two stayed in the emplacement beside the weapon through the night to prevent the Japanese from reoccupying it. Rooting in the darkness, Ruhl found a tunnel not far away. With no apparent thought that it might be occupied by extremely unfriendly tenants, the eccentric Montana boy crawled inside and explored its entire length with lighted matches. He discovered several woolen blankets and brought them back to his dumbfounded comrades.

As Suribachi's shadow spread into general darkness, Easy Company dug in for another cold, sleepless night. The fatigued boys knew what lay in store when the winter sun rose again. They knew that in the morning their battalion would have to assault the mountain. And that they would be part of the assault force.

Again, the star shells, the flares, and the searchlights conjured vast jumping shadows on Suribachi's sides to bedevil the boys' night-thoughts. As if to provide a soundtrack for those thoughts, a Japanese mortar shell hit an ammunition dump on the beach late in the night. The explosions continued for an hour.

By the end of this day, the 4th and 5th Divisions controlled only a mile and a half of the island. For this territory, the 5th Division had suffered some 1,500 casualties, and the 4th, about 2,000. And still, the Americans could not see their enemy; could see little evidence that they had inflicted casualties. For most of the young boys, it had not fully sunk in yet that the defenders were not *on* Iwo, they were *in* Iwo, prowling the sixteen miles of catacombs. Psychologically, it was as though they were shooting at—and getting shot by—phantoms.

And now, in the darkened land of the phantoms—in the madman's haunted house—the boys tried once again to sleep.

Nine

D-DAY PLUS TWO

Some people wonder all their lives if they've made a difference. The Marines don't have that problem.

—RONALD REAGAN

A STORM LASHED IN FROM THE OCEAN; blasts of wind; the surf at six feet. But this was nothing compared to the hell-storm about to erupt on the southern neck of the island. At eight-thirty A.M. a thin line of unprotected American boys would arise and rush directly at the most fortified mountain in the history of the world. Almost one third of them would be killed or maimed. But not in vain: Their charge would mark the beginning of the end for "impregnable" Suribachi—and thus for Iwo Jima itself as a factor in the war.

Soaked, cold, and fatigued, the Marines awoke and gazed toward the primitive mass of rock that held their fates. In the tense silence as first light broke, Easy Company lay poised for action on the 2nd Battalion's right flank. Easy faced a long, lethal gauntlet on the volcano's northeastern side. Dave Severance's boys would have to rush across two hundred yards of open terrain toward the mountain's base, with very little cover of any kind.

The guns trained down on the two hundred yards between the 28th Regiment and the mountain's base would soon make those yards the worst killing ground in the Pacific. Only after the battle would Americans grasp the full extent of what had been concentrated against them. Suribachi's interior had been hollowed out into a fantastical seven-story subterranean world, fortified with concrete revetments and finished off with plastered walls, a sewer system, and conduits for fresh air, electricity, water, and steam. As many as 1,300 Japanese soldiers and 640 navy troops filled each of the

---

Chapter opener: Official U.S. Marine Corps emblem.

various rooms and tunnels. They were armed with guns of every conceivable size and design.

The terrain below this fortress—the ground between the Marines and the mountain—was not only barren of natural cover, it lay in the teeth of overlapping ground-fire. At the mountain base stretched a welter of reinforced concrete pillboxes and infantry trenches. The firing ports of the pillboxes were angled so that the Japanese shooters could see one another and offer mutual support with their spewing machine guns.

At a little after seven-thirty A.M. the Marines' own artillery opened its earth-shattering barrage. Hot "friendly" metal streaked low over the Marines' heads, splintering the rock on the side of the mountain. The boys on the perimeter ducked under the lethal salvos; shrapnel was a fickle friend. "Ask for all of it!" Harry the Horse had yelled at his operations officer. There was no reason to hold back; after this day, there would be no space between the Marines and the enemy to aim shells. The combat could be hand-to-hand.

Toward the end of the barrage, forty carrier planes screamed in low, drilling the mountain with rockets that exploded at an earsplitting pitch. Some of the bombs landed a football field's length away from the crouching Marines.

The planes pulled away; H-Hour drew near: eight A.M. The boys braced themselves for the cry of "Attack!" that might usher in their last moments on earth.

But no attack order came.

The problem was tanks. Colonel Liversedge had expected several to arrive to cover the assault, but none had appeared. Rearming and refueling problems and Japanese mortar harassment had kept them pinned down. Harry the Horse delayed the assault until eight-fifteen, hoping that at any moment the mechanized monsters would grind into view.

Nothing.

At eight-thirty, Colonel Liversedge made a harrowing decision. Despite the crucial absence of armor to cover the charging boys, he could afford to wait no longer. He gave the order to go.

An electric current of pure terror pulsed across the regiment. The Marines could see that the tanks were not in the field. No tanks; no large bulky shapes to protect the boys against fire from the pillboxes as they ran. No tanks; nothing but bodies against bullets. A certainty of death filled the air. No jaunty war cries came from the veterans. Richard Wheeler experienced a pang of utter hopelessness: "I could feel fear dragging at my jowls."

Lieutenant Keith Wells would later admit to a memory from his boyhood in his father's slaughterhouse: an awareness, among the cattle, as the doors closed behind them, of what lay in store.

And then the heroes of the day began literally to stand up and be counted.

One of the first was Lieutenant Keith Wells of Easy Company's 3rd Platoon. Wells did not tell his men to follow him. He simply got to his feet, waved his gun toward the mountain, and began running. "I just thought it was pure suicide," he later recalled.

His mute example stirred the troops. Behind him, hundreds of scared boys stood up, leveled their rifles, and advanced against the mountain. To the left of Wells's 3rd Platoon (with Doc Bradley) was Lieutenant Ed Pennel's 2nd Platoon (with Mike, Harlon, Ira, and Franklin) matching Wells's advance step-by-step.

The mountain exploded back at them, a screaming death.

Harlon, Doc, Ira, and Franklin swept forward with the rest of Easy Company, in the vanguard of the attack. Immediately, Japanese shells and bullets began cutting the Americans down. Amidst the din, the air was cut with kids' strangled voices calling, "Corpsman! Corpsman!"

Officers and enlisted men crumpled together under the hail-stream of steel; were blown to bits; were machine-gunned where they crouched; were sliced open by hot shards.

Clusters of men were raked, and raked again. In Corporal Richard Wheeler's area, a mortar shell killed Corporal Edward J. Romero, an ex-paratrooper from Chicago. Wheeler dove into a crater and had scarcely recovered his wits when another shell exploded, ripping the future writer's left jawline apart. As the blood spurted, Corpsman Clifford Langley—who had treated a jaw wound on D-Day—hurried to Wheeler's side and applied compresses. Then Langley gave aid to a wounded man nearby. As he was closing his pouch and preparing to leave the crater, Wheeler's rifle in his hand, yet another mortar shell burst upon them. This one ripped Wheeler's left calf apart and drove shrapnel into Langley. The young corpsman ignored his own wounds and once again dressed Wheeler's laceration. Then they both realized that the shell had done its worst work on the wounded man nearby; both his legs had been ripped open, and he lay on his stomach, conscious but slowly dying.

It wasn't over yet. Now a fourth mortar hurtled in; it landed with a thump—a dud. Had it been live, it would have killed everyone near it.

Corpsman Langley—his clothing now soaked with his own blood—once again methodically closed his pouch, grabbed Wheeler's rifle, and went on his way.

William Wayne saw a bullet take a buddy's face off. "His teeth were just lying there," Wayne said. "If I'd thought about it at the time it would have driven me crazy."

Yesterday's heroes became today's dead. Don Ruhl's eccentric bravado finally got the better of him. It happened early on. Ruhl and his platoon guide, Sergeant Henry Hansen, were in the forefront of a charge that reached the brushy fringe of the mountain's base. They rushed past bunkers that had been blasted by the bombing, but soon found themselves at close quarters with active defenders. The two leaped atop a disabled pillbox and emptied their rifles into a cluster of Japanese who were hurling hand grenades. As they blasted away, a grenade clunked down between them.

Eyewitnesses recalled that Ruhl, who was near the roof's edge, could easily have slid over the side and escaped harm. But that was not his nature. He sized up Hansen's position—helplessly isolated near the center of the roof—and acted: With a shout of warning—"Watch out, Hank!"—he flung himself on the charge.

Sergeant Hansen recalled seeing the charge land, realizing he was trapped, flattening himself out ("hoping the fragments would pass over me") and hearing Ruhl's warning almost in the same instant. "I heard [the] muffled explosion," Hansen said in his official report of the incident. "I pulled Ruhl off the bunker, but he was dead. I am positive that had it not been for the self-sacrifice of his life, I would have been killed or seriously wounded."

Among the first to reach Ruhl's body was Doc Bradley, who held the dead boy in his arms while he examined him for signs of life.

For his bravery, Don Ruhl received a posthumous Medal of Honor.

The chain reaction of slaughter continued on. When Wheeler received his jaw wound, a comrade named Louie Adrian, a Spokane Indian, scrambled out of that foxhole and dove into another. There crouched his best buddy, Chick Robeson. The two Washington boys had enlisted together, traveled to Camp Pendleton together by train, and shared a tent in training. On liberty in California one night, feeling no pain, they fell asleep on a beach; they awoke when a huge wave crashed over them.

Now the two comrades were shoulder to shoulder, firing and tossing grenades, taking turns popping up and down in the cold, driving rain. "I came down to reload and Louie went up," Robeson recalled. "Then a bullet got him right in the heart. He fell and turned yellow with death. Louie was my best friend. My link with home. I was staring at him when our corporal yelled, 'Move, Chick! Move! Move!' "

Left: Harlon Block at Camp
Pendleton. *Above:* Ralph "Iggy"
Ignatowski.

Franklin Sousley with his
mother, Goldie, on his last
night home.

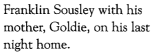

Corpsmen Vince Sagnelli, Jack
Santos, and Jack Bradley. At
Camp Tarawa, Hawaii, 1944.

Ira Hayes and
L. B. Holly on
Guadalcanal,
1943.

Ira Hayes in his
USMC paratrooper
gear.

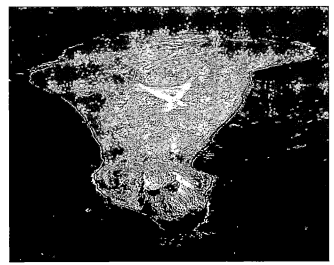

Iwo Jima, 1945.

D-Day, February 19, 1945—to the beaches, with Mount Suribachi in the background.

Top: D-Day, February 19, 1945. Amphibious landing units en route to Iwo.
Bottom: D-Day, February 19, 1945. U.S. Marines land on the beaches of Iwo.

Howlin' Mad Smith congratulating Boots Thomas on the first flagraising.

Rifleman on Mount Suribachi, with the landing beach below.

The first flagraising atop Mount Suribachi, February 23, 1945. Hank Hansen (without helmet), Boots Thomas (seated), Harold Schrier (behind Thomas), Louis Charlo (hand visible grasping pole), Jim Michaels (with carbine), and Chuck Lindberg (behind Michaels).

The first flag is lowered as the second is raised.

This cropped version became photography's most reproduced image.

The original Rosenthal photo, shot in a horizontal format, February 23, 1945.
Front row, left to right: Ira Hayes, Franklin Sousley, John Bradley, Harlon Block.
Back row: Mike Strank (behind Sousley) and Rene Gagnon (behind Bradley).

The posed "gung ho" shot, under the replacement flag. *Left to right:* Ira Hayes (seated), unknown, Harold Schrier, Franklin Sousley (rifle in right hand), Mike Strank (thumbs in pocket), Doc Bradley (in shadow, to Strank's left), Clarence Garrett, Grady Dyce, Howard Snyder, Hank Hansen (in cap), Phil Ward, Fred Walscak, Harold Schultz, Harold Keller, Tom Hermaneck, Gerry Smith (on knees with gun raised), Mike Larson (with pistol on knee).

And so seventeen-year-old Chick Robeson stood up and charged forward. He was a Marine, and he had work to do.

The 2nd Platoon, fighting hard on the left, found itself under a concentrated mortar barrage. Ira, Franklin, Harlon, and Mike zigzagged from one shell hole to another as they bore forward, looking for any sort of protection. Around them, their friends were suffering and dying as Easy took a cluster of casualties. A mortar round blew two boys to bits. An artillery round landed near Tex Stanton. The concussion blew Tex ten feet in the air; he fell to earth with deep burns on his legs and hips.

And still they advanced. Even as their casualties mounted at a rate that would have caused panic and retreat in nearly any other attacking force, these Marines remembered their training at Camps Pendleton and Tarawa and kept moving forward. Stoically, they followed their assigned roles and maintained the intricate teamwork of the great assaulting organism. The riflemen and machine-gunners who survived the charge aimed their fire at individual blockhouse ports, often mere slits in the hardened igloos. And as the enemy ducked (if the enemy ducked), the surviving demolition squads and the flamethrowers moved in through the chattering cross fire to get close enough for extermination.

In the midst of the carnage, Doc Bradley ran through the chaos, doing what he could in this landscape of blood. Just thirty minutes into the charge, the wet terrain was strewn with American bodies. Now the peaceable newsboy ignored the bullets and tried to save lives.

He watched a Marine blunder into a cross fire of machine-gun bursts and slump to the ground. Doc did not hesitate. His telltale "Unit 3" bag slapping at his side, my father sprinted through thirty yards of saturating cross fire—mortars and machine guns—to the wounded boy's side. As bullets whined and pinged around him, Doc found the Marine losing blood at a life-threatening rate. Moving him was out of the question until the flow was stanched. The Japanese gunfire danced all around him, but Doc focused his mind on his training. He tied a plasma bottle to the kid's rifle and jammed it bayonet-first into the ground. He moved his own body between the boy and the sheets of gunfire. Then, his upper body still erect and fully exposed, he administered first aid.

His buddies watching him from their shell holes were certain that he would be cut down at any moment. But Doc Bradley stayed where he was until he thought it was safe to move the boy. Then he raised a hand, signaling his comrades not to help, but to stay low. And then my father stood up into the merciless firestorm and pulled the wounded Marine back across the thirty yards to safety by himself. His attention did not flicker until the Marine was safely evacuated.

This action—so heroic that two sergeants and Captain Severance came forward to report it—earned him his Navy Cross, an honor he never mentioned to our family. It was one of the bravest things my father ever did, and it happened on one of the most valorous days in the history of a Corps known for valor.

Among the many heroes on the field, none surpassed the sustained courage of Lieutenant Keith Wells, Don Ruhl's 3rd Platoon leader and the man who had stood up to inspire the initial charge.

Wells took a terrific hit in the early fighting. It happened as Easy, slogging with ferocious intent toward the entrenched defenders, outpaced the unit on its right flank and began taking fire not only from the front but from the side as well. Soon the company was pinned down by grenades and bullets from a blockhouse in its path. Worse, it came under a pinpoint barrage of close-in mortar fire. Two kids volunteered to the rear for more grenades; they were gunned down from the blockhouse. Flamethrowers Chuck Lindberg and Robert Goode rushed to the scene but could not get through the mortar fire to the emplacement. Then a shell burst near Lieutenant Wells, wounding him and four other men, including William Wayne.

Wells suffered shrapnel wounds to his legs and lost some of his clothing. Doc Bradley darted to his side, injected him with morphine, and told him to get the hell to the rear. Wells would have none of it. His unit had begun the morning with forty-two men; twenty-five now remained. No one could be spared. The feeling had returned to his legs and he decided to stay in the field, in command.

Lieutenant Wells's determination drove his men to new heights of valor. Lindberg and Goode arose with their deadly flamethrowers and, ignoring the sheets of fire directed at them, stalked toward the pillbox. Soon the two were squirting their molten fire streams in all directions. They not only incinerated dozens of Japanese—the smell of burnt flesh floated on the damp wind—their liquid fire turned several pillboxes into infernos, causing Japanese ammunition to explode in great bursts.

Chuck Lindberg later recalled the hazards of lugging a tank that carried seventy-two pounds of jellied gasoline—napalm—under twelve hundred pounds of pressure. "The shot only lasted six seconds," he recalled. "We fired in short bursts. It was dangerous work. A lot of guys bought the farm trying that." Lindberg's steely calm and ferocious concentration led him to heights of accomplishment that few others attained. His day's work earned him a Silver Star.

The roar of tank treads now competed with the din of artillery all along the Marines' front, as dozens of them belatedly joined the front line.

Shielded by the armored bulk, infantrymen could rush ever closer to pill-boxes and bunkers without being exposed to fire. The inhabitants of those hovels—those who were not gunned down or scorched to death—began to flee toward the mountain. The Japanese first-line defenses were crumbling.

But the price of this victory remained high, and heroes continued to suffer. Five of the flagraisers fought side by side, led by Lieutenants Wells and Pennel. And now Pennel himself was a lacerated casualty, needing rescue. He was dashing from shell hole to shell hole when a shell landed between his legs and blew him a distance of thirty feet. His left heel was blown off, his right buttock and thigh gouged out, and his left shin pierced by shrapnel. Half a century later, Pennel told the story with detached humor:

"I was semiconscious. I heard someone screaming. Then I realized it was me. I felt liquid running down my butt and I thought my life-juices were running out. I looked between my legs to see what I had left. It was OK. It was my damaged canteen leaking.

"A medic came by and gave me a brandy and a shot of morphine. I took my helmet off and put it over my genitals. I laid there in a depression like a soup tureen for hours—parts of my body blown off, no clothes, helmet over my privates. I laid there with everything exploding around me."

An amphibious tractor tried to reach him. It hit a mine and blew up, killing the boys inside. Several hours later, four Marines approached him with a poncho. They rolled him onto it, each grabbed a corner, and they set off for the beach. A bullet wounded one of the carriers and Pennel toppled heavily to the ground. The remaining three men dragged him to the beach.

He lay there on a stretcher until darkness. "I felt exposed," he said, "like I was on a platform for all to see. Those flat-trajectory shells would skim straight in, making a roaring sound in the dark: *Foom! Foom! Foom!* Guys were being killed all around me. It was complete chaos."

Finally Lieutenant Pennel was loaded with some other wounded boys onto a long pallet. An amtrac rushed them to an offshore hospital ship, where the pallets were hooked with wires and winched up to the main deck. "A wire broke that was pulling the pallet just before mine," the lieutenant remembered. "Those guys screamed and just sank to the bottom."

Lieutenant Pennel's ordeal was not yet over. As a doctor examined him, a Japanese shell crashed onto the deck and skittered into the fuel bunker. The doctor turned and stood with his stethoscope pressed to the bunker, listening to the shell as it rolled around, doubtless wondering whether he and everyone nearby was about to be blown up. But it was a dud.

"It had been a long day," Ed Pennel told me later.

————

Soaked with blood, nearly immobilized by pain, Keith Wells continued to direct the 3rd Platoon's attack through the late morning. But he grew weak. He fell once, dashing to elude gunfire, and reopened his festering wounds. Immediately Doc Bradley was at his side. Doc dosed him up with morphine again, meanwhile screaming, "Enough! Get out of here!"

Wells willed himself to stay in the field another half hour, directing assault groups and rallying his men. Finally, half delirious with pain and confident of victory, he turned his command over to Platoon Sergeant Ernest Boots Thomas and made for an aid station in the rear. He got there by crawling. He was awarded a Navy Cross.

As rainy morning wore into afternoon and the fighting bogged down, the Marines continued to take casualties. Often it was the corpsmen themselves who died as they tried to preserve life. William Hoopes of Chattanooga was crouching beside a medic named Kelly, who put his head above a protective ridge and placed binoculars to his eyes—just for an instant—to spot a sniper who was peppering his area. In that instant the sniper shot him through the Adam's apple. Hoopes, a pharmacist's mate himself, struggled frantically to save his friend. "I took my forceps and reached into his neck to grasp the artery and clinch it off," Hoopes recalled. "His blood was spurting. He had no speech but his eyes were on me. He knew I was trying to save his life. I tried everything in the world. I couldn't do it. I tried. The blood was so slippery. I couldn't get the artery. I was trying so hard. And all the while he just looked at me, he looked directly into my face. The last thing he did as the blood spurts became less and less was to pat me on the arm as if to say, 'That's all right.' Then he died."

The near-misses were nearly as ghastly, especially the ones that resulted in other deaths. Donald Howell's buddy Walter Gust took a piece of shrapnel in the side of the head. It did not fracture his skull, but for a moment he was incoherent, flailing around. Howell and some buddies tackled him and were taking him to a corpsman when another round exploded, blowing Howell into the air and nearly taking Gust's arm off. The Marines reloaded Gust onto a stretcher; then a machine-gun burst killed the stretcher-bearers and ripped apart Gust's other arm. "I was watching this," recalled Howell, "and there was nothing I could do about it. Walter survived. He lived near me for years. I was the best man at his wedding."

————

By late in the bloody afternoon, the conquest of the mountain seemed within the Americans' grasp. Marine discipline and the sacrificial bonding of ardent young men was prevailing over concrete, steel, and thick volcanic rock. But the Japanese—even as their ingenious fortifications crumbled or were scorched hollow—were not quite done with their own desperate resolve. As the 28th continued to inch forward, Navy observation planes above the battle radioed that a swarm of Japanese had emerged from inside the mountain and was forming up for the dreaded banzai attack.

Within minutes, American planes were swooping in low to strafe the area. Their tremendous roar, and the concussion of exploding rockets, reverberated among the close-by Marines.

Finally the planes banked and vanished, and for a few moments the battlefield was silent, tense with expectation.

It was Sergeant Mike Strank, with the 2nd Platoon now on the left side of the line, who broke the spell. Leaping to his feet, the Czech-born Marine bellowed: "Let's show these bastards what a real banzai is like! Easy Company, charge!"

With that, the bone-tired, battle-scarred Marines got to their feet and once again slogged forward into the line of fire. To the right of the 2nd Platoon, the 3rd, commanded now by Boots Thomas, joined the footrace to Suribachi.

Boots Thomas was the next hero to shine. With rough terrain stalling the tanks some seventy-five yards to the rear, the twenty-year-old Floridian saw that his riddled unit was grievously exposed once again. In the thick of battle, a daring solution came to him. He sprinted back, through fire, to the nearest tank, and, still out in the open, directed its fire against the stubborn pillboxes. Then he dashed back to the front to exhort his men. A bit later he headed for the tanks again. He repeated this action several times.

His example paid off. The 3rd Platoon virtually annihilated the very enemy that had been massing for devastation of its own. As darkness on this triumphant, bloody day was setting in, Thomas himself identified the weak spot in the defensive line and personally led the breakthrough to Suribachi's steep flank, waving his knife aloft in victory. Boots was recommended for a Navy Cross, which was awarded.

Suribachi had not fallen, not quite, not yet, but victory now seemed inevitable. The wet day ended with the 28th Regiment poised in a vast semicircle around the battered volcano's base, gathering its strength for the finishing assault, expected to come the next morning. For Easy Company, it had been a day of grievous loss and historic valor: For its day's work, the badly decimated unit would receive a Medal of Honor, four Navy Crosses, two Silver Stars, and a number of Purple Hearts—one of the most decorated engagements in the history of the United States Marine Corps. These honors were paid for in blood: Casualties for the day amounted to thirty percent of Easy's strength.

Easy Company had actually moved a little too far and too fast for its own nighttime protection. Dave Severance's boys had penetrated past some active Japanese units, and spent the night isolated from the battalion. They huddled on a strip of jagged, rocky terrain at the southern base of Suribachi, the roaring surf of the Pacific below them on the opposite side. Dave Severance set his command post as close as possible to the mountain, so that he would have a line of sight up its flank. In the late evening, searchlights from the offshore destroyer-escort ships revealed something that looked like Japanese moving into view above Easy. As the ships began tattooing the volcano's flanks with 40mm shells, Captain Severance moved his command post back thirty yards to the water's edge, for a better view of the volcano's slopes. It was a good thing he did: The next morning's light would reveal that the original CP site lay buried under several tons of rocks from a bombardment-triggered slide.

Low on ammunition and food, Easy's troops munched what was left of their chocolate bars and waited for yet another dawn on Iwo Jima.

The Marines had paid for their advances across all fronts on the island with heavy losses. Official casualties for the battle now stood at 644 killed, 4,168 wounded, and 560 unaccounted for. Howlin' Mad Smith himself was sobered by what he had witnessed. "Watching the Marines cross that island," he later told a newspaper reporter, "reminded me of the charge of Pickett at Gettysburg."

But the horrors of this day's fighting did not end with the darkness.

Just as dusk fell, an air raid signal alerted the ships offshore. To Don Mayer of Portland, nineteen then, it made a spectacular show: "Every ship was firing thousands of tracers," he said. "It was more beautiful than any Fourth of July you've ever seen."

To the boys on board the task force ships, the sight was not quite so beautiful. Cecil Gentry, a radio operator on the USS *Lawrence Taylor*, could not move when the order to "Hit the deck!" came from his captain. "I was transfixed," he said. "I just stood there. One plane flew right over my head. I could see the face of the Japanese pilot. You could see the fear of death on his face. His lips were pulled back over his teeth."

This pilot immolated himself against the USS *Bismarck Sea*, adjacent to the *Lawrence Taylor*. Four of the ship's own torpedoes detonated in the concussion, and the great ship exploded in huge sheets of orange flame and rapidly sank, its bow turning straight down as it slid under the rough waves laced with rain. The men of the *Taylor* managed to rescue about 120 of the 800 crewmen from the water. Other rescuers managed to save hundreds more. Cecil Gentry recalled watching corpsmen amputating sailors' legs with razor blades, saws, and meat-cutters from the galley. But more than 200 were lost as the Japanese planes strafed the waters.

Back on land, the chilled, hungry, and exhausted Marines faced a different kind of nocturnal menace. Fear of infiltrators—the fear of the dancing shadows—had preoccupied the Americans on each night since D-Day. On this night, the fear took on more justification than ever before. On this night, the madman in the haunted house unleashed all his ghouls.

"Prowling wolves" was the name that General Kuribayashi had given his teams of stalking, crawling night-murderers; now, desperate to save their mountain fortress, they crept out in force.

At around nine P.M., up north with the 26th Marines, Thomas Mayers of the Bronx was surveying the terrain from his foxhole when a flare exploded in the mist. It illuminated a horrible sight, accompanied now by screams: Two Japanese slashing two helpless boys in the next foxhole with bayonets. Their names were Crull and Dortsch. Mayers and his buddy leaped to their feet to take action. One of the "wolves" wheeled and hurled a grenade at them; it was a dud, but it struck the other Marine in the head and knocked him unconscious. Mayers squeezed off one round before his rifle jammed. The predators were now advancing on him. The twenty-year-old private groped for his hand grenades. The Japanese were so close that throwing the explosives was out of the question; Mayers ripped out their firing pins, scattered them at the edge of his foxhole, and ducked.

The enemy soldiers howled and collapsed, their legs full of shrapnel. Mayers climbed from his foxhole, and with his knife cut their throats. Then he sprinted to the other foxhole. Crull was dead. Mayers shouted to the lacerated Dortsch: "Do you have any guns?" "Yes," the boy murmured. "Crull has a .45 in his shirt." Mayers snatched the weapon. It was slathered with Crull's blood and would not fire.

Two more Japanese were now upon Mayers. He rolled a few more grenades at them and ducked through the explosions, and then finished them off with his knife.

Ten

D-DAY PLUS THREE

It wasn't a matter of living or dying or fighting. It was a matter of helping your friends.

—CORPSMAN ROBERT DEGENS

A LULL AFTER THE HELL-STORM of the previous day. And a terrible day for capturing a mountain. The heaviest and coldest rains since D-Day lashed at the surviving Marines. The surf, whipped by twenty-knot winds, rolled in on nine-foot crests. The rain made a black stew of the volcanic ash underfoot and waterlogged many of the Americans' weapons.

Easy Company, clinging wetly to its isolated post, began D+3 by nearly getting wiped out by friendly fire.

"The Navy sent their carrier bombers in to bomb the volcano," as Captain Severance recalled it. "The pilots must have seen us as 'live Japanese targets,' and started dropping hundred-pound bombs on our positions."

Severance ordered red flares fired to warn the bombers off. No one could find cartridges for the rifle grenade flares. The bombs fell nearer. Radio connections to battalion headquarters had gone dead. More explosions. Desperate for relief, Severance put in a call to Harry the Horse himself, on the colonel's private radio frequency.

"Redwing Six!" the captain shouted. "This is Bayonet Easy Six! Friendly planes are bombing the hell out of us! Over!"

Back came the courteous reply from one of the colonel's radiomen: "Bayonet Easy Six, this is Redwing Six. You are not authorized to come up on this frequency. Out!"

Luckily for Easy Company, Lieutenant Colonel Chandler Johnson

---

Chapter opener: Mike Strank (far left) giving instructions to his men.

happened to be standing near the radio operator. He personally saw to it that the Navy planes were diverted before they caused any casualties.

Now that it was wide-awake, Easy Company prepared for a day of consolidation as the American ground troops waited out the weather. Lieutenant Colonel Johnson ordered Severance to reorganize and resupply his unit. The captain sent a patrol around the southern base of Suribachi to seek a linkup with the 3rd Battalion and to probe for enemy soldiers in the caves along the base of the volcano.

As the day progressed, sporadic firefights broke out around the volcano's base on the west side. Easy's peerless flamethrowers, clicking death in six-second bursts, scorched out some caves on the south and east sides.

Suribachi was surrounded now by American troops, and the invaders' heavy equipment operated almost without resistance. Tanks, howitzers, and other big-bore weapons slammed "Hot Rocks" as though it were a target on a firing range. Battalion officers moved their command posts up to the brush-line at the base of the slopes. Amphibious vehicles churned back and forth between the beaches and the front, bringing food and ammunition at will. Demolitions specialists converged on pillboxes and bunkers with a vengeance, relishing their payback for the volume of slaughter those emplacements had dealt out.

Sometimes a concealed Japanese soldier, seeing that his position was overrun, would make a sudden desperate break through the Marines for safety. His fate would usually be an M1 rifle bullet. One Japanese officer brandished his samurai sword as he made his break for it: a bad mistake. A Marine, seething with four days' worth of grief and terror, grabbed the blade out of the samurai's hands and sliced its owner to death with it. The Marine's hands were badly lacerated but he held on to the sword as a souvenir.

Many of the enemy simply remained in the ground. Their muffled voices, and the sounds of their movement, added an eerie note to the mopping-up exercises. "We could hear them talking and moving right under our feet," one Marine recalled. "Right under what we'd thought was solid rock. We'd dig down and find a rafter. Then we'd lower explosives or pour in gasoline. Then they made a lot more noise."

The combat-weary boys dealt in various ways with the memories of what they'd seen and done. Some talked to chaplains. Some lost themselves in their duties. For Ira Hayes, it was his edgy gallows humor that provided the shield against utter darkness. As Easy Company regathered itself at the base of Suribachi, Ira grew absorbed in shaping little mounds of earth with his hands. To Joe Rodriguez, they looked like fresh-dug graves, and in fact that seemed to be what Ira intended. When Franklin Sousley wandered past, Ira made a show of playing "Taps." Then he said to the Kentuckian: "This is just in case I'm not around when you get it."

"Franklin just kicked the mounds over," Rodriguez recalls.

The impending conquest of Suribachi was far from the only action on Iwo Jima. To the north, the main force of Marines had been battling with equal valor and sustaining equally severe casualties.

By the end of D+3, the volcano known as Hot Rocks was surrounded, except for a four-hundred-yard gap on the western coast. Surrounded, but still dangerous: Some of the defenders who remained were still determined killers, and no one knew when or where one might emerge with a grenade or a machine gun. As night fell, however, the Japanese themselves greatly reduced that danger via a highly uncharacteristic action: voluntary abandonment.

It involved only half the remaining force, but it amounted to an acknowledgment that the mountain fortress was finished. The order was given by Suribachi's commanding officer, Colonel Kanehiko Atsuchi. As one hundred fifty soldiers burst from the mountain in a desperate race to join up with the forces to the north, they were cut to pieces by Marines only too happy to deal at last with a visible enemy. Only about twenty-five made it through the gauntlet. When they arrived at the headquarters of the Japanese navy guard, their reception was not much better. The captain in charge, Samaji Inouye, accused their lieutenant of being a traitor and unsheathed his sword to behead the man. The lieutenant meekly bowed his neck, but a junior officer stopped him before he could swing his blade. Captain Inouye then collapsed in uncontrollable sobs. "Suribachi's fallen," he moaned. "Suribachi's fallen."

Earlier that afternoon, the American command had reached the same opinion, in a different frame of mind. Harry the Horse Liversedge received orders that the mountain be seized. Harry paid a visit to Colonel Johnson at his 2nd Battalion headquarters and issued a terse command: "Tomorrow we climb."

Eleven

"SO EVERY SON OF A BITCH ON THIS WHOLE CRUDDY ISLAND CAN SEE IT!"

I saw some guys struggling with a pole and I just jumped in to lend them a hand. It's as simple as that.

—DOC BRADLEY

IT HULKED ABOVE THEM STILL, before daybreak on the fifth morning, this primitive serpent's head that had struck them down in swaths. Amputated from the body, bombed, blasted, bayoneted, burnt, Suribachi at last lay silent after four days of being killed. But was it dead? Was the grotesque head finally a carcass, or was there venom still inside, and strength to lash yet again? There was only one way for the Marines to find out. They would tread on the head, and see whether it writhed.

February 23, 1945, dawned cold and stormy like the other days on Iwo Jima; but by midmorning the rain had stopped and the skies were clearing.

Hot Rocks glowed early. Navy planes lit it up with napalm at dawn. "It was a sheet of flames," remembered Donald Howell, who had relaxed with *House Madam* before the invasion. "An amazing pounding," agreed Max Haefele. But around nine A.M. the pounding stopped. The serpent's head lay mute and enigmatic. And the dangerous probing by foot began.

The pugnacious Colonel Johnson, wearing his trademark soft cap with the visor flipped up, called for two four-man patrols to reconnoiter routes up the northern face of Suribachi. Only Fox Company's patrol made it to the top. The leader was Sergeant Sherman B. Watson; the others were George Mercer from Iowa, Ted White from Kansas City, and Louis Charlo from Montana.

Tensely, grabbing at roots and rocks for balance, braced for ambush at every step, Watson's patrol felt its way upward amid the smoking rubble.

Chapter opener: The first U.S. flag being carried up Mount Suribachi.

The serpent lay dormant; the hostile fire never materialized. With the courage and discipline born of combat, Sergeant Watson and his boys ventured all the way to the volcano's lip and even risked a look into the crater—a satisfying mass of wreckage—before scrabbling back down to the base and reporting to Chandler Johnson.

As he observed Sergeant Watson descending, Colonel Johnson calculated he could risk a larger force and grabbed a field telephone. He cranked it to full battery power and yelled an order through the fuzzy wires to Dave Severance, who was bivouacked with Easy Company, still hugging the rocks on the southeastern point: "Send me a platoon!"

Severance surveyed his troops. The 2nd Platoon—Mike with Harlon, Franklin, and Ira—was off on a probe around Suribachi's base. The 1st was encamped several dozen yards away. So Severance chose the survivors of the 3rd (Doc's platoon), the closest to Colonel Johnson's command post, to become the first American platoon to climb the mountain. The ranks of the 3rd had been shredded by combat, so Severance augmented the platoon with twelve men from his Machine Gun Platoon, and several 60mm mortar section men. This increased the platoon strength to forty men.

Harry the Horse Liversedge himself picked the leader: First Lieutenant H. "George" Schrier, Severance's executive officer. Liversedge had known Schrier when they served in the Marine Raiders together, admired his combat experience, and valued the lieutenant's knowledge of how to direct air, artillery, and naval fire by radio. No one was ready to believe that the serpent had finished striking.

Just before the forty-man patrol began its climb, Chandler Johnson turned to his adjutant, Lieutenant Greeley Wells, and asked Wells to hand him something from his map case. Then Johnson called Lieutenant Schrier aside and gave him the object.

"If you get to the top," the colonel told Schrier, "put it up."

What Johnson handed the lieutenant was an American flag, one that Greeley Wells had brought ashore from the USS *Missoula*. The flag was a relatively small one, measuring fifty-four by twenty-eight inches.

Dave Severance never forgot the wording of that command. "He didn't say 'when you get to the top,' " the captain pointed out. "He said 'if.' "

The platoon made ready to start its trek. I imagine my father looking around for his buddy, Ralph Ignatowski. Iggy. A Marine staff sergeant named Louis Lowery, a photographer for *Leatherneck Magazine*, asked permission to come along and record the ascent. The boys in the unit glanced upward, measuring what lay ahead.

It was Boots Thomas—appropriately—who got the unit moving: "Patrol, up the hill! Come on, let's move out!"

"I thought I was sending them to their deaths," Dave Severance would later admit to me. "I thought the Japanese were waiting for a larger force."

As the forty-man line snaked upward, gained altitude, and grew visible against the near-vertical face of the mountain, it attracted attention. Marines on the beaches and on the flat terrain to the north turned to watch. Even men aboard the offshore ships put binoculars to their eyes to follow the thin line's winding trek. Nearly everyone had the same thought: *They're going to get it.*

The men on the march shared this sense of dread. Harold Keller happened to glance at the two stretchers being sent along as the platoon fell into line. "I thought to myself, *We'll probably need a hell of a lot more than that,* he recalled.

Doc Bradley, shouldering his Unit 3 bag, was another who wondered how many would return alive. "Down at the base, there wasn't one out of forty of us who expected to make it," he told an interviewer not long after the battle. "We all figured the Japanese would open up from caves all the way up to the crater."

And my father had an additional concern: "All the way up, I kept wondering, how the devil was I going to get the casualties down?"

Don Howell marked the slow, wary progress. "We inched our way up," he recalled, "blowing caves as we went. We'd see a cave ahead of us, pull the pin on a grenade, and throw it inside." As he passed the cave entrances, Howell could see that they were strewn with empty sake bottles—the Japanese liquor of choice—and bags of plain rice.

Phil Ward never forgot how the platoon wound its way cautiously, single file. "There was no trail, and there was a lot of blasted rock. We zigzagged our way up. We had to get on our hands and knees and crawl a couple of times. We had heavy weapons and two men had heavy flamethrowers on their backs. We were all scared."

One of the flamethrowing Marines was Chuck Lindberg. Even he was braced for instant bloodshed. "We thought it would be a slaughterhouse up on Suribachi," he later said. "I still don't understand why we were not attacked."

As the Marines climbed, they beheld Iwo Jima for the first time from the perspective of the Japanese. Spreading below them in panorama were the landing beaches and the armada at anchor in the ocean; the narrow neck they had secured at such cost; the enemy airstrip; and the rising terrain of the main bulk to the north. And the small figures that were their comrades, gazing back up at them. How close, how intimate, how eerily serene it all must have looked to them.

About two thirds of the way up, Lieutenant Schrier sent out flankers on either side of the main unit for cover. "We were tense," said Robert Leader, "thinking the enemy would suddenly jump out, or one of us would step on a mine. But it was completely quiet. Not a shot was fired. It took us about forty minutes to get to the top."

Sergeant Lowery documented the ascent with his cumbersome camera. At one point he asked a Marine to unfold the flag, so he could get a photo of it being carried up.

The patrol clawed its way to the rim of the crater at about ten A.M. Looking down into the bowl, the boys of the patrol saw devastation: Japanese antiaircraft guns fused together by the heat of American bombing; twisted metal; pulverized rock. Robert Leader could not suppress a smile of glee as he spotted two large drop-tanks—jettisoned fuel tanks from Navy planes. "I got a chuckle thinking of the Japanese watching those tanks come down," he said.

Leader's next impulse probably expressed the attitude of every young Marine who had faced the mountain: "I said to Leo Rozek, 'Gee, I have to pee.' Rozek said, 'Great idea.' So we both peed down the hill. I said, 'I proclaim this volcano property of the United States of America.' "

The spit-and-polish Hank Hansen took this in, and was indignant: "Knock that off! Who do you think you are?" Leader had a ready answer: "I'm an American citizen!" Hansen changed the subject: He relayed a request by Colonel Liversedge that Leader, as the platoon's unofficial artist, make sketches of everything around him. Leader set to work.

Then Boots Thomas came up with an order of his own: "See if you can find a pole to put the flag on."

Leader set aside his sketchpad—he'd bound his drawings together with surgical tape supplied by Doc—and he and Rozek scoured the rubble at their feet. The Japanese had constructed a catch-system for rainwater on the crater's surface, and fragments of pipe lay scattered about. Rozek, rummaging in the mud, found a fragment of usable length. He and Leader lugged it upright. The two discovered a bullet hole in the pipe. The rope could be threaded through that. They "manhandled" the pole, as Leader put it, up to where Thomas was waiting.

Then, knowing that this was an important moment that would be photographed, the patrol's brass took over.

Lieutenant Schrier, Platoon Sergeant Thomas, Sergeant Hansen, and Corporal Lindberg converged on the pole. They shook the folded flag out and tied it in place. Lou Lowery documented the proceedings with a steady succession of camera shots. He moved in close, suggested poses, cajoled the boys into self-conscious grins with his patter.

Louis Charlo joined the four. At ten-twenty A.M. they thrust the pole upright in the gusty wind, the first foreign flag ever to fly over Japanese soil. Lowery, wanting added drama for his shot, motioned to Jim Michaels, who crouched dramatically in the foreground with his carbine.

Then, a glitch: Lowery shouted, "Wait a minute!" to the posing Marines. He'd run out of film and needed a second to reload. Lindberg scowled and grunted at him to hurry it up: Men holding flags were easy targets.

With a fresh roll of film in his camera, Lowery called for a final, posed shot: Hansen, Thomas, and Schrier gripping the flagpole as they stiffly circled it; Lindberg and Charlo watching them from a couple of paces off; Michaels adding drama in the foreground with the gun.

As Lowery clicked this exposure, an amazing cacophony arose from the island below and from the ships offshore. Thousands of Marine and Navy personnel had been watching the patrol as they climbed to the volcano's rim. When the small swatch of color fluttered, Iwo Jima was transformed, for a few moments, into Times Square on New Year's Eve. Infantrymen cheered, whistled, and waved their helmets. Ships offshore opened up their deep, honking whistles. Here was the symbol of an impossible dream fulfilled! Here was the manifestation of Suribachi's conquest. Here was the first invader's flag ever planted in four millennia on the territorial soil of Japan.

Chuck Lindberg, a man not much given to sentiment, would remember it as a big wave of noise washing over them; it gave him a happy chill, the likes of which he'd never experienced before or since.

Robert McEldowney of Roanoke, Illinois, had watched the patrol's ascent from the landing beach; now he joined the wild hooting and yelling as he savored the crowning moment. "It was a thrill," he said. "When they put that flag up, I'll never forget—the entire island erupted with cheers. It sent a chill up and down my spine."

Max Haefele watched too, through his binoculars. "It felt great," he said. "When the flag went up, there was a lot of noise all over the island."

Many of the young Marines, in their giddiness, assumed that the battle of Iwo Jima was over. In this they were drastically mistaken. Robert Leader was one combatant who did not make this assumption. Amid the jubilation, he experienced a chill of a darker sort than Lindberg's or McEldowney's. "When I saw the flag I thought it was a bad idea for us up there," he remembered. "It was like sitting in the middle of a bull's-eye."

Leader's misgivings quickly proved prophetic. Just moments after the Stars and Stripes went up, Hot Rock's summit got hot again.

The first Japanese emerged from his tunnel with his back to the Marines. Harold Keller spotted him at once and fired his rifle three times from the hip. The fallen figure was yanked back into the hole from where he'd come. Another sniper immediately popped up and aimed his rifle at the Marines; Chick Robeson gunned him down. Next was a maddened Japanese officer, who leaped into view with a broken sword; an alert Marine dropped him.

Now the crater briefly came alive with ordnance. The serpent was not completely dead after all. Hand grenades started to arc out of several enemy caves. The Marines took cover and began hurling grenades of their own.

Photographer Lou Lowery was standing near the flag when a Japanese soldier stuck his head out of a cave and lobbed a grenade. Lowery dove over the volcano's rim and rolled and slid about forty feet down the steep, jagged side before he could break his fall. He suffered several cuts to his flesh, but was not seriously injured. His camera was broken, but his film was safe. Lowery decided it was time to head back down to find another camera.

The firefight lasted several minutes, and no American casualties were taken. And then the invisible enemy was silent once again.

After things had settled down, some of the young Marines grew fascinated with the view down below. Donald Howell found a working pair of large artillery field glasses, amazingly intact, in the rubble. He propped them up on their tripod, gazed through them, and was startled by what he could see. "They gave you an amazing view of the beaches," he recalled. "They [the Japanese] could see our every move." When eighteen-year-old James Buchanan had his turn, the war fell away for a moment and he was taken with boyish wonder: "I looked through them and could see all of Iwo. It was beautiful."

For others, the morning exacted grimmer duties. Chuck Lindberg remembered that he and his comrades spent the ensuing hour securing the mountain. "We used the flamethrowers or demolition charges for the caves we couldn't walk into, and we walked into whatever caves we could. We burned them out. We didn't know what side the Japanese would be coming up from, so we had to work fast."

Only later would the Marines comprehend just how much danger still festered inside Suribachi on the morning of February 23. Rummaging through an opened cave for souvenirs a few days afterward, Lindberg and Chick Robeson uncovered a sickening sight: the bodies of at least 150 Japanese, freshly dead. They had died of self-inflicted wounds.

"The stench was so foul that we had to put on gas masks," Robeson recalled. "We went in with a small flashlight, and found it to be a large cave in two parts. Dead Japanese lay all about—so thick we had to tread on some. Many had died by holding grenades to their stomachs.

"Why these Japanese hadn't tried to bolt from the cave and overwhelm the flagraising patrol is a mystery," Robeson continued. "They had our men outnumbered four to one. What made the situation even more unaccountable was that there were other occupied caves on the summit. We'll never know the number of Japanese who could have hurled themselves against our patrol. But there were surely enough to have killed every man in it."

There is one persuasive explanation for those self-annihilated soldiers, and it speaks to the corruption of Bushido that was wrought by Japan's malignant military regime. A traditional samurai might expect to die in combat and be honored for it. He might kill himself to atone for a moral mistake or a failure of courage. But suicide as an expression of ultimate sacrifice for one's country was not a traditional samurai value. This was a construct of a deranged military establishment cynically bent on extracting the maximum utility from its *issen gorin*.

While the 3rd Platoon was taking control of Suribachi's summit, other things were going on down below.

The Secretary of the Navy, James Forrestal, had decided the previous night that he wanted to go ashore and witness the final stage of the fight for the mountain. Now, under a stern commitment to take orders from Howlin' Mad Smith, the secretary was churning ashore in the company of the blunt, earthy general. Their boat touched the beach just after the flag went up, and the mood among the high command turned jubilant. Gazing upward at the red, white, and blue speck, Forrestal remarked to Smith: "Holland, the raising of that flag on Suribachi means a Marine Corps for the next five hundred years."

Forrestal was so taken with the fervor of the moment that he decided he wanted the Suribachi flag as a souvenir. The news of this wish did not sit well with Chandler Johnson, whose temperament was every bit as fiery as Howlin' Mad's. "The hell with that!" the colonel spat when that message reached him. The flag belonged to the battalion, as far as Johnson was concerned. He decided to secure it as soon as possible, and dispatched his assistant operations officer, Lieutenant Ted Tuttle, to the beach to scare up a replacement flag. As an afterthought, Johnson called after Tuttle: "And make it a bigger one."

At about this same time, a short, nearsighted, mustachioed wire-service photographer named Joe Rosenthal was struggling through a bad morning indeed.

Rosenthal, covering the invasion for the Associated Press, had landed on Iwo at around noon on D-Day and had risked his life to get stirring action shots through the days of combat that followed. But on the morning of February 23, nothing seemed to go right for him. He slipped on a wet ladder and fell into the ocean between the command ship and a landing craft. Fished out, he unzipped his camera—a bulky and durable 35mm Speed Graphic—from its waterproof bag, and clicked off a shot of Forrestal and Smith looking resolutely toward the beach.

As he was approaching Iwo Jima in an LCT in the company of Bill Hipple, a magazine correspondent, the boatswain told Rosenthal he had just heard on his radio that a patrol was climbing Suribachi.

"The hell you say," Hipple said.

"That's what I heard," the sailor said.

Hipple and Rosenthal headed toward the mountain, being careful to avoid marked mines, until they reached the command post of the 28th Regiment. There they encountered two Marines who were also combat photographers: Private Bob Campbell, who worked with a still camera, and Sergeant Bill Genaust, who had a movie camera loaded with color film.

"I think we'll be too late for the flagraising," Genaust remarked. But Rosenthal had come too far to turn back. "I'd still like to go up," he said, and talked Campbell and Genaust—who were armed—into making the ascent with him. The three men shouldered their cameras and hit the steep trail.

While Lieutenant Tuttle was off searching for a replacement flag, Chandler Johnson decided that Lieutenant Schrier, up on the mountain, could use a wired connection with the base for his field telephone, whose battery signal was growing weak. He rang up Dave Severance at Easy Company and ordered a detail to reel out a phone wire. The 2nd Platoon had just trooped in from its probe around the mountain's base. Severance ordered Mike, Harlon, Ira, and Franklin to the battalion command post to tie in a telephone wire that the fire team would then unreel up the mountain. Strank said simply, "Let's go!" The boys were tired, but nobody asked the young sergeant where they were going; nobody complained. As Ira later wrote, "We were certainly uneasy."

The captain also dispatched his runner, nineteen-year-old Rene Gagnon, to the command post for fresh SCR-300 batteries for Schrier.

They reached Colonel Johnson's field headquarters just as Lieutenant Tuttle hurried into view. He was carrying an American flag that he had obtained from LST-779 on the beach. As it happened, this flag—which at ninety-six by fifty-six inches was a good deal larger than the one now planted on the mountain—had been found in a salvage yard at Pearl Harbor, rescued from a sinking ship on that date which will live in infamy.

Tuttle handed the flag to Chandler Johnson, who in turn gave it to Rene to put inside his field pack. "When you get to the top," the colonel told Mike, "you tell Schrier to put this flag up, and I want him to save the small flag for me."

With their cargo of telephone wire, batteries, and American flag, the five boys set off up the mountain, unreeling the wire as they climbed. Doc had remained atop the mountain.

They reached the rim around noon. Mike reported to Lieutenant Schrier and explained the delivery of wire and batteries, and Johnson's desire to preserve the first flag. As Rene handed Mike the replacement flag, the sergeant decided an explanation was in order.

"Colonel Johnson wants this big flag run up high," he told the lieutenant, "so every son of a bitch on this whole cruddy island can see it!"

Mike directed Ira and Franklin to look for a length of pipe. He and Harlon started clearing a spot for planting the pole, and Harlon began stacking stones.

On his descent from the crater, Lowery encountered Joe Rosenthal, Bill Genaust, and Bob Campbell picking their way upward. Lowery told the group that he'd photographed the flagraising. The three photographers considered turning around and heading back. But Lowery had a different idea. "You should go on up there," he said. "There's a hell of a good view of the harbor." The three photographers trudged on.

A good view of a different sort greeted Rosenthal when he reached the summit, a little after noon: the American flag, in close-up, snapping in the strong breeze. "I tell you, I still get this feeling of a patriotic jolt when I recall seeing our flag flying up there," he told an interviewer some years later.

Then Rosenthal spotted another interesting sight toward the far side of the crater: a couple of Marines hauling an iron pole toward another Marine, who was holding a second American flag, neatly folded.

Rosenthal's fingers instinctively went to his Speed Graphic. Maybe he would get a flagraising photograph after all.

The pole that Ira and Franklin were dragging was a length of drainage pipe that weighed more than a hundred pounds. As they approached the

site, Lieutenant Schrier suggested that Mike's team do the job. The lieutenant wanted the replacement flag raised simultaneously with the lowering
of the first one.

Mike attached the flag to the pole. Schrier rounded up some Marines to
lower the first pole, and then stood between the two clusters of flag groups,
directing them.

The three photographers milled about some distance away, near the volcano's outer rim. Each of the three looked for a good vantage point. Campbell walked away and moved into position a short distance down the
hillside, almost directly below the first flag, so that he could shoot upward at
it as the Marines took it down. Genaust, almost shoulder-to-shoulder with
Rosenthal, about thirty yards from the second flag, had a few feet of color
film left in his camera, and decided to wait for the right moment to use
them. The five-foot-five Rosenthal had put down his Speed Graphic and
was bent over, piling up stones and a sand bag to stand on and improve his
shooting angle. His camera was set at a speed of 1/400th of a second, with
the f-stop between 8 and 16.

No one else on the summit paid much attention to what was going on.
The action had all the significance of a new football being tossed into a
game in progress.

It all happened in seconds. Genaust's movie camera recorded it all. In
the solitude of my living room, I have watched those few seconds again and
again, in slow motion. Here is how it unfolded:

Harlon braced himself above the target spot in the rubble-strewn ground,
ready to receive the base of the pole. Mike, at the other end, in charge,
guided it toward him, the pipe over his right shoulder.

Mike held the large flag wrapped around the pole to keep it from flutter-
ing in the strong wind until the pole was planted.

Mike and his four squad-members circled closer to the pole. They raised
their feet high with each step, to get clear of the debris. It looked as if they
were walking in deep snow.

Ira walked toward the pole, facing Mike, his back to Genaust's camera
frame. He said something to Mike that was lost in the strong wind. Ira
was wearing his Indian-style blanket stuffed through his military belt on
his rump.

Mike saw Doc Bradley walking past with a load of bandages in his arms
and asked him to come and help. Doc dropped the bandages and moved to
the pole, directly between Mike and Harlon.

Franklin walked to the pole from the foreground of Genaust's camera frame.
Rene approached the group from behind, to the right, his rifle slung over

his shoulder. He stood behind my father, who was in front of the pole in the movie frame.

The boys converged in a cluster behind Harlon, who bent low at the base. Doc gripped the pole in the cluster's center.

Rosenthal spotted the movement and grabbed his camera.

Genaust, about three feet from Rosenthal, asked: "I'm not in your way, am I, Joe?"

"Oh, no," Rosenthal answered. As he later remembered, "I turned from him and out of the corner of my eye I said, 'Hey, Bill, there it goes!' "

He swung his camera and clicked off a frame. In that same instant the flagpole rose upward in a quick arc. The banner, released from Mike's grip, fluttered out in the strong wind.

Rosenthal remembers: "By being polite to each other we both damn near missed the scene. I swung my camera around and held it until I could guess that this was the peak of the action, and shot."

And then it was over. The flag was up.

Campbell had gotten the shot he was after: the first flag going down, in the foreground of his frame, and the second one going up, off in the distance. Genaust had gotten the footage he wanted: a routine, spontaneous color sequence of the replacement flagraising.

Only Joe Rosenthal was unsure. The AP man didn't even have a chance to glimpse the image in his viewfinder. "Of course," he later said, "I couldn't positively say I had the picture. It's something like shooting a football play; you don't brag about it until it's developed." He'd captured 1/400th of a second out of four seconds of fluid motion. He had no idea whether he'd gotten a blur, a shot of the sky, or a passable photograph.

The six continued to struggle with the heavy pole in the whipping wind. The pole was fully upright. Harlon raised his hands up the pole and gripped it baseball-bat style, using his weight to force it into the ground. Ira did the same. Then Franklin added his heft. Mike anchored things.

Within a few more seconds the flagpole was freestanding, the cloth snapping and cracking in the wind. After a moment, Franklin and some of the others began looking for rocks to add support. Doc offered ropes he'd brought along to tie casualties to stretchers, and they secured the pole.

No one paid attention. It was just a replacement flag. The important flag—the first one raised that day—was brought down the mountain and presented to Colonel Johnson, who stored it in the battalion safe. It bore too much historic value for the battalion to be left unguarded atop Suribachi. The replacement flag flew for three weeks, eventually chewed up by the strong winds.

A few moments after the raising, Joe Rosenthal did what Lowery had done a couple of hours before him. He called several Marines over to cluster around the pole for a standard, posed "gung-ho!" shot. Lieutenant Schrier helped gather a crowd of boys for this photograph. Mike, Ira, Doc, Franklin, and fourteen other Marines posed proudly beneath the flag, waving their arms, rifles, and helmets.

Ira Hayes is smiling in this shot—his face creased with a wide, happy grin. He is the only seated figure among the eighteen.

Mike is standing next to Lieutenant Schrier. His lips are puckered, as if he is yelling a joyous "Whoaa!"

Franklin and Doc are behind Mike, one peering over each of his broad shoulders. Franklin has a triumphant smile and is thrusting his carbine in the air.

Doc Bradley would later say, "We were happy!" and in this shot he looks it: He has a big smile as he waves his helmet with his right hand.

Joe Rosenthal was satisfied with this posed shot. He felt certain that with all these smiling young boys facing the camera, and the landing beaches visible below, he had a photograph that would make the papers back home.

But the AP photographer would have to wait several days before he knew. That night, his film was flown to Guam for developing. If there were any good shots, they would be transmitted by radio signal to New York.

Several months later, the 2nd Battalion filed its "Action Report" for its role in the Battle of Iwo Jima. In describing the events of February 23, the report covered the reconnaissance patrol of the early morning. It covered Easy Company's fifteen-man patrol around the southern tip of the island (the 2nd Platoon). It covered Lieutenant Schrier's expedition up Suribachi with the forty-man patrol from Easy, and the planting of the first American flag at ten-twenty A.M. It mentioned the blowing-up of caves, the recovery of the Japanese binoculars, the sporadic resistance by fleeing Japanese.

The Action Report made no mention of a second flagraising. It was, after all, only a replacement flag.

Twelve

MYTHS

"All the News That's Fit to Print"

The New York Times

LATE CITY EDITION

VOL. XCIV...No. 31,809.   NEW YORK, SUNDAY, FEBRUARY 25, 1945.   TEN CENTS

AMERICANS DRIVE FOUR MILES BEYOND THE ROER;
OUR CARRIER AIRCRAFT SLASH AT TOKYO AGAIN;
MARINES WIN HALF OF IWO'S CENTRAL AIRFIELD

WMC DASHES HOPES OF EASED CURFEW; MAYOR ACTS TODAY

Germans Are Gloomy About U.S. Offensive

BIG FORCE STRIKES

Tokyo Indicates '1,600' Planes Hit in Waves— Sky Fights Swirl

5TH FLEET OFF COAST

Military, Naval and Air Bases Are Targets, Nimitz Announces

JAPANESE OVERRUN

Marines Smash Through Maze of Defenses in Bloody Iwo Battle

REACH PLATEAU'S TOP

Drive to Strip's Center, Widen Beachhead, Mop Up on Volcano

OLD GLORY GOES UP OVER IWO

31 TOWNS ENTERED

1st Army Captures Half of Dueren as 9th Drives On East of Juelich

4,000 CAPTIVES TAKEN

Third Army Clears 21 More Places in 5-Mile Gain Along Saar

JOINT ARMS BOARD SHAPED IN MEXICO

Inter-American Parley Likely to Set Up Defense Council

—U. S. Backs Proposal

EGYPTIAN PREMIER SLAIN IN CHAMBER

Eisenhower Points New Push At Knockout Blow in West

Here's one for all time!

—JOHN BODKIN,
THE AP PHOTO EDITOR IN GUAM

THE EXHAUSTED CONQUERORS of Mount Suribachi spent the ensuing four days resting on the brittle skin of the dead serpent. Some explored and blew out caves and tunnels. Some wrote letters home.

They had beaten the mountain. And so they thought the battle was over for them. At least they were safe—or safer than they had been for nearly one hundred hours. They had to be alert for the occasional Japanese infiltrator who prowled by night. But now the Japanese were mainly destroying themselves and one another. At night the boys listened to this morbid business being conducted below them in the hollowed-out seven stories of Suribachi. "As we lay in our foxholes trying to sleep, we could hear them blowing themselves up with grenades held to their stomachs," remembered Chick Robeson.

Joe Rosenthal's pack of film from February 23, with its twelve exposures, together with a pack he had started shooting the day before, began to work its way through the military channels back to America. First it was tossed into a mail plane headed for the base at Guam, a thousand miles south across the Pacific. There the film would pass through many hands, any of which could consign it to a wastebasket. Technicians from a "pool" lab would develop it. Their mistakes were routinely tossed aside. Then censors would scrutinize it; and finally the "pool" chief would look at each print to decide which was worth transmitting back to the United States via radiophoto, and which to discard.

Chapter opener: Papers across the country ran The Photograph on February 25, 1945. This shot is from *The New York Times*.

Of the twelve exposures from the pack taken on the twenty-third, two were ruined by streaks from light that had leaked through the camera housing onto the film. These two were adjacent to the tenth frame, the one Rosenthal had clicked off without looking into the viewfinder. For some reason the light hadn't marred that one.

Three days after the flagraising, my father found time to write home. He mentioned his concern for his brother Jim, then fighting in Europe, and for his father, who had suffered a heart attack. But for the sake of his worried mother, this twenty-two-year-old, caught in one of history's most ferocious battles, was only reassuring:

Iwo Jima
Feb 26, 1945

Dear Mother, Dad & all,

I just have time for a line or two, I want to tell you I am in the best of health. You know all about our battle out here and I was with the victorious Co. E. 2nd Batt 28th Marines who reached the top of Mt. Suribachi first. I had a little to do with raising the American flag and it was the happiest moment of my life.

I've been worried about Dad. I hope he is out of the hospital and up around again. I imagine you were a bit worried because you didn't hear from me. I can't write very often so please don't be alarmed if you don't receive mail frequently.

I hope the news from Jim is for the best and that you're all in good health & happy.

About an hour after we reached the top of the Mt. our Catholic Chaplain had Mass and I went to Holy Communion. I sure did my share of praying and it really gave me much security.

I'd give my left arm for a good shower and a clean shave, I have a 6 day beard. Haven't had any soap or water since I hit the beach. I never knew I could go without food, water, or sleep for three days but I know now, it can be done.

I'll write a longer letter when I get the chance, good luck and give everyone my regards.

> *Your loving son,*
> *Jack*

Seventeen-year-old Chick Robeson more accurately described the fear all of them must have felt: "I was never scared so stiff in my life before.

When the Japanese mortars and artillery starts dropping, I just can't help but shake like I was freezing but I guess everybody else does the same thing."

Franklin wrote to Goldie, offering her a harrowing kind of reassurance: that she shouldn't worry, even though bullets had been whizzing through his clothes.

Iwo Jima
February 27, 1945

Dearest Mother,
   As you probably already know we hit Iwo Jima February 19th just a week ago today. My regiment took the hill with our company on the front line. The hill was hard and I sure never expected war to be like it was those first 4 days. I got some through my clothing and I sure am happy that I am still OK.
   This island is practically secured. There is some heavy fighting on one end and we are bothered some at night. Mother you can never imagine how a battlefield looks. It sure looks horrible. Look for my picture because I helped put the flag up. Please don't worry and write.

Your son,
Franklin Sousley
US Marine

Like Rosenthal, Franklin hoped the posed "gung-ho" shot in which he appeared would make the papers back home.

And Rene took a moment from his rounds to jot a note to his sweetheart, Pauline Harnois:

Now that I can tell you, I was in action on Iwo Jima and that is the reason for such a delay in writing. I am still fine and some of my buddies are still with me, some are dead or wounded. After seeing all this it makes me realize what freedom really means.
   I got your pictures with the evening gown aboard ship so I put them in my helmet and carried them with me. They're not banged up too much. You still look beautiful, darling.

The Marines on Suribachi could not know it, but Americans back home were following their every move. Iwo Jima had become the number-one front-page story in newspapers across the country. And it had become the most heavily covered, written-about battle in World War II.

Readers who just days before had never heard of the sulfur island were by now as familiar with its contours as with their own backyards. As the war in Europe was thundering to an end, correspondents had migrated from that theater to the Pacific to record the growing conflict. Their dispatches flooded the newspapers, which churned out "extra" editions, and radio bulletins. Movie theaters showed newsreels of the assault, sometimes updating them daily as new footage arrived. For the first time in history, the radio networks carried live broadcasts from a beachhead under fire.

The news was stunningly fresh. In all invasions before Iwo, news copy had "hitchhiked" back to America on whatever transportation was available. Usually it had been flown to Honolulu on hospital planes evacuating the wounded. In this haphazard system, newsmen first had to wait until an airstrip was clear to accommodate the aircraft. Then they had to see that their dispatches made it aboard a plane; after that they could only hope the material would reach Navy press headquarters once the aircraft landed at Pearl Harbor.

It was a time-consuming process. Often days went by before news hit the home front. Tarawa's three-day battle was over before the first on-the-spot account of the fighting reached the mainland. Fully eight days had elapsed after the Saipan invasion before the first photo reached the U.S.

But at Iwo Jima, the process was accelerated, and streamlined. Daily editions during the week of February 19 brought battle accounts within twenty-four hours of actual time. Papers told the story in bold headlines, pages of background stories, and numerous maps and diagrams. Suddenly, civilians clustered in coffee shops and gathered around water coolers were bantering expertly, tossing off terms such as "Green Beach," "Suribachi," and "Kuribayashi" with ease.

Their expertise was formed abruptly. There had been no advance hint that an invasion of this magnitude was brewing. Iwo Jima burst onto the front page of The New York Times on Monday, February 19, under the bold lead headline: U.S. MARINES STORM ASHORE ON IWO ISLAND.

On the following day and for the rest of the week, Iwo Jima remained the number-one news story. Tuesday's main headline in the Times blared: MARINES FIGHT WAY TO AIRFIELD ON IWO ISLE; WIN 2-MILE BEACHHEAD; 800 SHIPS AID LANDING.

Below this appeared an enlarged photo of Iwo Jima with eighteen strategic points identified. The dominant feature was Mount Suribachi, festooned with an artist's rendering of a Japanese flag sitting atop it.

It hardly seemed to matter that General Patton was racing across Germany, or that President Roosevelt was sailing back from a historic summit conference in the Crimea. All other news was secondary to that from Iwo.

Wednesday's headline offered a hint of triumph: MARINES CONQUER AIR-FIELD, HOLD THIRD OF IWO.

This was tempered a bit by General Holland M. Smith's somber front-page quote that made plain the scale of the bloodletting: "The fight is the toughest we've run across in 168 years."

On Thursday the banner headline brought sobering news: MARINES HALTED ON IWO, NEAR FIRST AIRFIELD.

And on page four of *The New York Times*, in an article headlined MARINES' HARDEST FIGHT, the grisly statistics began to unspool:

> *Now the Marines have come to their hardest battle, a battle still unwon. Our first waves on Iwo were almost wiped out; 3,650 Marines were dead, wounded or missing after only two days of fighting on the most heavily defended island in the world, more than the total casualties of Tarawa, about as many as all the Marine casualties of Guadalcanal in the five months of jungle combat.*

Americans recoiled. This was worse than anything their boys had suffered in World War II: worse than Tarawa, worse than Normandy, worse than on the beachhead at Anzio. There was no doubt that the Marines were in the bloodiest battle since Gettysburg. The statistics were staggering: Iwo's four days of fighting worse than Guadalcanal's five months! It was as though Babe Ruth's sixty-homer season had been eclipsed in one game.

The news text may have accelerated in its race around the globe, but in 1945, it still took news wirephotos two extra days to complete the journey. Thus, the hopeful *Times* headline of Friday, February 23—MARINES TAKE SURIBACHI, CHIEF POINT ON IWO—was not accompanied by any photos of the seizure.

Readers must have been heartened as the news proclaimed: VOLCANO IS SEIZED—MARINES PUT FLAG ATOP SURIBACHI'S CREST, but any joy was tempered by JAPANESE HIT BACK—OUR CASUALTIES AT 5,372.

Saturday, February 24, brought a still more sobering headline: MARINES GAIN SLOWLY IN CENTER OF IWO.

Americans must have gone to sleep that Saturday night with heavy hearts. Normandy had been a wrenching experience; on the other hand, the beaches were captured in just a day. The casualties there had not been as heavy as on Iwo, and the reader was comforted by the knowledge of a quick victory.

But the Pacific's largest D-Day was terribly different. Five days of unthinkable casualties filled each morning's headlines. Americans combed the columns for a hint of hope. The sudden wave of uncertainty in the Pacific, so hard upon the triumphal news from Europe, created a sickening anxiety.

And then, as unexpectedly as news of the invasion itself, a radiant image of victory burned its way around the curve of the earth.

One of the first to notice it was John Bodkin, the AP photo editor in Guam. On a routine night in his bureau office, he casually picked up a glossy print of the "replacement" photograph. He looked at it. He paused, shook his head in wonder, and whistled. "Here's one for all time!" he exclaimed to the bureau at large. Then, without wasting another second, he radiophotoed the image to AP headquarters in New York at seven A.M., Eastern War Time.

Soon afterward, wirephoto machines in newsrooms across the country were picking up the AP image. Newspaper editors, accustomed to sorting through endless battle photographs, would cast an idle glance at it, then stand fascinated. "Lead photo, page one, above the fold," they would bark.

News pros were not the only ones bedazzled by the photo. Navy Captain T. B. Clark was on duty at Patuxent Air Station in Virginia that Saturday when it came humming off the wire. He studied it for a minute, then thrust it under the gaze of Navy Petty Officer Felix de Weldon.

De Weldon was an Austrian immigrant schooled in European painting and sculpture. He was assigned to Patuxent's studios to paint a mural of the Battle of the Coral Sea.

De Weldon could not take his eyes off the photo. In its classic triangular lines he recognized similarities with the great ancient statues he had studied.

He reflexively reached for some sculptor's clay and tools. With the photograph before him he labored through the long night. By dawn, he had replicated the six boys pushing a pole, raising a flag.

The next morning, Sunday, February 25, millions of Americans were similarly transfixed by the image. People would always remember where they were the moment they saw the photo, as others would later remember President Kennedy's death. The flagraising photograph signaled victory and hope, a counterpoint to the photos of sinking ships at Pearl Harbor that had signaled defeat and fear four years earlier.

Men and women bent down sleepily to their doorsteps, took one look, and called back into the house, "Hey, look at this!"

City pedestrians handed three cents to a street news vendor, took a few steps, then turned back and bought another copy.

Charles Sweeney, who later dropped the atomic bomb on Nagasaki, would write that his Catholic mother allowed only two images to be hung on the family's dining-room wall: Jesus and FDR. Until the morning she saw the flag photo, that is: She framed it and hung it as the revered third icon on the wall.

Many a mother with a son in the Pacific wondered if her boy was in the photo. But for Harlon's mother, Belle, back in Weslaco, Texas, there was no doubt. She was sure.

Early that morning Harlon's brother Ed Block, Jr., home on leave from the Air Force, stepped onto the family porch and stooped to retrieve the Sunday edition of the Weslaco *Mid-Valley News*.

He had just sat down in an easy chair in the living room and lifted the paper in front of him when Belle breezed into the room. As she passed behind him, she glanced at the paper. Then she stopped. She leaned over Ed's right shoulder, put her finger on the figure in the photo thrusting the pole into the ground, and exclaimed: "Lookit there, Junior! There's your brother Harlon!"

Ed did a double take, looking hard at the photo. The figure Belle was pointing to was unidentifiable, just the back of a Marine with no side view. The caption read only *Old Glory Goes Up Over Iwo,* and the articles provided no names.

"Momma," Ed declared, "there's no way you can know that's Harlon. That's just the back of a Marine. And besides, we don't even know Harlon is on Iwo Jima."

"Oh, that's definitely Harlon," Belle insisted as she slid the paper from Ed's grasp. And as she strode into the kitchen, her eyes fixed on the photo, Ed could hear her saying, "I know my boy."

The photograph's impact spread like a shock wave. That same Sunday, February 25, a columnist for *The New York Times* launched into a piece devoted to "the most beautiful picture of the war." A writer for the *Times-Union* of Rochester, New York, home of Eastman Kodak and a city where the visual vocabulary of photography was a familiar language, proclaimed the image "a masterpiece comparable to Leonardo's 'Last Supper.' "

The receptionists at major newspapers reported something unusual the week of the photo's appearance. Their switchboards were jammed with callers seeking reprints. Soon publishers were issuing "Special Extra Editions," one featuring the photograph "In Color!" while another promised "Printed on heavy paper, suitable for framing!" They couldn't print enough. All sold out.

No one knew who the flagraisers were, but Joe Rosenthal was an instant celebrity. On February 27, the *Times* ran a huge photo of Joe, identifying him as the photographer "who has earned nationwide praise for his picture."

Mr. A.B.R. Shelley of Raleigh, North Carolina, saw the photo and immediately wrote a letter to the editor of the *Times,* who published it on February 28:

On the front page of the Times *of Feb. 25 is a picture which should make a magnificent war memorial. It is the picture of the Marines of the Fifth Division raising Old Glory atop Mount Suribachi. There are war statues aplenty, but most of them are fictional. Reproduced in bronze, this actual scene should make good art and a fitting tribute to American men and American valor.*

By national consensus, it was a beautiful image. But for those who wanted facts, what, exactly, did it represent? No one suspected it, but the photograph suggested a very different reality from that being experienced by the Marines back on Iwo Jima.

On the same day the replacement photo appeared in the U.S., Boots Thomas was summoned from his battle post to General Smith's command ship. There, he was interviewed by a CBS radio correspondent. The interviewer didn't touch upon the Rosenthal photograph. He had not learned of its existence. Even if he had, he would not have brought it up: After all, it was only a replacement flagraising. It held no significance to those on Iwo Jima. To everyone on the island, "the flagraising" referred only to the one Boots was involved in.

In his interview Boots told the modest truth: His patrol walked up the volcano's slope encountering no opposition, and put up a flag as photographer Lowery recorded the scene.

But a number of elements came together to create an altogether different set of perceptions for the folks back home.

First, thousands had cheered the initial flagraising atop Suribachi, but from a distance. Only a few were close enough to see exactly who the raisers were. No one paid attention to or cheered the replacement flagraising. And no one cared who raised it. For most of the Marines on the island, there was only one flagraising.

Second, because civilian Rosenthal's AP photos traveled faster than Marine Lowery's military photos, only one flagraising was represented in the papers back home.

Third, because the replacement flagraising was essentially a nonevent, little was said about it. So readers back home assumed there was only one flagraising: the one they beheld on the front pages of their newspapers.

Fourth, reporters safe on ships miles from Suribachi and editors half a world away not only failed to report the full range of facts, they inadvertently created a confusing myth about the flagraisings that continues to this day.

There was the matter of that almost mythical image of the mountain. Nearly all aerial photographs featured Mount Suribachi; maps highlighted it, and news reports emphasized the enemy fire raining down from it. Thus, even though the rocky northern end of the island would prove to be the costliest part of the battle, it was natural for the reader to assume that once Mount Suribachi, the high point on the island, was taken, the battle would quickly end.

Then there was the shifting emphasis of reportage as the assault on the volcano wound down. The distant reporters had lavished great detail on the fierce fighting that led the Marines to the base of the mountain. Then they added three days of fanciful and garbled accounts of a murderous fight up Suribachi's slopes. But they never mentioned the actual, quiet walk up Suribachi on that Friday morning of February 23. On that day, lacking any supporting photos of the conquest, the editors substituted a photograph of Marines pinned down on a hill far to the north. This only added to the false impression that Marines had been pinned down on Suribachi's slopes.

On Saturday, February 24, the day after the flagraisings and the day before the photo appeared, correspondents continued to embellish the myth of the battle of Suribachi:

SURIBACHI REACHED IN A FIERY BATTLE

WAY TO VOLCANO'S BASE BURNED WITH
FLAMETHROWERS PRIOR TO SCALING OF VOLCANO

ASCENT MADE BY MARINES AS JAPANESE
HURLED GRENADES AND POURED BULLETS ON THEM

The boys of Easy Company would have howled at these gross exaggerations, but the *Times* copy just kept it up. Suribachi was the devil incarnate, "seeping steam and volcanic fumes," and the Japanese "were rolling grenades down the steep tawny cliffs to burst in the faces of advancing Marines" as the embattled Marines "called for ropes and stretchers to lower the wounded over the sharp cliffs."

These were the myths and inaccuracies that shaped Americans' perceptions of the battle in the days before the photograph appeared. When it did spring into the nation's consciousness on that Sunday morning, the photograph fused with the accumulated myth, and seemed to depict a final triumph in the very teeth of battle.

The *Times* was not through yet. It continued to fan the flames of hilltop heroism with the report that Boots Thomas "broke out the ensign, which was about three feet long, while his company was under intense enemy sniper fire."

———

How to explain this travesty of accuracy? How could an unopposed forty-five-minute climb up a hill and a quiet flagraising be portrayed as a valiant fight to the death?

The Marines were not to blame. None were quoted as sources, and none have since been blamed for the misleading hyperbole.

Quite simply, the press faltered in its duty. It replaced reportage with romanticism. Carried away by the daily valor of the Marines, working at a safe but obfuscating distance, and swept up in its own fantasy of a swashbuckling fight for a mountain, reporters invented the heroic fight up the slopes, and the flagraising among whizzing bullets, out of whole cloth.

In later months and years, when the myth was found to be just that, other reporters focused their suspicions on the men on the mountain. Then a new myth, an antimyth, took root, fanned by later complacent reporters who made no effort to root out the true story.

The flagraising did not signify the end of the battle. It was just beginning.

Easy Company's sector was secure but no place was safe on the small island. Distant giant guns in the north showered the mountain with nerve-shattering nighttime shells.

Dave Severance, hardly an officer given to panic, recalled one especially severe barrage. "It was my first experience with heavy artillery," he said, "and I was scared as hell. I crowded myself against the edge of the crater so hard that I gradually inched myself right up over the top."

On Wednesday, February 28, the 28th Marines received orders to prepare to move north. Their assignment was to relieve the 27th Marines at the 5th Division front on the heavily embattled west coast of the island.

The order to leave the mountain quickly changed Easy's mood to one of apprehension. "My twenty-first birthday is coming up March 10," Boots Thomas observed to a friend, "but I'll never see it."

And on that evening, Tex Stanton dropped into a foxhole that he and Mike Strank had prepared a little while earlier. Mike was already there, and Stanton at once sensed something different about him.

"He was lying limp, hobo-style, on his back with his hands behind his head," Stanton remembered. "And he was quiet. Now, Mike was always active, always talking, and I had never seen him still. So I asked, 'What's the matter?' Mike answered, 'Oh, nothing. I was just wondering where we're going with all this.' "

Tex Stanton felt a chill. He was so affected that he jumped out of the foxhole. "He was talking about his death," Tex maintained years later. "Mike knew he was going to die."

The northern battlefield beckoned. The idyll atop Suribachi was about to end. Harold Keller, looking through binoculars toward the fighting in the distance, summed up what Easy would face the next day. Asked later by a fellow Marine what he saw, Keller responded simply: "The Japs had all the cover, and our men got clobbered."

Thirteen

"LIKE HELL WITH THE FIRE OUT"

They are saying, "The generals learned their lesson in the last war. There are going to be no wholesale slaughters." I ask, how is victory possible except by wholesale slaughters?

                              —EVELYN WAUGH, IN HIS 1939 DIARY

HAROLD KELLER COULD NOT KNOW how right he was. He was peering through his lens into bad territory: an open furnace of violence that would soon beggar the suffering and dying thus far.

No one could have predicted the horrors to come. In fact, much of the world would assume—given 4,574 U.S. casualties and the triumphal raising of the American colors on February 23—that the Battle of Iwo Jima was over. In fact the reverse was closer to the truth.

For Easy Company, and for many thousands of other Marines, the real Battle of Iwo Jima was only about to begin.

"Dearest Mother," Harlon wrote to Belle in Weslaco early on March 1, the day of Easy Company's plunge into the asylum. "Just a few lines to let you know I'm OK. I came through without a scratch. Oh yes, I saw Carl Sims just before we hit. He is OK. I guess you're pretty anxious to hear from me by this time. This isn't much but it's all I could get. I will write more later."

The real battle would be waged exactly on General Kuribayashi's terms. It would be a battle of attrition on terrain that had no front lines; where the attackers were exposed and the defenders fortified; where Japanese infiltrators stalked the night; where every rock, every ditch, every open stretch of ground could conceal a burrowing, suicidal enemy. And where brave

---

Chapter opener: A Marine on the beach of Iwo Jima.

Marines trained to advance despite any conditions and all losses would advance yard by bloody yard for four more hellacious weeks, until the smell of death staggered the burial crews and the survivors on both sides resembled ragged phantoms more than living, vital young men.

They would advance, and die, largely bereft of their nation's good wishes or sympathy. Attention had now begun to shift away from Iwo Jima, even as the great bulk of the bloodletting began. The flagraising on Suribachi had given the press corps a convenient symbol of a "happy ending." Some seventy war correspondents had accompanied the armada to the island; for the first, drama-soaked week, they had remained on the scene and sent hundreds of thousands of words back to their newspapers, magazines, and radio networks—not to mention countless photographs and newsreel images.

But now the majority of these seemed to consider the story over. Having badly distorted the facts of the ascent up Suribachi, and having fatally garbled the true story of the flagraisings from the safety of their distant ships, the gentlemen of the press—or most of them—withdrew. There were other war zones to inspect, other exotic locales for their datelines.

Now the agony would have its veil of privacy. Now the valor would go uncelebrated.

Easy Company, reunited with its patrol that descended Suribachi the night before, was ready to join the great offensive on the northern plateau. Now the dying would begin in earnest.

Easy plunged into action with the rest of the 28th Marines along the island's embattled west coast, in the 5th Division's zone of operations. It was nasty business. The terrain—rocky plateaus abutting on steep cliffs, shallow ravines; "like hell with the fire out" in the words of one correspondent— offered the usual absence of cover. The 28th threw all three of its battalions onto the line, and the hidden Japanese gunners resumed their harvest. Easy had to cross rough, exposed ground against a heavily fortified ridge.

The Japanese ordnance showed no respect for heroes.

Among the first to get hit was Chuck Lindberg, shot through the arm. Doc Bradley was instantly at his side. ("The only time I saw your dad on Iwo, he was running," Pee Wee Griffiths told me. "Somebody was screaming and he was running.") The heroic flamethrower's war was over. He was evacuated from the island.

A few minutes later Mike Strank's dark prophecy came true.

Mike was leading Ira, Harlon, Franklin, and some other Marines across a dangerous strip of ground when a cluster of Japanese snipers opened up on them. Jesse Boatwright took a bullet in the stomach, a nonlethal wound but enough to slam him into a shell hole. His buddies scrambled for cover. Mike and some others dove behind an outcropping that seemed to give them solid protection from three sides. Its only exposure was toward the sea, where the American destroyers lay at anchor. As sniper fire continued to rake the area, Mike sized up the situation with a veteran's detachment. Pee Wee Griffiths, L. B. Holly, and Franklin bent toward their leader, awaiting orders.

Mike talked to them about possible escape routes. Then he seemed to drift into a private place. He broke his own silence after a moment with a cryptic remark to L.B.: "You know, Holly, that's going to be one hell of an experience." L.B. waited for him to continue, then finally asked: "What are you talking about?" Mike did not reply; he only pointed to a dead Marine who sprawled a few feet from the group.

"He was telling me he would die," Holly reflected many years later. "And sure enough, two minutes later, Mike was dead."

Joe Rodriguez watched it happen at close range; he was nearly killed himself. "Mike hollered at me to come over," he recalled. "He was on one knee with Franklin and the other guys around, getting ready to draw a plan in the sand to get us out of there. But before he could get a word out, a shell exploded."

Franklin and Holly were bowled over by the blast, but were uninjured. Pee Wee was hit in the face and shoulder and temporarily blinded. Rodriguez woke up a few seconds later with "a warm feeling in my chest, unable to move my legs."

Mike Strank did not wake up.

The shell got Mike where he gave it. The impact tore a hole in his chest and ripped out his heart.

No Japanese could claim credit for this kill. Almost certainly, the round had come from a U.S. destroyer offshore; it sliced through the only unprotected side of the outcropping. The Czech immigrant to America, born on the Marine Corps birthday, serving his third tour of duty for his adopted country, the sergeant who was a friend to his boys, was cut down by friendly fire.

Melvin Duncan, just nineteen, reached down and cradled Mike in his arms. Now, at seventy-two, Melvin's emotional comment recalls the esteem he and the others felt for Sergeant Mike: "If there had been some way I could have died in his place, I would have done it."

L. B. Holly gently replaced Mike's helmet on his head and whispered to the lifeless form: "Mike, you're the best damn Marine I ever knew." Then Holly took Mike's watch off and gave it to Harlon, who had idolized Mike. Now Harlon was "Mike," the squad leader.

And then the war went on.

———

Progress was slow and lethal across the rocky, windswept plain. The 28th had moved out at nine A.M. By nine-thirty it was taking harassing fire from the rear. Seven hundred yards inland, on a front that ranged from two hundred to five hundred yards wide, the regiment was caught in a harsh landscape of outcroppings and ravines. Below the surface was the labyrinth of caves and tunnels. As one combatant later wrote: "If a heavy aerial bomb happened to hit an entrance, smoke would puff out of the other entrances, sometimes an astonishing distance away."

The 28th was pinned down for four hours, its crouching boys getting picked off with sickening regularity, before it could start moving again.

And movement without cover offered only more danger. Easy, strung out in a long line, scampered across the hard rock toward the island's northern tip. The gunfire directed at them was intermittent but deadly. My father was following Hank Hansen across a crust of exposed ground when he saw Hank crumple up. No one had heard a shot, and at first Doc thought the sergeant had tripped and fallen. But Hansen did not get back up, and as the other Marines scattered, Doc ran to him and pulled him into a nearby shell crater.

The bullet had entered Hansen's back and exited through his abdomen. "It was a bad wound," my father told a magazine interviewer a few months later, "but one thing you learn out there is not to give up. I yelled for somebody to hold the plasma bottle while I put a battle dressing on. For me, it was the luckiest thing I ever did."

Hansen was dying, but Doc's cry for assistance saved his own life. Tex Hipps came sliding into the crater to assist the corpsman. Then he glanced over Doc's shoulder and shouted, "Watch out, Bradley!" Four Japanese, one brandishing a sword, were charging him, screaming, "Banzai!" Hipps dropped the sword-wielding officer and one soldier with his M1; the other two retreated. Now two Marines came tearing onto the scene, hurling grenades at the Japanese, who were disappearing into a hole. After it was cleaned out, ten enemy bodies were discovered.

But Hank Hansen was dead. Like too many young boys, he died in Doc Bradley's arms. My father slipped Hank's wristwatch off, vowing to pass it on to his friend's mother.

Harlon Block's tenure as the heir to Mike Strank lasted until dusk.

As twilight settled in, the rawboned Texan moved among the boys of what was now his squad, giving orders for everyone to dig in and align themselves with a good field of fire.

Tex Stanton had secured himself in his foxhole when Harlon—his helmet characteristically tilted to one side—walked up to the rim and asked, "Where's Hauskins?"

"Over there," Stanton replied, and then: "You'd better get down, Harlon."

"Then Harlon just exploded," Melvin Duncan remembered. "He was blown into the air; there was dust and debris all around him."

Stanton could see that Harlon had been sliced from his groin to his neck. The All-State pass-catcher, the boy who'd ridden along the banks of the Rio Grande on his white horse, stood there a moment, his hands filled with a heavy redness. He gave a strangulated scream: "They killed me!" He struggled with his intestines for a moment longer, then rolled to the ground and died facedown.

His back—which formed one of the most galvanic contours in the flagraising photograph—now lay limp and exposed to the setting sun. His letter to Belle—saying that he had come through without a scratch—had not yet left the island. Its postal cancellation would not be stamped until March 14.

On the day Mike and Harlon died, Congressman Joseph Hendricks of Florida stood up on the floor of the U.S. House of Representatives to introduce a bill authorizing the erection of a monument. It would be a tribute "to the heroic action of the Marine Corps as typified by the Marines in this photograph. I have provided in the bill that this picture be a model for the monument because I do not believe any product of the mind of the artist could equal this photograph in action. Never have I seen a more striking photograph."

At the same time, Maurine Block was imploring her mother, Belle, not to keep telling everyone that it was Harlon in the photograph at the base of the flagpole. It was just the back of a Marine. No one could be sure which one.

But Belle was sure. Her reply to Maurine was a mother's: "I changed so many diapers on that boy's butt. I know it's my boy."

The mission of Easy Company on March 2 and 3 was to advance. Their objectives were a series of low, stony ridges cut through with shallow ravines, filled with piles of rubble. Japanese shooters populated these ridges, using natural cover as well as their maze of caves and tunnels.

The weather turned raw and stayed that way: rain, gusts of chilling wind. The boys clutched their ponchos and shivered. At night the island was bathed in the lurid light of flares. "Things were going off all the time," Glen

Cleckler remembered. "You'd always wonder if the next one was going to fall on you."

By March 3, some 16,000 of the original 22,000 Japanese defenders were still alive. The Americans had taken 16,000 casualties, with 3,000 dead. On this day, the 2nd Battalion's feisty colonel, Chandler Johnson—who had saved the original flag on Suribachi for his men—was blown to bits, a collarbone here, another fragment there. He was one of four of the 28th's seven officers who were killed that day.

Other heroes continued to die. Sergeant Boots Thomas, who had led the thrust to the mountain's base and was interviewed on CBS radio, took a field telephone handed to him by Phil Ward. As he answered the call, a sniper shot his rifle out of his right hand. Thomas did not flinch. The next shot ripped through his mouth, killing him instantly.

The fighting was cramped and vicious. Five men of the 5th Division were awarded the Medal of Honor on this day, a record unmatched in modern warfare.

Corpsman George Wahlen, twenty, of Ogden, Utah, was one of those. He was finally pulled off the field after refusing to leave his comrades even though he had suffered the third of three serious wounds. The first, a grenade blast on February 26, had temporarily blinded him in one eye; he ignored it, as well as the other grenades that sent fragments through his butt and legs. On March 2 a mortar shell tore a hunk of flesh from his right shoulder; he kept on ministering to wounded men around him. Finally, on March 3, a mortar splintered his right leg. "I heard other guys crying for help," Wahlen told me years later. "I tried to walk over to them but couldn't. I bandaged myself up and gave myself a shot of morphine." With his foot barely attached to his leg, he crawled fifty yards to give first aid to another fallen boy before he was pulled from the battle.

"Why?" I asked Medal of Honor recipient George Wahlen. "Because I cared for my buddies," he answered.

It was on March 4 that the lacerated, exhausted Marines saw the first demonstration of why they were fighting and dying on the ugly little island. A crippled B-29 returning from an attack on Tokyo, the *Dinah Might*, became the first American plane to make an emergency landing on Iwo Jima. Nearby Marines watched with astonishment as the crew leaped from the aircraft and kissed the ground. The ground was shaking with artillery fire. As far as the leathernecks were concerned, the crew had just landed in hell. They got a different perspective when one of the crewmen, thankful he had been spared a crash-landing in the Pacific, shouted: "Thank God for you Marines!"

Rain and chilly winds buffeted the troops that day. Bill Genaust, who had recorded the replacement flagraising with color film and who had asked Rosenthal, "I'm not in your way, am I, Joe?" walked into a "secured" cave to dry off. The last thing he did was turn on his flashlight. He was thirty-eight and left behind a wife of seventeen years. His body was never recovered.

Joe Rosenthal landed on Guam on that day, and inadvertently created the myth that his now-famous photograph was "staged."

As he later recounted:

"When I walked into press headquarters, a correspondent walked up to me. 'Congratulations, Joe,' he said, 'on that flagraising shot on Iwo.'

" 'Thanks,' I said.

" 'It's a great picture,' he said. 'Did you pose it?'

" 'Sure,' I said.

"I thought he meant the group shot I had arranged with the Marines waving and cheering, but then someone else came up with the flagraising picture and I saw it for the first time.

" 'Gee,' I said. 'That's good, all right, but I didn't pose it. I wish I could take credit for posing it, but I can't.'

"Had I posed the shot, I would, of course, have ruined it. I would have picked fewer men, for the six are so crowded in the picture that one of them—Sergeant Michael Strank—only the hands are visible."

This conversation would haunt Rosenthal for the rest of his life. Some of the correspondents listening to him assumed that he was talking not about the "gung-ho" photograph, but about the previous frame, the one that was now famous. Soon a false and damaging slur was making the rounds: that the replacement-flag photograph, now universally understood as the *only* flagraising photograph, was bogus, staged. (Lou Lowery's shot of the original raising, delayed in its transmission to the United States, never made an impact on the public consciousness.)

The slur accelerated on the jealousy of some rival photographers, who were only too happy to see questions raised about the photo that had eclipsed all their work, and on the indifference of the news media about checking its facts. *Time* magazine, on its radio program, *Time Views the News*, broadcast the "staged" interpretation of the photograph without bothering to verify the rumor. As soon as he arrived back in the States, Joe Rosenthal did his best to set the record straight, and his wire service, the

Associated Press, demanded and received a public apology from *Time* about the error. It would be the first of many false claims, followed by press apologies. Joe Rosenthal's 1/400th-second exposure would bring him nearly as much frustration in life as it brought satisfaction.

Back on the island, Don Howell had his moment of crisis and valor. Finding himself and some comrades surrounded by Japanese in an enclosed area, Howell turned himself into an acrobatic killing machine. As he ran backward over the treacherous ground, dodging bullets, he coolly slipped a belt of ammunition from his shoulder and delicately fed it into his machine gun, sprayed withering fire into the attackers as his buddies dashed to safety. This action earned Howell a Navy Cross.

The Marines were taking terrible casualties, but at least one Japanese saw clearly how it would all end. General Kuribayashi sent a radio message to Tokyo: Iwo Jima would soon fall, the steely martinet reported, resulting in "scenes of disaster in our empire. However, I comfort myself in seeing my officers and men die without regret after struggling in this inch-by-inch battle . . ."

My father's luck continued to hold. Sometime on March 4 he narrowly escaped death once again.

He was treating a wounded Marine in a shell hole, my father told my brother Tom, when he glanced up to see a Japanese soldier charging him with a bayonet.

"I shot him with my pistol," John Bradley recalled later.

"What did you do then?" Tom asked him.

"I finished my job and ran to the next one."

"You didn't check to see if he was dead?"

"That wasn't my job."

But some of those closest to Doc were not so lucky. After this incident Doc returned to his platoon, but he could not find his special pal Iggy.

Ralph Ignatowski had been walking with Doc just before he went to help the Marine in the shell hole. Now he was gone. Doc asked a few Marines in the area about Iggy's whereabouts. No one knew.

The next day, the 2nd Battalion was relieved. Captain Severance took Easy Company back south, toward Suribachi. He was taking them swimming. The gesture was pure Severance: one minute the stern, unflappable field leader, dispensing intelligent, low-key orders under heavy fire; the next, a sensitive and thoughtful shepherd of his boys, in the same mold as Mike Strank. Dave Severance would be awarded a Silver Star for his masterful guidance of Easy Company throughout the Iwo Jima invasion.

Now, on the western beaches, across the island from the landing side, Dave's battle-scarred kids stacked their rifles and plunged in. It must have seemed surreal to them; it does to me, as I try to imagine it: a cadre of grimy, battle-hardened Marines facing mutilation and death in their dirty fox-holes transformed in a moment to a gaggle of naked boys swimming and splashing in the ocean. While they frolicked, the March 5 edition of *Time* magazine headed for the newsstands. It carried The Photograph, with the caption:

OLD GLORY ON MT. SURIBACHI

TO RANK WITH VALLEY FORGE, GETTYSBURG AND TARAWA

The boys in the ocean might have felt that they had somehow slipped off the edge of the earth, into a realm far beyond the reach or knowledge of their loved ones. They would have been amazed to know the true story: that the eyes of America were upon them as they struggled. The accompanying article in *Time* made this clear: "No battle of World War II," it declared, "not even Normandy, was watched with more intensity by the U.S. people."

During Easy's interlude in the Pacific surf, my father continued to wonder about Iggy. He asked around; none of the other boys had seen him lately. The mystery gnawed at him. Teamwork was encoded into the Marines' behavior. Iggy would not have simply left the company without saying something to someone, without having a reason.

A less mysterious departure was that of Admiral Spruance. The naval chieftain sailed from the island on March 5. Twenty-one days of battle remained.

The following day, Easy Company remained near the western beach.

On March 7, Easy moved out again, headed for the northern killing fields.

Representative Mike Mansfield of Montana, a future Ambassador to Japan, took the House floor on that day with a proposal that fired the imagination of his colleagues. A national Bond Tour—the seventh since the war began—was being organized to raise money for the war effort. The governmental sale of war bonds to the public had financed America's involvement in both world wars. Bond Tours were elaborate coast-to-coast touring shows, organized by the Treasury Department. Crowds gathered in stadiums and in roped-off city centers to hear bands play and to watch Hollywood movie stars and war heroes make pitches for the purchase of bonds.

Mansfield called for the flagraising image to be adopted as a symbol of this tour, so that "we as a people would do our part in keeping the flag flying at home as they have done in keeping it flying on foreign battlefields." His motion carried with great enthusiasm.

On the same day, a twenty-four-year-old Navy nurse named Norma Harrison, from Mansfield, Ohio, landed on Iwo Jima—the first of seven landings she would make there. She was a specialist in treating combat wounds in an airplane. She remembered the view as her plane circled, waiting to land: "I could see the island surrounded by ships as far as the eye could see. When a battleship fired, I could feel the concussion five thousand feet up. It was like living in a newsreel."

Once she was on the ground, Norma's newsreel turned gritty. "There was no time to be afraid. The wounded were in a large tent, on stretchers. I had never seen such injuries."

Norma and the other nurses (there were no doctors aboard) helped load the torn and broken boys onto the plane. "It was noisy from the shelling," she recalled to me, "but the patients were quiet. Death was quiet on those airplanes. A corpsman and I saw a guy die, and we decided not to cover him because the other guys hadn't noticed it. Those were quiet trips."

Norma Harrison remembered how stunned and grateful—"tickled to death"—the wounded boys were to see a woman. One boy asked her if she had any lipstick. "Yes," she answered, wondering why the kid would want to know.

"Would you please put some on?" the boy asked her. "I'd like to see a woman put lipstick on."

Ensign Harrison would continue as a nurse for many years, in war and in civilian life. She saw many varieties of wounded and injured men. She administered to men of the Navy and the Army. But these Iwo Jima Marines would always be distinct in her memory.

"The difference was their spirit," she said. "Not one of them was ever beaten. The Marines had esprit de corps. They were burned and injured and full of shrapnel. They were hurting. But they were never beaten."

On March 8, the Marines of Easy Company found Iggy. He had been grabbed, probably from behind, and pulled into a cave full of Japanese soldiers. As the company medic, it was my father's job to deal with what remained of Iggy's body after three days of brutal torture. I feel certain that the shock my young father must have experienced added greatly to his near-total silence, for the rest of his life, regarding his memories of the war.

Chick Robeson got hit toward dusk on March 8—in the act of saving my
father's life. Doc had run into the open once again to treat a wounded Marine. When he was finished he called for covering fire. Chick and several
others stood up, exposing themselves to view, and raked the ridge as Doc
scurried toward them. A Japanese bullet blew Chick's BAR out of his hand
and shredded his little finger. Doc was on him, patching him up, almost as
soon as he reached safety. Robeson later recalled that as a surgeon operated
on him that night, he asked, "Son, how would you like to get off this island?" It sounded good to Chick.

The 28th spent the next day clawing its way northward for about
150 yards, at alternating intervals of monotony and danger. The
rough terrain stripped them of tank cover. Seven men died in the 2nd
Battalion.

The day after that was a virtual repetition.

To Representative Homer Angell of Oregon, orating elegantly on the
House floor, the flagraising photograph represented "the dauntless permanency of the American spirit." Half a world away, the boys did not look so
dauntless. By this point in the campaign—a point far beyond anything most
troops in history had endured—the Marines' combat efficiency was showing
signs of deterioration, and the boys themselves had begun to resemble
ghostly remnants of a fighting force.

Scruffy beards matted their faces. Their fatigues were ripped and thick
with accumulated sweat. One of their number would later write that their
lips were puffed and black and their mouths hung open, as if they were having trouble breathing.

Their daily routine—impossibly dull and impossibly terrifying—was
turning them into human robots. Each day was the same: a morning artillery bombardment, then a crawling, slow advance over exposed terrain,
then an afternoon bombardment, then another advance. At dusk the boys
scuttled into shell holes or ravines for shelter. The next morning, it all
started over again.

They had gone deeper into the dark universe of combat than anyone before them. As Richard Wheeler would later write: "The Marines were now
being required to perform in a way almost beyond human endurance, both
physically and psychologically. History is filled with examples of high casualties in battle, but few armies with front-line losses of over fifty percent
have been ordered to keep attacking, especially in the face of heavy fortifications. No troops with less esprit de corps than these Marines could have
kept going."

One of the Marines who hardly ever betrayed a hint of the pain or exhaustion he felt was Ira Hayes. Jack First recalled Ira as stoic and focused
throughout the ordeal. "I spent a few nights with him in a foxhole," First
said. "He was quiet; he never said much." Lloyd Thompson agreed. "I would
shout, 'How you doing, Chief?' when I'd see him," he said. "Everybody
respected him as a soldier." And Phil Ward, who shared a foxhole with
Ira for a week in the north, maintained, "I was glad to have him looking
out for me."

But sometimes even Ira's veneer cracked. Bill Ranous recalled: "One
night a Japanese came close to our foxhole and Ira shot him dead. The next
morning I could see sorrow on Ira's face as he looked at the dead man. He
was moved."

As the boys slogged through their seemingly endless operation on Iwo
Jima—as they resigned themselves to the leaden permanency of an eternity
spent in hell—the effects of what they had accomplished began rapidly to
change the contours of the Pacific War.

On March 9 more than three hundred B-29's, liberated from harassment
out of Iwo's airstrips, launched the first of the great firebombing raids on
Tokyo. They dropped more than sixteen hundred tons of incendiary bombs
that destroyed sixteen square miles of buildings, killed nearly 100,000 people, wounded 125,000, and left 1.2 million homeless. The casualty figures
from this and other firebombing raids would be higher than those caused by
the nuclear attacks on Hiroshima and Nagasaki five months later.

The next day on Iwo my father's actions once again caught the eye of
Dave Severance. A man fell injured as Doc's platoon was repulsed by Japanese fire. Severance, in his report recommending my father's Navy Cross,
wrote what happened next: "As a second attack was launched, Bradley ran
forward under the covering fire of the attacking platoon, rushed to the side
of the casualty and remained there in the midst of the enemy's tremendous
volume of defensive fire until he had verified that the man had died of
his wounds."

The Marines inched forward on Iwo's hard shell; killed; died. On
March 11 two companies covered twenty-five yards and took thirty-three
casualties; on the 12th, they were stalled, with twenty-seven casualties. It
had become that kind of war.

A U.S. Senator, Joseph O'Mahoney of Wyoming, expressing a rising sentiment from around the country, arose in the Senate and called for a postage
stamp to be issued commemorating The Photograph.

And on this day Doc Bradley's war came to an end.

Sam Trussell, who was wounded along with Doc, remembered it. The two were crouching at the base of a cliff with some other Marines. They thought they were protected by an overhang, but the mortar shell that got them smashed against flat rock and sent steel splinters flying. "I was blinded," Trussell recalled, "and Doc pulled me back into the hole. Then he worked on a guy whose legs were torn up. Then he guided me to the aid station. I heard some guys talking about Doc's bloody legs, but I couldn't see how bad he was hit."

My father had taken shrapnel wounds to his right thigh, calf, and foot, and to his left foot. This did not stop him at first. Rolla Perry recalled glimpsing him as he ran past the enclosure: Both his legs were bleeding, but he was busily treating five other wounded Marines.

Dave Severance would later write, in his report on Doc, that "I observed him repeatedly running to any sector of the company zone of action to render first aid," and that "it would be hard to estimate the number of lives he saved by his prompt and skillful administration of medical aid, carried out with complete disregard for his own safety, nor to fully express how stimulating his devotion to duty was to the morale of those who served with him and were treated by him."

Doc was rushed to the Battalion Aid station for emergency treatment, then on to the field hospital, where some of the fragments were removed. The next morning he was loaded onto a plane for Guam, and then sent to a hospital in Hawaii.

In the Pacific killing grounds, Doc Bradley was just another casualty, one of thousands. But back in the United States, millions of people were scrutinizing his profile in The Photograph, wondering who he and the other flagraisers were. The *New York Sun* had superimposed a drawing of the famous "Spirit of '76" illustration in one corner of the photo. After it hit the newsstands, 48,000 people sent in requests for copies.

The day after my father departed, Rene Gagnon fired his rifle for the first time.

He and a buddy had wandered into a cave, assuming it was empty—a mistake that had cost many Marines their lives. The two boys found themselves facing a lone Japanese soldier with his rifle aimed at them. As he told his son, Rene Jr., many years later, the New Hampshire mill kid had a blinding thought in the split second that followed: "We all have mothers. We're all human. Why does this have to be?"

Rene had his own rifle, but he hesitated. He hoped, against all reason, that the Japanese would lay down his weapon. Instead, the enemy soldier fired. Rene's buddy dropped dead. In the next second it would be Rene's turn. He squeezed the trigger, and the Japanese crumbled.

Rene stood in the cave, trembling. This was what the battle had come down to. To his son, he later recalled thinking: "Why did I have to do this? Looking down a barrel into someone's eyeballs and having to kill him. There's no glory in it."

Glory, though, was on the mind of Senator Raymond Willis of Indiana, who was moved by The Photograph. On March 13 Willis urged his colleagues to move with "utmost haste" in creating legislation to honor "the all but unbelievable valor" of the Marines in the Pacific.

The next day the schoolchildren of Tokyo—those who had survived the firebombing—made a special radio broadcast to the surviving defenders of the island. They sang "The Song of Iwo Jima," which began:

> *Where dark tides billow in the ocean,*
> *A wing-shaped isle of mighty fame*
> *Guards the gateway to our empire:*
> *Iwo Jima is its name . . .*

On March 14, Admiral Nimitz proclaimed Iwo Jima conquered and that "all powers of government of the Japanese Empire in these islands are hereby suspended." Two days later Nimitz declared Iwo officially secured, and that organized Japanese resistance had ended.

"Who does the admiral think he's kidding?" steamed Marine Private Bob Campbell when he heard of this. "We're still getting killed!"

That same day, the 5th Division's cemetery, where Mike and Harlon now lay, was dedicated. Howlin' Mad Smith's eyes filled with tears as he said to his aide: "This is the worst yet."

President Roosevelt heard of the ceremony on his way to address Congress on the Yalta summit. "The Japanese warlords know they are not being overlooked," he said, in an aside to the legislators. "The Japanese know what it means that 'the United States Marines have landed.' And I think I may add, having Iwo Jima in mind, the situation is well in hand."

James Buchanan recalled those closing days a little differently. "We were trapped!" he said of his unit. "Getting shot at constantly. I was a private, and replacements were reporting to me. There was no one else left."

On March 16, General Kuribayashi radioed Tokyo: "The battle is approaching its end. Since the enemy's landing, even the gods would weep at the bravery of the officers and men under my command."

On that same day, Louis Ruppel, the executive editor of the *Chicago Herald American*, had a brainstorm. He composed it into a telegram that he sent to FDR that same day. Louis Ruppel's idea was that the flagraisers captured in Joe Rosenthal's famous photograph—which had already been designated the symbol for the Seventh Bond Tour—be brought home as stars of the tour.

This situation was unique: The Photograph had created such a stir that the President of the United States was about to anoint the flagraisers government-approved national heroes. Yet no one knew who they were, or what they had done.

On March 17, Japanese Prime Minister Kuniaki Koiso went on the radio to announce the defeat of General Kuribayashi's defenders on Iwo Jima.

But the bullets and shells were still flying. Amidst all his command duties, Captain Dave Severance of Easy Company began to receive some relayed requests that at first only annoyed and distracted him: Could he please provide the names of the Marines in The Photograph?

"I must confess, I shared little interest in the subject at the time," Severance told me. "We were fighting for survival, covering an area big enough to engage a full company, but manned now by two small platoons commanded by corporals or sergeants. Naming the flagraisers was a subject far from my mind."

By this time, newspaper clippings of the flagraising photograph had made their way to the island. Keyes Beech, a Marine correspondent, was one of many journalists who saw a story in finding the flagraisers. But the Easy boys who had been atop Suribachi that day were by now either casualties or scattered in the northern fighting. Only the runner, Rene Gagnon, was available to help with the identification.

Rene scrutinized the blurred figures. His best guess was five names: Franklin Sousley, Mike Strank, John Bradley, himself, and Henry Hansen. Rene had determined that Hansen was the figure on the far right, ramming the pole into the ground with his back to the camera. Ira Hayes was not mentioned.

On March 18 Tex Stanton, who had endured and witnessed so much travail, received his final wounds.

"I was lying in my hole," he recalled to me, "where I had been for four days. Whenever I raised my head they shot at me." He did not hear the round that got him. "It was just rocks and dirt everywhere." Ira and Franklin, sharing a foxhole nearby, fell under the same mortar barrage. They saw what happened to Tex.

Tex's memory of what happened next was matter-of-fact: "I tried to get up," he said, "and looked down and saw that both my feet were gone. But

I didn't want to leave. I wanted them [the corpsmen] to leave me with my buddies."

Rolla Perry, who also saw the impact, confirmed this. "I saw Stanton fly out of the hole," he said, "and when he landed his one foot was gone and the other was dangling. It was very sad to see him without feet, trying to reach his BAR so he could keep supporting his platoon, even though most of the original men were no longer there. I had always felt safe when he was firing near me, for he was the best. When the stretcher team loaded him up and started for the rear, I heard him say, 'You can't take me away. My old buddy Perry needs me.' "

As terrible as Tex's wounds were, many boys on the island would have gladly traded places with him. He had no feet, but he'd received a "million-dollar wound"—a ticket off the island. Unlike so many who were still fighting, he would survive. The battle had become so brutal, and these teenagers so brutalized, that the sacrifice of an arm or a leg made good sense to them now.

So saturated were their minds with visions of death that when they were splashed with the blood of a stricken buddy—as so many of them were—they perceived it as a kind of hallucinatory dream. Only years after the war ended would these dreams transform themselves for some into nightmares.

By March 21, the invasion force on Iwo Jima had been attacking for thirty-one consecutive days—a sustained effort unique in modern warfare. Their daily mission was unchanged: move on to one more ridge. A battle for yards, feet, and sometimes even inches. Brutal, deadly, and dangerous combat aimed at an underground, heavily fortified, nonretreating enemy. Five days of fighting remained, but no one could know that. Sleep-deprived, undernourished, inured by now to the routine of constant death, the boys shuffled forward. Their alertness, their finely tuned instinct for self-preservation, had inevitably deteriorated into a trancelike state.

Perhaps that explains what happened to Franklin Sousley.

Franklin had grown in battle, his comrades had observed. He'd seemed to get older and bigger. The last time L. B. Holly saw him, the young boy from Kentucky was cradling a wounded Marine between his legs as a corpsman gave first aid. A hell of a good Marine, Holly thought. A very considerate boy.

But then Franklin lost his focus for just a moment.

It happened at about two-thirty in the afternoon. The island had nearly been secured. Some Marines were already reboarding the transport ships offshore. General Keller E. Rockey was busy dedicating the 5th Division cemetery. And Franklin Sousley simply wandered into a road.

It was a known area of Japanese sniper fire. Perhaps Franklin forgot that.

Perhaps he figured the Japanese had stopped shooting. Perhaps he was day-dreaming about Marion.

The shot got him from behind. As the boys around him dove to the ground, Franklin swatted absently at his back, as though brushing away a blue-tailed fly. Then he fell.

Someone shouted to him: "How ya doin'?" and Franklin answered back, "Not bad. I don't feel anything." And then he died.

The glassy-eyed Marines had been inflicting heavy enemy losses for many days; but, as usual, these losses were mostly concealed from the Americans' view. But now the signs were inescapable: Final victory was near. General Kuribayashi's abandoned blockhouse was blown up on the day Franklin died. The job required four tons of explosives. Donald Howell, advancing with a unit at the very northern tip of the island, watched as a nearby tank aimed its flamethrower at a bunker, routing the Japanese inside. As they ran for their lives, Howell cut them down with his machine gun. "They were just piling up," he remembered. "I was shooting them as fast as they came through. I got sick to my stomach; I vomited; I was a mess for an hour and a half. It was just the thought of what you were doing to another human being. They weren't doing anything to me, and I couldn't take it. It was different than shooting someone who was threatening you."

The defenders grew reckless in their desperation. Enemy infiltrators were everywhere at night now, providing easy targets for Marine sharpshooters. A banzai charge on the night of March 22 faltered with fifty of the sixty attackers gunned down. Area after area on the northern plateau was declared "secure"—each area having been won at appalling cost.

"We are still fighting," Kuribayashi radioed on March 22. "The strength under my command is now about four hundred. Tanks are attacking us. The enemy suggested we surrender through a loudspeaker, but our officers and men just laughed and paid no attention."

It was Kuribayashi's last dispatch. His body was never found.

The next day, Frank Crowe looked on as two surviving platoon leaders met anxiously with Dave Severance. "They were murmuring about the losses, and about the inability to finish off the enemy," Crowe recalled. "They intimated that they and their men were about at the end of their rope. The captain listened to them, then quietly gave orders for the next day's fighting. His calm manner had a strong effect. The feeling of hopelessness changed to one of quiet resolve."

The tall, dignified captain was a good deal more ravaged than he appeared. He had received word from home that day that his wife had given birth to a stillborn baby boy. Sometime later, Severance learned the bad news about a corporal in his platoon, one Dave Bowman, whose wife also was expecting. Bowman was giving a final briefing to the platoon leader who was relieving him so that he could head for the offshore transport and passage back home. As he talked, he was shot dead.

This was too much for Severance. "I went off to an area all by myself and cried," he told Richard Wheeler. "I eventually regained my composure and moved on."

Three days after that, the war was over for Easy Company.

Easy's original total force on Iwo Jima was 310 young men, including replacements. On March 26, Captain Severance led his 50 survivors on a tour of the newly dedicated 5th Division cemetery. And then they traveled by a small boat to the transport, the *Winged Arrow*, for the trip back home. They had to climb a cargo net to get aboard. Many were so weak that they had to be pulled over the rail by sailors.

When I asked Severance, many years later, exactly how it finally ended, he thought for a moment and then replied: "We had all the real estate."

Severance was the only one of six Easy Company officers to walk off the island. Of his 3rd Platoon, the one that first scaled Suribachi, only Harold Keller, Jim Michaels, Phil Ward, and Grady Dyce came through the battle untouched. Easy Company had suffered eighty-four percent casualties.

Of the eighteen triumphant boys in Joe Rosenthal's "gung-ho" flagraising photograph, fourteen were casualties.

The hard statistics show the sacrifice made by Colonel Johnson's 2nd Battalion: 1,400 boys landed on D-Day; 288 replacements were provided as the battle went on, a total of 1,688. Of these, 1,511 had been killed or wounded. Only 177 walked off the island. And of the final 177, 91 had been wounded at least once and returned to battle.

It had taken twenty-two crowded transports to bring the 5th Division to the island. The survivors fit comfortably onto eight departing ships.

The American boys had killed about 21,000 Japanese, but suffered more than 26,000 casualties doing so. This would be the only battle in the Pacific where the invaders suffered higher casualties than the defenders.

The Marines fought in World War II for forty-three months. Yet in one month on Iwo Jima, one third of their total deaths occurred. They left behind the Pacific's largest cemeteries: nearly 6,800 graves in all; mounds with their crosses and stars. Thousands of families would not have the solace of a body to bid farewell: just the abstract information that the Marine had "died in the performance of his duty" and was buried in a plot, aligned in a row with numbers on his grave. Mike lay in Plot 3, Row 5, Grave 694; Harlon in Plot 4, Row 6, Grave 912; Franklin in Plot 8, Row 7, Grave 2189.

When I think of Mike, Harlon, and Franklin there, I think of the message someone had chiseled outside the cemetery:

> When you go home
> Tell them for us and say
> For your tomorrow
> We gave our today

Most of the Japanese dead lay sealed in caves where they would be mummified by sulfur fumes. Decades later, many would be found perfectly preserved, their eyeglasses still on. Some survived and fought on. One who surrendered months after the Marines left later emigrated to Brazil, too shamed to live in Japan. The last two defenders surrendered in 1949.

In the 1,364 days from Pearl Harbor to the Japanese surrender, with millions of Americans fighting on global battlefronts, only 353 Americans were awarded Medals of Honor, the nation's highest decoration for valor. Marines accounted for eighty-four of these decorations, with an astonishing twenty-seven awarded for just one month's action on Iwo Jima, a record unsurpassed by any battle in U.S. history.

The American victory unquestionably hastened the end of the war. In the ensuing months, about 2,400 distressed B-29 bombers, carrying 27,000 crewmen, would make emergency, lifesaving landings on the island.

This knowledge provided some comfort to the boys who had fought on Iwo Jima. Some.

"We who survived to the end were lucky," said Robert McEldowney. "Just lucky."

"It wasn't a matter of living or dying or fighting," said Corpsman Robert DeGeus. "It was a matter of helping your friends."

"Tell your readers," Corpsman William Hoopes advised me, "that I was wearing Marine Corps green dungarees. Mine were stiff with dried blood, and they cracked. And it wasn't my blood."

To Tex Stanton, it was an island of heroes. "If you got a medal," he said, "your citation read that you did something 'above and beyond the call of duty.' Well, I saw plenty of heroes on that island. And I figure if you spent just twenty-four hours there, you were doing something 'above and beyond' just to survive."

One of the last things Danny Thomas did before leaving the island was find Chick Harris's grave. Chick and Danny had been the "Buttermilk Boys"— the two friends who were too young to drink liquor on liberty. Danny had run past his severed, dying pal on D-Day.

Now Danny knelt beside the place where Chick lay buried and made a silent promise: a promise that had nothing to do with wars or flags or nations or the Century of the Pacific that the Battle of Iwo Jima had forged.

"I promised I'd drink a toast 'of buttermilk' to him," Danny said.

Fourteen

ANTIGO

Where seldom is heard
A discouraging word.
And the skies are not cloudy all day.
                   —"HOME ON THE RANGE"

I KNEW NOTHING OF ALL THIS, growing up in Antigo. I knew almost nothing of it until after my father's death in 1994.

World War II had been over less than ten years when I was born. Yet from a boy's perspective in this small, tree-shaded town, it might as well have been fought in the Middle Ages—a vivid, glorious, exciting story, filled with images of great battleships and planes and tanks and men charging forth in rounded helmets, all backgrounded somehow by the Stars and Stripes. Vivid and glorious, but already distant, a kind of myth. I played soldier with my neighborhood friends and sang "From the Halls of Montezuma," and thrilled to all the war movies on TV. As I grew a little older I devoured history books; I learned all about Eisenhower and MacArthur. But I never linked any of this to my own life, or my father's life. My brothers and sisters didn't, either. The Allied Expeditionary Force, Spearhead—these were about as connected to Antigo as Benny Goodman or Betty Grable.

This sense of distance was a little strange, of course, given that we all knew, early on, that our father was a figure in the most famous war photograph ever made.

But that's all we knew. Our father himself never mentioned the photograph. He didn't encourage anyone else to mention it. No copies of it existed in the house. The names Mike, Harlon, Ira, Franklin, and Rene were unknown to us. As was the name Iggy.

Chapter opener: James Bradley seated on the lap of his father, John Bradley.

And so the war, and The Photograph, floated at the edges of my child-hood, somewhere between reality and distant dream.

This was real: We lived at 321 Fifth Avenue, in the second-largest house in town. A black-shuttered white frame house that felt as though it had been there for all time and would continue there for all time, with three squat stories and a big front yard crowned by an old maple tree, and the backyard where we played football and catch-one-catch-all.

And this was real: Our dad was the owner of the McCandless, Zobel & Bradley Funeral Home, and one of Antigo's leading citizens. We never thought to wonder why Dad's name came last on the funeral home's name, given that he was the sole owner. It was just part of the way things were. Like our garageful of bikes. Or the old St. John's Church and St. John's Catholic School, where Dad had gone as a little boy, two blocks away. Or the Antigo River, two blocks in another direction. Real things; timeless things. Things that just were.

My father had come home from the war and looked up his third-grade sweetheart, Elizabeth Van Gorp of Appleton, and married her in May of 1946, and moved with her to Milwaukee, where he worked at a funeral home while studying mortuary science. They set up housekeeping in a chauffeur's quarters above a four-stall garage. In 1947 their first child, Kathy, was born, and John heard of an opening at the Muttart McGillan Funeral Home in Antigo. He brought Betty and the baby to his hometown. He probably carried all the money he owned in his pocket.

Seven years later, at the age of thirty-two, he was able to make one of the biggest commercial purchases in the county's history: the McCandless & Zobel Funeral Home.

He got on the front page of the Antigo *Daily Journal* with that purchase. Before long, people in town were calling it the Bradley Funeral Home. But officially it was McCandless, Zobel & Bradley.

Dad kept those original names in it as long as he owned the business—nearly forty years. McCandless & Zobel meant something to the history of the town, to its memory of itself. That was more important to John Bradley than advancing his own name.

Dad bought the funeral home along about my first birthday, in February 1955. I was the fourth of the eight Bradley kids. Before me there were Kathy, Steve, and Mark. Afterward we were joined by Barbara, Patrick, Joe, and Tom. I still have my birth bill from the hospital on a wall in my study. John Bradley paid it in full the month after I was born. I cost $71.90.

Our house on Fifth Avenue must have been built in the 1910's. It looked like it could survive a nuclear attack. It featured a big formal living room; a big formal dining room; a den; and a family room. The sunroom had a stone floor with a radiator underneath it.

Ours was a real working household. Everybody pitched in. We all had special tasks. When I was a little boy, my special task in winter was to get up every morning at five A.M. and go look outside the window to see if it had snowed. I had a particular window on the second floor, where my bedroom was, that was just right for this. It gave me a view to the telephone lines. There often was three feet of older snow already on the ground at five o'clock in the morning, and sometimes it was hard to tell if fresh snow had fallen. But I always could. If I focused on the telephone lines, even in the dark, I could see whether they supported thin parallel lines of fresh snow.

If there was fresh snow, I'd wake my two older brothers and we'd bundle up and set out on foot down to the funeral home, about a six-block walk, often through unplowed streets. There we'd get to work with our shovels.

The funeral home was a large corner property, and we had a lot of pavement to shovel off: a sidewalk, the large stair-stepped entrances, the huge parking lot. It was all manual labor; there were no little gasoline-powered snowplows back then. We'd arrive before sunup and work our way through what seemed like tons of snow. And after we were finished there, we got to come back to the house and do the walk and the driveway.

Two big snow-shoveling jobs before school. Only then could we dive into breakfast: the French toast, pancakes, and eggs Mom would have ready for us.

But it was fun. We never questioned it, never complained. It was part of Dad and Mom's "System."

They never called it that. But it existed. And I think it was brilliant. Brilliant and necessary. My parents had eight children to raise and a business to run. So as each of us got older, we took on a new level of responsibility. Washing the dishes. Keeping the lawn mowed. Helping out with the housecleaning. It was never something we complained about, or tried to negotiate. We just did it, because that was the way the family ran. We helped one another. We were a functioning, interdependent unit. It was our duty.

I think that Dad incorporated this concept of a System into his whole life—though if you put it to him that way, he wouldn't recognize it. He saw his role in the funeral business as being one of service. People always ask what it was like being a funeral director's son: Did you see a lot of dead bodies? Did you have to watch them get embalmed? It was never like that. My Dad wasn't an embalmer; he had assistants who did that. He was a diplomat. He was a psychiatrist, a psychologist, a counselor.

If you lived around Antigo and your father died, you called John. If you had a problem with the Social Security Administration, John would help you with that. You didn't know how you were going to pay that doctor bill? John Bradley would have a plan.

He focused on the needs of the families. Very often he would work until ten o'clock at night. He'd come home for dinner, take a short nap, and then go back. Nights were when the wakes occurred. He could have had an assistant handle those, but he was nearly always there himself.

He would stand at the top of the stairs inside the entrance to the funeral home greeting the people who came to mourn. He knew an astonishing number of these people by name. People from out of town, people he hadn't seen in years, would brighten a little when he not only hailed them by name but inquired about personal details they'd forgotten they'd told him— marriages, illnesses, newborn children. This must have required some effort on my father's part, but I'm sure it was never a strain. And it was never insincere. Ever. He cared about these people, their struggles and triumphs, their opinions. And the people sensed his caring.

I remember the first time I went on a call with my father to pick up a deceased person. I was about twelve years old. Dad said, "OK. We're going in that house, and we're going to pick up this lady. There'll be family in there, and they'll be crying." And then he said: "I just want you to act as if that is your mother you are picking up. We're going to treat her like she's your mother."

In the same spirit of service, my dad was president of just about everything in his hometown: school board, PTA, Lions, Elks. He was just a leader. But it benefited his business, too. He built one of the larger funeral homes in the state of Wisconsin—which is very close to impossible to do when you're in the small town of Antigo. But then, John Bradley was the funeral director of choice for counties around.

He cut a dignified figure in the town, but there was no vanity connected to his elegance. After he died, my mom gave me a money clip of his that bore his initials, "JHB." She commented that a salesman must have given it to him, because it would have been too flashy for him to have his initials inscribed. I countered, "But Mom, Dad had tailor-made suits, tailor-made coats, beautiful shoes. He always spent on his appearance."

She answered: "Yes, but that was for the business. He had to look good for his business." She was right: All his life he drove new Cadillacs. But those shiny new cars were used at the funeral home. After he retired he drove the smallest, least-equipped Chevy station wagon.

He ran his funeral home with a total commitment to quality and service. Everything was spotless, meticulously maintained. Once, when I was working there, he told me to clean the car that had just been used to deliver left-over flowers to the nursing homes. I cleaned and cleaned and shined and shined. At last I proudly announced that it was ready for his inspection. My dad walked to the garage, his wingtips crunching the tiny stones on the blacktop. He opened the back door, raised the floor, took the spare wheel out, and pointed to a single flower petal.

"I thought you said this was clean," he said. I got the message. I thought that was fair. Clean to the highest standards.

And the highest standards had to be met when dealing with the public. It wasn't about subservience or projecting a false image, it was about rendering true service. He didn't articulate it but you understood that people were important. They deserved respect.

My dad's natural leadership set an unspoken standard in the household. My older brothers were presidents of their class. In grade school and high school, the morning announcements were often read by a Bradley. The spokesperson for the school was a Bradley. I was president of my class for six, seven years in a row. It was an assumed thing. The Bradleys were leaders.

Dad never seemed to cultivate his leadership. He led a conservative life. He was not a star in any sense. But everyone liked John Bradley. Maybe part of his secret was that people felt safe talking to him. Maybe it was because of the way he listened to them. Those big ears of his, that got even more prominent toward the end of his life, were more than mere decoration.

He was a believing, practicing Catholic. He went to Mass every Sunday, he confessed his sins, he believed the dogma. "Jeepers Christmas!" was the worst oath he ever swore. Church for him was a bright soothing presence. The priests were figures of respect. The sacraments marked births and adulthood and death. All of it was straightforward, practical, solid—just like John Bradley. Thanks to him, we were a devout family. We all knelt down and said the Rosary. It wasn't that Dad insisted we do these things. He never spoke to us about faith. But his actions always spoke louder than words.

His actions, in fact—the day-to-day actions of his long, quiet, worshipful life as a pillar of the Antigo community—spoke so loudly that the words we all wanted to hear never broke the surface: the words that would explain to us what the war had been like for him. What Iwo Jima had been like. And what it was like to have been a figure in The Photograph. This was the way John Bradley wanted it. His actions would be what defined him to us. The words we sought would have to come from someplace else.

For decades—for an entire generation—those words remained unspoken.

And so they grew unimportant, at least most of the time. We all knew about the photo, but we knew of no story behind it to give it meaning for us. Statues had been made with John Bradley's figure in them, but my father wore no statue-shaped belt buckles; he lit no cigarettes with a statue-shaped lighter. His Navy Cross he kept out of sight; none of us knew he had been awarded it until after he had died.

Neither I nor any of my five brothers and two sisters ever read a book about Iwo Jima while my father was alive.

How could we be so incurious? It wasn't ineptitude. We knew how to obtain facts. We understood how to use libraries. As we grew older we all attended universities, with their great resources. How could we have persisted in this state of not knowing?

The answer, I think, lies in the attitude of unimportance my father projected toward the subject. "The subject," for him, could never merely be the battle of Iwo Jima. Always, it would have to be complicated—adulterated—by his unwanted fame as one of the flagraisers. Thus it became unimportant. Importantly unimportant.

"Reading a book on Iwo Jima at home would have been like reading a *Playgirl* magazine," my sister Barbara remarked once. "It would have been something I had to hide."

And so it was only outsiders, strangers, who brought the subject up with him. Mostly these were the newspaper and broadcast reporters who phoned once a year, every year, in early February, near the anniversary of the flagraising. Dad never expressed anger or exasperation to these annoying inquirers. One of his strategies for avoiding that was to enlist us, his family, in handling as many of them as possible. We were trained never to put our father on the line when the calls came in. Instead, we were to tell the television networks and national newspapers that John Bradley was "unavailable, fishing in Canada."

My father never went fishing in Canada. Often, as we gave this excuse, he was sitting across the table from us.

I don't remember him ever articulating why he did not want to speak to the callers. The best he could do was to give a barely perceptible shake of his head as if he were dealing with a common inconvenience like hay fever or nearsightedness. It was his personal affliction.

Or call it his aberration—that 1/400th of a second that welded him to a national fantasy. My father was a man firmly anchored to the world of real things, real values. He had no interest in theorizing, conjecture, highblown sentiments. The Photograph represented something private to him, something he could never put into words. It didn't represent any abstraction such as "valor" or "the American fighting spirit." Probably, it represented

Mike, Harlon, Ira, Franklin, and Rene, and the other boys who fought alongside him on Iwo Jima, boys whose lives he'd saved or tried to save.

He never disparaged The Photograph. He just never said anything about it.

John Filbrandt, an Antigo man who knew my father the longest, from the time they attended kindergarten together until my father's death, once told me of the one and only time he heard my father say anything about the flagraising. A stockbroker had come from another community to make a presentation to their investment club. Someone tipped the stranger off about John Bradley's past. The broker hurried over to my father.

"I understand you are one of the men who raised the flag on Iwo Jima!" he began with a bright look in his eyes.

Effortlessly, my father neutralized the man's intrusive thrust without disturbing the social atmosphere. "Yes," he replied gently, "that was a long time ago." And steered the conversation to other things.

I suspect he had an inventory of these preemptive phrases to deflect inquiries while not offending. Once he countered a query of mine with: "If only there hadn't been a flag on that pole."

That pole. He always called it a "pole." This reference is a key to the man and his view of the act. John Bradley was a sturdy and simple man, and plain, like the pole he raised. Helping Mike Strank with a pole—that's what my father did. The phrase "raising Old Glory" was much too grand for my father and what he thought he did that day. Indeed, in his only interview, conducted by an Iwo Jima documentary team in Chicago in 1985, he revealed that he could have done without the heroic mantle all his life:

> *Q: Considering all the fame the photograph achieved, if you had to do it all over again, knowing it would become famous, would you have jumped in as one of those six men?*
>
> *A: No, I don't believe I would. If I knew what was going to come of that photo I am sure I would not have jumped in and given them a hand putting that flag up.*
>
> *Q: Why?*
>
> *A: I could do without the pressure and the contact by the media. I'm just a private man and I'd like to leave it that way.*

And he was at least consistent. When I began my search for my father's past I asked my mother to tell me everything he had ever said to her about Iwo Jima.

"Well," she answered, "that won't take long. He only spoke of Iwo Jima once, on our first date. I was probing him for details, and he spoke for seven or eight disinterested minutes. All the while he was absentmindedly fingering his silver cigarette lighter. And that was it. The only time he talked about it in our forty-seven-year marriage."

My brother Mark had to ask him about it for a history assignment once. My father's answer was: "We were just there, we put a pole up, and someone snapped a picture." End of interview.

My sister Kathy hit a similar wall when she asked Dad to speak about Iwo Jima to her grade-school class. "Dad looked down, cast his eyes away, shook his head in the negative, but didn't say anything," she recalls. "I went to Mom and asked her about it and she said, 'Your father feels the real heroes are the men who died on Iwo Jima.' "

Why did he almost never speak of his past, and then only painfully, between long, excruciating silences?

A lot of easy answers come to mind.

"The press" covers one category. Dad deeply distrusted journalists, and with some reason. He'd been astonished, as a young man, to see how frequently reporters embellished interviews with him, even making up quotes when it suited their flowery visions. "They have the story written before they interview me," was his oft-repeated opinion of the Fourth Estate.

And they never got the heart of it right. They never understood the true essence of the flagraising. The press always insisted upon writing about the event in extremes, never in the realistic middle. Dad remembered ("Jeepers Christmas!") how the papers had reported the flagraising as one of the valorous deeds in man's history—the Marines slogging up the murderous slopes to plant the symbol of victory in a hail of gunfire.

The real story, as Dad saw it, was simple and unadorned: A flag needed to be replaced. The pole was heavy. The sun was just right. A chance shot turned an unremarkable act into a remarkable photograph.

"You never know what they're going to ask or how they're going to portray it," he told Mark a few years before he died, in explaining why he'd turned down a CBS affiliate's request for an interview. The station management had agreed to any condition: They would try to get Walter Cronkite or Charles Kuralt, as Dad preferred; they'd keep the interview in a vault until after his death if he wished; they'd let him in on the editing. Anything. He refused.

There were other plausible reasons: Iggy, for example. The pain and anger of remembering what had happened to Iggy, and of the pilgrimage Doc had made himself make to Iggy's parents after the war, to give them reassurances.

I'm sure that Iggy's memory fueled Dad's silence somewhat. On the other hand, I saw no other evidence that the war had embittered him. Bitterness was not part of his nature. He never spoke disparagingly of "Japs" or "Nips" or "the enemy," or even "the Japanese." Save for one terse remark to my brother, in explaining why he did not want to visit Japan, John Bradley did not continue to fight the war after he had returned home.

What was it, then?

I've come to believe that the answer may have been as uncomplicated, as unmysterious, as John Bradley himself. I think my father kept his silence for the same reason most men who had seen combat in World War II—or any war—kept silent. Because the totality of it was simply too painful for words.

Some veterans cope with pain via alcohol or drugs. Others seek psychiatric counseling—or don't seek it. Here is where I think my dad may have been a little different: He coped by making himself not think about the war, the island, his dead comrades. He coped by getting on with life.

He seemed almost to have erased it from his memory. During the conversation when he told me about the day Iggy disappeared, he seemed almost unable to recall Iggy's name. During his one TV interview, asked what he thought was the best thing about being a flagraiser, Dad was stumped. He'd never given it a thought. In that same interview he offered an amazing number of inaccurate details: where he'd taken his training as a corpsman, the exact circumstances of his getting to the flagpole.

He had simply forgotten.

But forgetting had not come easily for John Bradley. It had taken him a while to forget. He may have spoken about Iwo for only seven or eight disinterested minutes to Elizabeth Van Gorp on their first date. But after they were married, my mother told me, he wept at night, in his sleep. He wept in his sleep for four years.

His family, friends, and community all understood that he wanted to be known for who he was, not for a larger-than-life image. He was comfortable with himself; he didn't need any embellishment. And so his family, friends, and community closed around him to protect him from the inquiring world. In 1985, during the fortieth anniversary of the flagraising, John's hometown paper printed an article about what it was like not writing articles on their most famous resident:

> *Newspaper and broadcast stations from around the country contact Antigo* Daily Journal *editors, demanding to know why the newspaper hasn't written a story on Bradley.*

> *Managing Editor Gene Legro, who has worked for the newspaper for almost forty years, said the paper had given up trying to interview Bradley because he didn't want to be interviewed. He wants to be left alone. He wants his privacy and he's entitled to that, Legro said.*
>
> *"Do you want to know about Bradley?" Legro asked. "He's a nice guy."*

We kids respected our dad's wish not to talk about The Photograph, but sometimes our curiosity led us to explore what evidence there was of his wartime experiences. I remember a time when I was about six, rummaging in the attic among boxes of clippings about Doc Bradley that my mother had saved. (The three cardboard boxes we discovered after his death were not among these.) The clippings had to remain in the attic. Dad would have never tolerated these things being brought downstairs, displayed, talked about.

I found a photograph of the original statue erected in honor of the photo and dedicated November 10, 1945. I found a newspaper clipping about my dad's appearance in an Appleton court in 1946 on a speeding charge. The story told how the judge dismissed the case when he learned he was dealing with "John Bradley of Iwo Jima."

And finally I found a full-page newspaper ad from the Seventh Bond Tour, which he had participated in. It screamed: "You've seen the photo, you've heard him on the radio, now in person in Milwaukee County Stadium, see Iwo Jima hero John H. Bradley!"

Hero. In that misunderstood and corrupted word, I think, lay the final reason for John Bradley's silence.

Today the word "hero" has been diminished, confused with "celebrity." But in my father's generation the word meant something.

Celebrities seek fame. They take actions to get attention. Most often, the actions they take have no particular moral content. Heroes are heroes because they have risked something to help others. Their actions involve courage. Often, those heroes have been indifferent to the public's attention. But at least, the hero could understand the focus of the emotion. However he valued or devalued his own achievement, it did stand as an accomplishment.

The moment that saddled my father with the label of "hero" contained no action worthy of remembering. When he was shown the photo for the first time, he had no idea what he was looking at. He did not recognize himself or any of the others. The raising of that pole was as forgettable as tying the laces of his boots.

The irony, of course, is that Doc Bradley was indeed a hero on Iwo Jima—many times over. The flagraising, in fact, might be seen as one of the few moments in which he was not acting heroically. In 1998 Dr. James Wittmeier, my father's medical supervisor on Iwo, sat beside me silently contemplating my request for him to explain, or speculate on, why my dad never talked about that time. Finally, after many long minutes, he turned to me and softly said, "You ever hold a broken raw egg in your hands? Well, that's how your father and I held young men's heads." The heads of real heroes, dying in my father's arms.

So he knew real heroism. He could separate the real thing from the image, the fluff. And no matter how many millions of people thought otherwise, he understood that this image of heroism was not the real thing.

My father did not want his life dictated by what happened inside people's heads when they saw The Photograph. The Photograph represented something to people that had no validity for John Bradley. Beautiful, elegant, inspiring, yes. The most reproduced photographic image in history, yes. A model for the world's tallest bronze monument, certainly.

And yet misunderstood. Fundamentally, crucially misunderstood. Unrepresentative, in fact—at least when judged against the thousands upon thousands of split seconds that Doc and his buddies witnessed during that battle.

Antigo, the peaceable kingdom of my childhood, would be my father's lifelong refuge from all this: a place of clarity and simple goodness, where people understood one another for who they were and what they actually did. Where hard work, service, and love of family counted, and not myth or fantasy.

Antigo would be the one place in America where The Photograph did not distort things. Where its extraordinary power was overshadowed by the power of ordinary life.

But my father's longed-for reentry into this peaceable world was not to happen as quickly as he wished.

On the second-to-last day of March 1945, in one of his last acts as President before he died two weeks later, Franklin D. Roosevelt issued a secret order to Marine Headquarters in the Pacific. It was an order that further magnified the image's impact in American life—further magnified the distance between John Bradley, the man, and Doc Bradley, the figure in The Photograph.

Fifteen

COMING HOME

Nothing except a battle lost can be half so melancholy as a battle won.
—DUKE OF WELLINGTON

IN SIX POCKETS OF AMERICA, six mothers waited for word.

They did not yet know one another—or that they were soon to be forever linked by happenstance and history. At the end of March 1945 they were simply six random mothers among the 100,000 or so who waited for word from the Pacific. The newspapers, the radio, the newsreels at the movies had made it clear that a cataclysmic battle had occurred. Who survived, who was lost—this was still the great mystery.

Six mothers: to be linked, for a while, with a seventh, through a painful accident of misidentification.

In Weslaco, Texas, Belle Block felt that the word, in a sense, had already arrived, and the word was good. The Blocks had still not received Harlon's March 1 letter reporting that he had "come through without a scratch." But Belle felt secure. She felt an almost mystical connection to her boy because, as she was telling everyone, he was in the famous photograph. No one believed Belle; they asked her how she could know. But she did know, and because she knew, she felt somehow that Harlon was alive. Somehow The Photograph assured her that Harlon would not be killed.

On a windblown day, toward the end of the month, a telegram from the Commandant of the Marine Corps arrived, tolling otherwise.

———

Chapter opener: Rene Gagnon, his fiancée, Pauline Harnois, and Rene's mother, Irene Gagnon.

But even as grief, borne of telegrams, began to flow into households such as the Blocks', a different kind of current, a current of exaltation, gathered its own momentum in the nation. This current was borne of The Photograph. The Photograph seemed to illuminate the air around it; it released pulses of hope and pride and often tears in people who glimpsed it—even hard-headed people who would not think of themselves as susceptible to "inspirational" imagery.

The public needed to touch The Photograph, own it somehow, and place it among sacred objects. The San Francisco Chronicle offered "Color Versions Hand-Painted by Trained Artists," and sold out in a day. The California Legislature passed a resolution calling on the Post Office to issue an Iwo Jima Flagraising stamp to honor the bravery of the American fighting man. The AP in New York had established a "Joe Rosenthal desk" to handle the flood of inquiries about the photo. When the press wrote of it now, it was the "historic photo," the "famous photo," showing the "heroic" Marines raising the flag. There was almost no discussion of the facts surrounding the flagraising. The facts didn't matter. The photo looked heroic, and that was enough.

It was certainly enough for the Treasury Department. A two-front world war and the secret and fabulously expensive building of the atomic bomb had drained the national coffers. Filling them up again was not a simple matter of confiscation. In the 1940's concept of American democracy, war expenses were considered outside the normal federal budget. A wartime government was obliged to take its case repeatedly before the citizenry, keeping it accurately informed and hoping for a patriotic volunteer response.

War bonds were the chief mechanism for this volunteer funding, essentially a citizen's loan to the government. Purchase of a bond, at the issue price of $18.75, gave the government temporary use of the buyer's money; the buyer in turn could expect a yield, in ten years, of $25. The government stimulated these purchases through periodic national public relations efforts known as War Loan Drives. Each drive included newspaper and radio ads, direct mailing, and, as its centerpiece, a coast-to-coast barnstorming show featuring celebrities, war heroes, marching bands, and patriotic orators. These were known as Bond Tours.

Bond Tours had worked splendidly in the past. But this war had already produced six of them; and, with the European conflict drawing to a close, Treasury officials were concerned about the public's response to a seventh. The American people had dug deeply so far. Now, in March 1945, with Allied forces advancing toward Berlin, who could measure the sense of urgency that remained in an exhausted populace—or the reservoirs of wealth that still remained after six rounds of giving? Would there be enough to finance the unfinished business against the fanatical Japanese military in the Pacific—a conflict that still promised bloodshed on a massive scale? The Treasury Department was leaving nothing to chance.

Planning for the Seventh Tour had begun months before, a mammoth undertaking. Millions of volunteers were ready to move the glittering show through America. Now the anxious organizers at Treasury moved to secure the one element that could make The Seventh shine like no other tour ever: the presence of living figures from the beloved flagraising icon.

The President himself lent his influence to the plan.

Martha Strank was at home in her New-World "palace" at 121 Pine Street, Franklin Borough, Pennsylvania, when the Western Union deliveryman knocked. Telegrams were never welcome to women such as Martha. Two of her sons were on active duty: Mike on Iwo Jima, and Pete, a sailor aboard the USS *Franklin* in the Pacific.

Her young son John later described the way Martha stood in the doorway trying to figure how to deal with the presence of the Western Union man, the piece of yellow paper he held, the bad news she was certain it bore.

"She was so upset that she told the man, 'You open it,'" John recalled. " 'I can't do that,' he responded. 'But I want you to,' she said. She was pleading. He opened it and read it to her. She fainted.

John told me decades later:

"Her hair turned white within a couple of months. It had been coal black before Mike died."

As the Treasury Department shaped its theme for the "Mighty 7th," it enjoyed the wholehearted support of Madison Avenue. Some twenty-two of America's best advertising agencies volunteered their ideas and marketing skills. Case-hardened professionals who had delighted in no-holds-barred competitions to sell soap, sedans, and cigarettes now pooled their talents to sell hope and patriotism. Along with the six million volunteers—about four percent of the total population—it was a mobilization of civilian talent as vast, in its own way, as the mobilization of the armada for the invasion itself. As graphic artists, copywriters, designers, and photographers created stunning and informative posters, brochures, and print advertisements, veteran account executives gave up their spare time to devise distinct campaigns for every imaginable population segment: farmers, housewives, factory workers, fishermen, business leaders—all were targeted with separate appeals.

In every campaign, however, there recurred the same luminous anchoring image.

It was an image the public had fallen in love with, seeming to find in it an affirmation of the national purpose at its very origins that no politician, no history book had ever matched. The Photograph had become The Fact. It had, in a way, become its admirers. The Mighty 7th would make this triumphal joining complete.

And now the ailing Roosevelt made the gesture that would assure this joining. On March 30 the popular President, who as a distant caped figure had watched the boys of the 5th Division train for Iwo Jima a seeming lifetime ago, issued a confidential order that was radioed instantly to Marine Headquarters in the Pacific: TRANSFER IMMEDIATELY TO U.S. BY AIR . . . 6 ENLISTED MEN AND/OR OFFICERS WHO ACTUALLY APPEAR IN ROSENTHAL PHOTOGRAPH OF FLAGRAISING AT MOUNT SURIBACHI.

President Roosevelt's order found the survivors of Easy Company four days out of Iwo aboard the *Winged Arrow*. Marine correspondent Keyes Beech's cursory investigation had identified only one flagraiser on the boat: Rene Gagnon. Mike, Franklin, and the misidentified Hank Hansen were dead; Harlon had not yet been considered; and no one was sure about Doc. Ira was on the boat, but no one yet realized that he was a flagraiser. If Ira had his way, no one was going to.

Ira knew that he was in the photo, and he knew that Rene knew; and Ira had looked into his own soul and found no pleasure in this knowledge. He just wanted to stay with his good buddies. Ira sought Rene out and took him aside. The intense combat veteran told the teenage errand-boy that he didn't want to go on a Bond Tour. And furthermore, that if Rene revealed that Ira was in The Photograph, Ira would kill him.

This made an impression on Rene.

By concealing his identity, Ira was disobeying his Commander in Chief—a dire breach of discipline for a Marine. But Ira could think of no other choice. What were these people thinking? Could they possibly understand the insane difference between what he and his buddies had just endured, and what they were now asking him to do? The idea of going around the country being congratulated for his presence in a photograph, following a month of witnessing death and incessant killing, simply did not connect with his rural, tribal, almost nineteenth-century frame of reference. His memories of Iwo Jima had nothing to do with The Photograph. It certainly didn't jibe with what it meant to be a Marine. And his grasp of the larger American culture had no grounding in the emerging power of media or the photographic image.

It must have been like coming home from hell, and finding that he had arrived on the wrong planet.

Whatever the motivation, Rene was not about to challenge the baleful veteran. He agreed to keep Ira's secret, and the *Winged Arrow* churned for Eniwetok in the Marshall Islands. There, on April 3, Rene bade farewell to his comrades-in-arms. He climbed aboard a priority flight for the States. Thirty-four years later, Rene could still crow about how a colonel was asked to give up his seat so he could board. "Me, a lousy private, bumping a full bird colonel!"

He wouldn't be a "lousy private" much longer. Soon he would be the most famous fighting man in America. Among the three surviving flag-raisers, he would be the first to face the flashbulbs. Doc, his legs peppered with shrapnel, had been evacuated to Guam and now he lay convalescing in a hospital in Honolulu. Ira, keeping mum, was still with Easy, on a transport ship bound for Hilo. Rene was on a date with destiny all by himself.

He landed in Washington on Saturday, April 7. A waiting car rushed him directly to Marine Corps Headquarters. There, in a large conference room scattered with note-taking staff people and dominated by a blown-up reproduction of the Rosenthal photograph, the Marine brass pressed the new hero for the identities of the flagraisers. As he had done for Keyes Beech on the island, Rene offered five names: Strank, Bradley, Sousley, the misidentified Hansen, and himself.

But the enlarged photo showed six figures. "Who is the sixth man?"

Rene froze, staring at the photo for long silent minutes. Yes, he eventually admitted, it appears there are six. "Who is the sixth man?" Rene's hands began to shake. He knew who it was but had promised not to tell, Rene informed his interrogators. Impossible, they countered, they were all under Presidential orders.

Slowly, painfully Rene finally gave up his secret. Orders were flashed to the Pacific to bring back the sixth man. Ira's days as just another Marine were over.

Meanwhile, a Manchester *Union-Leader* newspaperman, alerted by an AP wire story, knocked on Irene Gagnon's front door. Rene's mother cried with relief and joy to learn her only boy was not only alive, but a hero.

The reporter suggested that he drive Irene to Pauline's house for a photo of the hero's mother and girlfriend together. And so, across the front page of the April 7 *Union-Leader* were splashed two oversized photographs: Rene's formal Marine Corps portrait and a shot of an "electrified" mom and fiancée: Irene Gagnon and nineteen-year-old Pauline Harnois.

When the reporter asked Pauline if she knew Rene was in the famous photo, she replied without hesitation: "I was almost sure in my heart that it was Rene. I guess," Pauline concluded, "it was woman's intuition."

Her intuition must have been remarkable, because Rene is almost completely obscured in the photo. Only the tip of his helmet, one knee, and his hands are visible behind John Bradley's figure.

Within days Pauline, the day-to-day worker in the Chicopee mills, was enjoying a new national nickname: She was "The Sweetheart of Iwo Jima."

On Sunday, April 8, the Marines released the identification of the six figures as given by Rene. The next day the photo reappeared in newspapers across the country, this time with a name linked by arrow to each flag-raiser, save one. The AP copy provided detailed biographies of five of the boys: Hank Hansen, Doc, Ira, Rene, and Mike. Only Franklin, killed on March 21, remained unidentified, pending notification of his mother.

On Monday, April 9, his mother was notified.

Goldie's last name was no longer Sousley. She'd remarried, to a man named Hensley Price. Nor did her household have a telephone. Still, the Marines found her with prompt efficiency.

After Goldie got the news, it spread fast around the region.

Marion Hamm had graduated from high school by now, but in her bedroom she still kept Franklin's formal Marine portrait.

She learned of Franklin's death while at work as a secretary. "When I found out, I was so sad," she told me in her direct, plainspoken way. "I went home from work and took all his letters, the insignia from his hat he had sent me, everything, and walked it over to Goldie's house. I gave it all to her. I said, 'I thought you might want these things.' "

Young J. B. Shannon, who had accompanied Franklin on his last train trip out of Hilltop—the trip on which Franklin promised, "When I come back, I'll be a hero"—remembers the moment he heard: "I was thirteen years old, plowing our field, breaking up the soil to plant tobacco. My mother came out and told me that Franklin was dead. I was very broken up. I unhooked the horses; I couldn't work anymore."

But it was Goldie's own reaction that Hilltop would remember the longest, and with the greatest sorrow. Goldie, who still put in long days of farm work, just as she had when Franklin was a little boy. Goldie, who had beamed her radiant smile through all of it; who always had an encouraging word for others.

Her freckled son had inherited that smile, and a reminder of it was on display in her living room: a glossy photograph of Franklin in uniform, movie-star handsome and smiling to beat the band. People who knew her said that Goldie often turned that photograph over to read the words he'd written on the back:

> *To the kindest friend I ever knew,*
> *The one I told all my troubles to.*
> *You can look the world over, but you won't find another*
> *Like you, my dear Mother.*
>
> > *Love,*
> > *Franklin*

The telegram came to the Hilltop General Store. Because Goldie didn't have a phone, a barefoot young boy ran it up to her farm.

Fifty-three years later Goldie's sister Florine Moran told me that the neighbors could hear Goldie scream all that night and into the morning. The neighbors lived a quarter-mile away.

In Pennsylvania, the news of Mike Strank's death was followed quickly by the revelation of his place in the iconic image. Brother John remembered how. "We were walking home from a memorial service for Mike," he said. "We saw people all around our house. It was mass confusion with neighbors and local press. I was wondering, 'What's happening?' Then they told us the story had just broken that Mike was in the photo."

Far to the northwest, in rural Wisconsin, Kathryn and Cabbage's neighbors called with their congratulations. Cabbage basked in his son's fame, but Kathryn—closer to her son in temperament—worried about appearing immodest.

Soon, she found something else to worry about. When she had learned her Jack was in the photo, she reread some of the recent days' press coverage about the event. She discovered the AP story datelined "Pearl Harbor" about Rene coming home, which had reported: "There are six men in the historic photo—five Marines and one Navy hospital corpsman." Then the dispatch added the chilling sentence: "The Navy man later lost a leg in battle."

Yet another error: The Navy man had not lost a leg. But he was indeed bedridden in a Honolulu hospital when he first glimpsed The Photograph. Years later, he recounted his reaction.

"I thought, 'Holy man, is that ever a terrific picture!'" he recalled. "There was a lot of confusion. We weren't sure who the flagraisers were. I couldn't pick myself out. It was such an insignificant thing at the time."

Insignificant to the boys in the Pacific, but not to the America that awaited their return. Doc Bradley's life was about to start changing fast. Just before it did—on the eve of his homecoming—Doc received a visit from his longtime friend Bob Connelly.

"I searched for your dad in the hospital there," Connelly told me. "I was walking through a ward when someone shouted at me. There he was, with his legs bandaged. He was very alert, very talkative. He told me that in the beginning of the battle he'd call for guys to cover him and heads would pop up, giving him covering fire. But as the battle went on, the replacements were too scared to cover him.

"He told me of running out to pull a wounded guy in and how he turned his back to the firing Japanese to protect his jewels.

"He talked about all the bodies laid out on the beach and how the Polish kid from Milwaukee was tortured. How they hammered his teeth, cut out his tongue, poked out his eyes, cut his ears off, almost dismembered him.

"He was aware that the photo was causing a ruckus. I admired his Marine boots. He said, 'Take them. The Marine Corps will give me anything now.'"

On the same day, April 9, word reached the *Winged Arrow* that Ira's days of anonymity were over. Sergeant Daskalakis was livid. "Why the hell didn't you tell me that you were in the photograph!?" he demanded of Ira. Ira could only shrug and mutter, "Oh, I don't know."

The transport put in at Hilo on April 12. Three days later, Ira reluctantly climbed aboard a plane for Marine Headquarters in Washington.

In Boston, the newspapers unknowingly began to perpetuate the single most tragic and painful of all the errors that adhered to the flagraising on Iwo Jima. The coverage offered solace—temporary solace, as it proved—to Hank Hansen's grieving mother, Mrs. Joseph Evelley. Mustering a smile, she proudly held The Photograph for a reporter to see:

"See, see the photograph," Madeline Evelley insisted. "That's my son, with his left hand gripped around the flag's staff. Henry put the American flag up on Iwo Jima."

In Weslaco, Belle Block remained unconvinced by this assertion. When Ed Block, Sr., showed the photo to her, with Hansen's identification attached, she just shook her head. "I don't care what the papers say," she repeated for perhaps the hundredth time. "I know my boy."

Joe Rosenthal, a modest man who did not seek attention, continued to struggle with the price of his new fame. He always made clear that his photo was of the second raising; never discounted the factor of luck. Yet the occasional detractor surfaced, amidst the general flow of praise.

A commentator on the NBC Blue network baldly asserted that the image had been "carefully posed" by Joe. The assertion was later retracted, and the photographer tried to take it in stride. "It wouldn't have been any disgrace at all," he told *The New Yorker* in its April 7 issue, "to figure out a composition like that. But it just so happened I didn't. Good luck was with me, that's all—the wind rippling the flag right, the men in fine positions, and the day clear enough to bring everything into sharp focus."

Before the flagraisers were known, the photo stood for a great military victory. Now, with names attached to all six figures, the public began to see in it a manifestation of eternal American values.

At the outset, it was Rene who satisfied America's thirst for humanizing details of the figures in The Photograph. With Ira impenetrable and John Bradley not yet in focus, it was the lean-faced, dark-browed Manchester boy, his mother and fiancée at his side, who confirmed the fondest elements of American wartime myth: the fighting hero as wholesome boy-next-door, eager for marriage, picket fences, and Mom's cooking.

The governor visited the Gagnon house and sat at Irene's kitchen table. Rene addressed a wildly cheering New Hampshire Legislature. He visited a local Cub Scout pack and signed hundreds of autographs.

The crowning event was scheduled for Thursday, April 12. Rene awoke that morning excited by the prospect of a boy's dream come true: His hometown was going to throw a parade in his honor. Bands, church leaders, and politicians from around the state were flocking into Manchester to take part. The disconnected kid from a broken family, the mill-factory "doffer" who had become a Marine Corps runner, had made it to the top of that world. Instead of drifting down Elm Street alone, on his way to the movies, looking at his reflection in store windows, Rene Gagnon was going in style, in an open limousine. And the crowds would do the looking.

It was not to be. A preliminary banquet went off as planned at six P.M. But then a shocking announcement changed everything. A news bulletin had flashed across the radio airwaves and was relayed to the banquet hall. The President was dead. Franklin Delano Roosevelt had succumbed to a cerebral hemorrhage at Warm Springs, Georgia. He had been wearing a certain dark cape when the seizure hit him, as he sat for a portrait in the living room of his cottage there.

Rene's ride in the open limousine never happened. The letdown would form a motif for his abbreviated life: The parade he always sought would never quite get under way.

Jack Bradley slipped back into America without much fanfare. When he arrived in Bethesda he called home, speaking with his parents for the first time in months. He talked matter-of-factly of his wounds, and of how he was brought back to Washington by Presidential order. After the conversation, Kathryn was strangely sad. For a long time, she kept the reason to herself: She thought her son was trying not to hurt her feelings by speaking of the leg he had lost.

In Wisconsin, the State Senate passed a resolution on April 12, praising "John Bradley" as one who "helped plant the American flag on Mount Suribachi." "Doc" was the nickname he would soon put aside, along with his wartime mementos. "Jack" he would still remain to his family and his Wisconsin friends; but it was as "John" he'd be introduced to all who met him from now on.

On Thursday, April 19, the final living flagraiser touched down in Washington. Ira arrived to find Rene, down from New Hampshire, and John, over from Bethesda on his crutches, awaiting him. Up to now the three had been serving the War Department. But now, by Presidential order, their services were transferred to the Treasury Department in a new battle, this one for money. And the Treasury Department did not believe in a gradual start: On the following day the three were to meet the new President, Harry Truman, in the White House.

During Ira's initial briefing at Marine Barracks, at Eighth and I Streets, he was shown the enlarged photograph of the flagraising. Ira spotted the error of identification immediately. The figure at the base of the pole was not Hank Hansen; it was Harlon Block. Ira remembered what Rene Gagnon and John Bradley could not have remembered, because they did not join the little cluster until the last moment: that it was Harlon, Mike, Franklin, and himself who had ascended Suribachi at midmorning to lay telephone wire; it was Rene who had come along with the replacement flag. Hansen had not been a part of this action.

Ira acted on his first impulse, which was to set the record straight. He pointed out the error to the Marine public relations officer who'd been assigned to keep an eye on the young Pima. The officer's response stunned Ira: He was ordered to keep his mouth shut. It was too late to do anything; the report had already been released.

L. B. Holly, who kept in touch with Ira for years afterward, told me: "When he got to Washington, Ira told them it wasn't Hansen, that it was Harlon. A corporal told Ira to be quiet, that everyone had been identified. Ira later told me he was very upset to be ordered to lie. He said he complained but there was nothing he could do."

Ira was ill at ease upon his reunion with Rene. He did not kill his former Easy Company mate, as he had sworn to do. But he didn't forgive him for snitching, either. He gave the younger boy the silent treatment, speaking to him only through my father.

The American public never glimpsed this rift. To the crowds, the boys were like the Three Musketeers. Except that they had a different collective name: Sometimes they were the "Iwo Jima flagraising heroes"; usually, they were simply "the heroes."

It must have felt surreal to the boys. Heroes? They had just returned from the protracted horrors of one of the deadliest and most intense battles in history, where heroes around them had acted with unimaginable bravery, suffered, and died almost by the minute. And here was an American populace driving itself into a frenzy over . . . what? Over an accidental photograph of a forgotten moment, an insignificant gesture in a month filled with significant ones.

As Ira would write, in wonderment, in a letter to his parents: "It's funny what a picture can do."

The first day of their official "heroism" began early and accelerated rapidly. Up the White House stairs, past the saluting guards, down the historic halls lined with applauding government employees, and into the Oval Office at 9:15 A.M. sharp. The new President already had risen from his desk to welcome them.

"I was very nervous before going in to meet the Commander in Chief," John told the *Boston Globe* afterward. "But after I got in, I felt no different than going into an office in my own hometown to meet a local businessman."

The boys presented Mr. Truman with the "first" copy of the official Bond

Tour poster in a gold frame. Truman, smiling, asked the boys to point themselves out on the poster as photographers clicked off photo after photo—
front-page news for the next day and publicity beyond value for the
Seventh Bond Tour. The President thanked them for the important duty
they were about to perform for their country. He grasped John's hand and
then Rene's, calling them heroes. Then he turned to Ira and said, "You are a
true American because you are an American Indian. And now, son, you are
a true American hero."

Next on their itinerary was the U.S. Senate. Senator A. B. "Happy" Chandler of Kentucky informed his colleagues that the heroes of "one of the
great pictures of American history" waited outside the chamber: "I ask
unanimous consent that the three young men be escorted into the Senate
Chamber so that they may be honored." The boys trooped in, the Senate
stood in recess, and its august members rose and applauded, then lined up
and jostled like so many Cub Scouts to meet John, Rene, and Ira. In the
midst of these high good feelings, Ira Hayes briefly revealed his unvarnished
side—the self-conscious outsider who could never quite learn to disguise his
honest bluntness.

A Senator from a Western state hurried up to him, hand outstretched,
babbling on in what he apparently believed to be the authentic Pima
tongue. Ira stared stonily at him for a moment, then inquired, with a terrible directness, "What do you want?"

The moment passed, and Speaker of the House Sam Rayburn swept the
boys toward a luncheon in their honor at the Capitol.

That evening, Rayburn escorted them to Griffith Stadium for the
Washington Senators' season-opener against the Yankees. Spectators' eyes
turned to the three uniformed young men, one of them on crutches, as they
settled into choice box seats not far from home plate.

The Speaker threw out the first ball. Then, before the first batter stepped
in, a spotlight bathed the three boys in a silvery glow as the public-address
announcer's words echoed around the stadium:

"Ladies and gentlemen! You've all seen pictures of six Americans raising
our flag on Iwo Jima! Three of them survive! These are the three—Marine
Private Gagnon, Marine Private Hayes, and Pharmacist's Mate Second
Class Bradley!"

Some 24,000 fans rose and gave the boys an ovation.

As the three survivors came to terms with their unreal celebrity life, in Weslaco the Blocks were finally coming to terms with Harlon's very real death. Belle had finally admitted to herself that Harlon wouldn't come back. But she was as insistent about Harlon's rightful place in The Photograph as Ira was desirous of escaping his.

Belle's husband was imprisoned inside his stoic German grief. Harlon and Ed Sr. had become friends in the year they drove those oil trucks together. And Ed had lived vicariously through Harlon's exploits on the football field.

Ed didn't cry, didn't express his grief in words. But a friend of his son Corky, Dale Collins, remembered noticing a sign of the pain Ed kept inside:

"In church there was a table in front with little U.S. flags representing the boys of the congregation that had gone off to war. If they were killed they got a gold flag. I'll never forget that Mr. Block would sit in a far right pew, positioned so he couldn't see Harlon's flag."

But life had to go on: the lives of the survivors, the life of the nation. The grieving Ed Block could never have imagined the great burden that Harlon's three comrades carried with them as they prepared for the marathon of the Seventh Bond Tour. Quite likely, the boys themselves did not fully imagine it.

But others did. At the end of the boys' meeting with Harry Truman, Treasury Secretary Morgenthau lingered with the new President—just long enough to present him with some dire numbers. The war had now devoured $88 billion out of a fiscal year budget of $99 billion. But government revenue receipts totaled only $46 billion.

It was critical that the Seventh Bond Tour bring in some big numbers.

Sixteen

THE MIGHTY 7TH

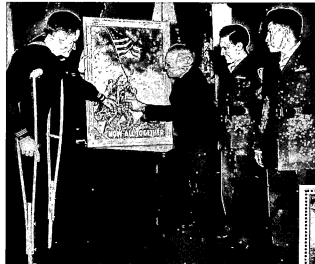

Left: Oval Office, April 20, 1945. Doc Bradley, Harry Truman, Rene Gagnon, and Ira Hayes with the Seventh Bond Tour poster. *Below:* Iwo Jima three-cent stamp, issued July 11, 1945. More than 150 million were sold.

A smoke before raising the flag for 50,000 fans in Soldier Field, Chicago, May 20, 1945. *From left to right:* Ira Hayes, Jack Bradley, and Rene Gagnon.

Doc Bradley raises the flag as Rene Gagnon and Ira Hayes look on in Times Square, New York City, May 11, 1945.

Wall Street, May 15, 1945. The flagraisers with the "Gold Star" mothers. *From left to right:* Madeline Evelley (mother of the misidentified Hank Hansen), Goldie Price (Franklin Sousley's mother), Martha Strank (Mike Strank's mother), Rene Gagnon, Doc Bradley, Ira Hayes, Emil Schram (president, New York Stock Exchange).

Doc Bradley and Rene Gagnon greeted by the Lockheed Girls at the Los Angeles airport June 9, 1945.

Harlon Block's funeral cortege, Weslaco, Texas, 1947. The casket is flanked by Harlon's Weslaco Panthers teammates.

Ira, Nancy, and Jobe Hayes.

Pauline, Rene, and Rene
Gagnon, Jr., dedicate the
Iwo Jima Motel, Arlington,
Virginia.

Elizabeth Van Gorp marries
John Bradley, May 4, 1946.

Pauline and Rene Gagnon en
route to Iwo Jima, 1965.

John Wayne and John Bradley on the set of *The Sands of Iwo Jima*, 1949.

John Wayne hands Rene Gagnon the flag as Ira Hayes and John Bradley look on.

Left: Felix de Weldon sculpting Rene Gagnon. *Below:* De Weldon with Rene Gagnon, Ira Hayes, and John Bradley.

Top: U.S. Marine Corps Memorial, Arlington, Virginia. Bottom: Dedication of
the U.S. Marine Corps Memorial, November 10, 1954. From left to right: John
Bradley, Goldie Price (mother of Franklin Sousley), Richard Nixon, Belle Block
(mother of Harlon Block), Rene Gagnon, Ira Hayes.

Ira Hayes in jail,
Chicago, 1953.

Rene Gagnon.

John Bradley,
Memorial Day
parade, Antigo,
Wisconsin.

Iwo Jima today.

The Bradleys with com-
memorative plaque atop
Mount Suribachi, April
1998. *From left to right:*
Betty, Steve, James, Joe,
and Mark.

The Bradleys in a Japanese blockhouse, Iwo Jima, 1998. *From left to right:* Steve,
Joe, James, Mark, and Betty.

It's funny what a picture can do.
                                    —IRA HAYES

FOURTEEN BILLION DOLLARS, TO BE EXACT. That was the monetary goal set by Treasury for the Seventh Bond Tour. Seven billion from companies and businesses, and seven billion from individuals.

Fourteen billion: a sum equaling the highest goal of any of the eight bond drives of World War II. A sum larger than the government's expenditures in prewar 1941 and equaling a full quarter of its budget for fiscal 1946.

Fourteen billion to keep feeding, clothing, sheltering, and arming the millions of men and women still fighting World War II, and provide more planes, ships, and tanks for their effort. Fourteen billion for a war that was costing $250 million a day; $175,000 a minute; a war being waged mostly now against a Pacific enemy whose population was still replacing its armies' destruction rate of a quarter million men a year.

Fourteen billion to be solicited from a population of 160 million: nearly one hundred dollars, on average, from every man, woman, and child in America. This in a country where an annual income of seventeen hundred dollars comfortably supported a family of four; where a Harvard education cost a thousand dollars; where a hotel room in New York could be had for three dollars; where a good breakfast cost thirty-two cents.

A mountain of money that must have seemed as formidable, in its own way, as Suribachi. And now the three surviving flagraisers would lead the charge to take that mountain.

Bond Tours enjoyed a cherished place in American tradition of the

---

Chapter opener: The Seventh Bond Tour poster.

time. Their goal was twofold: to call attention to the wartime need for purchasing government bonds, and to stimulate citizens to leave their homes and offices and head for one of the many "buying booths" scattered about towns and cities, where the actual paper could be purchased. That was where the color and pageantry came in.

National in scope, local in flavor, Bond Tours combined the old-fashioned elements of vaudeville, the county fair, the Fourth of July parade. And they anticipated some of the flash and crowd-pleasing fervor that would accrue, not too many years later, to Elvis, the Beatles, and the Rolling Stones.

As families gathered, squinting and waving flags along the Main Streets and Broadways of the nation, columns of soldiers and marching bands would troop past, followed by open vehicles filled with waving movie stars and decorated war heroes. Mock battles would be fought in city parks and athletic stadiums. And speakers' platforms would display a lineup of politicians, celebrities, and local heroes, many of them missing an arm or a leg, everyone exhorting the crowds to be a part of things, support their country, buy a bond.

This was the ponderous challenge—and the incomparable excitement—of reaching a mass public in an age before television: a great roving road show that would personify the war's realities and deliver them to Americans' home precincts. An effort by the government to communicate almost face-to-face with as many of its citizens as possible, and to make its case for voluntary sacrifices, rather than simply confiscate the needed money through taxes. A gargantuan feat of popular democracy, the likes of which have since vanished from the culture.

The Seventh Bond Tour—the Mighty 7th—would have all the features of the six previous drives, and more. The Mighty 7th would have as its emblem the most famous image in the history of photography. And the 7th would exhibit, for public view, three of the six figures from that almost-holy frieze.

As the Seventh moved toward its May 9 kickoff in Washington—it would storm through thirty-three cities before winding up back in the nation's capital on July 4—The Photograph's mystical hold on the nation continued to deepen.

Detached—liberated—even from the merely factual circumstances that produced it, The Photograph had become a receptacle for America's emotions; it stood for everything good that Americans wanted it to stand for; it had begun to act as a great crystal prism, drawing the light of all America's values into its facets, and giving off a brilliant rainbow of feeling and thoughts.

An entrepreneur offered the Associated Press $200,000 for the rights to the photo. A Congressman, W. Sterling Cole of New York, declared that it should become "public property"—it meant too much to the nation to be used for mere commerce. The AP finally decided to donate the rights to the photo to the government, with royalties going to a sailors' retirement fund.

The sculptor Felix de Weldon went to work on a larger model of his flag-raising monument. And in Times Square, the crossroads of the world, a five-story flagraising statue was being installed.

On Tuesday, May 8, the newspapers trumpeted the biggest news yet in the war: Germany had surrendered. And still a development regarding The Photograph worked its way onto the front page of *The New York Times*: Joe Rosenthal had won a Pulitzer Prize.

A Pulitzer submission for work done in 1945 normally would not be eligible for a prize until 1946. But for the first and only time the trustees of Columbia University suspended the rules "for this distinguished example," declaring "Joe Rosenthal's famous photograph of the flagraising on Iwo depicts one of the war's great moments," a "frozen flash of history" caught by his camera.

Bright sunshine and soft spring breezes graced the Mighty 7th's opening ceremonies in Washington the next day. As military brass glittered, tubas *oom-pahed* and flags undulated overhead, members of the President's Cabinet and of both Houses assembled outside the Capitol Building to wish the tour godspeed.

After some speeches and introductions, the crowning event unfolded. As official Washington silently saluted, the Marine Band played "The Star-Spangled Banner." Rene stood at ramrod attention, while John and Ira pulled a guide rope to hoist the American flag over the Capitol dome. In raising it there, the boys were introducing a new national relic into American history.

Within a few hours, Ira, Rene, and John—now "immortal heroes"—would hit the road with their sacred relic to inspire the populace.

They boarded a train bound for New York. As they traveled, Treasury Secretary Morgenthau and Commandant Vandegrift commented on their journey in a national broadcast from a Washington studio with Bob Hope as host. Hope then sang a duet with Bing Crosby via a remote hookup with Hollywood. The song was one that disc jockeys all over the country would play for months afterward: Crosby's recording of "Buy, Buy Bonds."

The boys did not travel unsupervised. Accompanying them was their chaperon: Keyes Beech, the Marine correspondent. Ira explained Beech's role in a letter home to his parents: "Four of us are on this trip. Gagnon, Bradley and Tech. Sgt. Beech, who is watching over us and taking care of our traveling business. He's a swell guy and I like him."

Ira liked Beech for a number of reasons, including several wrong ones. Paramount among them was the fact that Keyes reinforced Ira's soggy notions of a good time. George McArthur, Beech's good friend in later life, told me, "Keyes was a big drinker. He was a drop-dead alcoholic until he joined Alcoholics Anonymous in the 1960's. He used to tell me that he and Ira drank every night on the Bond Tour and that his main job was to get Ira to the scheduled events."

The boys disembarked at Grand Central Station to a huge applauding reception committee. They gaped at blowups of the Bond Tour poster that papered the cavernous Main Hall. Whisked ten blocks up Park Avenue to the Waldorf-Astoria, the boys passed likenesses of themselves that seemed to cover just about every surface in the city.

Nearly every New Yorker had beheld those likenesses. The bond poster fluttered from street lamps; it adorned buses and taxicabs; it festooned the windows of banks, factories, post offices, and department stores. In the most tangible of ways, the boys' reputation had preceded them.

Another reproduction of the image was draped above the Waldorf's entrance. As the boys entered the lobby, the staff of the world-famous hotel lined their path and applauded.

As soon as he'd settled in his room, a dazzled John Bradley grabbed a sheet of Waldorf stationery and dashed off a note home:

> Dear Mom, Dad & all,
>   We just arrived at New York and look where we're hanging our hats. Boy, what a swanky joint. I couldn't pay for room if I had $100. All our meals are free and valet service also . . . I'm really all excited about the whole affair so if I don't sound like myself, you'll know why.

At about the same time, Ira was likewise scribbling away:

> Dear Parents and Brothers,
>   We just arrived here in NYC about 2 hours ago from Washington. I can't hardly realize I'm here in the most famous hotel in the world. But I am . . .
>   Tomorrow is a big day. We go to the Roxy Theater in the morning and

*make an appearance. Then we go to Times Square to unveil the monument
of the flagraising on Iwo, which is 25 feet high. And then the dinner to be
held in our honor in the evening. Then we leave for Philadelphia and Boston
and back here in New York. So you see we will be busy.*

> *Your excited but happy son . . .*
> *Ira H. Hayes*

New York City's bond sales goal was $287 million, and the boys' schedule
was crammed. They commenced their roles as tour celebrities on Thursday
morning with an autograph-signing session at the Roxy Theater in Times
Square. Their admirers crowded the lobby, gaping at the boys beneath a
huge enlargement of Rosenthal's photograph, which had been wedged between smaller portraits of Roosevelt and Truman.

Meanwhile, fund-raising events blossomed around the city. At the Astor,
representatives of the ready-to-wear industry enthusiastically pledged to
raise $100 million. Life insurance executives, dining elsewhere, pledged the
efforts of thirty thousand New York area agents to the cause.

But the big show unfurled Friday, May 11, in Times Square. There, with
Mayor Fiorello La Guardia and tens of thousands of New Yorkers looking
on, the five-story Iwo statue was unveiled. The *Times* coverage the next day
featured a photograph of John raising the flag over the statue as Rene, Ira,
Commandant Vandegrift, and the mayor saluted.

Again and again, despite abundant opportunity, the three boys refused to
pick up the theme of press and speechmakers and portray themselves as
valiant warriors who hoisted the colors against sheets of enemy fire. New
York reporters threw the first of many chances to them. But the three chose
instead to tell the unadorned truth: They had simply put up a replacement
flag. A bit sourly, perhaps, the *Times* reported that the three "looked a bit
harried and confessed that appearing for the Seventh War Loan Drive 'is
not as much fun as it would seem.' "

Clearly, modesty wasn't enough for the aggressive urban press. Glory was
the thing that sold papers. The press wanted tales of blood-and-guts heroism from the living icons in front of them. It was my father who finally cut
the reporters off at one impromptu press conference. They should just report the truth, John Bradley said: "It took everyone on that island and the
men on the ships offshore to get the flag up on Suribachi."

Ira learned to take refuge from such ordeals in his beloved bottle. His
drunkenness created acute demands on his equally bibulous chaperon. At a
banquet that night, Beech struggled to keep the befogged Ira conscious
enough to "say a few words" when his turn came. Beech later wrote:

There is something disconcerting about presenting to an audience a man who is gently snoozing at your side. But the Chief always came to life when I mentioned his name.

He would stand, acknowledge the introduction with a prodigious yawn, which invariably brought a mass response from the audience, then sit down and go back to sleep.

Ira was a hell of a good fighting man, but he wasn't the kind of guy you'd pick to send on a Bond Tour. His drinking, Beech believed, was a defense against his own insecurity.

On Saturday, cheering crowds in Philadelphia got a glimpse of the boys as their motorcade sped to Independence Hall, where they posed for the flash-bulbs in front of the Liberty Bell. The press fished for a fantastical story, but the three offered the only one they could remember, mostly about the first flagraising.

And once again, the press probed for a hotter angle. One reporter, offering no proof, mentioned a rumor that the photo was posed. The boys, refusing to go along with the hyperbole, fired back that "the picture was entirely spontaneous."

The next stop was Boston, where a shocking discovery reminded every-one how real, and how close, the war could be: Three German submarines had been captured just off the coast, and were being towed into Boston Har-bor for surrender.

All of which gave fresh significance to the Bond Tour. The Massachu-setts goal was $700 million, and Hollywood stars—including Joan Fontaine and Jane Wyman, then the wife of Ronald Reagan—had been trickling into town to add glamour to the festivities.

Miss Fontaine and Miss Wyman found themselves upstaged by a most brazen amateur. As the Boston press corps milled in a roped-off area at South Station on Sunday morning, waiting for the boys' train to arrive, an attractive young woman appeared out of nowhere and marched up to them. In a distinct New Hampshire accent, she informed the reporters that she was here to meet her "hero-fiancé," and suggested that they might want to get a photo of the happy reunion.

It was Pauline, who had made the trip from Manchester to Boston on her own initiative. When the train pulled in, she swooped forward to greet the nonplussed Ira, John, and Rene as they alighted. And became the star of the day.

Her bold ploy did not go over well with the other two. Ira, whose discomfort amidst women was deeply ingrained, thought it vulgar for Pauline to be pursuing Rene so publicly. John, the conservative Catholic, did not approve of an unchaperoned single woman in their midst.

None of it mattered to Pauline, who recognized her ticket out of the mills. Almost as soon as Rene had come home, she'd begun pressuring him to marry her.

Irene Gagnon tried to protect her son from Pauline's onslaught. "Irene told my dad, 'Don't get married so young, don't be stupid,'" Rene Jr. told me. "'You're traveling on the Bond Tour. Wait. Come home and think it over.'

"But Pauline pushed him. When my dad came back as a hero, my mother lived on it. That meant she could travel and do more things. It became a big deal in her mind."

A torrential downpour did not keep 200,000 Bostonians from lining the parade route to applaud. The movie stars rode in jeeps that carried large placards identifying them; the boys rode in an unmarked car. No ID was needed.

They raised the flag over the statehouse with the governor, and with 100,000 Bostonians observed simulated military maneuvers on the Boston Common. Speaker after speaker spoke of the boys' gallantry.

And again, it was Ira who provided the unscripted spark. After the governor had introduced him as "the only man here who can claim to be a real American," Ira strolled to the microphone and brought the house down with: "I'm an Indian and I'm damn proud of it."

Ira was a curiosity to the press as well. The *Boston Globe* printed a story about how the "full-blooded Pima Indian from Arizona . . . feels more at home with a tommy gun in his hand than he does before a microphone." The thrust was that "with the memory of his many buddies killed and wounded on Iwo Jima and with plenty of war against the enemy Japs still ahead of us, Ira didn't want to come back."

This made for stirring copy, but wasn't quite accurate. Ira liked many things about the Bond Tour, especially the late nights. In fact he enjoyed almost everything about the tour except his main assignment: talking to the press and public.

On Monday afternoon, May 14, the three "heroes" rolled back into New York for ceremonies that would spotlight a dramatic Wall Street war-bond pledge of staggering proportions. An added tier of distinction marked this return visit: Joining Ira, John, and Rene on the speakers' platforms would be the mothers of the three fallen flagraisers.

John Strank escorted his mother, Martha, from Franklin Borough, Pennsylvania, to the city. "My dad was just so broken up after Mike's death that he couldn't go," John recalled. "It was a challenge for my mother. She worried that her English was not good enough."

From Hilltop, Kentucky, Goldie—now Mrs. Hensley Price—arrived. She'd never before been more than 150 miles from home, she told a reporter. And from Somerville, Massachusetts, Mrs. Madeline Evelley, the mother of Hank Hansen, still identified as the sixth flagraiser, traveled to the city with her daughter Gertrude.

The combined entourage checked in at the Waldorf, where politicians and military brass doted on them. At dinner in the ballroom that evening, the Duke and Duchess of Windsor, perhaps the most famous couple in the world, petitioned a waiter for introductions to the three survivors.

But for Ira, John, and Rene, the personages who mattered were the three bereaved "Gold Star" mothers. ("Gold Stars" were banners displayed in the window of a slain serviceman's home.) "I remember Ira Hayes grabbing my mother; he was so emotional, he wouldn't let her go," said John Strank. "He was sobbing. It took a few people to get him off her."

My father and Mrs. Evelley gravitated toward each other. John had been Hank's close friend. He had rushed to Hansen when he was shot, and had tried to save his life. And now, here in the dash and glitter of a far different world, John at last was able to make the quiet gesture he had pledged to make amidst the smoke and slaughter of Iwo Jima: He withdrew from his pocket the watch that he had slipped from dead Hank's wrist, and placed it in Madeline's hands.

The next morning the mothers and the boys were ushered onto a reviewing balcony at the New York Stock Exchange. Trading was halted as the ticker sign flashed, WELCOME IWO JIMA HEROES, and the traders erupted in applause.

Thousands more awaited the group outside as marching bands encouraged a festive mood. Wall Street was jammed and office workers peered from their canyon windows through the sea of Bond Tour posters.

At the stroke of noon the music ceased, and the crowd hushed as three matronly women wearing dark orchids and dazed expressions were escorted to the platform.

Reporters noted the instant when the three women and the three Marines touched fingertips, a moment that "caused onlookers to fall silent and avert their eyes." The *Times* observed that "The survivors did not look at the posters, nor did the mothers of the fallen comrades."

The New York Stock Exchange president then announced a stunning pledge: The Wall Street Broker-Dealer Syndicate had committed itself to raise one billion dollars for the Seventh War Loan—enough to finance creation of a Superfortress fleet of sixteen hundred B-29's, geared to the destruction of Japan.

For the six guests of honor on the platform—the three flagraising "heroes" and the three bereaved mothers—this moment must have throbbed with wildly competing emotions.

The boys, so recently returned from battle, had not yet recovered from its ravages. My father was crying in his sleep. Ira was drinking hard. And Rene had developed a tic that would never go away. Yet here they were, the inspirations, at least in part, for an outpouring of wealth that might save thousands of American lives.

As for the mothers, they were still in a haze of grieving. From the families of the three, I have often heard it remarked that their grief could never end: The fact of The Photograph obliged them to relive it over and over again.

Massive throngs, a "million-dollar cast" of Hollywood stars, and three days of patriotic fervor awaited them in Chicago, where several hundred thousand public and parochial schoolchildren had become volunteer bond salespeople. The local sales goal was $327 million. Humphrey Bogart was in town, and Lauren Bacall, and Ida Lupino. And Pauline Harnois. Once again the New Hampshire girl elbowed her way into the spotlight, showing up unannounced on Friday as the train pulled in. Rene, sensing Ira's scorn and John's quiet disapproval, tried to make the best of it.

On Saturday, May 19, 100,000 cheering people crammed themselves into the Chicago Loop for a massive rally. Beside a huge painting of the familiar image, the boys went through their paces.

Again, it was John Bradley who injected the thoughtful note. Responding to the official welcome, my young father stepped to the microphone and repeated the terse message he had delivered in other cities:

"Men of the fighting fronts cannot understand the need for rallies to sell bonds for purchase of seriously needed supplies. The bond buyer is asked only to lend his money at a profit. The fighting man is asked to give his life."

The people in the crowd listened, and dug deep.

The crowning display was set for Sunday—"I Am an American Day," as sponsored by the Hearst newspapers. At Soldier Field, Hearst had financed the construction of a miniature Suribachi. Fifty thousand people would pour into the great stadium near the shores of Lake Michigan to watch a parade and glimpse such stars as Pat O'Brien, Forrest Tucker, and Henny Youngman.

But the real stars of the day would be three young men who had never made a movie, never recorded a song, and never told a joke before a microphone. And the 50,000 who came to watch them were moved by emotions far more profound than mere celebrity worship.

These, after all, were the Americans who formed the solid home front of World War II: the men and women who worked assembly lines to build the tanks and guns; who gave sons and daughters to the conflict; who collected paper and bottles and scrap iron for the war effort; who as priests and ministers gave solace; who as day-to-day citizens sacrificed their luxuries and their necessities in the cause of victory. Now, on one glorious afternoon, these solid-core Americans could flow together into one large red-white-and-blue celebratory mass—could stand in the sunshine with the heroes in the "immortal" frieze, and be as one with them.

One of the heroes, however, had been reenacting other pursuits. Ira turned up missing throughout Saturday night; the police finally found him walking the Loop after a night of drinking. Over his protests—he'd already raised one flag on Iwo, he didn't know why he had to raise another—Beech and others hauled him back to the hotel, poured ice water over him, and "slapped him into something resembling sobriety." The flagraising at Soldier Field was an hour away.

For the triumphal tour around the stadium in an open Cadillac, Beech made sure to wedge Ira between John and Rene so that he would not fall out. Observing all this from the reviewing stand was Commandant Vandegrift. Reports had reached the commandant that "the Indian" was creating a bad name for himself and the Corps. Something, it was clear, was going to be done about Ira Hayes.

He wobbled through the flagraising reenactment, joining John and Rene in hoisting the famous flag. And then Ira Hayes packed his bags and, with the others, made ready to hit the road again.

After several days in Detroit and Indianapolis, the tour returned to Chicago. From the Palmer House, on May 24, Ira wrote to his parents anticipating future stops in St. Louis and Tulsa; marveling at the gift of the $21 pen he was using to write the letter, and closing that he had to go down to breakfast. It was to be his last letter, and his last breakfast, on the tour.

Later that morning a Marine colonel telephoned Keyes Beech with an order to bring Ira to his office. In the reception area, Ira slumped in a chair with his hands in his pockets. When the colonel and a Marine captain arrived, the captain told Hayes to stand up. Sullenly, the young Pima got to his feet and faced the bad news.

He was to rejoin his unit, Easy Company, in the Pacific, Colonel Fordney told him. The orders had come from the commandant, Vandegrift. Ira was silent at first. Then he asked if he could visit his mother in Arizona en route. The colonel snapped that it would not be possible, and thrust a United Airlines ticket toward Beech.

The Marine Corps and Bond Tour officials gave Ira a face-saving cover—one that ironically confirmed his press image as a fighting man who yearned for active duty: He was being sent back overseas "at his own request."

The next morning as Rene, John, and Keyes Beech headed for St. Louis, Ira stopped off in San Francisco and wrote a letter home. Self-revealing in a way that few of his "tough-guy" statements to the press were, it showed the embarrassment, hurt pride, and frustrated yearning of a still-young, still-tender, and deeply wounded man:

> *Dear Parents & Brothers;*
>
> *This may shock you but do not be afraid. At the present I'm in San Francisco just got in this morning from Chicago. And leaving this morning for Pearl Harbor.*
>
> *There's supposed to be some show out there that's why Gen. Rockey wants me back there just for it. Then back here again to rejoin Gagnon, Bradley and Beech. So do not worry.*
>
> *Today Bradley & the others are in St. Louis and I sure wish I was with them. But that has to wait till later.*
>
> *Well I'll close here as I have a few things I'd like to do.*
>
> *God Bless all of you & please for my sake do not worry.*
>
> > *Your Loving Son & Bro.*
> > *I.H.H.*

The "show" that Ira alluded to was nothing less than the contemplated invasion of Japan, which was then in its building stages. By suggesting that the commanding general of Spearhead required his participation, Ira was making a grandiose—and tortured—grasp at camouflaging his humiliation.

Accumulated folklore has it that Ira was an innocent corrupted by the Bond Tour, that he hated every minute of it. But the truth is that when released from his promotional duties, he only wanted back on the tour.

St. Louis, Tulsa, San Antonio, Austin, Portland, Seattle. The cities began to blur. But the popular adulation, amplified by the newspapers, contrasted acutely with how the boys saw themselves. "We are not heroes," John

Bradley insisted in El Paso. He continued to insist that "anyone on the island could have been in the picture," and that "we didn't do anything out of the ordinary."

Rene was likewise humble: "Someone yelled, 'give us a hand,' so I did," was his typical interview line. He emphasized repeatedly that theirs was the second flagraising of the morning.

In fact, the boys had little to say about the replacement flagraising itself. There was, after all, little to say. The act had been so insignificant at the time, they had paid it little heed. John and Rene emphasized repeatedly that they "didn't know anything at all" about the presence of any photographer, and had as yet not even met Joe Rosenthal—"the guy who got us into all this." The boys talked far more about the first flagraising—recounting the efforts of Boots Thomas, Lieutenant Schrier, photographer Lou Lowery, and the rest.

None of it really registered. Ordinary prose, it seemed, no longer sufficed. The Photograph had transported many thousands of anxious, grieving, and war-weary Americans into a radiant state of mind: a kind of sacred realm, where faith, patriotism, mythic history, and the simple capacity to hope all intermingled.

And it reflected the epic regard in which the public held the boys—a regard that manifested itself repeatedly in the massive crowds the boys drew; the almost universal wish to touch them.

Meanwhile, some four thousand miles to the west, a fallen "immortal" was reconciling himself once again to the military life.

Ira had rejoined Easy Company in Hawaii—where the 5th Division was training for the invasion of Japan—clinging to the face-saving story that the Marines had allowed him: He "wanted to be with the boys."

He had breezed in with a swagger that he perhaps did not feel, a seabag full of autographed glossies of showgirls, and a greater thirst than he'd shown before the Bond Tour. "He had changed," said Lloyd Thompson, the first Easy man to spot him, grinning, in front of the company's office tent. "He'd get drunk and create problems. He was fairly straitlaced before."

His buddies had spilled out of their tents and greeted him with thumps on the back, and for a while he reigned as the toast of the 28th Regiment. But soon his comrades noticed that Ira was not really with them. "He'd take his allotment of six Saturday afternoon beers and take off alone," Thompson remembered. "He never drank with us."

Truth to tell, there were more strangers than buddies in the outfit now. The boys he'd cared about the most were dead.

"I can never forget them," he wrote to his parents from Pearl Harbor, carefully embroidering the fiction of a voluntary return.

> . . . *I know there are lots of persons who think I am crazy for coming back when I could have stayed in the States forever. But as I said before, I have a reason . . . Nobody would understand it but me. There was a strong urge in me to come back. And I felt it was my Lord, still by my side. And now I am back, more confident in myself and stronger in mind and I am unafraid. For I still have Christ to look up to . . .*
>
> *The bond tour was really fun for a while. We found out it would not be so easy after a week on the road . . . It got so boring and tiresome.*
>
> *And the people were so bothering. I couldn't stand much more, especially newspaper reporters and photographers.*
>
> *Over here I feel a lot better. I feel like my own self, just another Marine, and that's the way I want it.*
>
> *Please do not feel hurt over the quick decision I made . . .*

Appleton, El Paso, Houston, Dallas, Phoenix, Tucson, Denver, Milwaukee, Atlanta, Greensboro, Tampa, Columbia, Charleston, Richmond, Norfolk. As the tour headed south, June deepened toward July; the weather turned hot, and fatigue and numbness overtook the boys. It was all train stations, airports, flashbulbs, adoring faces, unfamiliar beds, no sleep, the same old questions. Luxury was no longer a sumptuous banquet, a well-appointed suite. Luxury was a good shave, a hot bath, a square meal. Fastidious John grew focused on his laundry. It never seemed to catch up with his schedule. In the final weeks, laundry came to dominate the concerns of local rally chairmen: The boys had decided that until their fresh clothes had been delivered, they would give no interviews to the press. Service improved markedly.

Asked for a third time whether The Photograph had been posed, John replied evenly: "I did not know the picture was being taken. If I had, I would have gotten the hell out of there and I would not be on this tour."

As the tour neared the final phase of its eight-week loop around America, John and Rene could not have fully appreciated the scale of what they had accomplished. The Mighty 7th was exceeding all expectations. With the invasion of Okinawa now commanding the headlines, and patriotic fervor running high, the tour was inspiring subscriptions at a rate that would astound the nation when they were finally totaled.

———

The Bond Tour revenues would have immediate use. America was pouring every resource into the Pacific War. At the beginning of June, President Truman had announced doubling to seven million the troop strength pitted against Japan—higher than the U.S. deployment in Europe at its peak. All strategies pointed to an invasion of the Japanese home islands. An expeditionary force of 770,000 was being assembled for the first wave alone, the landing set for Kyushu. (Normandy had required 175,000.) On June 18, Truman's military advisers presented the President with horrifying projections: Up to 35 percent—nearly 270,000—of these men would be killed or wounded in the first thirty days of fighting. After 120 days, the time allotted for occupying the island, U.S. casualties could reach 395,000.

That was the first wave. The second—an invasion of Honshu and the capture of Tokyo, projected for March 1946—would require a force of one million. And would exact hundreds of thousands of casualties.

On the night of July 4, the nation's capital was a tumult of the rockets' red glare, the bombs bursting in air. Some 350,000 spectators—a larger crowd even than would assemble for Martin Luther King's March on Washington eighteen years later—turned their faces upward to watch fireworks explode and spread their contrails over the Washington Monument, turning the Potomac's surface, for nearly an hour, into a mirror of reds and whites and yellows and greens. The fireworks filled the night sky with the outlines of the American flag, the face of President Truman, and the Iwo Jima flagraising scene.

The Mighty 7th had completed its triumphal circuit of the nation; it had come back home.

It was over.

Rene reported to Marine Headquarters the next day. He was given a short leave before his transfer back to San Diego. On July 7 he married Pauline in Baltimore, in a ceremony performed by the Vice Chancellor of the Catholic Archdiocese there, the Reverend F. Joseph Manns. John Bradley served as best man. Irene Gagnon did not attend.

Pauline accompanied Rene as far west as Pasadena. By November 7, he was on active duty in Tsingtao, China.

By the end of the summer, the final totals for the Mighty 7th were in. The tour had not just met its goal; the tour had nearly doubled it: Americans had pledged $26.3 billion. This was equal to almost half of the 1946 total U.S. government budget of $56 billion.

When I spoke with a Treasury Department source by telephone to confirm these figures, the official marveled over the size and accomplishments of the Mighty 7th. He fell silent for a moment as he shuffled some papers on his desk. Then he said, simply: "We were one then."

Nor was the outpouring of riches inspired by the image at an end.

An Iwo Jima commemorative stamp was issued on July 11, the anniversary of the founding of the Marine Corps Reserve. It was the first stamp to feature living people. Even Presidents had to die to get their image on a stamp. It immediately broke post office records for first-day sales, topping 400,000. In time, 150 million stamps would be printed, making it the best-selling stamp in history up to that time.

John Bradley, again being treated at nearby Bethesda for his wounds, sat quietly among the dignitaries—the only one of the six figures present—during the Washington ceremonies that opened the sale of the stamp. Presented by the postmaster with the first sheet off the presses, he managed a simple "Thank you" before sitting down again.

He listened as the postmaster proclaimed: "We honor the individuals here depicted, who by God's mercy still live among us. But they are not represented on this stamp as individuals. In the glorious tradition of the Marine Corps, they submerged their identities, giving themselves wholly to the United States of America."

I can only imagine the thoughts that must have coursed through my father's mind as he heard these words: my father, age twenty-one, two years out of his adolescence, who had never wished more fervently for anything than he wished for the day he could return to Wisconsin, marry, start a family, and open his funeral home—the quiet dream that had sustained him through the long months in the Pacific, who indeed "gave himself wholly to the United States of America."

My father was now listening to the news that his identity would never again be his own: that it would remain, in some irretrievable way, the property of the nation.

He would not be able to leave the image. The image would not leave him.

He was a figure in The Photograph.

Seventeen

A CONFLICT OF HONOR

That's Harlon. I know my boy.

—BELLE BLOCK

IN WESLACO, TEXAS, at about the time the Bond Tour was looping
back east for its triumphal finale, Ed and Belle Block were packing their
belongings for a private journey west. They were moving to California—
to Loma Linda, where the Seventh-Day Adventist Church had its
headquarters.

Loma Linda was Belle's idea. In fact, she'd insisted on it. Daughter Maurine, now Maurine Mitchel, lived there with her husband and two daughters. Ed Jr. was stationed nearby in the Air Force. But just as important for
Belle, Loma Linda was somewhere besides the Valley. Belle had never adjusted to the sapping humidity, the isolation, the endless milking, of farm
life in south Texas. Ed had adjusted fine; it was the life he knew in his bones,
the only life. But he did not resist his wife's strong desire to leave. Sorrow
and solitude had steered the Blocks' marriage into trouble, and Ed hoped
that maybe a move away from their memory-laden environs could make
things better. He hoped that at least she could leave behind her preoccupa-
tion with Harlon as a figure in the flagraising photograph. And he harbored
the secret hope that someday, when the grief had finally eased down, he and
Belle might come back home.

The stresses had begun even before they had learned of Harlon's death.
They had already sold their house when the telegram arrived. But the bad
news had only hardened Belle's determination. "Harlon's death exploded

---

Chapter opener: Harlon Block and his mother, Belle, taken while Harlon was on furlough.

Mom from the Valley," Maurine later recalled. "She couldn't go on; there was just too much hurt. She used to say, 'Everything bad that ever happened to me happened in the Valley.' "

On the surface, Belle remained the cool and focused prairie matriarch. At age fifty she was a handsome woman, straight-backed and conscious of her breeding, her thick black hair pulled tightly into a bun, her hazel eyes appraising behind her round spectacles. But people who knew her well understood that something in her had been broken. Something in all of the Blocks. "Harlon's death tore that family apart," remembers Travis Truitt, a friend of Harlon's in Weslaco. "It was like taking a glass and dropping it on a concrete floor—it just shattered them."

So in June 1945, while the nation celebrated the grand tour of the surviving flagraisers and their patriotic show, Ed and Belle quietly loaded up their car and, with their young sons Mel, Larry, and Corky in tow, left Weslaco, Texas, heading for California.

In late July, the Big Three leaders of the Allied nations—Winston Churchill of Great Britain, Harry Truman of the United States, and Josef Stalin of the Soviet Union—met in Potsdam to map out the closure of the Pacific War. Blockades and carpet-bombing were quickly ruled out: Clearly, the malignant Japanese war machine would capitulate only to direct and cataclysmic force. This machine would have to be broken, at nearly any cost. The Allied leaders settled on an invasion of Japan.

It would be the largest and costliest operation in the annals of warfare: 1.5 million combat troops committed to the initial assault waves, with reserves bringing the total to 4.5 million. The projected casualties beggared the imagination: a million Americans; half a million British.

Churchill, Truman, and their aides conferred discreetly on one further, just-emerging alternative: the one whose detritus still floated in the high winds above the testing ground at Alamogordo Air Base in New Mexico, where it had fissioned into human history only days earlier, at five-thirty A.M., on July 16.

"The decision whether or not to use the atomic bomb to complete the surrender of Japan was never an issue," Churchill later wrote. "There was unanimous, automatic, unquestioned agreement . . . nor did I ever hear the slightest suggestion that we should do otherwise."

On July 26, the Allied leaders issued their Potsdam Declaration: Japan must surrender or face "utter and complete destruction."

Japan ignored the ultimatum. It still numbered 2.5 million active troops and a civilian population that could be conscripted into a suicide defense force. "One hundred million hearts beating as one" was the slogan. The Rising Sun would fight to the last *issen gorin*.

Hundreds of thousands of young American men, including veterans of both the Pacific and the European Theaters, braced themselves for likely death on the shores of Kyushu and Honshu. Easy Company trained with the 5th Division at Camp Tarawa for its role in "The Big One." At mail call, Ira Hayes received an imposing package: a commemorative sheet of flagraiser stamps signed by President Truman, Commandant Vandegrift, and John Bradley. He barely glanced at it before crumpling it and tossing it in his seabag.

With her new husband on active duty in Tsingtao, China, Pauline Harnois— now Mrs. Rene Gagnon—returned to her life as a mill worker in Manchester, New Hampshire. Among her fondest possessions was a formal color photograph of Rene in his full-dress Marine uniform.

"My mother always told me she married him in that uniform," Rene Jr. told me. "But when I was older I saw an old news photograph showing him in a casual uniform at his wedding. That was typical of my mother. She always had to maintain a certain image of him, of what things should be like."

Loma Linda did indeed bring Belle some measure of peace. The family bought a small house, and Belle busied herself with church life and her children while Ed scouted for farmland.

Belle's fixation on Harlon's place in the photograph, though, remained unshakable. In fact, it grew stronger. One of the first items she unpacked in their new dwelling was a copy of the photo. And for the rest of her life she wore a scarf pin fashioned from Harlon's paratrooper wings.

Her heart continued to harbor the belief that it was her son in the photo. One day she received a visit from a student from the old hometown of Weslaco, Russell Youngberg. "She showed me the photo," he remembered, "and told me it was Harlon there putting the pole in the ground. I thought to myself, 'How can she be so sure?' "

California was less welcoming to Ed. It proved as bad a fit for him as Texas had for Belle. He could not believe the price of land out there; it dwarfed his small nest egg. A stranger to the local banks, he was unable to secure a loan. The dream of a farm began to wither. Frustrated and miserable, he told Belle one day: "I've got to make us a living. I'm going back to Texas."

Whatever hopes he might have harbored about Belle were dashed when she replied: "Go. But I'm not." Ed picked up a used Model A on the cheap, threw his luggage into it, and hit the long road back to the Valley.

"He always thought that eventually she would come back there to him," Maurine said. "I think she broke his heart."

Through the summer of 1945, Iwo Jima continued to serve the purpose for which it had been wrested from the Japanese: to provide air cover and an emergency landing strip for the B-29 bombers flying from their base in Tinian to their targets in Japan.

In the dim predawn light of August 6, 1945, the pilot of one of those bombers, on his first mission to the Japanese homeland, puffed his favorite Bond Street tobacco through a Kaywoodie briar pipe as, through the broken clouds ahead, Iwo loomed into view. At 5:55 A.M. he made a spontaneous loop around Mount Suribachi as he waited for two other B-29's to catch up with him. Looking down from the cockpit of the plane he had named after his mother, the pilot ruminated that the horrendous battle had been worth its costs: "The island, which had become Japan's prime defensive outpost, lay directly on the route our bombers flew on their mission from the Marianas to Tokyo. Without it, our mission would have been more difficult."

Within twelve minutes the other two B-29's had joined him. At 6:07 the three bombers dipped their wings in a departing salute to Mike, Harlon, Franklin, and the thousands of other boys buried below.

The pilot was one of thousands who flew to Japan unimpeded because the Marines had conquered the sulfur island. But there was something different about his flight. Secured in his jacket were twelve cyanide tablets: one for each crew member, in case they were shot down. They were on a mission whose secrets were too vital to be divulged under Japanese torture.

The pilot's name was Paul Tibbets. His plane was the *Enola Gay*. His payload was a single weapon nicknamed "Little Boy." His target was Hiroshima.

John Bradley spent the last half of July and part of September at Bethesda Naval Medical Center outside Washington, undergoing treatment for his legs that had been delayed by the Bond Tour. In mid-September he was given a leave, and hurried off at once to Appleton.

He played a round of golf with Bob Schmidt, the hometown friend and fellow corpsman who saw burial duty on Iwo. "We didn't speak of Iwo Jima," Schmidt remembered, "other than to remark what good buddies the

Marines were. We were out to enjoy ourselves and neither of us talked about the war."

A day or so later, Betty Van Gorp was out on a date at a dance club. "Jack came in with some other guys and sat in the same booth with us," my mother told me. "We hadn't seen each other for years, and we caught up. My date didn't dance, so Jack asked me to dance."

A couple of weeks after that, Betty saw Jack again. He showed up with another male friend of hers at the courthouse, where Betty was employed as a social worker. They chatted, and the two men left. Not too many minutes after that, Betty's work phone rang. It was Jack. He wanted to take her out to dinner the next night.

"I later learned that some men were waiting in a car outside Jack's house to take him to a speaking engagement," Betty said. "Jack was late and the men were impatient. He was calling my number and the line was busy. The others kept calling, 'Come on!' But Jack kept dialing till he got through to me. He spoke to me in a relaxed way, as if he had all the time in the world."

Jack took Betty to Jake Skall's nightclub in Appleton, driving his cousin Glen Hoffman's car. "Over dinner I asked him about the flagraising," my mother said. "He had a lit cigarette and he started playing with his silver lighter, looking at it, distracted. He told it like he must have told it many times; like a speech, nothing personal, just the facts. 'People call us heroes, but we're not.' 'It was just another thing to do that day.' Things like that."

Later they went to a dance club and chatted with high-school friends. On the way home Jack invited Betty to a movie the following night—his last night in town—and she said okay. Her impression of him, she recalled, was that he was mature, that he had been through a lot, and that his responsibilities for people's lives had required him to make important, snap decisions far beyond his young age.

Fifteen minutes into the movie the next night, Jack asked Betty: "Do you mind if I step outside and have a cigarette?" He came back in a few minutes, but went out twice more to smoke. Finally, Betty asked him: "Would you like to leave?" Jack said yes.

Not long after that, Jack was holding Betty tightly in his arms and telling her, "I love you with my whole heart and soul." Betty was touched; taken by the way Jack said those words, "heart and soul." No one had ever said that to her. "I knew he really loved me," she said.

John left the next day for more surgery on his shrapnel wounds at Bethesda Naval Medical Center.

When his surgery was complete, his obligations as a figure in The Photo-graph resumed. November 10, 1945, would mark the 170th anniversary of the Marine Corps. To commemorate it, Felix de Weldon had struck a twenty-five-foot statue of the six boys. De Weldon, John, and Commandant Vandegrift would dedicate it in front of the Navy Building on Connecticut Avenue in Washington. That night, John would be interviewed coast-to-coast on the NBC Blue network, his last "hero" broadcast before he left the service. "If you are not busy at 9:30 P.M. Saturday," he humbly wrote to Betty, "perhaps you could listen in."

In this valedictory broadcast, flanked in the studio by Commandant Vandegrift and Secretary of the Navy James Forrestal, John focused his re-marks not on himself but on his comrades, the Marines. "The thing that no corpsman will ever forget is that no matter how badly hurt they were, they never complained," he said. "We lived with them and buddied with them, and it wasn't a question of taking care of a patient, but of looking after your friends. That's the way I will always feel about the Marines."

Three days later he was discharged. He was twenty-two and had spent thirty-four months, a seventh of his life, in the Navy—the outfit he'd joined so that he would not have to fight on land.

He made straight for Appleton. He proposed to Betty and they were en-gaged on December 3. In January 1946, he began classes in the Wisconsin Institute of Mortuary Science in Milwaukee, while working part-time at the Weiss Funeral Home there. The life he had dreamed of in California, in Hawaii, on the sulfur island, was becoming a reality. The life before that was already fading into the ether.

Ira boarded a ship from Japan, after a month with the occupational forces, on October 25, to return home. It was his eleventh and last military trans-port. He landed at San Francisco on November 9 and was discharged from active duty at San Diego on December 1, 1945. Just turned twenty-two, he had spent thirty-nine months of his life as a Marine, twenty-three of them in three overseas tours.

Pete Strank, one of Mike's two younger brothers and a Navy man, came home too, in a sense. In another sense, Pete never came home.

Pete had resembled Mike: big, at six foot four; boisterous, handsome with a white-toothed smile; full of life.

That had changed on March 19, 1945, when Pete's ship, the USS *Franklin*, sixty miles off the coast of Japan, took a hit by a kamikaze dive-bomber carrying two five-hundred-pound bombs. The *Franklin*, loaded with fully fueled and armed fighter planes, became a bomb herself, a thirty-thousand-ton floating bomb. She burst into an inferno of explosions and Niagaras of ignited gasoline; the massive concussions lifted her out of the water and shook her from side to side. As the black smoke formed itself into a mushroom cloud, 724 crewmen perished.

No one thought the *Franklin* would survive. But she did, a husk of her former self; she limped back to the United States as the most heavily damaged warship in U.S. naval history, her crew the most decorated. Pete survived in a similar way—a husk of his former self. His wife, Ann, told me, "Pete's nerves were shot. His hands shook and his behavior was erratic. He drank too much after the war, trying to forget."

He would moan in bed at night next to Ann. Once she nudged him and he sprang up, his hands seizing her neck. "The only thing he ever told me about the Navy," Ann said, "was that a kamikaze hit his ship and they shoveled body parts up with coal shovels."

And John Strank, the third brother, told me: "I lost two brothers in the Pacific War."

Nineteen forty-six was the first year in more than a decade and a half that dawned with the world at peace. Like John Bradley, millions of returning servicemen plunged into the dreams they had deferred: marriage, parenthood, a new house, perhaps college on the GI Bill.

Many of these young men made stress-free transitions into the peacetime world. Don Mayer was among the tens of thousands who entered college. "It was great," he said. "Our tuition and books were paid for and we got sixty-five dollars a month on top of it." Jack Lucas finally began his high-school career—the only Medal of Honor winner to enroll as a freshman. Robert Leader, after recovering from his grievous wounds and the long day lying helpless under fire on the Iwo beach, reentered college and eventually became a professor of fine arts at Notre Dame. "No guilt," he insisted many years later. "I did my best and it was the right thing to do." And Donald Howell spoke for many when he declared, "I just got on with my life after Iwo Jima. There was a job to do, and we did it and that was it. If you want to lie around and feel sorry for yourself, you can."

But for many other veterans, it was not that easy. For many, there would be no peace. For many, the word "dream" would mean something entirely different. Many, like Pete Strank, left parts of themselves behind, in the dreamscape war that would never end.

"Life was never regular again," Tex Stanton said. "We were changed from the moment we put our feet in that sand."

Corpsman George Whalen, a Medal of Honor winner on Iwo, did not grow aware of the trauma he had suffered until the battle had ended. "I had nightmares in the hospital after Iwo," he told me. "I would scream in my bed. They had to put me in a private room because I would wake up the other guys. I had dreams of my platoon sergeant with his face blown away, his legs gone."

For Danny Thomas, no amount of toasting could ever quite put "Buttermilk Chick" to rest. "After a while the dreams started," he said. "And the one that kept coming back—you know how the surf comes in on a beach, rolling back and forth? I see that surf coming in on Iwo, and there are the bodies of my friends, just rolling back and forth. And there's nothing I can do for them."

James Buchanan found it hard to concentrate on things. "I felt life was very short," he said. "I didn't value anything other than life and my family. I lacked incentive. I couldn't take anything too seriously."

Corpsman Cliff Langley could not stop the nightmares. "I would be facing death," he said, "I would come close to being killed, and then it didn't happen. If I would wake up, get right up out of bed, it would finish. But if I laid there, the nightmare would continue. This went on for years."

Wesley Kuhn, the theatrical "Kissing Bandit" from Appleton, found the nights hard, too. "When I traveled on business," he said, "I would check into a hotel room, and one of the first things I did was lay my K-Bar knife on a chair next to my bed."

John Bradley seemed to have escaped the demons of the wartime dreamscape. In the first months of his return, he wrote constantly to Betty from Milwaukee and the mortuary institute, and there was no Iwo Jima in the letters; the letters were suffused with serenity and happiness, a kind of luminous normality: "Gee I just can't seem to keep my mind on this schoolwork and that's bad in a way. The good thing about it is I'm always thinking of you and wishing myself with you."

Serenity and happiness. And yet even after the two were married, John Bradley continued to weep in his sleep for four years.

Rene returned from China in April 1946. He came home with hopes of benefiting from his "hero" cachet and realizing a dream of his own: to become a state police officer.

He thought he could do it with "connections," but Rene did not meet the qualifications for the job, and no one in the New Hampshire state police department seemed inclined to give him a courtesy appointment based on his reputation. Soon Rene was back at work with Pauline in the Manchester mills.

Ira resumed his life at the Pima reservation south of Phoenix. He moved back into his family's adobe house. Nancy kept a print of the flagraising photograph on the wall, but Ira did not encourage conversation about it.

Neither did his father, Jobe. "Jobe was very quiet, he hardly talked at all," recalled Sara Bernal, the niece who lived for a time with the Hayes family. "He worked in the fields chopping weeds, harvesting cotton. He did what he had to do. He never said anything about the flagraising. And Ira was just like his dad."

He found menial jobs, day-labor work: picking cotton, stacking ice in an ice plant. Eventually he bought a dwelling of his own: a room in an abandoned barracks that during the war had housed Japanese-Americans who had been relocated. He bought it for $50, using his privilege as a veteran.

If Ira thought that he could come all the way back to his former life—if he thought the hoopla over the flagraising photograph would die down now that the war was ended—he was wrong.

"Tourists would drive all over the reservation looking for me," he would later tell a reporter. "They'd spot me in the field, rush up to me with their cameras and ask, 'Are you that Indian that raised the flag on Iwo Jima?' "

Inevitably, perhaps, Ira turned again to the anesthetizing relief that he had sought during the Bond Tour.

"We'd work in the fields together and drink afterwards," recalled Arnold Charles, a friend from those days. "We drank anything, mostly Tokay wine and Coors beer. We had to drink on the streets because it was illegal for Indians to drink in the bars. The police could see us outside drinking, and we'd get thrown in jail in Phoenix for being drunk and disorderly."

Arnold Charles recalled Ira as easy to get along with, a nice guy. But Ira's cousin Buddy Lewis remembered Ira's trip wire.

"His favorite expression when asked about Iwo was, 'That's a bunch of bullshit,' " said Lewis. "He would say it to shut the conversation down. When people called him a hero, he'd just say, 'Yeah, yeah,' and walk away."

Ironically it was Ira's "hero" cachet that made access to liquor easier. Someone was always buying for him. In Phoenix, he found, he would not get kicked out of the skid-row bars around Third and Jefferson; the proprietors were proud to have this particular Indian on the premises.

Yet he remained a loner. As his drinking continued, he would sleep in alleys, along railroad tracks. His face grew heavy and his features thickened. The arrests piled up: drunk and disorderly. "Ira was a nice guy," Buddy Lewis said, "but he changed when he got drunk. He had a split personality. He was mean when he was drunk. He would laugh, but he went ape-shit over the subject of Iwo Jima. He didn't want to talk about it."

Servicemen's weddings were commonplace events in the spring of 1946, but on Sunday, May 5, a photograph of one of them made newspapers across America. Its caption read: "One of the flagraisers on Iwo Jima, John H. Bradley of Appleton, Saturday married a hometown sweetheart, the former Elizabeth Van Gorp, in St. Mary's Catholic Church there."

After a honeymoon night in Milwaukee's snazzy Pfister Hotel, they set up housekeeping in the city. John had rented a chauffeur's quarters above a four-stall garage of an elegant house at Lake Drive and Linnwood Avenue, a wealthy section of town. He began working full-time at the Fass Funeral Home.

Reporters, book authors, and collectors of memorabilia tracked him down and made constant demands on his time. But the young husband and quiet civilian was already separating himself from such things. "It was either a matter of granting interviews full-time or trying to make a living for my family," he remarked in a rare interview near the end of his life. "So I decided to make a living for my family and treat everyone the same: no interviews for anyone."

From the earliest days of their marriage, John and Betty made a ritual of saying their nightly prayers silently together. "Then one night I asked him what his prayers were," my mother recalled. "They were similar, so we started praying aloud.

"After doing this a number of times, I heard him finish with some extra words. I asked him, 'What did you say?' He was embarrassed, and answered, 'Oh, I just said, "Blessed Mother, please help us so everything turns out all right." ' We were both silent for a minute and then he added, 'It's something I said on Iwo.' "

John's other nightly habit, though, was something he refused to talk about at all. When Betty would ask him about it in the morning, he would simply turn away.

"He'd be sleeping, his eyes closed," was the way my mother remembered it. "But he'd be whimpering. His body would shake, and tears would stream out of his eyes, down his face."

Ira's life trickled into barren ground: working the fields by day, drinking in Phoenix at night, sleeping it off in the streets, coming home to his silent, watchful parents, staring wordlessly out into the starlit distance. No one tried to intervene in his troubles; it was not their way. Nancy always had a hot meal for him. Jobe offered mute acceptance.

Then one day in May of 1946, Ira Hayes decided to act on the thoughts that danced in the night sky.

He said nothing to anyone. He probably dressed in the type of clothing he wore for any normal workday: a short-sleeved cotton shirt, open at the collar; blue jeans with the cuffs rolled high in the style of that time; work boots. He walked off the Gila River reservation and out to the Pearl Harbor Highway. But instead of hitching the forty miles north to Phoenix, he thumbed his way south toward Tucson.

At Tucson, he headed east along sun-baked two-lane highways, through little towns named Dragoon and Wilcox and Bowie, then across the New Mexico line and towns named Lordsburg and Deming. He would have ridden in the backs of farm trucks, in the cabs of big rigs, alongside any driver who would pick up an Indian. He would never have told any of them his name.

He would have slept where he was tired: maybe in the Las Cruces city park, maybe in an abandoned car out in the desert. Crossing the Texas border north of El Paso, he would have passed within seventy-five miles of Alamogordo.

At San Antonio, Ira would have looked for lifts heading due south: toward the knife-blade tip of Texas where the Rio Grande empties into the Gulf of Mexico. Where the miracle of irrigation had promised that citrus orchards and cotton fields would overtake the sagebrush. Toward the Rio Grande Valley. Toward the little towns where a good buddy of his had once played on an undefeated football team and gone horse-racing bareback with his Mexican pal Ben Sepeda.

At Weslaco Ira would have asked around about the whereabouts of Ed Block. (He almost certainly did not know that the Block family had left town, and that Ed had come back alone.) No one would have paid much attention to his questions: He could have been another laborer, looking for work on Ed's cotton farm.

He had hitchhiked more than thirteen hundred miles in three days.

With his directions, Ira hitched back north out of Weslaco for a few miles, then walked west off the main road two more miles to an unmarked crossroad. Looking north from there, he could see Ed Block's cinder-block house about fifty yards away across the red dirt.

He walked up the driveway and knocked on the door. No one answered.

Ira turned his gaze to the cotton field, where a lone figure was bent over in the hot sun. Ira knew all about cotton fields.

He approached the figure silently, from behind. When he was near him, he softly asked: "Are you Mr. Block? Harlon's father?"

Many years later, Rebecca Salazar—who eventually became Ed's second wife—still vividly remembered the excitement in Ed's voice when he reached her by telephone.

"He was almost breathless," Rebecca recalled. "He asked me, 'Do you know that Indian in the flagraising photo?' I said, 'Yes . . .'

"And Ed went on, 'Well, he was here today! He just left. He just walked up and started talking to me about Harlon, how they were good friends. He talked about Harlon playing football, about driving the oil trucks with me. He knew everything! He and Harlon had been good buddies.' "

Rebecca Salazar continued to reconstruct the call from Ed: " 'I didn't know what to say. I was speechless. And he asked me if I knew Harlon was in the photo, the guy putting the pole in the ground. I told him we had suspected it. Ira said it was definitely him, that Harlon and he had been together going up the hill, that Ira knew it was Harlon. He said that there was confusion in Washington about the photo and when Ira tried to set it straight, they hushed him up. He was pretty mad about it and he wanted to set the record straight.' "

Apparently the conversation out in the cotton field did not last long. As Ed told Rebecca, "Once he knew that I knew Harlon was in the photo, he just said, 'Okay, well, I guess I'll be off.' We shook hands and he walked out of the field.

"I was so stunned I didn't even think to ask him where he was going or where he came from. I should have offered him something to eat, seen if he needed a place to sleep. But I wasn't thinking clearly. He was just standing there before me, talking about Harlon, and then he was gone."

Belle—haunted Belle, ravaged Belle, tireless, fixated, unrelenting Belle—had been right all along.

It took fourteen days before Ed mustered the courage to pick up the phone and call his estranged wife in California. When she received the news, Belle was matter-of-fact about it. She wrote to Ira for confirmation and received a handwritten note in response:

> . . . God knows how happy I was to get your letter!
>
> I knew your son very well. I'm writing this cause I know, I was there and I saw. Harlon was in on this picture.

But how they fouled up the picture, I don't know. I was the last man to come back to the states for this 7th Bond Drive . . . when I did arrive in Washington D.C. I tried to set the thing right but some Colonel told me not to say another word as the two men were dead, meaning Harlon and Hansen. And besides the public knew who was who in the picture at the time and didn't want no last minute commotion.

. . . It did not seem right for such a brave Marine as your son, not to get any national recognition.

Not long after that, Harlon's friend Leo Ryan returned to his hometown and paid a visit to Ed Block. "He told me that Ira Hayes had visited him and that Harlon was in the photo," Leo recalled. "He pointed to the figure in the photo and said, 'This is my boy, and I'm going to do my best to get him recognized.' "

On August 16, 1946—the first anniversary of the victory over Japan—the city fathers of Buffalo, New York, invited the three surviving flagraisers to participate in a day of patriotic ceremonies. John demurred: He had made his rules, and besides, Betty was now in the late stages of an ill-fated pregnancy. Ira and Rene accepted. But if they expected to relive some of the euphoria of the Bond Tour, they were mistaken. It wasn't the same, and neither were they.

A photograph in *The New York Times* told it all: There they were, Ira and Rene, raising Old Glory one more time, but there was something forlorn in their attitudes. And the ravages of drink and hard living were etched on Ira's fleshy face.

The story began, "Two men who took part in the historic Iwo Jima flagraising sounded a note of sadness and disillusionment today as Buffalo jubilantly celebrated the first anniversary of V-J Day." Noting that Rene "felt some disappointment about not seeing all those promises fulfilled that were made when the war was on," the article gave full play to Rene's burst of self-pity:

"*And I'm not saying it because it's just my case,*" *he continued. "It isn't. It's the same for other fellows, too.*

"*I had no success in my attempt to obtain a police or fire department job in Manchester,*" *Gagnon continued. "I can't find a place to live in my own town. I have to live with my wife's relatives in Hooksett, about eight miles away.*"

The article did not take note of this, but no evidence exists that Rene had sought out the training that would have made him eligible for such jobs. Clearly, this youngest and most naive flagraiser—he was still only twenty-one in 1946—had assumed that his "hero" mantle was a kind of appointment for life, complete with compensation. During the tour, John Bradley could see it coming. "All the bigwigs on the tour would slap us on the back and promise us a job if we ever needed one," he told me once. "I didn't think much of it, but Rene's eyes lit up. He thought he had it made."

Meanwhile, Ira was telling a slightly different tale of woe: "I want to be out on my own," he told reporters, "but out in Arizona the white race looks down on the Indian as if he were a little man and I don't stand a chance anywhere off the reservation unless I come East."

Such self-pity is not uncommon among people in the grip of alcoholism. But Ira's next remarks perhaps touched the true source of his very legitimate torment: "Most of our buddies are gone," Hayes observed. "Three of the men who raised the flag are gone. We hit the beach on Iwo with 250 men and left with 27 a month and a half later. I still think about that all the time."

In that oft-repeated lament, I believe, lay the key to the locked-up sorrows of Ira Hayes.

But even as Ira continued to brood about his lost buddies, and continued to pour alcohol over his grief, the seeds of his most singular act of moral heroism were beginning to bear fruit. His 2,600-mile hitchhiking odyssey of the previous spring, from the Gila River reservation in Arizona to Ed Block's south Texas cotton field and back—had put in motion a series of events that quickly reached the highest levels of the U.S. Marine command.

After hearing of Ira's visit from Ed, Belle Block acted immediately. She composed a letter to the Congressman from the Weslaco district, Milton H. West, signing herself "Mrs. E. F. Block," and using Ed's address in the Rio Grande Valley:

> In studying the picture of the famous flagraising on the peak of Suribachi I was convinced that the Marine at the base was my son, and began writing to several Marines that I was acquainted with to inquire if my son was the one in the picture and have received assurance from them that it was, but could not get definite proof until I got in touch with Ira Hamilton Hayes one of the survivors of the flagraising and received a lengthy letter from him identifying and verifying that it was my son . . .

The Congressman forwarded both letters to Commandant Vandegrift, requesting an explanation. The commandant bestirred himself and dispatched an aide to the Pima reservation in Arizona to obtain an identification affidavit from Ira.

The aide interviewed Ira on December 10 in Phoenix, and found Ira's deposition persuasive. Among other things, Ira recalled with clarity how it was Harlon who had piled stones to form a base for the pole. Then he drew the colonel's attention to some photographs made of Hank Hansen as he helped raise the first flag on Suribachi that morning, along with Lindberg, Thomas, Michaels, Charlo, and Schrier. He pointed out that Hansen was wearing a cloth cap, not a helmet, and that he also wore crossed bandoliers and parachute boots with the trousers tucked in—all these details in contrast to the figure at the base of the flagpole.

"That's definitely Harlon Block," was the way Ira summed it up.

The Marine Corps sent Ira's deposition, along with the photographs, to John and to Rene. Both affirmed that the figure in question was not Hank Hansen and that it probably was Harlon Block.

On January 15, 1947, almost two years after the photo appeared, Commandant Vandegrift mailed a two-page letter addressed to "Mr. and Mrs. Block." He confirmed that a mistake had been made: Henry Hansen was not in The Photograph. On the evidence and by consensus, the Marine thrusting the pole into Mount Suribachi was Harlon Block.

Vandegrift blamed the mix-up on the photographer, Joe Rosenthal, and not on the Marines, as had Ira. As for the twenty-three months of anonymity for their son, when attention to the photo had been at its peak, the commandant could muster only a stiffly worded *harrumph:* "It is exceedingly regretted that an incorrect identification should have been made."

No matter what the wording, Belle Block had been vindicated. With nothing more than the rear view of a blurry figure in a wirephoto from six thousand miles away, she had instantly recognized her son.

Perhaps, in the end, it did not entirely matter that the Marines confessed their error to Belle at all. "I am sure," said Maurine, "that no matter what the government said, Mother would have gone to her grave insisting that was her son Harlon on that photograph."

Belle knew her boy.

Eighteen

MOVIES AND MONUMENTS

If everything isn't black and white, I say, "Why the hell not?"
                                                    —JOHN WAYNE

THEY WERE NO LONGER BOYS NOW; they were postwar men. And
still, everything they did was news.

In 1947, the year the Cold War began, the nation still looked to the figures in The Photograph for reassurance. In February, on the second anniversary of the flagraising, wire-service photographs went out showing John in a
suit arranging flowers in a funeral home; Ira as an Arizona farmer in an open
work shirt; Rene in an undershirt, working in the hot Chicopee mill. When
John graduated from the Wisconsin mortuary school, when Rene Jr. was
born in Manchester, when Kathleen Bradley was born in Milwaukee, when
John found a job in his birth town of Antigo—when all these things happened, the flashbulbs popped and the headlines told the tale.

Ira continued to make headlines of a darker kind. His arrests for drunkenness in Phoenix and surrounding towns piled up. The local newspapers
highlighted the arrests until they grew so commonplace they were no longer
a novelty; then they dropped Ira's scrapes with the law into the police log,
with the rest of the petty-crime news.

To the reporters and tourists who never left him alone, he remained tol-
erant, if distant. Ira took to stuffing an American flag in his back pocket
while working in the cotton field, to satisfy the inevitable request of the
strangers with their cameras. But he'd never talk about the event. Or the
war. Not to the tourists. Not to Nancy and Jobe. (Nancy later recalled that
Ira had tried to unburden himself to her once or twice, but had ended up

---

Chapter opener: The Marine Corps Memorial being assembled.

sobbing.) Not to anyone, except perhaps to his best friend. His best friend, according to his cousin Buddy Lewis, was the bottle.

After a while, it was not the tourists who plagued him as much as it was his neighbors on the reservation. The other young Pimas, when they broke their usual stoicism, liked to rib Ira in the wry, almost mocking style that flavored their culture's humor. "Iwo Jima hero!" was the inescapable salutation. Ira had used this agitating kind of wit on his own Marine buddies. The difference lay in the subject matter. Probably no phrase in the English language was as torturous to Ira Hayes as "Iwo Jima hero."

"It wasn't just that Ira had seen others do much more than he, and pay for it with their lives," said Urban Giff, a fellow ex-Marine and later a Pima leader. "His problems were made worse by the fact that in our culture, it's not proper for a person to seek recognition. I think he always struggled with this."

Struggled, and drank. And slipped a little further into the darkness.

Ira was hardly alone in facing the demons that the darkness held.

Betty Bradley learned to cope with John's nocturnal weeping. But she was still taken aback one day when, tidying up the contents of John's dresser, she discovered a large knife in one of the drawers. "I asked him why he had it, and he just said, 'Oh, I don't know,' " my mother remembers. "He wasn't a hunter; he had no use for that knife other than for protection."

If the knife represented one layer of nighttime protection for John, the two martinis he often took before bedtime represented another. "He'd never get tipsy," Betty said, "but I always wondered if he needed to have a drink to get him past his wartime memories."

The memories floated through the nights of many veterans. For some, they spilled into the daylight hours as well. Danny Thomas was in medical school when the flashbacks started.

"I'd be sitting there in class looking normal," he said, "but I wasn't seeing what was there. I was seeing Chick on the beach, all the death on Iwo. It was like a movie screen wrapped around me. I thought I was going crazy. I went to Health Services. They hypnotized me and that cut out the flashbacks and I couldn't remember the dreams. I knew I was still having them because I'd wake up wet from sweat. But I couldn't remember them."

For George Wahlen, the Medal of Honor became a guarantee that the memories would never go away. "People want you to talk, the mayor wants to have a parade," he recalled. "I was always being asked to speak somewhere, introduced as a hero. I didn't feel comfortable with it."

Eventually George Wahlen hit on his own way of finding relief from the constant attention. In 1948 he enlisted in the Army and spent twenty years there.

In January of 1947 the U.S. government began the long process of transporting the bodies of the Marines slain on Iwo Jima back home.

Franklin Runyon Sousley's remains were returned to his mountaintop community in Kentucky. The boy who had promised that he would come back a hero was buried on May 8, 1947, with honors in the small Elizaville Cemetery on a sunny, breezy Saturday. A Marine escort accompanied the coffin, and local veterans fired a rifle salute as it was lowered into the soil. A local newspaper correspondent wrote that the "volleys of shots echoed and re-echoed. The soft notes of the bugle went out over the little village . . . and from somewhere in the distance came an echoing bugle. Strong men choked with emotion and women wept." The governor of Kentucky stepped from the crowd and took Goldie Price's hand in his.

In the fall of 1947, Belle Block returned to the Valley—but not, as Ed had hoped, to reunite with him. She came to witness the burial, in the Weslaco city cemetery, of Harlon.

She had driven from California, with her sons Mel and Larry, along the "river route" to El Paso, and from there down to the tip of the Texas knife-blade. With Ed at their side, they joined a crowd of nearly 20,000 that had gathered on a hot windless day to watch the caisson bear Harlon's flag-draped coffin along Texas Avenue. Behind the caisson walked more than one hundred veterans, followed in turn by their families and friends in cars. Holding the reins of the horses that pulled the caisson, and walking on both its sides, were Harlon's fellow Panthers: surviving members of the undefeated football team he'd played on; the boys who had enlisted en masse in January 1943.

Among them were Glen Cleckler, who had fought on Iwo, and Leo Ryan, who'd been temporarily blinded at Tarawa. Leo watched the ceremony with a veteran's detachment. "It had little to do with Harlon," he said later. "It was Marine Corps pomp and glory. The real meaning of Harlon—the religious fact of his being, that boy going through the halls of the high school—that was for his friends to remember."

Cleckler felt the same way. "We guys who'd enlisted talked for an hour afterwards. Somebody said, 'If old Harlon was looking at this he'd have a good laugh.' Everybody was seeing him as a hero, but he was just Harlon to us."

From the perspective of half a century, Leo Ryan permitted himself to re-visit that hot windless day. As it all came back, he said through tears: "All we had between the enemy and us was a pair of green dungarees. And I thought of Harlon out there leading young boys, sealing holes, fighting an unseen enemy, sleeping in a rocky hole. I wondered how many people think of the seriousness of this. So much is taken for granted. I hoped the efforts of guys like Harlon would be appreciated in the future."

Ed and Belle were civil toward each other that day, Mel Block recalled. But when it was all over, his mother got in the car and the three of them drove back to California. Belle never returned to the Valley.

Mike Strank was buried at Arlington. Interment in the National Cemetery seemed fitting for the young man known universally as a "Marine's Marine." A busload of his family and friends came down from Franklin Borough for the occasion, on which thirteen other boys were also buried. Mike's father, Vasil, consented to come—Vasil, who had not been able to cope with the Bond Tour. So did Pete, who could not talk about his time in the service or bring himself to look at The Photograph. John, Martha, and young Mary completed the family presence.

The Arlington ceremony did not provide closure for the afflicted Strank family. As with John Bradley, but lacking his resolve to keep the outside world at bay, the Stranks endured for years afterward the calls and visits from veterans groups, reporters, the curious. One visitor, in the fall of 1948, was Harry S. Truman, storming through his legendary reelection campaign. Leaving his entourage at the doorstep, the President trooped into the living room of the tiny duplex that Vasil and Martha had scrimped to acquire many years earlier. As he took leave of Mike's parents, Truman noticed young Mary standing quietly by the door. He bent down and said to her, "It was an honor to meet your parents."

Ralph Ignatowski's remains were put into the earth of the National Military Cemetery in Rock Island, Illinois.

Like most mothers of dead servicemen, Frances Ignatowski could not restrain her need to know what had happened to her son. She wrote letters of inquiry. No one would tell this mother the awful truth about her Ralph. But eventually she found out.

Julia Heyer, Ralph's sister, told me of that terrible time: "My mother could barely eat for six months. We were all so indescribably sad. We couldn't talk about it. There was just a quiet in the house."

There is confusion within the Ignatowski family over how their mother learned the details of Iggy's death so many years ago. But brother Al Ignatowski told me his mother spoke of "a man from northern Wisconsin," who came to their home in Milwaukee and told Frances and Walter of how the Japanese had captured Ralph.

The "man from northern Wisconsin" could only be my father.

The last two Japanese defenders on Iwo surrendered on January 8, 1949. They emerged from the caves clean and well fed. They decided to give up after reading, in a fragment of the U.S. Army newspaper *Stars and Stripes*, of how American forces were celebrating Christmas in Japan. This told them that the war was over. For four years they had foraged food and clothing in nighttime raids on the compounds of American occupation troops on the island.

The Photograph continued to maintain its hold on the American imagination. In four years it had metamorphosed from an image of hope in battle, to an icon of victory in World War II, to a symbol of the pride Americans now felt as citizens of the world's new superpower.

In early 1949, Republic Studios announced that production was under way on an ambitious motion picture depicting the role of the Marines in the Pacific War. As contrasted with earlier, wartime morale-boosting "quickies," this film would have the scope and stature of an epic. Its price tag was more than one million dollars, the largest in Republic's history. The studio chief, Herbert Yates, "nearly had heart failure" at the prospect of such an investment, as the director, Allan Dwan, recalled it. But Yates gave his approval—on the condition that the lead role be played by Hollywood's emerging superstar of action films, John Wayne.

The movie would portray Marines training in New Zealand, fighting on Tarawa, on leave in Hawaii, and in the closing few minutes, landing on Iwo Jima. This required a huge budget, which necessitated a giant turnout at the box office. It was imperative that the movie capture the public's imagination.

So Republic Studios hatched a plan to have the three survivors raise their flag as the climax to the movie. Imagine—John Wayne and the flagraising! Soon, even though little of the movie concerned Iwo Jima, the flagraising image became central to its marketing. The image even overwhelmed the naming of the film, whose title became *Sands of Iwo Jima*.

To ensure that the flagraisers were aboard the project, Republic took no chances: It called out the Marines.

No doubt the Marines were well aware by now of John's reclusiveness and the unpredictability of Ira. So they moved shrewdly and efficiently. They contacted Ira, Rene, and John in turn, informing each of them that the other two had agreed to participate. Thus each man was given to understand that if he backed out, he would ruin the entire movie.

It worked. Certainly it worked on John Bradley, the one most likely to have resisted. "John didn't want to go to Hollywood," recalled his friend John Freidl. "He said the only reason any of them would come was because the others came." My mother agreed with this. "Jack went because he was told Rene and Ira would be there," she said. "He felt he should go, too."

But even in accepting, John did all he could to minimize attention to his moviemaking debut. He instructed Betty that if anyone in Antigo should wonder where he'd disappeared to for a few days in July 1949, he was simply away on a business trip.

Later, after returning from Hollywood, John gave the straight scoop in a letter to his old buddy from Easy Company, former corpsman Cliff Langley:

> *They didn't get us out to California to help make the picture. All that was a cheap publicity trick to get a little free advertising for the movie. Republic Studios is making the movie, we were out there only two days and most of that time was spent fooling around. I think they only took about two shots of the flagraising and that only took about ten minutes. If you think you will see real action like Iwo Jima by seeing the picture I really think you will be sadly disappointed. Chief Hayes says they have the picture so fucked up he isn't even going to see the movie.*

John had it figured right. The flagraisers' roles in the movie were minuscule. Their two scenes—one bunched around John Wayne as they receive orders, the other a quick glimpse of them pushing up a flagpole—required a total of only about thirty minutes of filming. Still, they had value to the Republic project: value as feature-story fodder. As the studio had guessed, reporters followed them everywhere on and off the set. And indeed the three generated so much copy that, combined with the movie's title and promotional art, the impression took hold that *Sands of Iwo Jima* would center on the flagraisers and their "immortal" action.

The survivors made little further news until September 1953 when the *Chicago Sun-Times* ran a shocking photo of Ira behind the bars of a Chicago jail. The headline read IWO FLAGRAISER JAILED AS DRUNK.

Ira had moved to Chicago to work as a tool grinder at an International Harvester plant. He worked diligently on the three-thirty-to-eleven-P.M. shift and maintained his own apartment. He was enjoying his anonymity until management featured him on the cover of their in-house magazine,

Harvester World. A three-page story blew Ira's cover, and the listing of his home address encouraged countless autograph seekers. For two days after the article appeared, the International Harvester switchboard was jammed. Ira's apartment phone rang off the hook day and night.

In the glare of celebrity all the old temptations resurfaced. "Will you say a few words at our dinner, Ira?" "Can I buy you a drink, Ira?"

Not surprisingly, there soon came to be nights when Ira did not make it back to his apartment and the ringing phone. The Chicago police soon grew as acquainted with him as the Phoenix police had been. "He was a hero to everyone but himself," one of them commented.

His superiors at International Harvester tried to accommodate his ever-more-frequent absences. They groped for ways to handle what was quickly turning from a public relations coup to a public relations embarrassment.

By the end of the summer, Ira himself solved International Harvester's problem. He left. "I quit there because I was drinking so much and I was ashamed to face my coworkers," he later said.

The arrests for drunkenness continued. Judges often assigned him to work crews in lieu of a fine. Pima leader Jay Morago remembered a stopover at O'Hare when he was returning to Arizona from a National Congress of American Indians conference in Washington. Rinsing his hands in the men's room, Morago glanced in the mirror and spotted a familiar figure sweeping the floor, dressed in prisoners' fatigues. "I walked over to him and said, 'Ira, hey, man, come back home,' " Morago recalled. "But Ira just said, 'We've had this conversation,' and moved away from me."

The more helpless and vulnerable Ira grew, the more brazen was the press's exploitation of him. On his fifth arrest, in September 1953, someone, probably a Chicago policeman, tipped off the *Sun-Times*. As he sat in his cell, an officer entered the block and called him to the bars: "You've got a friend to see you." But the man in the fedora was no friend. He whipped a camera from behind his back, and before Ira—who had risen in curiosity and was now gripping the bars—could react, he flooded Ira's face with a flashbulb explosion at close range.

Sun-Times editors, encouraged by the national interest in Ira, decided to make journalistic hay out of his plight. They put up bail money, installed him in an alcoholics' sanitarium, and proceeded to wring all the pathos from the story they could:

> This newspaper does not believe that Ira Hayes should spend a night in jail.
>   The Sun-Times *believes that the people of Chicago will feel the same way when they are told who Ira Hayes is.*
>   Do you think that Ira Hayes, hero of Iwo Jima, is worth a second

chance? The Sun-Times *will accept contributions to help him toward a
new life.*

So "saving Ira Hayes" through the "Ira Hayes Fund" became the *Sun-
Times's* sanctimonious mission. Newspaper sales rose as people scanned the
donor lists and the photos of prominent citizens counting the funds.

For his part, Ira gamely played along with the authorities' visions of his
recovery. In a letter home about that time, he wrote:

> *Well, I guess you know what happened. The whole country knows now. I
> got drunk, woke up in jail. No shirt, no shoes. The judge gave me [a fine of]
> $25 or 17 days in the workhouse.*
>
> *The Sun-Times came and bailed me out and took me to see the editor*
> *and I guess I owe him everything . . . They took me to the Hopecrest sani-
> tarium where they cure drunks. In 5 to 7 days they will help the patient to
> hate any kind of liquor. I was there 5 days and took 10 treatments and 16
> shots in the arm. My last four treatments were rough, but I was forced to
> take it if I really wanted to help myself, and of course I did.*
>
> *Like I said I was pretty sick. I threw up all the whiskey, gin, beer
> and wine they forced on me and automatically hated the taste of all
> of them. . . .*
>
> *So I was cured in their eyes. They had done their part. Now the real test
> is up to me . . . all I need is the will power. . . .*
>
> *So you see what a position I'm in. People have put their trust in me—so
> many people and so much trust—and now I've got to do good.*

Ira was the number-one story in many periodicals that fall, including the
lead national item in *Time* magazine's October 6 issue. The *Time* correspondent spilled much useless ink wringing his hands over whether Rosenthal's
chance shot had ruined this "big copper-colored kid," who as a youth ran
"barefooted across the Gila River Indian Reservation." If only the correspondent could have seen beyond his prejudices and preconceptions and
listened to Ira as he described the root cause of his problem.

"I was sick," he told *Time.* "I guess I was about to crack up, thinking about
all those other guys who were better than me not coming back at all, much
less to the White House."

Ira Hayes was not the only veteran of World War II who came home
drinking. He was not the only kid of any race who drank before he entered
the service. It seems clear that Ira, like millions of his countrymen, was pre-
disposed to problems with alcohol. But it is equally clear—at least to me—

that he did not drink because of The Photograph, because he was an Indian, or because enlightened white society had failed to save him from himself.

Ira drank—I think—for the same reason Danny Thomas sought hypnosis; for the same reason my father wept at night and kept a knife in his drawer. Ira drank to escape the images of horror burned into his brain on Iwo Jima. He drank because he walked off that island, leaving so many of his good buddies behind.

Elizabeth Martin, singer Dean Martin's estranged wife, hired Ira as her chauffeur and children's guardian after reading of Ira's plight in the *Chicago Sun-Times*. For months it was a fortunate match, Ira with his own room in Martin's Beverly Hills home, ferrying the children to and from school and other appointments. He seemed to have taken the cure.

Then the day after Halloween, in 1953, Mrs. Martin received a call at five A.M.: Ira had been arrested a block from the house. Drunk and disoriented, he had abandoned the car and tried to walk back to the safety of the house. He came within one cruising patrol car of making it.

She kept her faith in him; installed him in another sanitarium. He returned to work for her. A week passed. This time the call was from the Los Angeles jail. The alternatives given him by the judge were unsparing: either a jail term or a one-way ticket to Arizona.

The police escorted him to the bus terminal. He was weeping as he said good-bye to Elizabeth Martin.

On November 11—Veterans Day—Ira stepped off the bus in Phoenix. "There was no hero's welcome for Ira Hayes when he arrived," reported the *Phoenix Gazette*. But of course there were some reporters and photographers. And of course Ira supplied them with the quotes they demanded. "I guess I'm just no good," he said. "I've had a lot of chances, but just when things start looking good I get that craving for whiskey and foul up."

Arriving back in Jobe's and Nancy's household that same day, Ira learned that his brother Dean had been awarded the Silver Star for heroism in Korea.

The drinking went on. Ira's war would never end.

In December 1953, "Cabbage" Bradley—John's father—suffered the heart attack that killed him. He did not live to see his son immortalized in bronze.

I was born two months later, in February 1954, in Antigo, and was given Cabbage's name: James Joseph Bradley.

The Photograph's power surged along undiminished. The gigantic work of art it had inspired—the world's tallest bronze statue, the only monument in the nation's capital commemorating World War II—continued to take shape in Washington. Sculptor Felix de Weldon worked feverishly at it as the years went by; working in plaster to form the molding for a finished casting in bronze, the great mass to be established at Arlington National Cemetery.

De Weldon worked three years to create the six figures as nudes. Then he worked three more years to adorn them with uniforms and equipment.

When completed, the statue would rise a hundred and ten feet from the ground and would weigh more than a hundred tons. The six figures would average about thirty-two feet in height. Their rifles would be sixteen feet long. Its cost was $850,000—every penny of it covered by private donations.

The logistics of construction were as outsized as the edifice itself. Far from simply translocating from the studio to nearby Arlington, the sculptor's completed plaster mold would have to be broken down into component parts—eighteen one-ton sections for each plaster figure—and transported by truck to a Brooklyn foundry for casting into bronze. Then those massive bronze figures would have to be trucked back to Washington, there to be bolted and welded together into the final, unified piece.

On September 2, 1954, the great bronze elements—the Brobdingnagian bodies, stretched out and secured on three flatbed trucks—began their journey. They lumbered slowly out of Brooklyn and through the narrow streets of Manhattan, flanked by police escorts and tailed by press reporters and network TV crews. They thundered across the George Washington Bridge, and headed south to Arlington.

As the unveiling date, November 10, 1954—the shared birthdays of Mike Strank and the U.S. Marine Corps—neared, the three surviving flagraisers were summoned once more into the nation's spotlight. Rene and Pauline came down from New Hampshire. John and Betty Bradley arrived from Antigo. Ira showed up, alone.

The governor of Kentucky had proclaimed November 10 "Iwo Jima Day" in that state in honor of Franklin, and Goldie came to the ceremonies in Washington. All the surviving Stranks were there—Pete, John, Mary, Martha, and Vasil. Ed and Belle Block were reunited for the first time since

Harlon's burial at Weslaco, along with Maurine and Mel. Rene Jr. accompanied his parents.

It was to be the last contact among the families until I began making telephone calls forty-one years later, in 1995.

Joe Rosenthal arrived with his wife, Lee, and their two small children, feeling elated. Before the ceremonies he led his family on a walk around the monument's base—hoping to watch the expressions on their faces when they discovered his name there.

But the discovery never happened. Rosenthal's name had not been inscribed on the base. Neither, for that matter, had the names of the six boys. The only name that appeared on the giant edifice was that of the sculptor, de Weldon.

In the nation's memory, the flagraisers' transformation from individuals to anonymous representative figures had begun.

The face of the black granite did, however, contain an inscription. It was a quotation from Admiral Nimitz immediately after the battle, summing up the Marines' collective heroism on the island. The inscription read:

UNCOMMON VALOR WAS A COMMON VIRTUE

Seven thousand dignitaries swelled the grounds on the day of the unveiling. Marching bands and streaking military jets added to the great sweep of ceremonial pomp. President Eisenhower and Vice President Nixon sat on the speakers' stage, along with the Secretary of Defense, General H. M. "Howlin' Mad" Smith, and former Commandant Vandegrift—who found himself staring directly at Ira Hayes in the front row facing the monument.

The moment of unveiling arrived. The lanyard was pulled, the protective draping swung free, and the Iwo Jima memorial statue took its place amidst the sacred icons of the nation.

The survivors and their families sat staring at it, stunned.

"Awesome," was the way my father later described the moment. "The statue was just so huge, so impressive. I could hardly believe it was a reality."

Ira—who had wept upon meeting Martha Strank in New York during the Bond Tour—beheld the image, burst into tears, and buried his face in Goldie's lap.

Belle Block fought mightily to hold herself together.

After the ceremony, photographers and TV cameramen rushed toward the stage. They arranged the survivors and the dignitaries in various groupings. Amateur photographers from the large milling crowd joined in, and the requests for posing went on and on. One AP shot captured Ira, Rene, and John, Belle, Goldie, and Martha, and the Vice President. Published in *The New York Times*, it was the final image of the three men in a single photographic frame.

My young father stood, typically, at a remove, as the last great ceremony of his public life slowly dissipated; as the festive crowd and the beribboned generals drifted from beneath the gleaming monument and toward their cars. People around him noticed that he seemed already to have receded from the whirl of voices and faces around him. "He wouldn't keep a conversation going," said John Strank. "He'd answer a question politely, but wouldn't initiate anything. I heard him say, 'It was something that happened a long time ago . . .' "

Finally—echoing the Bond Tour itself, nine years earlier in Washington, the fireworks fading in that summer night—it was over. The President and Vice President had departed the speakers' platform; the generals and admirals were gone; the crowd thinned out. The three flagraisers prepared to take their leave of one another. They would never be together again.

Ira Hayes, Rene Gagnon, and John Bradley had fought in one of the great battles of World War II; of world history. They had planted a flag on a mountain in that battle. They had seen the image of that planting raised to the status of enduring national symbol, a gesture toward the founding ideals of the Republic. They had come home to America and helped raise a vast treasury to complete the conquest of their nation's enemies. Now they had witnessed their "immortal" collective image transubstantiated to bronze.

This ultimate public investiture had transported the three across a subtle boundary. It was the iconic image, now, and not the men, who were fixed in history. At last, the surviving figures in the photograph were released to their individual destinies.

Nineteen

CASUALTIES OF WAR

> The nicest veterans in Schenectady, I thought, the kindest and fun-
> niest ones, the ones who hated the war the most, were the ones
> who'd really fought.
>
> —KURT VONNEGUT, SLAUGHTERHOUSE FIVE

WITHIN NINETY DAYS of the statue's dedication, each of the survivors' lives went its separate way. Rene was "angling" to capitalize on his fame, my father fulfilled his singular dream of buying a funeral home, and Ira Hayes was found dead—dead drunk.

Pieced together decades later, these facts strike me as more than coincidence. It's as if fate chose them to serve the image: to create that happenstance tableau atop Suribachi; to storm the country with its banner under Presidential orders; to give it celluloid life; and then finally to institutionalize it in bronze.

Consider the Marine Corps Memorial as the ultimate transmutation of The Photograph. One hundred tons of bronze, requiring an act of both houses of Congress and the President's signature to so much as chisel another word in its base. That's as permanent as can be.

To me it's as if Ira, Rene, and John served the image from photo to film to bronze, and once it was safely in its final form, they were released to their individual destinies. Never again would they meet, never again would they serve The Photograph.

A week before Christmas 1954, Ira was arrested again in Phoenix for being drunk and disorderly. Someone figured out that it was his fifty-first such

---

Chapter opener: Goldie Price, the mother of Franklin Sousley, holding a copy of The Photograph.

arrest, dating back to April 4, 1941—one of two arrests he had experienced before entering the service.

A caseworker for the U.S. Indian Service, Pauline Bates Brown, tried to help him during his latest downfall. "His attitude was not bitterness," she remembered years later, "but some hurt that I couldn't sort out."

The dedication of the Iwo Jima monument at Arlington provided Ira with a brief moment of public dignity; his last, as things turned out. He quickly returned home to a routine that never varied: menial work, the bottle, the police, the jocular but tormenting question from his fellow Pimas: "How's the hero, Ira?"

On the frigid morning of January 24, 1955—one month shy of ten years since he raised a flag—Ira was found dead at the age of thirty-two.

He had walked over to an abandoned hut about three hundred yards from his small living quarters on the Gila River reservation, where he'd sat in on an all-night card game. The other players included Ira's brothers Kenny and Vernon, the White brothers Harry and Mark, and a murky, erratic character named Henry Setoyant. The men drank wine as they played. Ira was winning; Henry Setoyant was not pleased by that fact. By the early-morning hours, everyone was drunk, and Ira was the drunkest of all.

The White brothers were the first to call it an evening. Then Vernon and Kenny said, "Let's go home, Ira." But by that time Ira and Henry Setoyant were arguing, clumsily pushing each other. So Vernon and Kenny left.

It was Setoyant who came to the Hayes household with the shocking news the next morning. When they heard it, father Jobe, mother Nancy, and brother Kenny all raced across the hard bare ground toward the abandoned hut. They found Ira's body nearby, next to a disused rusting car: lying facedown in a pool of his own vomit and blood.

The coroner ruled it an accidental death due to overexposure in the freezing weather and too much alcohol.

Two thousand people, many of them weeping, gathered outside the Cook Presbyterian Church in Sacaton for services on January 25. Five American flags hung at the altar. At two P.M., six young Pima Marine Reservists bore Ira's coffin into the little church and up the central aisle past two rows of benches to the altar. Ira was dressed in a green Marine uniform. A choir sang hymns in Pima and then in English. The gray-haired pastor, Esau Joseph, likewise spoke in both languages. "We are gathered to pay final respect to our fellow tribesman," he told the mourners. "He was a good man; he wished harm to no human being. On foreign soil he fought that men may inherit peace—a peace which he himself has found only now."

The following day, Ira's body lay in state at the Arizona Capitol Rotunda. Thousands stood in line to pay tribute, overflowing the rotunda and spilling far outside the Capitol. The State Legislature stood in recess; Governor Ernest W. McFarland gave the eulogy. More than forty years later another former governor, Rose Mofford, said, "I remember it well. It was the biggest funeral I've ever seen in Arizona."

Nancy Hayes tried to maintain her self-possession. "He was always talking about the Marines," she told a reporter. "He was so proud to be a Marine." But she broke into sobs as she spoke.

He was buried on a snowy day at Arlington National Cemetery. The grave site was at the bottom of a hill off Pershing Drive, just down the slope from the small tombstone marking the burial place of the great World War I general John Pershing, and next to the fresh graves of thirty-four privates, noncommissioned officers, and cooks who had died in Korea.

Rene attended. When a reporter asked him about Ira, the old frictions slipped away. "Let's say he had a little dream in his heart that someday the Indian would be like the white man—be able to walk all over the United States."

John did not attend. But from his home in Antigo, he remarked that Ira's death "makes him truly a war casualty."

A book, two movies—one starring Tony Curtis, the other Lee Marvin—and a song by Johnny Cash would all later mythologize Ira's death. In these versions he died either because of Anglo society's exploitation of him; because of his guilt over staging a "phony" photograph; or because he was not elected to a leadership post within his tribe.

His brother Kenny Hayes, the only survivor of Ira's last drunken night, told me in 1998 he is convinced Ira died as a result of his scuffle with Henry Setoyant. That Ira died because of a fight with a fellow Pima. Whether Ira was pushed or tripped, what's clear is he was simply too drunk to break his fall and get up.

What's also clear—to me, at least—is that the notion he died young as a result of his fame is just bunk. Today a battle-scarred Ira Hayes would be diagnosed with post-traumatic stress syndrome, and there would be understanding and treatment available to him. But in the late forties and early fifties, Ira had to suffer alone. Suffer daily with images of and misplaced guilt over his "good buddies who didn't come back."

The Photograph will forever inspire paeans to glory and valor among those who see the figures as immortals. To those of us who knew them as ordinary men, there's another side to the story.

Imagine six boys from your youth. Line them up in your mind. They are eighteen to twenty-four years old. Select them now; see them. How many marriages, how many children will intersect their lives?

Now consider that other than my father, only one other flagraiser married. And that other than my family, the only offspring sired by the six young flagraisers was Rene Gagnon, Jr.

I bonded immediately with Rene Jr. ("pronounced 'Rainy,' like a wet day"), when he confided that his namesake regarded his participation in the most revered military moment in history as "as significant as going to the mailbox." I chuckled; it was something my father could have said. Of course, only a flagraiser could utter those words. Such a sentiment from a historian or even from another Marine who had fought on Iwo Jima would be sacrilegious.

Rene Jr. described his father's life as an existence torn by the knowledge he had done something quite ordinary on the one hand and the public's perception of him as an immortal hero on the other. And also by the neverland of his marriage to Pauline.

Late in his life, Rene complained of living a life of a celebrity one minute and a "John Doe" the next. This stress was a constant throughout his days.

"It was an emotional roller coaster," Rene Jr. said. "He would lead a normal life and then he would be invited to a parade, a function, and he would show up and be treated like a little god. The people meeting him at the airport gate, the drivers, the newspaper people, the autograph-seekers. Then it was over and he'd have to unwind for days, sometimes weeks, from being the 'hero' to leading a normal life. It was stop-and-go heroism."

But Rene never stepped away from his roller coaster. Acknowledging the cheers of a Rose Bowl crowd at halftime; dedicating another statue; appearances as a "mystery guest" on TV; another speech; waving from the convertible to the crowds lining the parade—he rarely said no. One minute the hero, and back home the airline clerk, an employee in his wife's travel agency, and finally a janitor.

So why couldn't he step away? There seem to be three explanations.

First was Rene's natural passivity, his blowing with the latest wind. "Mr. Gagnon, it would be a *great* honor and a *proud* day in our city's history if you would address our group." Heady stuff.

Second, Rene always expected his 1/400th of a second of fame would pay off. Soon after the 1954 statue dedication, Rene was searching for a sponsor for his nationwide speaking tour. In a promotional interview he admitted, "This [the experience] is all I have left. My wife and Junior need the things in life we haven't had." Rene was thirty-two years old.

A sponsor never came forward. The speaking tour never got off the ground.

Twenty-one years later in his last interview, Rene, at the age of fifty-three, was singing from the same sorry songbook. He bitterly inventoried his lost "connections"—the jobs promised him by government people when he'd been at the height of his fame, jobs that never materialized. "I'm pretty well known in Manchester," he allowed to a reporter. "When someone who doesn't know me is introduced to me, they say, 'That was you in The Photograph? What the hell you doing working here? If I were you I'd have a good job and lots of money.'"

And then there was Pauline. Probably the determining reason.

Lillian Lebel, an employee in the Gagnons' travel agency, remembers the divergent outlooks of Rene and Pauline: "Pauline loved the fact that he was famous. She liked the attention it brought to her. I remember how she was visibly excited about a 1975 trip to Washington, D.C. She went shopping for new clothes. Rene had an 'I couldn't care less' attitude. He didn't want to go, but Pauline insisted. If it was up to him, he would not have gone."

Even her own brother, Paul Harnois, admits: "She pushed him. She wanted the pride, she wanted to go on the trips, wherever there was an event. She enjoyed it more than him. He couldn't care less if he went and she cared a lot. It affected her big-time. Pauline pushed him to be a hero."

Pauline was like the public: She embraced the idealized image, never grasping Rene's conception of the ordinariness of his action.

"All he'd say was, 'I just happened to land there and we put up the flag and someone took a photo,'" was how Rene Jr. described his father's recollection. Exactly as my father recalled it. But Pauline could never accept such an ordinary interpretation.

Pauline figured Rene's fame as a transcendent hero was the vehicle to a good life. But when that vehicle did not perform to her expectations, she rebelled.

Rene Jr. remembered a visit in 1959 by his grandmother Irene: "My dad made a small mistake while fixing a door. My mother started screaming at him, 'You're stupid, you're ignorant, you're no good!' Grandma had enough. She stood and said, 'Take me home. This man built this house with his bare hands. He is talented, and the end of the world is not here!' My mother and Grandma never shared a room again."

Rene tried marriage counseling. But Pauline would send Rene alone to the therapist (after all, it was *his* problem!). He would try to get away, fleeing with an airline ticket to some exotic place. But he always came back.

One day in early October of 1979 Rene and Pauline tangled once again. In the aftermath, Rene Jr., who was then thirty-two, advised his father, "You have to resolve it with her."

"He just said, 'I have no answers. There is no way out. There is no escape,' " Rene Jr. later recalled. " 'No escape!' That shocked me."

Three days later, on October 12, a janitor at Colonial Village, Frank Burpee, discovered that the door to the boiler room of one of the buildings was jammed. He got a crowbar and pried it open. On the floor lay his fellow janitor, Rene Gagnon, dead. In his hand was the inside handle to the door. Apparently he had dislodged it as he grappled with the door in the throes of his heart attack.

No way out. No escape.

He was fifty-four.

Papers across the country ran the story on page one, with "Rene Gagnon" and "Iwo Jima Flag" umbilically attached in the headlines. Many of the stories noted that the only remaining survivor among the six flagraisers was John Bradley, fifty-six, a funeral director in Antigo, Wisconsin. But "Bradley was in Canada vacationing Saturday and couldn't be reached for comment."

My brother Steve was present when our father got the news. "Dad answered the phone at the funeral home and it was a reporter," he told me. "He got off the phone and said to me, 'Rene Gagnon just died, so I'm out of town, fishing in Canada.' The phones rang off the hook for a week, and he didn't answer them."

But the press knew, as it always did, where to find Rene. Reporters descended on Manchester. At the Phaneuf & Letendre Funeral Home, where his remains lay, a reporter from the *Chicago Tribune* named Mary Elson pushed her way toward the casket. Rene Jr. promised her an interview later. In it, he was typically thoughtful and compassionate as he analyzed his father's tortured life.

"There were a lot of heavy thoughts my father was not capable of understanding," he told Mary Elson. "He was just a young kid doing his part for his country, and suddenly everywhere he went, people were saying, 'You're a hero. You're a hero.' And he was thinking, 'What did I do?'

". . . He was happy he did it [raising the flag] and that he would go down in history. But he didn't do it to go down in history."

In her story, the *Tribune*'s Elson described the eulogy at Holy Rosary Church.

> *"We don't have to single out an event in his life," the pastor intoned, as a Marine honor guard stood by the flag-draped casket, lodged awkwardly between the first five rows of wooden pews.*
>
> *But of course the pastor did single out an event, equating the flagraising at Iwo Jima with man's continual battle with evil and concluding: "Rene Gagnon was respected by millions for what he stood for—a man that remains to us a sign of life, victory and courage." It was a majestic tribute and one with which Gagnon probably would have been the first to disagree.*

She had it right. Even in death, Rene was overshadowed by his photographic image.

He was interred in a mausoleum in Manchester. Because of his short length of service and his lack of medals, the government ruled that he was not eligible for burial at Arlington.

But the government did not reckon with Pauline. She mounted a telephone campaign, driving home the point to military officials that they did not want to deal with the adverse publicity that the disgruntled widow of an Iwo Jima flagraiser could generate. It took nearly two years, but on July 7, 1981, newspapers carried photographs of Pauline at the U.S. Marine Corps War Memorial, gazing up at her bronzed hero on the day of his Arlington burial.

"This is our thirty-sixth wedding anniversary, so the day has special meaning to me," she told the press. She added: "It is appropriate that Rene will be interred very near to the Iwo Jima monument. He will be just across the street."

The headstones for Mike and Ira at Arlington are similar to all the others there: simple white slabs that denote only their names, ranks, and birth and death dates.

But Pauline saw to it that Rene's stone was distinctive. On its back is a bronze relief of the flagraising and an inscription:

FOR GOD AND HIS COUNTRY
HE RAISED OUR FLAG IN BATTLE
AND SHOWED A MEASURE OF HIS PRIDE
AT A PLACE CALLED IWO JIMA
WHERE COURAGE NEVER DIED

Twenty
COMMON VIRTUE

> *There are no great men.*
> *Just great challenges which ordinary men,*
> *out of necessity, are forced by circumstances to meet.*
> —ADMIRAL WILLIAM F. "BULL" HALSEY

ONE OF MY DAD'S FINER QUALITIES WAS SIMPLICITY.

He lived by simple values, values his children could understand and emulate.

He had no hidden agendas; he expressed himself directly. He had a knack for breaking things down into quiet, irreducible truths.

"It's as simple as that," he'd say. "Simple as that."

But a flagraiser's existence wasn't always so simple.

In 1979, the *Chicago Tribune* writer Mary Elson was following up on Rene's death and surprised John Bradley at his desk at the McCandless, Zobel & Bradley Funeral Home.

He gave her about "ten agitated minutes of his time," puffing "nervously on a cigarette . . . sitting on the edge of his chair in the electric pose of a runner ready to bolt from a starting block."

He spent most of those ten minutes downplaying the perceived heroics of the flagraising. But in two of his sentences he revealed his thinking about that eternal 1/400th of a second. "You think of that pipe. If it was being put in the ground for any other reason . . . Just because there was a flag on it, that made the difference."

Here my father captured the two competing realities of The Photograph. It was an action of common virtue, not uncommon valor, as plain as a pipe.

Chapter opener: The original, horizontal version of the Rosenthal photograph.

But because of a fluke photo—a stiff wind, a rippling flag—this common action represents valor in the eyes of millions, maybe billions of people.

The reporter Mary Elson grasped none of this and wrote in the *Chicago Tribune* that John's pole comment was "an oddly irrelevant afterthought."

Odd? Irrelevant? A casual afterthought? I don't think so.

My dad had given Mary Elson the key to everything. *"Just because there was a flag on it, that made the difference . . ."* But just as the inquiring reporter in *Citizen Kane* had missed the significance of "Rosebud," Mary Elson remained oblivious to the revelation John had handed her.

By the early 1980's, the men of Easy Company were in their sixties. Their families grown, their work lives nearing an end, many of them felt an urge, long dormant, to reconnect with one another; to remember with their buddies.

Dave Severance became the catalyst for these reconnections. A career Marine, he had left the infantry to become a fighter pilot after World War II. He flew sixty-two missions in the Korean War, and won the Distinguished Flying Cross and four Air Medals before retiring with the rank of colonel in 1968. But as with anyone who had walked in the black sands, Iwo Jima would remain the defining event of his life. With the instincts of a company captain, Dave compiled a list of Easy Company veterans, searched for their addresses around the country, and began a newsletter round-robin that soon prompted several reunions.

Dave invited my father to all the reunions, but he never went. The burden of being an "immortal hero" and the press attention he'd attract made it impossible.

"I'd love to go," he told my brother Steve once, "but I couldn't just go and be myself and visit with the guys I wanted to. I couldn't just be one of the guys."

Perhaps there were other considerations as well. Perhaps they were similar to those revealed to me, through tears, by John Overmayer, a corpsman who had gone through medic training with John and was with him on Iwo.

"I stayed away from reunions at first; I didn't want to remember, but I'm glad now that I've been to a few," Overmayer told me. "I went through life wondering how I could be so proud of something that was so bad. I had twenty out of thirty of my guys killed within ten or fifteen minutes. I couldn't get them out. I was their nineteen-year-old doctor, priest, and mother. But I couldn't save them. It took two buddies to get me through that night. But the next morning, when someone cried 'Corpsman!' I got out of my foxhole and went to help him. I did it. I kept going.

"The number-one motivation on Iwo Jima was to stand with your buddies and not let them down. And all my life I was proud of that, but I couldn't talk about it. But after going to a reunion I found others who felt the same way. And now I feel better."

My father probably felt that need to seek out comrades for an affirmation of feelings. But his fame as a figure in The Photograph would not let him go.

Or maybe it was something else. Something too painful to reopen. In 1964, when he was forty and I was nine, my father hinted at why he couldn't talk about Iwo Jima. But I was too young to really understand.

My third-grade class was studying American history. When we got to World War II, there, on page 98 of our textbook, was The Photograph.

My teacher told the class that my father was a hero. I was proud as only a young son can be.

That afternoon I sat near the back door of our house with my history book open to page 98, waiting for Dad to come home from work. When he finally walked through the door, I jumped toward him before he'd even had a chance to take off his coat.

"Dad!" I exclaimed. "Look! There's your picture! My teacher says you're a hero and she wants you to speak to my class. Will you give a speech?"

My father didn't answer me right away. He closed the door and walked me gently over to the kitchen table. He sat down across from me. He took my textbook and looked at The Photograph. Then he gently closed the book.

After a moment he said, "I can't talk to your class. I've forgotten everything."

That was often his excuse, that he couldn't remember.

But then he went on: "Jim, your teacher said something about heroes . . ."

I shifted expectantly in my chair. I thought now I would hear some juicy stories of valor. Instead, he looked me directly in my nine-year-old eyes signaling that he'd like to embed an idea in my brain for the rest of my life.

Then he said: "I want you to always remember something. The heroes of Iwo Jima are the guys who didn't come back."

Simple as that.

Six years went by before I discussed the subject with him again. And for some reason, on one ordinary night—it was 1970—it all bubbled up to the surface. I asked him about Iwo Jima. And persisted through the initial silence.

And that was how I learned about one special hero of Iwo Jima. And about why he didn't come back.

It was just a normal evening in the Bradley household. Everyone else was asleep, except for Dad and me. He was forty-six then. I was sixteen, a high-schooler with pimples. The two of us were sitting up late, as we often did, watching Johnny Carson. For some reason that I've since forgotten, I brought up the subject that I knew by then was practically taboo. Iwo Jima.

Any information would have satisfied me. A couple of sentences. He'd never told me anything substantial. But as usual, on this night my father kept his silence, at least at first. I remember how he gave a half smile at me, then looked back at the TV—the blue screen reflecting in his glasses—then shook his head, sighed, glanced at me again.

On this night I decided not to let it go. After a long silence, I said: "Well, Dad, you were there. The Battle of Iwo Jima is a historical fact. It happened. You must remember *something*."

Again he listened to my question, then looked back at the TV. His mind was working, he heard me, but there was only silence.

I persisted. Finally he closed his eyes and dropped his head back against the headrest of his easy chair. Then he rubbed his forehead and said, "Geez." It sounded more like an anguished expulsion of air: *Sheeesh!!*

And then my father broke a long silence.

He said: "I have tried so hard to black this out. To forget it. We could choose a buddy to go in with. My buddy was a guy from Milwaukee. We were pinned down in one area. Someone elsewhere fell injured and I ran to help out, and when I came back my buddy was gone. I couldn't figure out where he was. I could see all around, but he wasn't there. And nobody knew where he was.

"A few days later someone yelled that they'd found him. They called me over because I was a corpsman. The Japanese had pulled him underground and tortured him. His fingernails . . . his tongue . . . It was terrible. I've tried so hard to forget all this.

"And then I visited his parents after the war and just lied to them. 'He didn't suffer at all,' I told them. 'He didn't feel a thing, didn't know what hit him,' I said. I just lied to them."

I didn't know what to say. I was young, unable to fathom the depths of emotion he had just revealed. And so we sat there for a few minutes in silence letting Johnny Carson's next guest change the subject.

Many years later, in researching my father's life, I asked Cliff Langley, Doc's co-corpsman, about the discovery of Iggy's body. Langley told me it looked to him as though Ralph Ignatowski had endured just about every variety of physical cruelty imaginable.

"Both his arms were fractured," Langley said. "They just hung there like arms on a broken doll. He had been bayoneted repeatedly. The back of his head had been smashed in."

Those were the relatively benign wounds. But they were not the worst of what had happened to Iggy, who had faked his urine sample to get into the Marines; Iggy, the proud Marine, the small, fresh-faced boy who had endured "Polack" ribbing with a good-natured smile.

My father remembered the worst thing. He kept the image alive under his many protective layers of silence and solitude. He never disclosed the worst thing to me, not on that night in front of the TV, not ever. But he mentioned it to my brother once, while I was in Japan.

Japan. How amazing it is that I found my way to that country—lived there—grew to love it—learned its history and studied its religious traditions—and did all of this without consciously connecting Japan to my father's past. Perhaps the currents of thought and motivation run deeper than we sometimes think.

I was hypnotically drawn into this old land, into what struck me as an almost mystically refined, cultured society. I'd arrived from a country where people joked about Japanese robot-workers building cheap cars, living in boxes, and eating rice and fish heads. What I found instead was an infinite lacing of social refinements that had evolved over centuries.

Here was a crowded island country smaller than California, but with 160 million people living on it. Eighty percent of that terrain was mountainous, compacting the available living space to an even greater density. Centuries of close living had distilled an elaborate system of courtesies designed to make this dense cohabitation enjoyable.

I grew more and more attuned to these rituals of humility and politeness. I didn't reflect on it at the time—indeed, not until many years later—but what I was experiencing was the irreducibly real Japan: the Japan that had existed before the militaristic epoch that culminated in the Pacific War, and that will continue into the next millennium. It was a Japan my father could never imagine.

Only now, years later, do I realize that the values of the Japanese and John Bradley were so similar. Quietness, politeness, integrity, honor, simplicity, devotion to family. Silent contemplation, looking inward for answers rather than prattling on.

———

I wanted my parents to come visit me in this Japan that I loved. I was sure they would see what fascinated me. I couldn't imagine any other reaction. I wrote them a letter of invitation. My mother responded that they couldn't make it. I never knew why or what my father's reaction had been—that is, until I spoke with my brother Steve in May of 1997, after Dad had died. He told me exactly what my father had said back in 1974 when he received my letter of invitation.

"It was at the funeral home," Steve told me. "Dad was agitated. He was jingling the change in his pockets like he did when he was upset.

"He said you had invited Mom and him to visit you in Tokyo. He didn't say anything for a long while. Then he blurted out, 'Jim wants us to come visit him. They tortured my buddy. The Japanese stuffed his penis in his mouth. I'm not too interested in going to Japan.' "

Memories of Iggy seemed to be always just under the surface. Maybe this accounts for my father's remarkable silence about the Battle of Iwo Jima and the flagraising. Maybe.

For many of the veterans, their memories of combat receded; supplanted by happy peacetime experiences. But there were others for whom the memories did not die, but were somehow contained. And for a few, the memories were howling demons that ruled their nights.

Among these last, a disproportionate number, I believe, are corpsmen.

It was the corpsmen, after all, who saw the worst of the worst. A Marine rifleman might see his buddy shot down beside him, and regret the loss for the rest of his life. But in the moment, he kept going. That was his training, his mission.

But the corpsman saw *only* the results. His entire mission on Iwo was to hop from blown face to severed arm, doing what he could under heavy fire to minimize the damage, stanch the flow, ease the agony.

The corpsmen remembered. And their memories ruled the night.

Danny Thomas, whose hypnotism in 1947 had ultimately proved ineffectual in blotting out the dreams, could never stop seeing the bodies at the edge of the water. "That's the thing I see in my dreams the most," he told me once. "How the tide and the motion of the waves would rock them.

"Just last night I woke up covered with sweat. I saw the shifting of the bodies on the Iwo Jima beach. My pajamas were drenched. I had to change. I still have to wring the sweat from my T-shirt on some nights.

"There's one body rocking on the sand that really grabs me. He's partially buried. His right shoulder and part of his face are sticking out of the sand. His right hand is moving in the tide as if it is beckoning: 'Follow me. Follow me.' I saw that guy on the second day."

All combat produces unshakable memories. But consider Cliff Langley, who as Corpsman Langley labored side by side with my father on Iwo—3rd Platoon, Easy Company.

He went on to serve in Korea and Vietnam with the Army. But there's one battle that rules: "The dreams have lasted for years. At seventy-three I still get 'em. I've been in three wars and I haven't got past Iwo yet."

After studying in Japan I was convinced I was an expert on Pacific history. At a Thanksgiving dinner at our family home in 1975, I was only too happy to enlighten my father and the assembled family as to the "real" reason we fought Japan in World War II: American insensitivity to Japanese culture and FDR's severing of their oil lines forced Japan—an industrial beached whale—to attack Pearl Harbor in self-defense.

The 350,000 "liberated" victims of the rape of Nanking and the millions who perished in the Asian Holocaust might have taken some exception to this point of view. But I was entranced with it, and confidently explained to the veteran of Iwo Jima seated across the table from me that it was his side that was to blame. Japan was the victim.

Typically, my dad did not take offense that day of thanks. He nodded thoughtfully, his glasses glinting, and reached for his knife to cut the turkey.

It would be years before I read of the atrocities the Japanese military machine had perpetrated on millions of people; years before I discovered that the "self-defense" rationale I was spouting off about had been rejected by the Tokyo War Crimes Tribunal as bogus.

John Bradley was fifty-two in 1975, and he knew a hell of a lot more about why we got into America's War than I did. But rather than challenge me, he just nodded.

He was secure in himself, his marriage, his family. He was a success-ful man. He owned a large home in Antigo, a summer cottage at Bass Lake several miles to the north, and a thriving funeral business.

He possessed the things that mattered most to him: not fame or adula-tion, but a large, secure family and the respect of his fellow townspeople, re-spect that devolved from years of hard work, his attitude of service, and his contributions to his community.

He could afford to nod in silent understanding and hand me another slice of turkey. In return for the slice of baloney I had just handed him.

John's heart was in bad shape by Christmas of 1993. Open-heart surgery, irregular heartbeat.

He was seventy, and had mortality on his mind. He wrote his own Christmas cards that year. He reached down through the years and sent them out to his Easy Company buddies. When I met and interviewed those men after his death, they told me that John had sporadically written little Christmas notes over the years. But his 1993 card was downright chatty and included a photograph of his extended family. Did he know it would be his last?

To Dave Severance, his old company commander, Doc confided: "I am not progressing as I should. My heart is not beating in its proper rhythm."

Betty, making the bed, discovered John's rosary beads under his pillow.

John Bradley's death of a stroke in January 1994 was reported around the world. All the newscasts spoke of John Bradley's passing, and we received clippings from as far away as Johannesburg, Hong Kong, and Tokyo.

Everyone in the world media reported that the last surviving flagraiser had died. But to us that title seemed distant, disconnected from our dad.

Fred Berner, editor of the Antigo *Daily Journal*, got it right when he wrote:

> *John Bradley will be forever memorialized for a few moments' action at the top of a remote Pacific mountain. We prefer to remember him for his life.*
>
> *If the famous flagraising at Iwo Jima symbolizes American patriotism and valor, Bradley's quiet, modest nature and philanthropic efforts shine as an example of the best of small-town American values.*

I will always remember my dad for a little favor at the very end of his life.

When he suffered his stroke, I was the only Bradley unable to drive to the Antigo hospital. I flew in from New York, the pilot holding the connecting plane in Chicago for me.

At about one A.M. on Tuesday, January 11, I pulled into the hospital parking lot. I had been traveling for seven hours.

I rushed into the Emergency entrance. The nurse on duty, who had never met me before, looked up and recognized one of "Johnny's boys." Without a word from me she said, "I'll take you to your father."

I heard him before I saw him: loud, labored breathing. Extreme heavy breathing like that which results in fainting or death. "He can't keep that up!" I blurted out to the nurse.

Approaching his bedside, I was struck by how good he looked in spite of the chest wheezing up and down. His color was up, and he looked like my dad of old, my healthy dad.

I tried to talk to him. But my words could not compete with his loud breathing. And I was crying, besides.

I silently thanked him for being a good man, a good father, someone whom I could admire. I told him all the reasons I loved him.

After about twenty minutes, I left the room to shed my winter coat and rinse my face. When I reentered the room about five minutes later, Dad's breathing had dramatically changed. His chest rose slowly now. Within a couple of minutes, his breathing slowed some more.

I summoned the nurse. She put an oxygen mask on Dad's face. I told her that the family had decided against intervention.

"This will just ease his last moments," she said quietly.

I telephoned my mother. Then Steve, who called Tom; both of them lived nearby. I telephoned Barb, Patrick, and Mark in Wausau, forty miles away.

Within twenty minutes the nearby Bradleys—Steve, his children Paul and Sarah, Tom, Joe, my mother, and me—were all by his side.

My mother cradled his head, brushed his hair, kissed his forehead. We all touched and kissed him. His breathing got weaker.

"Jack, are you leaving us now?" Betty Van Gorp Bradley whispered. "It's all right if you leave us when you're ready," his wife whispered. "It's all right, Jack."

At 2:12 A.M. on Tuesday, January 11, 1994, John Bradley took a small breath, exhaled, and died.

Several hours later, while my brothers were taking care of the arrangements, I sat peacefully in the dark looking at Dad, just sitting and thinking and, perhaps, praying. I noticed the nurse standing slightly behind me. The one who had eased my dad's last minutes.

"He waited for you," she whispered.

We both gazed at John Bradley for a few seconds.

She put her hand on my shoulder. "He waited for you," she repeated.

His wake was held in the funeral home where he had comforted so many. It was the largest anyone could remember. When the well-wishers shook our hands to express their condolences, we could feel that they were bone cold, chilled after waiting in the long line outside in the freezing winter.

We heard many stories about our father that evening, stories of silent kindness that he never brought home with him. But no one mentioned Iwo Jima or The Photograph. One woman said she had read the obituaries but did not know the war hero who was on the monument in Arlington or the sailor on the postage stamp. She said she knew a man who helped her parents with their parents' funerals and had become a friend of the family. She knew a man who had raised his family in Antigo and worked to make Antigo a good place to live. She said that was the man she would miss.

So John Bradley had achieved his goal and died as more than a figure in a photograph.

The morning after the wake, just before the church service, we had the closing-of-casket ceremony at the funeral home. This was the family's last chance to say good-bye to husband, father, father-in-law, grandpa.

Some of our family placed small personal items in his casket: a poem, a ring. I walked down the hall of the Bradley Funeral Home and entered my father's office. I faced the only photo hanging there. I gently removed it from the wall and returned to my father's side.

I turned to my family to get their attention. I held the photo high. All could see themselves in it, posed in a family reunion shot that John Bradley had never tired of bragging about.

"That is the only photo he cared about," I said, and then slid it into his casket.

We six "Johnny's boys" were his pallbearers. Rolling his casket up the aisle of St. John's, I was surprised that even though the church was packed to the gills, it was utterly silent. Like a void, more silent than when empty. The silence of a community's utter sadness.

At the end of the ceremony we all stood in our pews silently facing Dad's casket. The back doors to St. John's Church were opened. Outside, beyond the back door and down the steps, stood a lone bugler bathed in frigid sunshine. He played "Taps." The crisp and somber notes swept through the mourners and we wept.

Chiseled on John Bradley's simple gray headstone in the Queen of Peace Cemetery are the words he learned from his mother, the words that got him through Iwo Jima, the words he repeated with his wife every night before sleeping: Blessed Mother Help Us.

After he was gone, his actions continued to speak louder than words. I was stunned to learn that my father had been awarded the Navy Cross. Stunned. I read his citation over and over and was so proud of him and his life-saving actions on Iwo Jima.

I'll never truly understand the structure of my dad's wall of silence. Perhaps my daughter Alison's "Letter to Grandpa" comes close to describing the bewilderment and awe left in John Bradley's wake.

Alison was a fifteen-year-old high-school student with an assignment: Write a short letter to the person you admire the most.

She chose her Grandpa Bradley, who had been dead for three years.

Dear Grandpa,

You'll see on the envelope there is no address. I sat for a long time and wondered where to address it. Heaven? Is that where you are? I had no way of knowing, so I hope that this ends up getting to you.

I've been thinking a lot about you lately. I just have a few questions I need answered.

This past holiday Daddy took us to Washington, D.C., for a few days to learn more about you. Daddy told us stories of your youth.

He told us how as a young, unmarried man you boarded a cramped boat with thousands of other young Marines and shipped off to Iwo Jima to either live or die. World War II was such a horrible thing for your generation.

I saw the letter you wrote to your mother from Mount Suribachi. You described how filthy you all were and how you would give your "left arm for a good shower and a clean shave." How did you do it? I'll never know.

Finally, Daddy showed us the original footage of the flagraising in 1945. Over and over we saw you and your friends raise that flag.

This was our background to the trip, no more, no less.

But once in Washington, D.C., the enormity of the event and your contribution sank in. In our four days we climbed up your leg at the Marine Corps Memorial, had a personal tour of Congress, and a private tour of the White House.

I have finally obtained knowledge and understanding of the love and respect that the world has for you. In four days there I learned more about you than I did in the twelve years that I knew you.

Why did you not tell us about the Navy Cross?

And how about the time that Congress stopped and the Senate lined up to shake your hand? Why did you never sit us on your knee and tell us these stories?

The only answer I can give myself is that you were a quiet, modest, and honorable man who did not bask in glory. The only words that you ever spoke in front of a camera were, "I was in a certain place at a certain time. None of us are real heroes; we all just jumped in and lent a hand."

These words illustrate your feelings exactly. You just wanted a normal, ordinary family life with your wife and eight children. And that is exactly what you had. After you died a local newspaper wrote, "Bradley was the sole survivor of the flagraising for more than 14 years. He often was asked to attend banquets and dinners and give interviews. But Bradley was a quiet man who operated the Bradley Funeral Home in Antigo. He declined."

The article ends, "His silence has been honorable. And now it is eternal."

I write this letter exactly fifty-two years to the day since the flagraising on Iwo Jima. I sat for about an hour before I started writing to you and tried to picture exactly how you felt and what it was like being on that little island thousands of miles from home. To you there was no glory in an operation that cost two nations so dearly.

Every year on your birthday, Grandpa, we all go off to your grave and tell stories about how it was when you were alive. We always sing your favorite songs. Can you hear us?

My questions are pointless seeing as I'll never know the answer. I just needed to ask them. I cannot send this to you so it will go into my drawer, but wherever you are, heaven or otherwise, I do hope you receive my letter.

We are all healthy and our lives are going well.

Your loving Granddaughter,
Alison Bradley

In the saga of the figures in The Photograph, my dad came to play a unique role. He was the "last survivor" for fifteen years. For a decade and a half he was the only one.

And being the last survivor, he endured increased demands from authors, journalists, and documentarians. He politely refused all their entreaties. Until Betty asked. She wanted him to endure his first and last taped interview in 1985. "Do it for your grandchildren," she implored.

The transcript of this interview has never been published. I obtained it after my dad's death. My father answers the interviewer's questions carefully, weighing every word. Asked to describe his participation in the raising of a pole, John Bradley says:

When I came upon the scene, they were just finishing attaching the flag to the pole and they were just ready to raise it up.

I just did what anybody else would have done. I just gave them a hand.

That's the way it is in combat. You just help anyone who needs a hand.

They didn't ask for my help. I just jumped in and gave them a hand.

Then the last survivor smiles, and recalls his buddies:

Harlon: "A tall Texan. Always had a smile . . ."

Franklin: "We loved his stories told in that Kentucky brogue."

Rene: "I was best man at his wedding, you know."

Mike: "A great teacher. We all respected Mike."

Ira: "I always had a lot of respect for Ira Hayes. He was one great guy."

John then speaks for all the flagraisers, something he had never done before. He wanted to convey a message that he was sure the other guys would endorse: "People refer to us as heroes. We certainly weren't heroes. And I speak for the rest of the guys as well."

". . . certainly weren't heroes."

After spending five years researching their lives, the boys certainly seem like heroes to me. I admit it.

But I must defer to my father. He was there. He knew the guys, knew what they did. His hands were on that pole. And John was a straight arrow all his life. He said the same things about the flagraising at sixty-two as he had at twenty-two. And he was confident enough in his conclusion to claim the right to speak for the other guys.

So I will take my dad's word for it: Mike, Harlon, Franklin, Ira, Rene, and Doc, the men of Easy Company—they just did what anybody would have done, and they were not heroes.

Not heroes.

They were boys of common virtue.

Called to duty.

Brothers and sons. Friends and neighbors.

And fathers.

It's as simple as that.

ACKNOWLEDGMENTS

I was ten years old when the war ended. I thought the returning veterans were giants who had saved the world from barbarism. I still think so. I remain a hero worshiper. Over the decades I've interviewed thousands of the veterans. It is a privilege to hear their stories, then write them up.

—STEPHEN AMBROSE

Walking Harlon's football field with his brother Ed . . . listening to Mary describe her last time with Mike . . . standing with Kenny over the spot where he found Ira dead. How can I thank the flagraisers' relatives who accepted me as family? You gave me five more brothers.

Dad, now I know why you didn't talk about Iwo Jima. And I'm glad I know.

To my family, thank you for trusting me with this story. I tried to honor your trust by getting it right.

Dave Severance guided my search for the flagraisers' pasts. He demonstrated limitless patience for my endless questions, and this book could not have been written without his help. My life has been enriched getting to know this American hero.

Only one man in the world could get my mother to Iwo Jima. I asked that man to help me. "Of course," he replied. Marines are special people. And Charles Krulak is a special Marine.

Katie Hall of Bantam Books took a risk by acquiring this book, and edited it with professional and loving care. Her contribution will remain invisible to the reader, but I know and will always appreciate her superb efforts.

My agent Jim Hornfischer bravely took me on after I had managed to accumulate twenty-seven publishers' rejections. It was Jim's idea to team me with Ron Powers, whose reputation for quality was key to making this project a reality. Thanks, Jim and Ron!

To my many friends and supporters whose encouragement was never-ending—I wish I could add another chapter and list your names.

I have lived and worked in Japan and have warm friendships with a number of Japanese. Nothing I have written detracts from the deep respect I have for Japan and her people.

Easy Company member Jesse Boatwright made a remark to me once that reflects the sentiments of almost all the Marines and corpsmen who contributed to this book: "You might think we did something special there on Iwo, but we were just ordinary guys doing our duty."

To Mr. Boatwright and his comrades, yes, I understand your feeling that you were just doing your duty. And I hope you can appreciate the profound admiration I have for you and your actions out in the Pacific. You ordinary guys, you heroes of Iwo Jima.

James Bradley
January 2000
Rye, New York

INTERIOR PHOTO LIST
AND CREDITS

Chapter Openers

1: From the collection of Joseph Bradley
2: From the collection of Geneva Price
3: © Mary Craddock Hoffman
4: © USMC
5: From the collection of Geneva Price
6: © National Archives
7: © National Archives
8: © National Archives
9: © USMC
10: © Dave Severance
11: © National Archives; Louis Lowery, USMC photographer
12: © *The New York Times*
13: © National Archives
14: © C. R. Toburan
15: © AP/Wide World Photos
16: © U.S. Dept. of the Treasury
17: © Edward F. Block, Jr.
18: © USMC, DOD photo
19: © *The Courier Journal*
20: © AP/Wide World Photos

Photo Insert 1

Mike Strank, First Communion (from the collection of Mary Strank Pero)
Franklin Sousley (from the collection of Geneva Price)
Franklin Sousley's birthplace (© Leatherneck Magazine)
Rene Gagnon (from the collection of Rene Gagnon, Jr.)
Ira Hayes and father (from the collection of Sara Bernal)
Jack Bradley (from the collection of Elizabeth Bradley)
Harlon Block and brothers (© Edward F. Block, Jr.)
Jack Bradley and family (from the collection of Jean Bradley)
Harlon Block, Marine (from the collection of Catherine Pierce Foster)
Ira Hayes, Marine (from the collection of Kenny Hayes)
Rene Gagnon, Marine (from the collection of the Wright Museum)
Jack Bradley, Navy (from the collection of Elizabeth Bradley)
Franklin Sousley, Marine (from the collection of Geneva Price)
Mike Strank in camouflage (from the collection of Mary Strank Pero)

Photo Insert 2

Harlon Block (from the collection of Edward F. Block, Jr.)
Ralph Ignatowski (from the collection of Ruth Ignatowski Gaura)
Franklin Sousley and mother (from the collection of Geneva Price)
Jack Bradley, Camp Tarawa, Hawaii (© L. B. Holly)
Ira Hayes, Guadalcanal (© Robert Mueller)
Ira Hayes, paratrooper (© National Archives)
Iwo Jima, 1945 (photo by E. W. "Bill" Peck, from the collection of Carol Peck Sanders)
To the beaches (© National Archives)
Amphibious landing units (© National Archives)
U.S. Marines land (© National Archives)
Howlin' Mad Smith (© National Archives)
Rifleman on Suribachi (© National Archives)
First flagraising (© National Archives; Louis Lowery, USMC photographer)
First flag down (© National Archives; Louis Lowery, USMC photographer)
Rosenthal photo cropped (© AP/Wide World Photos)
Rosenthal photo horizontal (© AP/Wide World Photos)
Gung Ho (© AP/Wide World Photos)

Photo Insert 3

The boys and Truman (from the collection of Mark Bradley)
A smoke in Soldier Field (from the collection of Kathleen Bradley)
The boys in Times Square (from the collection of Fred Walcsak)
The "Gold Star" mothers (from the collection of Mary Strank Pero)
Doc Bradley and Rene Gagnon with Lockheed Girls (from the collection of Marge Abrahamson)
Harlon Block funeral cortege (from the collection of Leo Ryan)
Ira Hayes and parents (from the collection of Sara Bernal)
Rene Gagnon and family (from the collection of the Wright Museum)
John Bradley wedding photo (from the collection of Elizabeth Bradley)
Pauline and Rene Gagnon (from the collection of the Wright Museum)
John Wayne and John Bradley (from the collection of Elizabeth Bradley)
John Wayne hands flag (© USMC, DOD photo)
Felix de Weldon sculpts Rene Gagnon (from the collection of Elizabeth Bradley)
De Weldon with the boys (© UPI/Corbis-Bettmann)
USMC Memorial (© James Bradley)
Nixon with the boys (© AP/Wide World Photos)
Ira Hayes in jail (© AP/Wide World Photos)
Rene Gagnon (© AP/Wide World Photos)
John Bradley Memorial Day parade (© Antigo Daily Journal)
Iwo Jima today (© Marty Block)
James Bradley and family atop Suribachi (© Joseph Bradley)
Bradley family in bunker (© Joseph Bradley)

Endpapers

Large flagraising photo (© AP/Wide World Photos)
Six frames of the flagraising (© USMC; Bill Genaust, photographer)

NOTES

Two: All-American Boys

p. 39   *But as he later wrote*   Henry Dobyns and Frank W. Porter III, gen. ed., The North American Indian Series, *The Pima-Maricopa* (New York: Chelsea House Publishers, 1989), 31.

Three: America's War

p. 59   *Youth magazines carried*   Saburo Ienaga, *The Pacific War: A Critical Perspective on Japan's Role in World War II* (New York: Random House, 1978), 30.

p. 59   *"It was commonplace for teachers"*   Ibid., 31.

p. 62   *Everyone scrambled to be of help*   Gerald F. Linderman, *The World Within War: America's Combat Experience in World War II* (Boston: Harvard University Press, 1999), 91.

p. 65   *In less than a month*   Information about the Rape of Nanking taken from Iris Chang, *The Rape of Nanking: The Forgotten Holocaust of World War II* (New York: Basic Books, 1997).

p. 67   *"They were expendable"*   Ienaga, *The Pacific War*, 52.

p. 67   *"We'd give each"*   Holland M. Smith and Percy Finch, *Coral and Brass* (Nashville, TN: The Battery Press, Inc., 1989), 193. *Note:* This is my favorite book on the Pacific war.

p. 69   *Aware that the American individualistic ethic*   Linderman, *The World Within War*, 187.

p. 70   *When a recruit named Eugene Sledge*   E. B. Sledge, *With the Old Breed: At Peleliu and Okinawa* (New York: Oxford University Press, 1981), 5.

Note: Sledge's book is generally considered the best infantryman's account of the Pacific war.

p. 70   *"This is my rifle"*   Richard Wheeler, *Iwo* (Annapolis, MD: Naval Institute Press, 1994), 45. *Note:* If you read one book about the battle of Iwo Jima, this is the one. Also by Wheeler, *The Bloody Battle for Suribachi* is, I feel, the best book on the battle for Mount Suribachi. Mr. Wheeler served in Easy Company with the flagraisers, in the same platoon as Doc Bradley.

p. 70   *All militaries harden their recruits*   Thomas E. Ricks, *Making the Corps* (New York: Scribner, 1997), 19.

Four: Call of Duty

p. 77   *His early letters home*   Ira Hayes's letters are printed here courtesy of his brother, Kenny Hayes.

p. 78   *"He went from brown"*   Albert Hemingway, *Ira Hayes: Pima Marine* (Lanham, MD: University Press of America, Inc., 1988), 12.

p. 82   *"Never had men"*   John C. Chapin, Cpt., USMC, *Top of the Ladder*, Marines in WWII Commemorative Series, Marine Corps Historical Center.

p. 82   *"From seven o'clock"*   John A. Monks Jr., *A Ribbon and a Star: The Third Marines at Bougainville* (New York: Holt and Co., 1945).

p. 82   *"the closest thing to a living hell"*   Eric Bergerud, *Touched with Fire: The Land War in the South Pacific* (New York: Penguin Books, 1997), 66. *Note:* I consider this to be the best book on the land war in the Pacific.

p. 85   *"steak and eggs"*   Chapin, *Top of the Ladder*, 3.

p. 86   *"Though we spent"*   Hemingway, *Ira Hayes*, 28.

p. 86   *That night Ira's childhood*   Ibid., 32.

p. 93   *"As I slowly headed"*   James S. Vedder, *Combat Surgeon: Up Front with the 27th Marines* (Novato, CA: Presidio Press, 1984), 198.

p. 95   *" 'leap off the deep end' "*   Joseph H. Alexander, *Storm Landings: Epic Amphibious Battles in the Central Pacific* (Annapolis, MD: Naval Institute Press, 1997), 45. *Note:* Retired Marine Col. Alexander is the acknowledged expert on amphibious assaults.

p. 95   *"toughest of all military operations"*   Robert Sherrod, *Tarawa: The Story of a Battle* (Fredericksburg, TX: Admiral Nimitz Foundation, 1986), 67. *Note:* This is one of the finest books written about the Pacific war by one of the bravest correspondents in that war.

p. 96   *It would be forty-four years*   Alexander, *Storm Landings*, 53.

p. 96   *"The pillbox is forty feet long"*   Sherrod, *Tarawa*, 133.

p. 97   *Looking at these Japanese defenses*   Smith and Finch, *Coral and Brass*, 8–9.

p. 97   *A grief-stricken General Smith*   Sherrod, *Tarawa*, 139.

Five: Forging the Spearhead

p. 116   *"a huge hunk of green jade"*   Charles W. Tatum, *Iwo Jima: Red Blood, Black Sand: Pacific Apocalypse* (Stockton, CA: Charles W. Tatum Publishing, 1995), 79.

p. 116   *A local woman, a cook*   "Camp Tarawa, 1998," *Leatherneck Magazine,* July 1998.

p. 118   *"There were no saddles"*   Hemingway, *Ira Hayes,* 47.

p. 120   *Harlon wrote his mother a letter*   Harlon Block's letters are printed here courtesy of his sister Maurine Block Mitchel.

Six: Armada

p. 135   *"The Seventh Air Force dropped"*   Smith and Finch, *Coral and Brass*, 243.

p. 135   *"We thought it would blast"*   Ibid.

p. 136   *"The prolonged aerial bombardment"*   Ibid.

p. 141   *These tactics would capitalize*   Alexander, *Storm Landings*, 110.

p. 141   *"Fukkaku positions"*   Ibid.

p. 144   *"due to limitations on the availability of ships"*   Smith and Finch, *Coral and Brass*, 244.

p. 144   *"I regret this confusion"*   Ibid., 248.

p. 144   *"The cost in Marines killed"*   Ibid.

p. 145   *"Though weather has"*   Bill D. Ross, *Iwo Jima—Legacy of Valor* (New York: The Vanguard Press, 1985), 54.

p. 145   *"If the Marines"*   Smith and Finch, *Coral and Brass*, 245.

p. 145   *"Even though you"*   Ross, *Iwo Jima,* 33.

p. 145   *As Easy Company*   Ibid., 44–47.

p. 146   *"But no man who saw Tarawa"*   Sherrod, *Tarawa*, 149.

Nine: D-Day Plus Two

pp. 182–183   *Lieutenant Keith Wells would later*   John Keith Wells, *Give Me Fifty Marines Not Afraid to Die* (Abilene, KS: Ka-Well Enterprises, 1995), 207.

p. 183   *"I just thought"*   Ibid., 213.

p. 183   *Wheeler dived into a crater*   Richard Wheeler, *The Bloody Battle for Suribachi* (Annapolis, MD: Naval Institute Press, 1994), 112–113.

Ten: D-Day Plus Three

p. 197 "*Suribachi's fallen,*" *he moaned*   Wheeler, *Iwo,* 168.

Eleven: "So Every Son of a Bitch . . ."

p. 208 *Rosenthal, covering the invasion*   All Joe Rosenthal information about the flagraising is taken from "The Picture That Will Live Forever," *Collier's Magazine,* February 18, 1955.

p. 209 "*Colonel Johnson wants this*"   Wheeler, *Iwo,* 161.

Twelve: Myths

p. 224 "*My twenty-first birthday*"   Wheeler, *Iwo,* 186.

Thirteen: "Like Hell with the Fire Out"

p. 239 *By this point in the campaign*   Wheeler, *Iwo,* 220.

p. 239 "*The Marines were now being required*"   Ibid., 203.

p. 242 "*Who does the admiral*"   Tedd Thomey, *Immortal Images: A Personal History of Two Photographers and the Flag Raising on Iwo Jima* (Annapolis, MD: Naval Institute Press, 1996), 18.

Fourteen: Antigo

p. 257 *Indeed, in his only interview*   Interview transcript courtesy of Arnold Shapiro Productions, Inc.

Seventeen: A Conflict of Honor

p. 302 *In the dim predawn light*   Paul W. Tibbets, *Flight of the Enola Gay* (Columbus, OH: Mid-Coast Marketing, 1989), 216–219.

Twenty: Common Virtue

p. 352 *My father answers the interviewer's*   Interview transcript courtesy of Arnold Shapiro Productions, Inc.

BIBLIOGRAPHY

Alexander, Joseph H. *Storm Landings: Epic Amphibious Battles in the Central Pacific*. Annapolis, MD: Naval Institute Press, 1997.

Bartley, Whitman. *Iwo Jima: Amphibious Epic, A Marine Corps Monograph*. Nashville, TN: The Battery Press, 1988.

Bergerud, Eric. *Touched with Fire: The Land War in the South Pacific*. New York: Penguin Books, 1997.

Chang, Iris. *The Rape of Nanking: The Forgotten Holocaust of World War II*. New York: Basic Books, 1997.

Chapin, John C., Cpt., USMC. *Top of the Ladder*. Marines in WWII Commemorative Series, Marine Corps Historical Center.

Conner, Howard. *The Spearhead*. Nashville, TN: The Battery Press, 1987.

Dobyns, Henry, and Frank W. Porter III, gen. ed. *The Pima-Maricopa*. New York: Chelsea House Publishers, 1989.

Hemingway, Albert. *Ira Hayes: Pima Marine*. Lanham, MD: University Press of America, Inc., 1988.

Ienaga, Saburo. *The Pacific War: A Critical Perspective on Japan's Role in World War II*. New York: Random House, 1978.

Linderman, Gerald F. *The World Within War: America's Combat Experience in World War II*. Boston: Harvard University Press, 1999.

Monks, John A., Jr. *A Ribbon and a Star: The Third Marines at Bougainville*. New York: Holt and Co., 1945.

Newcomb, Richard. *Iwo Jima*. New York: Bantam Books, 1995.

Ricks, Thomas E. *Making the Corps*. New York: Scribner, 1997.

Ross, Bill D. *Iwo Jima—Legacy of Valor*. New York: The Vanguard Press, 1985.

Shay, Jonathan. *Achilles in Vietnam: Combat Trauma and the Undoing of Character*. New York: Touchstone Books, 1995.

Sherrod, Robert. *Tarawa: The Story of a Battle*. Fredericksburg, TX: Admiral Nimitz Foundation, 1986.

Sledge, E. B. *With the Old Breed: At Peleliu and Okinawa*. New York: Oxford University Press, 1981.

Smith, Holland M., and Percy Finch. *Coral and Brass*. Nashville, TN: The Battery Press, Inc., 1989.

Tatum, Charles W. *Iwo Jima: Red Blood, Black Sand: Pacific Apocalypse*. Stockton, CA: Charles W. Tatum Publishing, 1995.

Thomey, Tedd. *Immortal Images: A Personal History of Two Photographers and the Flag Raising on Iwo Jima*. Annapolis, MD: Naval Institute Press, 1996.

Tibbets, Paul W. *Flight of the Enola Gay*. Columbus, OH: Mid-Coast Marketing, 1989.

Vedder, James S. *Combat Surgeon: Up Front with the 27th Marines*. Novato, CA: Presidio Press, 1984.

Wells, John Keith. *Give Me Fifty Marines Not Afraid to Die*. Abilene, KS: Ka-Well Enterprises, 1995.

Wheeler, Richard. *The Bloody Battle for Suribachi*. Annapolis, MD: Naval Institute Press, 1994.

————. *Iwo*. Annapolis, MD: Naval Institute Press, 1994.

INDEX

Note: Page numbers in **boldface** refer to photos or illustrations

Ables, Chuck, 82
A Company, 160–61, 166
Adrian, Louie, 184
Amoskeag Mills, 44–45
amphibious tractors (amtrac), 136, 152, 153
amphibious warfare, 63–64, 106–7, 117, 143
Angell, Homer, 239
Antigo, WI, 20, 252, 254, 259–60, 261
Appleton, WI, 21–23
Arlington National Cemetery, 320, 326, 337
Army, U.S., 60–62
atomic bomb, 300–301, 302
Atsuchi, Kanahiko, 197

B-24 Liberator, 135
B-29 Superfort, 134–35, 234–35, 240, 247, 302
Bailey, Emogene, 26, 93
banzai charges, 141, 171, 189, 232, 245
BAR (Browning Automatic Rifle), 68, 105
Basilone, John, 64, 161
Basophy, Ann, 48, 51
Bataan Death March, 62

Beech, Keyes, 243, 268, 284, 285–86, 290
Bernal, Sarah, 39, 41
Bethlehem Steel, 49
Biggs, Aloise, 165
Bismarck Sea, USS, 191
Blandy, Vice Admiral, 145
Blankenburger, Ed, 151–52
Block, Belle (Harlon's mother), **297**
    attends memorial unveiling, 326, 328
    family and religion, 29–36, 80
    life insurance beneficiary, 119–20
    moves to California, 299–300, 301
    The Photograph, 221, 233, 265, 273, 301, 310–11, 312–13
    son's death, 265, 277, 319–20
Block, Corky (Harlon's brother), 300
Block, Ed, Jr. (Harlon's brother), 31, 37, 80–81, 115, 221, 299
Block, Ed, Sr. (Harlon's father)
    attends memorial unveiling, 326
    family and religion, 29–36
    moves to California, 299–300
    The Photograph, 273, 309–11
    returns to Texas, 301–2
    signs son's enlistment papers, 80
    son's death, 277, 319–20

Block, Harlon, **297**
   at Bougainville, 82, 87–88
   boyhood, 29–37
   in Honolulu, 124
   insurance beneficiary, 119–20
   Iwo Jima, 157, 163–64, 165, 176, 183,
      185, 230–31
      death, 232–33
      flagraising, 202, 208–11, 229
   The Photograph, 11, 268–69, 309–11,
      312–13
   recruitment and boot camp, 79–80
   religious beliefs, 32–34, 125
   thoughts of death, 92–93, 115, 124, 125
   training, 80–81, 103, 105, 114–15,
      119–20
Block, Larry (Harlon's brother), 300, 319
Block, Maurine (Harlon's sister), 31–32,
      115, 233, 299, 300, 302, 313
Block, Mel (Harlon's brother), 80, 300,
      319, 320
Block, Rebecca Salazar (Ed Sr.'s second
      wife), 310
blockhouses and pillboxes, 8–9, 96–97,
      142–43, 173
Boatwright, Jesse, 68, 69, 70, 106, 230
Bodkin, John, 220
Bond Tour (Mighty 7th), 281–95
   Boston, 286–87
   Chicago, 289–90
   description of, 282
   goals, 266, 281–82
   New York, 283–86, 287–89
   Philadelphia, 286
   planning, 237–38, 243, 266–68
   poster, 275–76, **279,** 284
   results, 293–94, 295
   song, 283
Boston, MA, 286–87
Boston Globe, 287
Bougainville, 82, 85–88
Bradley, Alison (John's granddaughter),
      351–52
Bradley, Betty (Van Gorp)
   childhood, 22–23, 158
   John's death, 349
   John's lack of vanity, 254
   John's war memories, 257–58, 303,
      318

marriage and children, 7–8, 252–53,
      303–4, 308
   visits Iwo Jima, 6, 7
Bradley, James J. "Cabbage" (John's
      father), 20–21, 83, 271, 325–26
Bradley, James (John's son, author), **1,**
      5–13, **249,** 345–46, 347
Bradley, Joe (John's son), 6, 8
Bradley, John Henry ("Jack," "Doc"), 351
   attends memorial unveiling, 326–28
   avoidance of the press, 4, 256, 258,
      259–60, 336, 341–42, 352–53
   Bond Tour, 283–94
   boyhood, 19–24
   children, **249,** 251–53
   community service, 254
   corpsman training, 84, 89–90, 139–40
   death, 348–50
   enlistment, 24, 82–84
   Ira's funeral, 333
   Iwo Jima, 151, 152, 162–63, 166, 172,
      176, 183, 184, 185–86
      flagraising, 201, 203, 210–11, 216
      northern plateau offensive, 230, 236,
         237, 239, 240
      wounded, 240–41
   letter from granddaughter, 351–52
   marriage, 303–4, 308
   mortuary business, 21, 252, 253–54, 304
   Navy Cross, 8, 185–86
   Navy discharge, 304
   part in *Sands of Iwo Jima,* 321–22
   The Photograph, 5, 268–69, 270, 272,
      293, 295, 352
   postage stamp ceremonies, 295
   religious beliefs, 19, 21, 109, 255, 308
   training camp, 103, 105, 107–8, 109,
      110, 111, 119
   treatment at Bethesda, 274, 295, 302,
      303
   visits Iggy's parents, 320
   war memories and silence about Iwo
      Jima, 4–5, 8, 10, 238, 251, 255–61,
      306, 308, 318, 343–47, 351–52
   Washington trip, 274–76
Bradley, Katherine (John's mother), 20,
      24, 271–72
Bradley, Kathy (John's daughter), 252, 258
Bradley, Mark (John's son), 6, 8, 258

Bradley, Mary Ellen (John's sister), 23–24
Bradley, Paul, 109, 161–62, 174
Bradley, Steve (John's son), 6, 8
Browning Automatic Rifle (BAR), 68, 105
Buchanan, James "Jim," 68, 109, 153, 156, 206, 242, 306
Buchwald, Art, 69
buddy system, 110
Buffalo, NY, 311
Burden, Winifred, 26
Bushido, 66–68, 207

Campbell, Bob, 208, 209–11, 242
Camp Pendleton, CA, 101–15
   amphibious training, 106–7
   flagraisers come together, 102–4
   hardships, 101–2, 108–9
   specialist training, 106
   weapons training, 105–6
Camp Tarawa, HI, 116–20
Castle, Jack, 118–19
Castorini, Guy, 156, 159
casualties, 167, 177, 185, 190, 246–47
caves and tunnels, 7, 141, 142, 203, 206–7, 247
Chandler, A. B. "Happy," 276
Charles, Arnold, 307
Charles, Jack, 86
Charlo, Louis, 201–2, 205
Chiasson, Roland, 165
Chicago, IL, 289–90
Chicago Sun-Times, 322–24
Chicago Tribune, 336–37, 341–42
Chicopee Manufacturing Company, 45
China, 59–60, 65–66
Christman, Phil, 172
Churchill, Winston, 57, 300–301
Civilian Conservation Corps (CCC), 53
Clark, T. B., 220
Cleckler, Glen, 36, 79, 80, 124, 233–34, 319
Collins, Dale, 277
Connelly, Bob, 23, 83, 272
corpsmen
   casualties among, 188
   D-Day, 161, 165, 166
   Japanese targeting of, 66, 139–40
   training, 89–90
   Unit 3 (pouch), 139–40

war memories of, 346–47
correspondents, 165, 208, 218, 230
"Courageous Battle Vow," 147–48
Crowe, Frank, 245
Crull (Marine), 191–92

Daskalakis, John, 173–74, 272
D-Day. See under Iwo Jima
DeGeus, Robert, 195, 247
Depression, Great, 19, 21, 31, 32, 53
Dollins, Ray, 162
Dortsch (Marine), 191
Duncan, Melvin, 231, 233
Dyce, Grady, 101–2, 106, 246

Easy (E) Company
   aboard the Missoula, 126
   Camp Pendleton, 103
   casualties and medals, 190, 246
   D-Day, 130, 152, 153–54, 157–58, 159
   D-Day + 1, 171, 172, 173, 175, 176–77
   D-Day + 2, 181, 183, 185, 189–90
   D-Day + 3, 195–97
   flagraising, 202
   northern plateau offensive, 224–25, 229, 230, 233–34
   reunions, 342–43
   swimming, 236–37
   trains for invasion of Japan, 301
Eldorado, USS, 135, 147
Elson, Mary, 336–37, 341–42
Emery, Gregory, 89, 157, 161
Enola Gay, 302
equipment and supplies, 127, 139–40
esprit de corps, 70–71, 239
Evelley, Madeline, 272–73, 288–89

Faulkner, William "Bill," 78, 86, 87
F Company, 201–2
5th Division, 102–3, 152, 154, 177, 230, 242
Filbrandt, John, 257
First, Jack, 240
flagraisers (See also Block, Harlon; Bradley, John; Gagnon, Rene; Hayes, Ira ; Sousley, Franklin; Strank, Mike)
   background differences and similarities, 17–19

flagraisers *(cont'd)*
  honored in Washington, 274–77
  identification of, 243, 268–75, 309–11,
    313
  last meeting, 333
  places in The Photograph, 10–12
  as representative of Iwo Jima and
    America, 12
flagraising, 201–12
  ascending Mount Suribachi, **199,**
    201–4
  first flagraising, 204–6
  myths and confusion about, 222–25
  second (replacement) flagraising,
    207–12
  See also Photograph, The
flamethrowers, 186
Flora, Aaron, 27, 94
Fogarty, Thurman, 162–63
Forrestal, James, 146, 207, 304
4th Division, 134, 152, 154, 177
Franklin, USS, 304–5
Franklin Borough, PA, 49–50, 51,
    52–53
Fredatovich, John, 131–32, 163–64
Freidl, John, 322
Fukkaku positions, 141

Gagnon, Henry (Rene's father), 43
Gagnon, Irene (Rene's mother), 43, 45,
    46–47, **263,** 269–70, 287, 294
Gagnon, Pauline Harnois (Rene's wife),
    263
  dating and marriage, 47, 131, 294, 301,
    335–36
  joins Bond Tour, 286–87, 289
  Rene's death and burial, 337
  Rene's identification as flagraiser, 270
Gagnon, Rene, **263**
  Bond Tour, 283–94
  boyhood, 42–47
  China duty, 294, 301
  death, 336–37
  enlistment, 47, 84
  hometown parade, 273–74
  Ira's funeral, 333
  Iwo Jima, 208–11, 217, 241–42
  marriage, 131, 294, 335–36
  part in *Sands of Iwo Jima,* 321–22

The Photograph, 11, 243, 268–69, 270
  postwar disappointments, 306–7,
    311–12, 334–36
  training, 89, 103, 105, 113–14
  unveiling of memorial, 326–28
  Washington trip, 269, 274–76
Gagnon, Rene, Jr. (Rene's son), 301, 334,
    335, 336
Genaust, Bill, 208, 209–11, 235
Gentry, Cecil, 190, 191
GI Bill, 305
Giff, Urban, 39, 318
Gila River Indian Reservation, AZ, 38
Goettge, Frank, 66
Goode, Robert, 186
Gramling, John, 165
Green Beach, 118, 130, 154
Griffiths, Pee Wee, 68, 70–71, 89, 230
Guadalcanal, 62, 63–65, 66, 68
Gust, Walter, 188

Haefele, Max, 174, 201, 205
Hamm, Marion, 27–28, 94, 270
Hansen, Henry "Hank"
  identified as flagraiser, 268, 269, 270,
    272–73, 274–75, 313
  Iwo Jima, 184, 204–5, 232
  mother joins Bond Tour, 288–89
Harnois, Anita, 47
Harnois, Paul, 335
Harnois, Pauline. *See* Gagnon, Pauline
    Harnois
Harris, Chick, 158–59, 248
Harris, Pee Wee, 231
Harrison, Norma, 238
Hawaii, 57–58, 62, 116–20, 123–25
Hayes, Ira Hamilton
  Bond Tour, 283–90
  Bougainville, 82, 85–87, 88, 90–91
  boyhood, 37–42
  brotherhood of Marines, 146
  Camp Pendleton, 103, 105, 110–12,
    114
  Camp Tarawa, 117, 118
  contacts Harlon's parents, 309–11
  death, 331–33
  drinking problem, 77, 284, 285–86, 290,
    307–8, 309, 322–25
  enlistment and boot camp, 42, 76–78

identification as flagraiser, 268–69, 270, 272
Iwo Jima, 157, 158, 161, 176, 183, 185, 196–97, 230–31
  flagraising, 202, 208–11
Marine discharge, 304
parachute training, 78–79
part in *Sands of Iwo Jima*, 321–22
The Photograph, 12, 274, 309–11, 313
postwar jobs, 307, 322–24, 325
receives flagraiser stamps, 301
rejoins E Company, 290–91, 292–93
silence and stoicism of, 37, 39, 240
unveiling of Iwo Jima memorial, 326–28
war memories, 307–8, 312, 317–18, 324–25, 333
Washington trip, 274–76
Hayes, Jobe (Ira's father), 38–39, 307, 309, 317–18, 332–33
Hayes, Kenny (Ira's brother), 38, 39, 332, 333
Hayes, Nancy (Ira's mother), 38, 39, 307, 309
  Ira after Bougainville, 90–91
  Ira after Iwo Jima, 317–18
  Ira's death, 332–33
  Ira's enlistment, 76, 77
Hayes, Vernon (Ira's brother), 332
Hendricks, Joseph, 233
heroism, 260–61, 275, 334, 343, 353
Heyer, Julia, 320
Hilltop, KY, 24–25
Hipple, Bill, 208
Hipps, Tex, 232
Hirohito, Emperor of Japan, 133
Holly, L. B., 231, 244, 275
Hoopes, William, 69, 71, 188, 247
Hotaling, Gage, 175
Hot Rocks. *See* Suribachi, Mount
Howell, Donald
  brotherhood of Marines, 107
  Iwo Jima, 151, 154, 188, 201, 203, 206, 236, 245
  Navy Cross, 236
  war memories, 305

Ignatowski, Al (Ralph's brother), 110–11, 320
Ignatowski, Francis, (Ralph's mother), 320

Ignatowski, Ralph "Iggy"
  death, 236, 238, 320, 344–45, 346
  friendship with Doc Bradley, 110, 258–59
Ignatowski, Walter, (Ralph's father), 320
Inouye, Samaji, 197
International Dateline crossing, 131–32
International Harvester, 322–23
issen gorin, 67, 137, 171
Iwo Jima, **1, 149, 169, 193, 227**
  air raid on offshore ships, 190
  American strategy, 118, 127–31, 135–36, 143–46, 160
  the armada, **121,** 125–48
  bombardment/air cover, 17, 135–36, 143–45, 152, 153, 182, 189
  burials, 175
  casualties, 167, 177, 190, 246–47
  D-Day, 151–69
  D-Day + 1, 171–77
  D-Day + 2, 181–92
  D-Day + 3, 195–97
  description, 6–7, 127, 130
  flagraising, **199,** 201–12, 222–25 (*See also* Photograph, The)
  importance to Allies, 134–35, 234–35, 240, 247, 302
  importance to Japanese, 132–33
  Japan announces defeat, 243
  Japanese defenses, 7, 8–9, 128–29, 130–31, 140, 141–43
  Japanese strategy, 137, 154, 156, 164, 169, 191, 229–30
  Japanese suicides, 206–7, 215
  landing, **149,** 154–60, 164–65
  maps, **128–29, 155**
  Marines' bodies returned home, 319–20
  medals awarded, 10, 247
  media coverage, 217–19, 222–24, 230, 237
  memorials and monuments, 220, 233, 283, 285, 295, 326–28
  northern plateau offensive, 197, 229–48
  revisited, 6–13
  Sands of Iwo Jima (movie), 321–22
  supplies and equipment, 127
  surrender of last Japanese defenders, 321
  See also Suribachi, Mount

Japan
atomic bomb, 300–301, 302
atrocities in China and Manchuria,
59–60, 65–66
corruption of Bushido, 66–68, 207
militarization of, 58–59
opinion of Marines, 65–66, 146
Potsdam Declaration, 300–301
radio broadcast from children, 242
seeks control in the Pacific, 60
Tokyo raids, 240
treatment of prisoners of war, 138–39
See also specific battles (e.g., Pearl
Harbor, Guadalcanal, Iwo Jima)
Johnson, Chandler, 103, 173, 195, 196,
197, 234
flagraising, 201, 202, 207, 208, 209,
211
Joseph, Esau, 332
Juan, Matthew, 41

Kaiama, Tsugi, 116–17
K Company, 86
Keller, Harold, 203, 205–6, 225, 246
Kelly (corpsman), 188
Kempei Tai, 138
Kentucky, 24–25, 319, 326
Kochi, Commander, 6
Koiso, Kuniaki, 243
Krulak, Charles, 6
Kuhn, Wesley, 158, 165, 306
Kurelik, Ed, 172
Kuribayashi, Tadamichi
"Courageous Battle Vow," 147–48
defense plan, 141–43, 154, 156, 164,
172, 229–30
description and background of, 133
expectations and goal at Iwo Jima,
136–37
messages to Tokyo, 236, 242, 245
presumed dead, 245

La Guardia, Fiorello, 285
Lane, Robert, 69, 71, 119
Langley, Clifford, 111, 322
Iwo Jima, 159, 162, 165, 166, 183,
344–45
war memories, 306, 347
Lawrence Taylor, USS, 190–91

Leader, Robert
about the Marine Corps, 69, 104, 147
Iwo Jima, 151, 156, 204, 205
reaction to Pearl Harbor, 62
war memories, 305
Lebel, Lillian, 335
Lee, Robert E., 171
Legro, Gene, 260
Lehrer, Jim, 71
LeMay, Curtis, 135
Lewis, Buddy, 41, 307, 308, 318
Lewis, Richard, 78
Lindberg, Chuck, 135, 186, 203, 204–5,
206, 230
Liversedge, Harry "the Horse"
Camp Pendleton, 103, 104–5
Iwo Jima, 157, 166, 172–73, 182–83,
197, 202
Lowery, Louis, 202, 204, 206, 209, 222
Lucas, Jacklyn, 174–75, 305
Luck, Hans von, 65
Lundsford (veteran Marine), 159

MacArthur, Douglas, 60–61, 134
Manchester, NH, 43–47, 273–74
Manchester, William, 191–92
Mansfield, Mike, 237–38
maps
D-Day, 155
Iwo Jima, 128–29
Pacific Theater, 55, 61
Marine Corps, U.S.
amphibious warfare, 63, 76, 95, 98
boot camp, 69–70
brotherhood, 107–8, 146–47, 161, 195
buddy system, 110
corpsman training, 89–90
emblem, 179
enlistment after Guadalcanal, 68
esprit de corps, 70–71, 239
formation of 5th Division (Spearhead),
134
Marines on the beach of Iwo Jima,
227
170th anniversary, 304
Raiders, 81, 132
recruiting poster, 73
See also specific battles (e.g., Bougainville, Guadalcanal, Iwo Jima)

Marine Corps Memorial, **315, 326–28**
Martin, Elizabeth, 325
Mayer, Don, 106, 175, 190, 305
Mayers, Thomas, 191–92
McArthur, George, 284
McEldowney, Robert, 205, 247
McFarland, Ernest W., 333
McNeil, Hector, 174
Medal of Honor, 234, 247
    Basilone, John, 64
    Lucas, Jacklyn, 174–75
    Ruhl, Don, 184
    Stein, Tony, 160–61
    Wahlen, George, 234
medals and awards, 10, 234, 247
    See also Medal of Honor; Navy Cross;
        Silver Star
medics. *See* corpsmen
Melville, Herman, 17
memories. *See* war memories
Mercer, George, 201–2
Michaels, Jim, 205, 246
Mighty 7th. *See* Bond Tour
Milstead, Kenneth, 111–12, 176
Missoula, HSS, 125, 126–27
Mofford, Rose, 333
Monahan, Esther, 41
Monks, John, Jr., 82
Morago, Jay, 323
Moran, Florine, 271
Morganthau, Henry, Jr., 283
mother, dying soldier's last word, 137
Mount Suribachi. *See* Suribachi, Mount

Navy, U.S.
    bombardment of Iwo Jima, 135–36,
        143–45, 152, 153, 173, 195, 201
    corpsmen, 66, 89–90
    pre-invasion bombardment of
        Bougainville, 85
Navy Cross
    Bradley, John, 185–86
    Howell, Donald, 236
    Mayers, Thomas, 191–92
    Pennel, Ed, 176
    Thomas, Ernest "Boots," 189
    Wells, Keith, 188
Neptune initiation, 131–32
New York, NY, 283–86, 287–89

New York Stock Exchange, 288–89
New York Sun, 241
New York Times, The, **213**, 218–20,
        221–22, 223–24, 285, 311
Nimitz, Chester W., 134, 135, 242, 327
Nishi, Baron, 142
Norris, Dana, 39, 41, 76

Olson, Donald, 96
O'Mahoney, Joseph, 240
Overmayer, John, 89, 90, 342–43
Ozment, Monroe, 158

Pacific Theater, World War II
    Bougainville, 82, 85–88
    Guadalcanal, 62, 63–65, 66, 68
    Iwo Jima. (*See* Iwo Jima)
    maps, **55, 61**
    Pearl Harbor, 57–58, 62
    Philippines, 60–62, 66
    Potsdam Declaration, 300–301
    Tarawa, 95–98, 218
Pagac, Joe, 80
Paine, Thomas, 75
Paramore, Roy, 174
Parrish, Vernon, 152
Pasquale, Eleanor, 41–42, 78
Pearl Harbor, HI, 57–58, 62
Pennel, Ed, 104
    Camp Pendleton, 103, 104
    Iwo Jima, 157–58, 176, 183, 187
    Navy Cross, 176
Perry, Rolla, 244
Philadelphia, PA, 286
Philippines, 60–62, 66
Phoenix Indian School, 41
Photograph, The, 210–12, **213**, 215–16,
        339
    Bond Tour poster, 275–76, **279**, 284
    monuments and memorials, 220, 233,
        283, 285, 326–28
    myth that it was staged, 235–36, 273
    postage stamp, 240, 266, 295, 301
    symbolism and power of, 220–22, 241,
        261, 266, 273, 275, 282–83, 292,
        321, 326, 328, 333–34, 341–42
    See also Rosenthal, Joe
Pierce, Catherine, 37, 79, 88, 92–93,
        120

pillboxes and blockhouses, 8–9, 96–97,
142–43, 173
Pima Indians, 38, 39–41, 42, 76, 78
postage stamp, 295, 301
posters, **73**, 275–76, **279**, 284
post-traumatic stress syndrome, 333
See also war memories
Potsdam Declaration, 300–301
Price, Goldie Sousely (Franklin's mother),
329
joins Bond Tour, 288–89
marriages, 25, 270
relationship with son, 25–26
son home on leave, 93, 94
son's death, 270–71, 319
unveiling of Iwo Jima memorial, 326,
328
Price, Hensley, 270
Prowling Wolves, 191
Puffer, Jack, 23
Puller, Chesty, 103
Pyle, Ernie, 65

Radebaugh, Robert, 113
Ranous, Bill, 114, 119, 159, 165, 240
Rayburn, Sam, 276
riflemen, importance of, 105–6
Rio Grande Valley, TX, 29–31
Robeson, Chick, 184–85, 206, 215,
216–17, 239
Rockey, Keller E., 244
Rodriguez, Joe, 104, 112, 123–24, 131–32,
159, 196–97, 231
Romero, Edward J., 183
Roosevelt, Franklin D.
attack on Pearl Harbor, 58
Camp Pendleton, 107
Depression programs, 53
Iwo Jima, 133, 167, 242
Seventh Bond Tour, 268
Rosenthal, Joe
blamed for misidentification of
flagraisers, 313
Iwo Jima, 157, 208, 209–11, 212
The Photograph, 211, 215–16, 222,
235–36
Pulitzer Prize, 283
unveiling of Iwo Jima memorial,
327

Rozek, Leo, 204
Ruhl, Don, 173–74, 176–77, 184
Ruppel, Louis, 242–43
Ryan, Jean, 92, 124
Ryan, Leo, 35, 36, 80, 124–25, 311,
319–20

Saipan, Marianas, 134, 136, 218
Salazar, Rebecca. *See* Block, Rebecca
Salazar
Schmidt, Bob, 175, 302–3
Schrier, H. "George," 202, 204–5, 209,
210, 212
Scott, George, 112
2nd Battalion, 173, 246
semper fidelis, 107–8
Sepeda, Ben, 33
Setoyant, Henry, 332, 333
Seventh Day Adventist Church, 32–33
Severance, Dave
Camp Pendleton, 103, 105–6, 114
E Company reunions, 342–43
identifying the flagraisers, 243
Iwo Jima, 157, 173, 195, 202–3, 208,
224–25, 240, 241, 245–46
on Iwo Jima's defenses, 131
Silver Star, 237
takes E Company swimming, 236–37
Shannon, J. B., 27–28, 29, 93, 94, 270
Shelley, A.B.R., 221–22
Shepard, Charles, 173
Sherrod, Robert, 96–97, 146, 165, 172
Shoemer, Bill, 84
Shutter, Carl, 21
Silver Star
Lindberg, Chuck, 186
Severance, Dave, 236–37
Sledge, Eugene, 70
Smart, Richard, 116
Smith, Holland M. "Howlin' Mad"
amphibious warfare, 63, 143
on the bombardment of Iwo Jima, 135,
143–44
description and background, 133–34
Iwo Jima, 154, 169, 190, 207, 219, 242
Tarawa, 95, 96, 97, 98
unveiling of Iwo Jima memorial, 327
Smith, Jerry, 157
Smith, Julian, 146

Solomon Islands. *See* Bougainville;
    Guadalcanal
Sousely, Goldie. *See* Price, Goldie Sousley
Sousley, Duke (Franklin's father), 25–26
Sousley, Franklin Runyon, **329**
  boyhood, **15**, 24–29
  enlistment, 28–29
  furlough, 93–94
  in Honolulu, 124
  Iwo Jima, 157, 176, 183, 185, 197,
    230–31
    death, 244–45
    flagraising, 202, 208–11, 217
  Iwo Jima Day in Kentucky, 326
  The Photograph, 11, 268–69, 270
  remains returned to Kentucky, 319
  sense of humor, 26–27, 88
  training, 88–89, **99**, 103, 105, 112–13,
    119
Spearhead, 103, 106–7
Spruance, Raymond, 144
Stalin, Josef, 300–301
Stanton, Tex
  boot camp, 88
  Camp Pendleton, 106, 108, 109
  enlistment, 68
  Iwo Jima, 185, 224–25, 232–33, 247–48
  war memories, 306
  wounded, 243–44
Stein, Tony, 160–61
Steinfort, Roy, 116, 157
Stoddard, George, 173
Strank, Ann (Pete's wife), 305
Strank, John (Mike's brother), 288, 326
  boyhood, 49, 50, 51–52
  Mike as a Marine, 54, 76
  Mike's death, 267, 271, 305, 320
Strank, Martha (Mike's mother)
  attends unveiling of memorial, 326, 328
  immigration, 48, 49
  joins Bond Tour, 288–89
  son's death, 267, 320
Strank, Mary (Mike's sister), 49, 52, 92,
    320, 326
Strank, Mike, **193**
  Bougainville, 85, 88, 91
  boyhood, 47–54
  Camp Pendleton, 103, 105, 108, 113,
    114

Civilian Conservation Corps (CCC),
    53
  death, 230–31
  enlistment and training, 54, 75–76
  in Honolulu, 123
  Iwo Jima, 157, 159, 165, 176, 183, 185,
    189, 202, 208–11, 230–31
  leadership qualities, 48, 104, 108, 132
  The Photograph, 11–12, 268–69, 270
  Raiders, 81
  religious beliefs, 51
  sense of humor, 108, 113, 131–32
  thoughts of death, 91, 93, 165, 224–25
Strank, Pete (Mike's brother), 49, 50,
    304–5, 320, 326
Strank, Vasil (Mike's father), 48, 49, 50,
    320
suicides, 206–7, 215
supplies and equipment, 127, 139–40
Suribachi, Mount (Hot Rocks), **1, 149,
    199**
  advancing toward, 171–77
  assault on, 181–92
  conquest and flagraising, 201–12
  description, 127
  fortification of, 156, 181–82
  importance of, 154
  isolating, 130, 154, 160
  Japanese abandonment, 197
  training for, 118
Sweeney, Charles, 220

Taft, D. M., 80
tanks, 156, 176, 182–83, 186–87
Tarawa, 95–98, 218
3rd Division, 134, 152, 154
Thomas, Danny
  Iwo Jima, 158–59, 166, 248
  Marine brotherhood, 161
  war memories, 306, 318, 346–47
Thomas, Ernest "Boots," 188, 189, 234
  flagraising, 202, 204–5, 222, 223–24
Thompson, Lloyd, 109, 159, 240, 292
Tibbets, Paul, 302
Time (magazine), 235–36, 237
Tokyo raids, 240
Tokyo Rose, 147
training for Iwo Jima, 101–15, 116–20,
    136

Treasury Department, U.S. *See* Bond Tour
Truman, Harry, 3, 275–76, 277, 300–301,
    320
tunnels and caves, 7, 141, 142, 203,
    206–7, 247
Turner, Kelly, 145
Tuttle, Ted, 207, 208, 209
28th Regiment
    assault on Suribachi, 130, 154, 172,
        181, 189
    Camp Pendleton, 103, 104–5, 108–9
    northern plateau offensive, 224, 230,
        232, 239

Unit 3 (corpsman's pouch), 139–40

Vandegrift, Alexander, 64, 283, 291, 304,
    312–13, 327
venereal disease testing, 108
Vonnegut, Kurt, 331

Wahlen, George, 234, 306, 318–19
Ward, Lyndolph, 160
Ward, Phil, 157, 167, 176, 203, 234, 240,
    246
war memories, 305–6, 318–19, 325, 333,
    346–47

Washington, D.C., 269, 274–77
Watson, Sherman B., 201–2
Waugh, Evelyn, 229
Wayne, John, 317, 321, 322
Wayne, William, 164, 165, 184, 186
weather, 171, 181
Weldon, Felix de, 220, 283, 326–28
Wells, Greeley, 202
Wells, Keith, 156, 162, 176, 183, 186,
    188
Weslaco, TX, 34, 124, 221, 319
Weslaco High School, 35–36, 79–80
Wheeler, Keith, 165
Wheeler, Richard, 172, 176, 182, 183
White, Ted, 201–2
Willis, Raymond, 241–42
Winged Arrow, USS, 246, 268, 269,
    272
Wisconsin honors John Bradley, 274
Wittmeier, James, 176, 261
World War II
    rationing, 62
    See also Pacific Theater, World
        War II

Young, Fergus, 103
Youngberg, Russell, 33